Teaching Primary English

The state of the art

Edited by

David Wray and Jane Medwell

London and New York

First published 1994
by Routledge
11 New Fetter Lane, London EC4P 4EE

Simultaneously published in the USA and Canada
by Routledge
29 West 35th Street, New York, NY 10001

Reprinted 1996, 1998

Typeset in Times by LaserScript Limited, Mitcham, Surrey
Printed and bound in Great Britain by
Mackays of Chatham PLC, Chatham, Kent

British Library Cataloguing in Publication Data
A catalogue record for this book is available from the British Library

Library of Congress Cataloging in Publication Data
A catalog record for this book is available from the Library of Congress

ISBN 0–415–08669–8 (hbk)
ISBN 0–415–08670–1 (pbk)

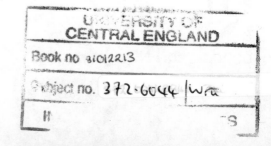

Contents

Part III Writing

Part IV Other themes and issues

Illustrations

Contributors

Roger Beard is Senior Lecturer in Education at the University of Leeds. He has taught in primary schools in several countries and has been involved as tutor and consultant to the Open University's reading and language courses. He has written and edited several books about aspects of literacy including *Teaching Literacy: Balancing Perspectives* (Hodder & Stoughton, 1992).

Greg Brooks is a senior research officer at the National Foundation for Educational Research in Slough. He has taught in France, Kenya, Essex and Northern Ireland and from 1981 to 1990 was responsible for the assessment of oracy in the Assessment of Performance Unit Language Monitoring Project.

Richard Fox is a Lecturer in Education and Primary Courses Coordinator at the University of Exeter. He taught in primary schools and spent some time as an educational psychologist before becoming a lecturer at Bath College of Higher Education. His research interests are in the development of children's writing.

Martin Hughes is currently Reader in Education at the University of Exeter. He has researched and written widely on the development and education of young children, and his books include *Young Children Learning* (with Barbara Tizard, 1984) and *Children and Number* (1986). His current research is on learning and social interaction and on the relationship between parents and schools.

Ann Lewis is a Lecturer in Education at the University of Warwick. She taught for ten years in primary and secondary schools before taking up her present post. She has carried out research into literacy, curriculum development and integration. Recent publications include *Primary Special Needs and the Curriculum* (Routledge, 1991), which was shortlisted for the 1992 TES/NASEN special needs book award.

Jane Medwell has taught in primary schools in Cardiff and Devon and is at present the PGCE Courses Leader at the College of St Mark and St John, Plymouth. She has researched into children's perceptions of reading, classroom contexts for writing and the use of word processors. Her publications include *Literacy and Language in the Primary Years* (with David Wray, Routledge, 1991).

Colin Mills is a Lecturer in Education at the University of Exeter. His teaching and research interests are in the areas of children's literature and literacy, gender and the general field of cultural studies and its relationship to schooling. He is the editor of *Language and Literacy in the Primary School* (with Margaret Meek, 1988).

Terry Phillips is a Lecturer in Education at the University of East Anglia. He has taught in several primary schools and been a teacher-tutor in a Norwich middle school. He has researched throughout his teaching career into children's responses to literature, small group discussion in the classroom, and the relationship between group talk and modes of thinking.

Frank Potter is a Senior Lecturer in Information Technology at Edge Hill University College, Ormskirk. He has taught in both primary and secondary schools and for his doctoral research investigated children's use of context in reading. More recently he directed a European Research Project on Word Processing and Literacy Skills and was President of the United Kingdom Reading Association 1989–90.

Bridie Raban is Professor of Primary Education at the University of Warwick and Director of the Research Centre for the Study of Early Childhood. She directed the National Curriculum Council funded evaluation project on the implementation of English at Key Stages 1, 2 and 3, and currently has responsibility for the early years tutors in the Department of Education at Warwick.

Denis Vincent is Reader in Education at the University of East London. He has carried out research and development projects in the field of literacy assessment and is the author of a number of published tests of reading. He is director of the East London Assessment Group which specialises in research into educational assessment and undertakes projects for government agencies and for educational publishers.

Margaret Wallen is a former teacher of English in secondary schools and of various subjects in middle schools. She was formerly Dorset Coordinator of the National Writing Project and the National Oracy Project and is currently team leader of the Dorset Curriculum Support Team for language.

David Wray taught in primary schools for several years before lecturing at Edge Hill College and University College, Cardiff. He is currently Senior Lecturer in Education at the University of Exeter. He has researched widely and published several books in the areas of literacy, language, educational uses of computers and teaching through project work, including *Literacy and Language in the Primary Years* (with Jane Medwell, Routledge, 1991).

Introduction

Teaching Primary English: The State of the Art is, without doubt, one of the riskiest titles one could select for a book. It invites debate and controversy in several ways.

First, the very reference to *Primary English* raises some important issues beyond simple nomenclature. This term would not have been used at all in the period from the post-Bullock late 1970s to the National Curriculum dominated late 1980s. Indeed, the book to which this current volume is a complement, our *Literacy and Language in the Primary Years*, still did not use it in 1991. The agenda has changed, however, largely because of the prescriptions of the National Curriculum, and a book which claims to reflect the *State of the Art* in this area has to take account of this agenda. One might, nevertheless, regret some of the implications to which the use of the term *Primary English* may give rise and as editors we should state here that we do not use the term to imply that this area should or could be thought of primarily as a discrete curriculum subject. English (or language and literacy) clearly underpins the whole of the primary curriculum (and indeed any curriculum). Language is both a medium, the control of which has to be learnt, and at the same time the means through which all learning is mediated. This view of English as process is, to be fair, enshrined in the requirements of the National Curriculum, although there are several voluble critics who would wish to see a greater emphasis upon English as a body of knowledge to be absorbed and a series of skills to be mastered.

A volume entitled *The State of the Art* also risks controversy with regard to the large claims such a title implies. We attempt in this book to bring together a cast of writers and researchers who might be expected, from their positions and reputations, to be at the forefront of current thinking in the particular areas about which they write. Such an attempt is, of course, fated to be only partially successful. The language and literacy area encompasses and is informed by such a wide range of research and critical disciplines that no single volume could really do it and its thinkers and developers justice. The contributors to this book *are* among the best known and most influential researchers and teachers in the area (in the United Kingdom). There are obviously others whose work could have been included.

The organisation of the book does itself make certain assumptions which need some explanation. As mentioned above, we have had to take account of the agenda currently before British primary schools in the early 1990s. This is reflected in two major ways. We have divided the book into parts in a manner largely determined by the organisation of the *English* National Curriculum for English. (We hope readers in Scotland and Northern Ireland will forgive this!) Thus the first three parts focus respectively on speaking and listening, reading and writing. The final part deals with some other important issues in primary English which are very much cross-modal. All this is not, of course, to imply that such divisions are anything other than convenient. A major lesson from the research and development of the past 15 years has, as we pointed out in our *Literacy and Language in the Primary Years*, been the importance of approaching the language area in a holistic way. A great deal of direct relevance to teaching has been learnt from seeing the parallels between, for example, learning to read and the development of writing. Oral language, of course, influences and is influenced by both these processes.

The other 'sign of the times' element to the book is the significant attention given to issues of assessment. There can be few periods of educational history in which this topic and its ramifications have had such a dominating effect upon the everyday classroom experience of British teachers and a state of the art volume clearly had to give it major treatment. For all the attention the assessment issue has had it is still plain, from the three chapters in this book, that there is more to be said about it and all three contributors give the topic innovative treatment.

As we hinted above, this book could easily have been twice as large as it is. We hope, however, that the collection of chapters we have included is found to be interesting, stimulating and useful. We see the book very much as a companion to *Literacy and Language in the Primary Years*, with the purpose of that volume being to chart out the important territory with which teachers of literacy and language need to become familiar. The present book is intended to provide for follow-up reading by those interested in filling in the details on their charts. We hope it fulfils that purpose.

Part I

Speaking and listening

Editors' introduction

In the National Curriculum for English it is the Profile Component Speaking and Listening which is, perhaps, closest to the hearts of many 'language' specialists. Since the pioneering work of Douglas Barnes in the late 1960s and early 1970s and the strong recommendations of the Bullock Report (DES, 1975) much theoretical attention has been given to the important role of talking in the learning process in all curriculum areas. Some of the key ideas now generally accepted about talk in the learning process were outlined in Chapter 1 of *Literacy and Language in the Primary Years* where we also examined the characteristic patterns of talk in classrooms. That these patterns appear, from a wide variety of research (Edwards and Westgate, 1987), to apply equally to contemporary classrooms as to pre-Bullock settings suggests that there are powerful forces operating to create a kind of classroom inertia in so far as classroom talk is concerned. These forces may include the self-perpetuating influence of 'classroom ecology' (Doyle, 1983) or 'continuity', in Mercer's terms (Mercer, 1990), which in turn is centrally derived from the belief systems of the participants in classroom discourse.

The beliefs held by many primary teachers are, suggests Martin Hughes in his chapter in this part, often characterised by a fairly negative perception of the linguistic capabilities of the children they teach, especially children from lower working-class backgrounds. Hughes found in his study that, despite an exposure to and knowledge of the findings of recent research into young children's language, which, by and large, contradicts the 'deficit model' of linguistic development, teachers persisted in their beliefs that this research did not apply to the children in *their* schools. Hughes' strategy for changing these teacher beliefs, which has a wide applicability in many educational contexts, was to involve them in action research with their children. The personally important evidence obtained during this process led to a marked shift in their attitudes towards their children's language capabilities and the classroom contexts and activities they subsequently devised.

In the final part of Chapter 1 of *Literacy and Language in the Primary Years* we went on to discuss the uses of group talk and to suggest some activities and contexts for it in the primary classroom. Terry Phillips' chapter here takes this much further. After surveying some of what is currently known about small group talk in educational settings he highlights some of the problematic areas in this knowledge and in its applications. He goes on to suggest several ground rules for strategies that teachers might use to enhance group talk in the classroom. Among these, most interestingly, is included the need to engage children in 'talking about their talk'. This metalinguistic approach finds echoes in several other chapters in this book.

Alongside an enhanced emphasis upon the place of speaking and listening in planned classroom activity goes, quite naturally, an awareness of the need to make useful assessments of children's abilities and progress in oracy. This would be true even without the requirements of the National Curriculum but, of course, these demands give an extra urgency to attempts to devise a workable approach to assessment in this area. The chapter by Greg Brooks is of significant help here. It reviews the findings and methodology of national approaches to the assessment of speaking and listening, and as well as suggesting that there is significantly more that teacher assessment can contribute to this process than has perhaps been realised, especially by teachers themselves, the chapter also suggests that there is mileage in involving the children in the process of assessing their own oracy. Brooks also discusses some of the common objections which are made to the assessment of oracy. As with other areas, it appears that assessment is not the overwhelming problem it is often taken to be, although it does clearly need some careful thinking on the part of teachers if it is to become more than just a set of 'bolt on' procedures and assume its most useful place as central to all classroom curriculum decisions.

REFERENCES

DES (1975) *A Language for Life*. London: HMSO.

Doyle, W. (1983) 'Academic work', *Review of Educational Research*, 53 (2), pp. 159–199.

Edwards, A. and Westgate, D. (1987) *Investigating Classroom Talk*. Lewes: Falmer.

Mercer, N. (1990) 'Context, continuity and communication in learning', in Potter, F. (ed.) *Reading, Learning and Media Education*. Oxford: Basil Blackwell.

Chapter 1

The oral language of young children

Martin Hughes

INTRODUCTION

The last few years have seen a renewed and rapidly increasing interest in the spoken language of young children. This is most clearly shown in the prominent place accorded to Speaking and Listening as a profile component of English within the National Curriculum, with the same weighting as Reading and Writing. At the same time, the value of oracy has been stressed by major national initiatives, such as the National Oracy Project and the Language in the National Curriculum (LINC) Project, which have emphasised the role of spoken language in helping children to make sense of their learning. The message for teachers is clear: developing children's oral language is now an essential part of their work.

It seems to be important, therefore, that teachers should have a clear understanding of the abilities which children already possess in the area of oral language when they first arrive in school at the ages of 4 and 5. For as Margaret Donaldson (1978) points out: 'teachers need to be clear not only about what they would like children to become under their guidance but about what children are actually like when the process is begun' (p. 15).

This point seems to be particularly appropriate to children's oral language, given that almost all children learn to talk long before they start school. It thus seems fairly uncontentious to hope that teachers have a clear understanding of what is known about children's spoken language when they first start school, and that they should draw on this understanding in their daily practice. As we shall see in this chapter, however, the issue is by no means as straightforward as it might appear. Indeed, there seems to be a gap of major significance between what many teachers believe about children's spoken language and what is known from recent research. This chapter first sets out the evidence that such a gap exists, and then attempts to understand how it has arisen. The chapter ends by looking at ways by which the gap might be reduced.

TEACHERS' PERCEPTIONS OF CHILDREN'S ORAL LANGUAGE

A rich source of evidence concerning teachers' perceptions of children's language comes from the Early Years Language Project, a project recently undertaken in the

South West of England by the University of Exeter and a local LEA. This project grew out of concerns expressed to the LEA about children's language by a group of headteachers from infant and primary schools in a large city in the region. Essentially, the headteachers claimed that children were increasingly entering their schools with spoken language insufficiently developed to benefit from what the school was providing. In response, the LEA seconded two local teachers and one advisory teacher to join a team of two LEA advisers and two university lecturers to investigate the issue more closely. More details of the project and its findings can be found in Cousins, 1990; Hughes and Cousins, 1988; Hughes, 1989; Goldsbrough, 1990; Hubbard, 1990; and Hughes and Cousins, 1990.

The first step taken by the project team was to carry out in-depth interviews with the headteachers and reception teachers of all schools in the city which admitted children at the age of 5. Altogether 69 headteachers and 88 reception teachers were interviewed. The interviews were concerned with the difficulties experienced by reception teachers, with the link between these and children's spoken language, with the nature and presumed cause of the children's language problems and with possible remedies.

When asked to outline the main problems facing them, the reception teachers made clear that language problems were high on their list of concerns. The most common problem, mentioned by nearly half the teachers and over a third of the headteachers, was that the children had limited spoken language. These limitations were said to take a number of forms. It was frequently stated that the children were unable to give explanations, to ask questions, to express themselves effectively, or to take their language above the level of mundane day-to-day requests. In addition, over a third of the teachers and headteachers said that the children were unable to listen: they did not seem to understand what the teacher was saying or were unable to carry out simple instructions. The teachers also commented on the children's poor vocabulary, the immaturity of their speech and their use of 'baby-talk'. About a quarter of the teachers expressed concern about the children's poor articulation, and it was remarked several times that many children had heavy accents or spoke with a strong local dialect. There were also a number of comments about the children's apparently poor grammar. These criticisms were illustrated by comments such as the following:

'The children have no language.'
'They use signs, grunts or gestures to express their needs.'
'I never presume they understand what I'm saying.'
'They do not talk in complete sentences, which makes it difficult to read and write.'

The teachers were asked what they thought were the causes of the children's language problems. By far the most common answer, given by around four-fifths of both the teachers and headteachers, was that the causes lay in the children's home environment. A large degree of concern was expressed about the amount and type of communication which took place at home, and several teachers commented that the parents just shouted or swore at their children. Many teachers felt they were battling against the unhelpful influence of the home environment, and particularly that of TV. Typical commments were:

'I feel that time at home with the parental model negates my teaching.'
'The parents can't construct a sentence properly, so it's not surprising the children can't either.'
'TV makes children unable to listen to a voice without a screen attached.'

More than half the teachers and headteachers related these linguistic limitations in the home environment to other apparent deficiencies in the quality of family life. Parents were frequently seen as neglectful and uncaring, and many were thought to have little interest in their children. However, such comments were by no means universal: about a third of the teachers made positive comments about the parents. This evident sympathy for the parents nevertheless placed many teachers in something of a predicament when asked to account for the language problems which they were encountering, a predicament which was summed up by one teacher as follows: 'I don't like to blame the parents – they try very hard – but we do get them straight from home, so what else can we blame it on?'

RECENT RESEARCH INTO CHILDREN'S ORAL LANGUAGE

These interviews indicated that the great majority of reception teachers and headteachers subscribed to what is often termed the language-deficit model. They believed that large numbers of children were starting school severely deficient in their spoken language, and that these deficiencies had their roots in the limited spoken language being used in the children's homes. These problems were most likely to be present in children from working-class homes, or from families suffering some kind of deprivation.

Such deficit theories of language are by no means new. Evidence presented in 1921 to the Newbolt Committee of Enquiry into the Teaching of English shows similar concerns to those expressed above:

Many children, when they first come to school, can scarcely talk at all. Sometimes, a witness told us, they cannot even name their eyes, ears, toes and so forth . . . the great difficulty of teachers in Elementary Schools in many districts is that they have to fight against the powerful influence of evil habits of speech contracted in home and street.

(Newbolt, 1921: 59, 68)

The language-deficit model became particularly prominent in the 1970s. At that time its proponents drew inspiration from the influential work of Bernstein (eg 1971), Tough (eg 1976), and the Bullock Report (DES, 1975), although none of these authors would necessarily agree to being labelled in this way. At the same time, the model was being questioned by other theorists. Linguists such as Labov (1972) argued that the language of urban lower-class black children in America was not so much deficient as different from that of their middle-class counterparts. Further support for Labov's views came from several British research studies which looked more closely at the language actually being used in the homes of young children (eg Wells, 1978, 1984, 1986; Tizard and Hughes, 1984). These studies painted a very different picture from that of the language-deficit theorists. Thus Wells (1978) concluded from his extensive recordings of children's language at home that:

> All but a very small minority of children reach the age of schooling with a vocabulary of several thousand words, control of the basic grammar of the language of their community, and an ability to deploy these resources in conversations arising from the many and varied situations that occur in their everyday lives.

> (Wells, 1978: 16)

Similarly, Tizard and Hughes reported from their study of 4-year-olds at home and at nursery school that:

> the conversations in the working-class homes were just as prolific as those in the middle-class homes. There was no question of these children 'not being talked to at home', and few signs of the language deprivation that has so often been described . . . the working-class children were clearly growing up in a rich linguistic environment.

> (Tizard and Hughes, 1984: 8)

The teachers interviewed in the Early Years Language Project were thus sub-scribing to a theory of language which is not supported by the findings of recent research. Why should this be?

One possible explanation is that the teachers were simply unaware of the relevant research findings. Indeed, there is some evidence to support this view. Our interviews revealed that a surprisingly high proportion of the reception teachers had not in fact trained for working with children of that age group. Many had set out to teach older children in junior or secondary classrooms, but had gravitated to working in the reception class as much by chance as by design. Moreover, many of the teachers had received their training at least ten years previously, when theories of language deficit were much more widely held. It seems likely, then, that many of the teachers had simply not been exposed to more recent work.

This, however, is not the whole story. Several teachers in the sample had in fact attended recent in-service courses at which alternative theories of language had been put forward – in some cases by members of the project team themselves. And yet, this exposure to more recent work had not led to a change in the teachers' views. Rather, it had been met by a reluctance to accept alternative evidence, and a more tenacious attachment to the language-deficit theories. Some teachers attempted to dismiss the newer evidence on various methodological grounds, such as the size and selection of the sample, the technique used to make the recordings and the geographical location of the studies. The following comments were typical of many:

> 'Tizard and Hughes' research was carried out in London, and Wells worked in Bristol: how relevant is that for us?'
> 'If you'd done the research in my school your findings would have been different.'

CHILDREN'S ORAL LANGUAGE AT HOME

In order to investigate this last possibility more thoroughly, the project team set out to make recordings in the homes of children living in the area where the interviews had taken place. Altogether, the homes of 19 children were visited in two areas of the city. Eleven of the children had just started at one school, while eight of the children were about to start at another school. The catchment areas of both schools were described by their headteachers as working class, and both schools were considered by their teachers to have a considerable number of children with language problems. A large proportion of the families contained only one parent, usually the mother. The occupations of the parents were either unskilled or semi-skilled, although not all the mothers were in paid employment. All the parents were interviewed about their child's language and some of the parents agreed to make tape-recordings of home conversations.

The interviews with the parents made clear that they did not share the teachers' beliefs about the children's limited spoken language. For example, the parents were asked if they considered their child to be talkative. This was usually met with much hilarity and cries of 'he never stops', or 'she rabbits on and on'. Only two of the children were described as not being talkative, and this was put down to shyness rather than any linguistic problem.

The parents' views were confirmed by listening to the tape-recordings of the home conversations. It was evident that there was a wealth of talk in the children's homes, and that this talk covered a wide variety of subjects. Conversations ranged over such diverse topics as why trains have a cowcatcher on the front, the dentist, starting school, animals, the human heart, fairy stories, why a milk-shake is frothy, birthdays, friends and relations. Particular attention was given to children's use of explanations, as many children had been said by their teachers or headteachers to be unable to take their language above the level of mundane day-to-day requests. However, in none of the homes was there any evidence to suggest that the child was unable to explain.

The following conversation, for example, was taped at a meal-time. Kevin and his father had earlier been working together in the shed. Not only does Kevin explain how he painted his wheelbarrow, but there is also evidence to show that he has a good awareness of colours and is able to justify his actions:

> M. (Mother) Well, are you going to tell me how you painted your wheel-
> barrow then?

K. (Kevin)	I painted it with silver and yellow because I didn't like it green.
F. (Father)	You primed it up first, didn't you?
M.	Didn't you like it green?
K.	No, 'cos I wanted it yellow. I wanted it yellow.
F.	It came out all right then, didn't it? Did you like doing that?
M.	Then how did you do it?
K.	With a gun.
M.	What?
K.	With a gun.
M.	A gun?
K.	A painting gun.
M.	Oh, what did you do?
K.	I painted it yellow, lift it up and stuck all the red on . . . I . . . and mixed it around and around . . . and after that . . . I put some, put some paper, put some paper on it and sellotape . . .
M.	What did you use sellotape for?
K.	For the paper on the windows.

Another comment frequently made about the children in school was that they seemed unable to listen. However, there was little evidence on the home tape-recordings to show that the children did not or could not listen – indeed the fact that they engaged in a variety of conversations and could respond appropriately would suggest that they did listen. There were instances on the recordings where the parent had to repeat herself, but this was rare and occurred in circumstances where the child was either absorbed in another activity or had to alter his or her train of thought to suit the adult.

Children's use of 'baby-talk' was commented on frequently in the school interviews. It was also suggested that many parents had limited expectations of their children's language, and allowed them to get away with immature speech. These claims were not borne out by the families whom we studied. The interviews with the parents indicated that baby-talk was disapproved of, and this was supported by evidence from the recordings. In the following extract, for example, Linda and her mother are talking about what Linda had been doing with her friends at playschool that day. Linda is describing lunch:

L.	Others had a beefyburger.
M.	The others had a beefburger?
L.	Me and Sarah 'ad cccccccake, ccccc-
M.	. . . you talking like that for?
L.	Cake, cccc-
M.	You talk properly.

Linda's mother does not overtly correct the use of the word 'beefyburger' but repeats the word in the correct form. However, she criticises the child directly for not articulating the word 'cake' properly.

The teachers had also commented on the use of what they termed 'bad grammar', giving as an example of this the failure to speak in complete sentences. The recordings of the children talking with their parents indeed showed evidence of non-standard forms of English, as well as examples of incomplete sentences. However, it should be pointed out that such features are frequent in normal everyday conversations. In the following conversation, for example, Ross's mother is explaining to him that when he starts school he will be eating school dinners:

R. You do 'ave to buy me a packed lunch box 'cos I go packed lunch.
M. Well, you'll stay to dinners like Neil [his brother].
R. That's school dinners.
M. That's school dinners like Neil, won't yer?
R. Yeah, an' you goin' 'ave to buy me a box.
M. Oh no, you won't need a packed lunch box if you staying school dinners 'cos they'll cook yer dinners in school an' give it to yer.
R. No they don't 'cos they 'aven't got a cooker.
M. They 'ave.
R. You wouldn't know.
M. Yeah.
R. You gotta make it.
M. No, mummy don't make it, they make it in school an' then you sit down with all the other children an' eat your dinner.

While Ross and his mother certainly use non-standard forms of English, they do so in a regular and consistent way. It is not so much that the conversation shows 'bad grammar', but rather that their speech reveals a slightly different syntactic pattern to that of standard English. Clearly, Ross and his mother do not have problems understanding each other; nor would the use of non-standard forms, in this instance at least, affect communication with others.

Many of the teachers had observed that the children seemed reluctant to ask questions in the classroom. In contrast, the home tapes revealed a number of occasions when the children persistently used questions as a way of increasing their understanding. What was particularly interesting, in view of the teachers' comments, was that such questioning frequently occurred when the children were watching television. The following example occurred when Richard saw a milk-shake on TV:

R. Hey Mum, when you shake it how does it get like that? How does it do that?
M. Make it all frothy?
R. Yeah . . . hasn't it got gases in it?
M. Not gas, no.
R. What's it got in it?
M. They put some stuff in it to put the flavour in and then you make it all up, it goes all frothy. You get bubbles on the top.

We saw earlier that the headteachers and reception teachers made a number of comments about deficiencies in the quality of family life, and in particular about the parents' lack of concern or interest in their children. Our recordings suggested a very different picture, in which the parents were evidently concerned for their children's welfare and interested in their ideas. This revealed itself in a number of ways. For example, we were impressed throughout the recordings by the parents' evident willingness and ability to enter into the child's world, not just in the 'make believe' sense, but also by looking at the world from the child's point of view. In addition, we were impressed by the evidently close relationships between the parents and the children. This was revealed in a number of conversations, but especially in this one which took place between Linda and her mother at bedtime:

L. I like you best.
M. You like me best?
L. Not when you shout at me.
M. Not when I shouts at you? (laughs) You should be good shouldn't you? Eh? 'cos if you was a good girl sometime I wouldn't have to shout at you would I?
L. You don't like shouting?
M. No, I don't like shouting at you and I don't like you being naughty.
L. Don't you? Don't you? Think it's a shame when I cry?
M. Do I think it's a shame when you cry? Sometimes.
L. Sometimes you don't?
M. Yes, sometimes I don't, 'cos sometimes you get sent to bed don't you?
L. When I get sent to bed don't you care?
M. Of course I care. Do you care?
L. Care about you.
M. You care about me?
L. Every day.
M. Every day?
L. Even when I'm being naughty.

The picture which emerges from the children's homes contrasts sharply with that emerging from the interviews with the local teachers. The teachers expressed concern about the amount of language which took place at home, about the children's limited use of explanations, their inability to listen, their use of baby-talk, their lack of vocabulary, their poor grammar and their use of questions, as well as about the parents' lack of concern for their children. In contrast, the home interviews and tape-recordings revealed the children to be competent conversationalists who used language in a skilful way to increase their understanding of the world, in the company of concerned and interested parents. While it must be admitted that the number of children recorded at home by the Early Years Language Project was relatively small, the picture revealed by these home recordings – and by the interviews with the children's parents – fits remarkably well with that emerging from other British studies, such as those of Wells and Tizard and Hughes.

Clearly there is a gap between the teachers' perceptions and the findings of research. But to say this is not to be critical of teachers, or to suggest that they are ignorant of recent research. The issue, as we have seen, is far more complex than that. In the next two sections we try to understand how such a gap has arisen, and how it might be reduced.

CHILDREN'S ORAL LANGUAGE AT SCHOOL

The issue becomes a good deal easier to understand if we broaden the picture and consider children's oral language in school. For, as several studies have now shown (e.g. Tizard and Hughes, 1984; Wells, 1986), young children frequently have difficulty in demonstrating within school the language abilities which they so readily display at home. This seems to be particularly pronounced for young working-class children, who are much less likely than middle-class children to demonstrate their true linguistic capabilities in the classroom. Faced with a silent or monosyllabic child, it is not surprising that a teacher will conclude that this child has 'little or no language', and that this must be because of some deficit in the home.

This point is well illustrated by the following conversation from the Early Years Language Project. The conversation features Kevin, the boy whom we saw earlier describing to his mother and father how he painted his wheelbarrow at home. The school conversation took place at 'large group sharing time', as Kevin's teacher tried to encourage him to talk about some paintings he had done earlier:

T. Kevin's got something to show, Kevin, haven't you? Sit down Louise, sit down lovie, that's right. Kevin, what did you want to show?

K. (no response)

T. Come on then . . . no not yet Richard, in a minute . . . yes alright, if you must, yes go on then. What did . . . Kevin wants to tell you all about his paintings . . . aren't they lovely children? He's . . . Sarah, Sarah . . . look here lovie, Kevin's . . . aren't they beautiful? What colour is it Kevin?

K. (no response)

T. This one? That wasn't very kind, that wasn't a nice thing to say. Kevin wants to tell you about his paintings.

K. (no response)

The intention here is not to criticise Kevin's teacher in her efforts to encourage him to contribute to the group discussion. Rather, the example is given to show how a young child can be relatively articulate in one situation but may say very little in another. On this basis, it would be quite reasonable for Kevin's teacher to consider that he had 'little or no language'. In fact, the teacher was aware of Kevin's abilities from other conversations. Earlier that day she had talked to him while he was actually painting:

K. I'll put a bit of red on that now.

T. That's dramatic now . . . all red. What happened there?

K. It's all red now, all red. More yellow now, yellow. I'm going to do another painting in a minute.

T. Have you nearly finished this one, then?

K. Yeah, I wanna do another one (very excited). Look, it's gone all orange now!

T. So it has. What did you dip it in?

K. Yellow and red, and it's gone all orange.

T. So it has. What a lovely colour, beautiful. Yes, it's lovely.

K. (happy and singing) All of my work. I got orange. Yellow dripping down again. But red now . . . Orange . . . orange. Oh, it's dripping on my red now, it's gone all yucky . . . blue. All yellow . . . all yellow now, yellow more yellow, some more yellow on the red. Orange some more, some more yellow on some blue . . . GREEN . . . GREEN. Look teacher, look what I done there. Teacher, I've done another one down there.

Interestingly enough, this conversation did not actually take place in the classroom during normal lesson time. Instead, it took place in the hall when the teacher was supervising a wet playtime. It seems that Kevin felt much more able to express himself linguistically in such a context – possibly because it felt closer to the more familiar context of home conversations than did 'large group sharing time'.

BRIDGING THE GAP BETWEEN THEORY AND PRACTICE

How might we bridge the gap between teachers' perceptions and the findings of research? From what we have seen already, it seems unlikely that simply inform-ing teachers about research findings will bring about change, particularly if these findings are seen as having little relevance to – or are even contradicted by – conditions in their own immediate circumstances. Instead, a different approach is needed, which starts from the reality of teachers' own classrooms. Such an approach was adopted by the Early Years Language Project, and is described in this section.

The approach adopted was to set up a study group of ten reception teachers who met regularly with one of the project members (Jacqui Cousins) over a period of about a year. Initial discussions within the group revealed their doubts about the validity of recent research into the language of young children. Speci-fically, the teachers doubted whether it could be assumed that most children were already competent talkers when they started school, and they wanted the oppor-tunity to observe, record and analyse classroom language for themselves – something which they had never done before. Accordingly, a method of working was evolved in which the project member spent a day in each of their classrooms in turn. During this day there were periods when the project member took charge of the whole class, leaving the teacher free to make observations and recordings of a particular child. At other times the project member made her own observations and recordings, and discussed the teacher's observations with her. The teachers brought transcriptions from their recordings to group meetings, and discussed them within the group.

One of the clearest benefits from this method of working lay in the changes which came about in the teachers' perceptions of the individual children whom they had chosen to observe. In nine cases out of ten these children had been selected because the teacher considered their spoken language to be poor (the other child was thought to have exceptionally good language). However, by the end of the project the teachers had clearly revised their opinions about these children:

'My relationship with this child improved from that short time that I concentrated on him. I think my attitude changed. I can't explain exactly what I mean, but I think I've been too convinced that he couldn't do things, and I haven't expected a lot.'

'I was assuming that there was little language at home but I don't know, do I? This is where I've got to listen more to the children's family. This child gave me a big surprise when I really listened to him.'

The recordings enabled the teachers to reconsider the value of certain activities for eliciting children's spoken language, and allowed them to reflect on their own use of language in the classroom. One teacher, for example, having recorded her target child playing a 'language game' concluded that:

'Those language games are a total waste of time in encouraging oral language. Out they go!'

Another teacher recorded herself talking to one child and reflected on her own use of language:

'Questions, questions, questions! All I do is ask questions of the poor child. I'm going to record myself regularly and concentrate on not asking questions, particularly "what colour is it?" '

In their discussions, the teachers recognised that conversations such as the one where Kevin had been painting during a wet playtime did in fact occur at school, often at the beginning or end of the day or when the children were changing for PE. What they found difficult was knowing how much importance to attach to them. One teacher commented that she felt guilty about having such a conversation because it took time away from the 'real work' of school. Another teacher was more forthright:

'This is just chat . . . filling in a few moments before lunch. It isn't the substance of their learning. We're too rushed to chat like that with all the children who need support with their oral language.'

Nevertheless, most of the teachers recognised the value of such conversations in giving them a different picture of the child's spoken language to that normally presented in the classroom. They also went on to consider how existing activities could be adapted to encourage more investigative and exploratory uses of language by the children.

One of the teachers in the group was the same teacher who had earlier been trying to elicit conversation from Kevin at 'large group sharing time'. As a result of her involvement in the project, she changed the way she organised such sessions in her reception class. First, she concentrated on keeping the number of children as small as possible. Second, she tried to keep eye-contact with the children who were particularly shy, so that they could see her non-verbal expressions and gestures and she was able to see theirs. Third, she chose topics which linked as closely as possible to their interests and experience. And finally, she made a particular effort to keep the focus of the group conversation on the topic in question, ignoring distractions and minimising her own questions.

The following conversation illustrates her new approach in action. Two of the children involved, David and Leanne, had both been extremely silent when they first arrived in school, and she was particularly concerned that they should make a contribution. The conversation took place after they had visited a wild area which David had discovered close to the playground. They had found some little creatures and brought them back to put them in a tank:

T.	I really enjoyed that, didn't you?
Ian	I did, I really did.
Sarah	I specially liked all they little baby snails.
David	I like they things, look, they . . .
Ian	Worms.
Leanne	I hates worms . . . yuk . . . I hates them all slimy.
T.	Well, they can't help being slimy, can they?
Louise	Why have they got slimy bits? Snakes 'ain't got slimy bits like they. When that man came from his zoo with snakes he told us they weren't slimy.
David	I touched a snake.
Ian	I touched a frog.
Leanne	I held the little owl and he pecks me.
T.	Well, why have worms got slimy bits? Louise asked us an interesting question there. Can anyone . . . ?
Richard	It's because they live in the ground and that can hurt if they not slimy . . . and snails is slimy when they moves.
David	Look, I can see all his slimy on the glass.
Kevin	That silly . . . drinks in glass.
Sarah	I'm thirsty.
Louise	I'm thirsty now.
T.	You can all have a drink in a minute. Let's just . . . let's just . . . who can help me to show the children the little snail climbing up the glass tank? Sit down lovie, so that we can see.

Sarah	Look at the little snail and there's his big mum in the grass.
David	I can see all the slimy on the glass.
Kevin	Is it like glue? Not glue like when we do sticking at school.
Sarah	Not that white sort of glue, like . . .
Richard	I did sticking, I made a big card for my Nan.
T.	So you did, but do you think this snail is really stuck with glue?
Peter	He's not stuck properly, he can still go up.
Ross	Yeah, he's going right up to the top of the glass.
Richard	And then he'll fall on the ground and a big bird'll fly in and eat him.
Sarah	Ah, poor snail . . . I feel really sorry for poor little creatures being ate.
Richard	That's what birds do to snails.
Ross	Then things eat birds and then all things get eaten up.
Richard	If things don't then they all die.
T.	Well, I don't think a bird will get this snail because he's in the classroom. I think we had better take them all back after, don't you?
Sarah	No, I don't want that little snail to get ate up . . . I want to keep him.
David	I want to keep all a they . . .
T.	Well we can keep them for a little while but we'll have to find them food.
David	Snails eat grass and leaves and things like that, don't they?

This conversation suggests that her new approach was more successful than her previous efforts. All the children were attentive, and those who didn't talk watched closely as the snails and worms moved in the tank. The teacher was pleased that she had been able to keep the conversation on the topic of the little creatures without dominating the conversation with her questions. At the same time she commented that she had almost felt a sense of guilt at allowing the conversation to continue for so long on this single topic.

The teachers' analysis of children's language in the classroom also led them to reconsider their assumptions about the language of the home. Four teachers wanted to initiate visits to the children's homes, and three wanted to establish more links with the families before the children started school. In most cases their headteachers were supportive and it was possible to implement these changes. Indeed one headteacher commented that:

> 'The changes in attitude towards the children's families have been remarkable and we are going to make closer links, a thing that I as a head have tried to get her to do in the past . . . there has been such a resistance.'

Those teachers who were able to initiate home visiting hoped that eventually they would be in a position to ask for a recording of a conversation in the children's homes. At the same time, other teachers were very hesitant about asking for a home recording, and felt that it would be seen by the parents as an invasion of their privacy. One teacher commented:

'There is the gap in really being able to listen to the child having a conversation at home because I haven't got a tape-recording of any. I haven't got the right to ask for one, and because I'm still not very confident at home visits I don't know how to ask the mum to do it.'

Another said:

'If gathering data from home was part of the normal procedure and everyone involved understood that it wasn't because Big Brother was listening in to private conversations then I would do it. I think it does fill in gaps but I'm prepared to say that children of all classes and cultures do use oral language and do talk to each other so do I need to add to my workload in listening to 30 tapes?'

Within the group attempts were made to link up the teachers' observations and new perspectives on children's language with the findings of recent research. Dissatisfactions were expressed about theories which they had held for some time, and there was a renewed interest in finding out about more recent theory. Four members of the group applied for courses to carry out further study, and three of them were successful. Finally, all the teachers made positive comments about the value of the work for them personally, and eight referred to their own increase in confidence as a result of the support provided within the group.

CONCLUSION

The overall conclusion which we would want to draw from this chapter is therefore a positive one. It seems that there is indeed a large gap between many teachers' theories about children's oral language and the findings of research. The gap is more understandable when it is placed alongside what is currently known about children's oral language in school. At the same time, the gap is not something which is fixed for ever. As our work with the ten teachers has shown, teachers' views can be changed if they are able to stand back from their practice and observe children, and to discuss their observations with others in a supportive environment. In turn, this can lead to changing their practice in ways which enable children to use oral language as readily at school as they undoubtedly do at home.

ACKNOWLEDGEMENTS

I am grateful to the other members of the Early Years Language Project (Mary Chessum, Jacqui Cousins, Marilyn Goldsbrough, John Gulliver, Graham Hammond and Lorraine Hubbard) for allowing me to use material from the project in this chapter; however, the views expressed here are not necessarily shared by other members of the team. I am also grateful to Louise Poulson for her critical comments on an earlier draft of this chapter.

REFERENCES

Bernstein, B. (1971) *Class, Codes and Control*. London: Routledge.

Cousins, J. (1990) 'Are your little Humpty Dumpties floating or sinking?', *Early Years*, 10 (2), pp. 28–34.

DES (1975) *A Language for Life. Report of the Committee of Enquiry chaired by Sir Alan Bullock*. London: HMSO.

Donaldson, M. (1978) *Children's Minds*. London: Fontana.

Goldsbrough, M. (1990) *Teachers' Perceptions of Language in the Reception Classroom*. Unpublished M.Phil. thesis, University of Exeter.

Hubbard, L. (1990) *Teachers' Theories of Language at Home and at School*. Unpublished M.Phil. thesis, University of Exeter.

Hughes, M. (1989) 'The child as a learner: the contrasting views of developmental psychology and early education', in Desforges, C. (ed.) *Early Childhood Education*. Edinburgh: Scottish Academic Press.

Hughes, M. and Cousins, J. (1988) 'The roots of oracy', in MacLure, M., Phillips, T. and Wilkinson, A. (eds) *Oracy Matters*. Milton Keynes: Open University Press.

Hughes, M. and Cousins, J. (1990) 'Teacher's perceptions of children's language', in Wray, D. (ed.) *Emerging Partnerships: Current Research in Language and Literacy*. Clevedon: Multilingual Matters.

Labov, W. (1972) 'The logic of non-standard English', in Giglioli, P.P. (ed.) *Language and Social Context*. London: Penguin.

Newbolt, H. (1921) *The Teaching of English in England*. London: HMSO.

Tizard, B. and Hughes, M. (1984) *Young Children Learning*. London: Fontana.

Tough, J. (1976) *Listening to Children Talking*. London: Ward Lock.

Wells, C.G. (1978) 'Talking with children: the complementary roles of parents and teachers', *English in Education*, 12, pp. 15–38.

Wells, C.G. (1984) *Language Development in the Preschool Years*. Cambridge: Cambridge University Press.

Wells, C.G. (1986) *The Meaning Makers*. London: Heinemann.

Chapter 2

The dead spot in our struggle for meaning

Learning and understanding through small group talk

Terry Phillips

'Understanding is the dead spot in our struggle for meaning; it is the moment-ary pause, the stillness before incomprehension continues.' (Sless, 1986)

WHY DISCUSS IN GROUPS?

Until very recently primary teaching in which small group discussion did not take place was almost unthinkable. Today, the value of small group discussions, along with other small group activities, is being questioned in some quarters by people who see it as inefficient and wish schools to abandon its use. Now is as good a time as any, therefore, to evaluate the educational significance of group talk, and to consider – where appropriate – some of the ways it might be put to more effective use. It certainly has to be recognised that small group discussion, like any other classroom activity, can be worthwhile or a waste of time. The fact that children are talking in small groups does not automatically mean that they are having a 'good' discussion. Nor does it follow that because some small group discussion is allegedly 'poor', such discussions are intrinsically flawed as a means of learning. We have to look at what children do when they talk together in small groups, consider whether it is valuable educational activity, and whether – even if it is valuable – it is the most valuable way that they could use the opportunity offered by working with peers.

GROUP TALK AS NOT-CLASS TALK

The by now familiar argument in favour of small group discussion in school is that it offers something that the class lesson does not. Class discussions, because they are mediated by an adult with power to control turn-taking, initiate topic change and determine exchange types, inhibit the number and range of contri-butions that students make to a conversation. Research has shown that teachers use language for a wide range of purposes (functions), including directing, informing, commenting, evaluating and eliciting answers (Sinclair and Coult-hard, 1975), while students use their talk almost exclusively to respond to questions (Barnes, 1976; Willes, 1980; MacLure and French, 1981). When teaching a whole class, teachers employ a range of linguistic strategies to create three-part interaction patterns, providing prompts to help children know when to offer an answer, and clues to guide them towards the 'correct' answer if it becomes obvious that first attempts are moving along the 'wrong' lines (Sinclair and Coulthard, 1975). Adults occupy the speaking role for a disproportionate amount of time, dominating interaction by taking twice as many turns as all the children put together (Bellack *et al.*, 1966; Flanders, 1970), and children achieve success by becoming aware of and competent at responding to the strategies that teachers use to direct them to 'right answers', 'relevant information' and 'proper understanding'.

Class lessons emphasise the procedural rather than the intellectual. The most obvious thing about the small group discussion is that it is not a class lesson. Among a group's three or four members there is no person with asymmetrical rights to control the conversation and determine the (reactive) role of the others. To engage successfully in small group discussion speakers have to employ social and conversational rules which they have learned in everyday interactions. To ensure that they take their turn appropriately they must listen actively for falling intonation at the end of a tone group (Halliday, 1970; Brazil *et al.*, 1980), note when an information unit is completed (Halliday, 1985; Butler, 1985) and watch to see where speakers drop their gaze (Swann and Graddoll, 1988). Where they depart from the main agenda of the conversation they must head off the potential disruptiveness with mitigations in which they excuse their action (Sacks *et al.*, 1974). And when they introduce a new topic they must either link it cohesively with previous utterances or warn that they are changing direction by using a 'gambit' such as 'if I can mention something else for a minute' (Keller, 1981). In the process they must learn to modify what they have discovered in both symmetrical and asymmetrical dyadic conversation about politeness – a major principle to which all speakers normally adhere (Grice, 1963) – and in particular must learn to exercise assertiveness without completely destroying the politeness principle.

By taking part in small group discussion children become involved in a great deal of 'conversational work', actively using conversational procedures from natural speech rather than reactively responding to institutionalised lesson routines. Because group members have to work together to construct a way of interacting that suits them all (or at least most of them), group discussion is sometimes difficult for the child who has become used to being directed. Inexperienced group members may initially be unable to cope with the extra and unfamiliar demands. One person may help the group to avoid the problem by taking on the role of surrogate teacher, another may attempt to overcome it with excessive caution leading to near silence, others may add to it by unintentionally interrupting at the wrong moment or becoming uncomfortably loud in an effort to gain a turn. Only with experience will peers learn to operate 'as a group', recognising and deploying the strategies that enable them to work together conversationally. There are bound to be a few small management problems at first but once the children have gained experience of the new way of working these will dissolve.

'SOMETHING MORE'

By minimising the need to concentrate on procedures, the small group offers all its members a better chance of getting a turn. But that fact alone is not sufficient reason for accepting the organisational upheaval that changing a class's ethos to include group work often requires. A much greater potential advantage to be had from the removal of procedural constraints is that students are freed to concentrate on their own purposes, and to initiate their own topics. Whether this potential is realised, however, depends upon the context in which the discussion takes place. Or rather, it depends upon three aspects of that context, namely:

(a) *the task*, as represented in the type of activity, the teacher's instructions and the children's comments;
(b) *the classroom language climate* and the relationship of the communication element of the task to it;
(c) *the learning culture* of the particular classroom through which the children have developed their expectations and attitudes about knowledge. It is worth looking at each of these in turn.

THE NATURE AND PURPOSE OF THE TASK

A task is not just what is being done by a group at the moment it is doing it, but also a whole set of concomitant notions of what and how the activity should be done. The *task frame* is to all intents and purposes part of the task.

Central among the framing agents is the teacher's definition of the task as represented in her words in setting out what has to be done. If the ostensible task is to complete a plan for the layout of tables at the summer fête and the teacher says, 'I would like you to discuss where to put the tables so that we can get as many different stalls into the available space as possible', she has set a slightly different task from the one motivated by the instruction, 'In 25 minutes I want you to give me a list of all the stalls we might be able to have at the fête.' The first instruction defines the task as being about a problem to be solved, the other about making a list, which may or may not have a problem-solving aspect.

Another major influence upon the framing of the task is the children's interpretation of the teacher's instructions. They will decide what she means in the light of their experience of previous analogous tasks. If they have found all discussions about what to include on a list to be for the sake of the exercise rather than as a planning stage for a real activity, they will interpret any instruction to discuss 'what to include' as such an exercise. If, on the other hand, they have found this sort of activity to be real in the past, with the possibility of an action outcome, they will interpret the task as being about achieving the outcome. There may well be some doubt in their minds as to what exactly the task is about, and so they may spend at least part of their discussion unofficially negotiating a definition of it as they might their first tentative attempts to become involved in a task they are slightly confused about. Some of the children may begin the discussion, for instance, in an *exploratory* mode, speculating about the possibility of having interesting new kinds of stall at their fête, while others adopt an *operational* (or practical activity oriented) mode, attempting to get the list of stalls completed as quickly and with as little fuss as possible. The discussion might continue in this way for five minutes or so, with the two definitions of the task in competition, until by tacit agreement both groups settle down into a predominantly *argumentational* mode to compile their list through explaining and justifying their choices to each other. (See Phillips, 1986, 1988 for a fuller description of these modes.)

A final frame is provided by the metalanguage used to set the task up, and to negotiate it once in progress. If the children are asked to 'discuss', the task is theoretically much broader than if they are asked to 'persuade'. If someone interrupts the group discussion by saying, 'Hang on a minute, you've got to "explain" why you want the coconut shy put next to the mother and toddler rest room', they have narrowed the task by referring to the metalanguage. Both the teacher's and the children's language about language are active influences upon the precise nature and function of the task.

One practical implication of the complexity of the task (and its often inextricable relationship with other aspects of the context) is that there is often a mismatch between a teacher's expectations about what will come out of a group discussion and what actually does. Research in progress suggests that teachers often decide after a discussion what it was that served as evidence that the children had got something useful from it. Often the outcome of a group discussion, although different from what the teacher intended, is worthwhile, but it is somewhat hit and miss to make that decision *post hoc*. There is clearly some merit in allowing time for all concerned to clarify their understanding of the task before the discussion proper gets under way. The first part of a peer group discussion may be spent negotiating that understanding; alternatively teachers may reduce some of the need for this by taking care when setting out the task. But because it is likely that children will always interpret tasks slightly differently from the way teachers do, perhaps the best way to achieve a common understanding of the task is for teacher and children to get into the habit of preceding all small group discussion with an interrogation of the task to find out what its purpose is, with questions such as, 'Why are we doing this?', 'What do you mean by "discuss" this time?', and 'What should we be able to do at the end?' or 'What should we know at the end?' (Phillips, 1992). Such interrogation of the task will help the group to decide whether they are supposed to be collecting new information, exploring an experience, planning a future activity or giving an account of a recent one, and whether this involves the cognitive activity of argument, hypothesis, collection, speculation or problem-solving. One legitimate criticism of some small group discussion would be that neither the teacher nor the children in the group know precisely enough what the task is. This is why interrogation of the task is time well spent. And there is a bonus. In closely questioning the purpose of the group discussion, it might be discovered that the task is inappropriate, or just a plain waste of time, in which case it can be abandoned and replaced with something more educative.

THE LANGUAGE CLIMATE

One of the ostensible reasons for introducing group discussion into the primary classroom is that it enables children to work at their own pace, participating fully in arranging their own schedule for finding out information and understanding it. The popular view of communication as the transmission and reception of messages persists, however, and interferes with the good intentions. The primacy of this view has not weakened over time, despite research which has shown that communication has a social purpose as well as an informational one, and that it is interactional and interpretative (Wells, 1981). Business training schemes, adult education courses, management courses and the National Curriculum all have so-called communication skills units that include such things as speaking clearly, listening attentively, being succinct and getting your message across. These are unambiguous indicators of the general view in society that 'good' communication is primarily instrumentally successful communication, communication with which the speaker can pass messages to the listeners with the minimum amount of fuss. Habermas has described this function of communication as *strategic* (Habermas, 1985). Despite claims to the contrary, the belief that the most important function of communication is its strategic one is prevalent in many classrooms. The consequence is that when children from these classes are asked to discuss in groups they realise from their knowledge of the classroom language climate that they are expected to make definitive statements about the world (that is, to deal in 'facts'), rather than to play with alternative notions of the world.

The alternative perception of communication is that it is an act of mutual interpretation for increasing understanding, or in Habermas's term it is *communicative* (Habermas, 1985). It is a perception that envisages all information as inherently 'arguable', that is, as a suitable subject for investigation with a view to achieving either clarification or falsification (Phillips, 1986). In places where this view is held speakers ask questions on the assumption that 'questioning indicates the existence of an unsettled issue, a difficult matter, an uncertainty, a matter for discussion [and it] opens possibilities and leads, in some sense, to uncertainty, for it throws what may have been thought secure into disequilibrium or imbalance' (Bergum, 1991). Where the transmissive view of communication pertains it skews the development of small groups as an alternative to class teaching towards the old activity of information acquisition and exchange. Where there is a communicative and interpretive perspective it tends to lead to small groups being treated as contexts where a fundamental discourse about knowledge and understanding can take place.

The language climate of a classroom does not change quickly. By focusing on quantitative aspects of interaction such as duration and number of turns, and quasi-qualitative aspects such as the balance of types of question and answer, research has failed to challenge the pernicious notion of knowledge as transferable commodity. Quantitative and quasi-qualitative studies of children's classroom talk have left understanding of it stuck in the doldrums of the transmissive view of knowledge. They leave unchallenged the assumption that knowledge can be passed on; they merely look at how it is passed on, and consider the implications of the passing on being carried out in one way rather than another. Although research has moved the language climate in many classrooms beyond the point where the quantity of pupil talk was so curtailed as to offer little opportunity for involvement in learning, and has even brought about an improvement in the quality of that talk by encouraging an increase in the range of functions children use, it has not been able to shift the major impediment to educative discourse, namely the view that the strategic function of language is paramount over its communicative function. In a school system where the emphasis is on stability, new evidence is treated selectively to reinforce existing views and prevent 'disturbance'.[1]

The alternative view of communication, held by this author, is that it is an interactive venture in which individuals cooperate to produce texts within socially determined frameworks. In this view, discussion is in part shaped by what the participants know society expects in a particular situation, and some regularly occurring types of discussion are tightly constrained by a set of highly formalised procedures. The more ritualised an event a discussion is, and the more often the speakers have taken part in similar discussions, the more the event will conform to the schematic structure 'normally' expected for that situation (Martin, 1984; Halliday and Hasan, 1985; Ventola, 1986). To quote Kress: 'The conventionalised forms of the occasions lead to conventionalised forms of text, to specific genres' (Kress, 1985). In the classroom, the group discussion as much as the class lesson is a ritualised event in which the speakers are constrained by previous practice; both have a schematic structure and are therefore recognisable classroom genres. The members of a small group will expect to talk to each other within a framework of socially constructed ground rules that they 'know' intuitively from their experience of living in the classroom culture. To that extent, their discussion is culturally determined. But within that cultural framework they are free to interpret what the other speakers say and do, as active meaning-makers. They can vary the 'official' schematic structure to suit their own purposes. After a while a group that is confident about its own standing fashions its own 'norms' and breaks out of the expected schematic structure. For instance, in response to the teacher's instructions a group of children will begin to 'prepare a case for the use of animals for health' according to all the 'rules' of argumentation. In the course of argumentative discussion children can become passionately involved in telling each other stories about neglected animals and so move beyond the traditional argumentative framework (Phillips, 1991).

In classrooms where the language climate reflects commitment to the view outlined above there is bound to be a different understanding of the purpose of group talk and its potential for learning. In this kind of climate there will be an expectation of active involvement in the construction of meanings. That construction process may be constrained by social genres that prevent unrestrained creativity, but because children may choose to behave differently from the 'norm', either by choice or through only partial familiarity with its pattern, the creativity is in no way predetermined by the genre. Speakers, social meanings and texts are in a dynamic relationship; speakers influence and shape their worlds as much as the world influences and shapes the text of their discussion.

THE RELATIONSHIP BETWEEN LANGUAGE CLIMATE AND LEARNING CULTURE

All communication occurs in a social context, and there is always a relationship between that context and the text of the conversation. Halliday has argued that the 'register' which speakers use takes account of the tenor and the field of discourse. By this he means that the language chosen recognises specialised terms, concepts and socially agreed ways of presenting what is being talked about (the field), and it reflects the formality of the relationship between the speakers (the tenor) (Halliday, 1978). Gregory and Carroll have suggested that it also reflects what they call the functional tenor, or overall purpose of the interaction (Gregory and Carroll, 1978). A 'register' is language appropriate to a particular context and is affected by field, interpersonal tenor and functional tenor; it is not a pre-specified language form, but is worked out between the speakers within a broad framework that they have learned to recognise from social interaction and conversation over time. The point can be clarified with an example. Speakers in formal contexts, meeting each other in an official capacity in order to discuss the buying and selling of a house, will use different language from the same people meeting each other informally to celebrate moving into the house. In each case, however, they will determine the precise form and function of the language as they go, producing two different texts that reflect the differing features of the situation. Halliday talks about texts and contexts, and looks at the systemic relation between them, but fully recognises the active agents creating the text. At the basis of his argument is a perception of communication as the social construction of meanings and a consequent denial of the view that it is about the transmission of context-independent information (Halliday, 1978).

To adopt a Hallidayan view of communication is not only to accept his claim that it is a process for socially constructing meanings, but also to acknowledge that it is the process by which the social is itself constructed. In plain English, and in direct relation to the topic of this chapter, this means that, when speakers in small groups talk together, they not only create meanings rather than transmit them, they also create the circumstances for changing the relationship between their new understanding and the thing they are talking about. By extension this means that children working in groups are, through their socially imbued language, active meaning-makers who are integrally involved in jointly shaping both their social and their intellectual worlds. Because 'The process of understanding is the result of an active, cooperative enterprise of persons in relationships' (Gergen, 1985), they cannot be passive receivers of knowledge. Through talk they are active agents in the process of knowledge construction because 'knowledge is no more and no less than the outcome of joint communicative action' (Penman, 1988).

THE LEARNING CULTURE, AND EXPECTATIONS ABOUT KNOWLEDGE AND UNDERSTANDING

Group discussion can be used to promote the dynamic exploration of knowledge, allowing the participants to treat it in a positive sense as transient, and therefore capable of continual reconception. Or it can be used to promote it as a set of discrete pieces of information to be captured, pinned down and admired like a dead butterfly. The culture of each classroom, of which the view of knowledge is part, will shape the expectations of every child in the class (Phillips, 1991). We need only compare one group of children in a product-oriented classroom with another group in a process-oriented one to see the difference. The children in the first class make lists without any great effort to justify the presence or absence of particular items on the list (Phillips, 1988). The children in the second class construct hypotheses together and argue passionately but constructively with each other (Phillips, 1987). Attitudes to knowledge exploration, in common with all other attitudes, are socially demonstrated by the fact that children in different classes provide significantly different accounts of what a socially defined concept like 'argument' is. Some describe it in terms which suggest it is a dispute between people with different opinions, some as an angry shouting match between people who have let themselves be carried away by their feelings, and others as an attempt to persuade rationally. Through their experience of typical adult responses to arguments, children learn the cultural meaning of concepts such as 'argument', and become acculturated with values about it. If the culture dismisses emotional and opinionated argument, despite the fact that such forms of argumentation often contribute usefully to an awakening of the possibility of challenging a particular point of view, it will be difficult for children suddenly to see it as on a par with sustained rational debate, no matter what they are told by an individual teacher on a given occasion. On the other hand, if the children's perception of argument is broadened to value emotions and opinions as much as justification and explanation, the world is rendered 'arguable' on many more fronts. Education is about pushing back the frontiers of understanding, and understanding is most likely to occur where the general approach is investigative and exploratory. In a truly educative culture, nothing is allowed to be taken-for-granted, everything is 'arguable', i.e. a suitable subject for interrogation.

Learning occurs when children are encouraged to enter uncharted territory, where ideas, values and experiences are up for exploration, where it is recognised that some things are only half known and that many things are uncertain, and where it is accepted that a few things are inherently problematic and are exciting to explore as problems. It occurs, in fact, where understanding is seen as a continuing process of exploration, where 'Understanding is the dead spot in our struggle for meaning; [it is] the momentary pause, the stillness before incomprehension continues' (Sless, 1986). When there is an imperative to look critically (or argumentatively) at what is not known, what is believed and what is opined about, learning takes place and small group discussion comes alive. In the best circumstances, that imperative comes through the task itself, its intrinsic value to the learner. As often, it is a cultural creation; children learn criticality by living in a climate where mutually supportive criticality is the order of the day. Given some guidance and half a chance, children imaginatively reconstruct possibilities by analogy with past events, through the use of anecdote and story. They picture possibilities by 'what if' hypothesising. They develop cases for and against by extending each others' suggestions (Phillips, 1986). But without a supportive framework for liberation, what Edwards and Mercer – following Vygotsky – call 'scaffolding' (Edwards and Mercer, 1987), they remain trapped in the teacher's definition of the situation and never become autonomous learners. Autonomous learning is more likely to happen in small groups, but without a supportive context and a worthwhile task the move to small group talk will not of itself bring it about.

CHANGING GROUP TALK FOR THE BETTER

In view of the understanding of communication described above, it is now possible to examine the case for small group talk in the primary classroom and to scrutinise its current use. First of all, it follows from the argument outlined that small groups are not necessarily the most convenient focal points for discussions whose object is to collect information. Small group discussion undoubtedly has some value as a means of facilitating the building up of a databank, because the combined knowledge and experience of the whole group is bound to be a greater resource than the knowledge and experience of any individual member. Individuals working alone can draw on reference books and electronic databanks to extend their resource base, but only in groups can children expect to find support and encouragement as they extend their information base. Small groups can usefully 'brainstorm' together (i.e. collect all the information on a particular topic), synthesise the collected information for themselves and re-order it for a different audience (Reid et al., 1989; Shreeve, 1992).

The greatest value of small group talk is, nevertheless, as an arena for the development of understanding and the pushing back of knowledge frontiers. Groups are natural arenas for intellectual exploration because they concentrate only minimally on procedures. This leaves children free to determine their own relevance (Phillips, 1988), to use anecdote to relate experience to the task as they see it and to construct (sometimes quite bizarre!) hypotheses about the world in order to explore it (Phillips, 1983). They do not have to worry, as they might in the class lesson, that the telling of anecdote and the tentative formulating of hypotheses tend to hold things up. Nor do they have to check that every piece of information is 'correct' and every concept fully developed to an adult standard, before they play with it imaginatively. Consequently they are able to take part in the discussion in order to develop understanding rather than to prove that they 'know'. They are able to explore, transform and reflect upon information, turning it from something inert to a living entity.

THE INTERACTION BETWEEN TASK, LANGUAGE CLIMATE AND KNOWLEDGE CULTURE: SOME CASES

The way that group discussion is affected by the relationship between the task and the context in which it is set can be illustrated by examining some cases from current research into the development of spoken language and new technology (SLANT). The SLANT project team which is carrying out the research, and of which this writer is a member, has been looking at the effect of computer software, teachers' instructions, language climate and knowledge culture on children's talk in small groups working with computers. It is investigating the claim that 'worthwhile discussion' is a particular bonus of cooperative work at the computer. To date it has found that there certainly is a substantial amount of talk between children working at the same program, but by no means all of that is of the same kind. By describing and analysing the varieties of talk that come out of computer-mediated contexts, the researchers hope to provide information on which teachers can base their judgements about the communicational and the educational worth of particular computer-mediated activities.

The first thing to note is that there is a range of types of task in the computer software and that therefore the programs themselves are key task-framing agents. The small group talk reflects that framing. Children working with adventure games spend much of their time talking about how to operate the keyboard, directing one another's actions and 'celebrating' successful moves when they happen. They spend only a small part of their time outlining how they see the choices before them, or explaining their reasons for opting in favour of one and dismissing the remainder (Phillips and Scrimshaw, 1992). It appears that the linearity of the program leads the children to construct the task as a series of simple (i.e. non-complex) steps to be passed through with minimum delay for discussion. Some simulations, on the other hand, produce a degree of case-putting and defending because they invite children to enter a realistic world where there is some advantage to be gained from convincing others (Phillips and Scrimshaw, 1992). Children constructing designs using Logo offer explanations for comments such as 'go there; turn up four' when there is some hiccup such as when a previous choice is being 'repaired' because it didn't lead to the expected outcome. At other times they talk about the immediate task, make unexplained suggestions and give each other instructions. The program sets up problems to be solved, but frames the task in terms of action rather than planning and reflection.

It is clearly evident that the program alone does not frame the discussion in these groups. The same sort of program activity results in very different kinds of group discussion in different classrooms. In one class, children using the word processor to 'write a letter to the local council complaining about litter' (the teacher's instruction) concentrate on the spelling, vocabulary and layout of their piece more often than the content, which they seem to take for granted will be a stitching together of whatever each of them contributes turn by turn to the conversation. Children in another class using the word processor to produce books for nursery school children spend a great deal of time discussing the plot, the audience and the style. Their teacher gave them a series of instructions over several days that concentrated their attention on the choices that needed to be made and this led to the task being framed for them in terms of exploration and decision-making. Although children in one class working at a problem-solving activity discussed their proposed solutions very little (see the Logo example above), children in another class tackling a practical but also imaginative problem, like the design of a picture using Paintspa, discussed their thinking at some length (Fisher, 1992). All these groups are influenced to some extent by the nature of the software. If a program is constructed as a series of self-enclosed sub-activities, there is no necessity for the group to reflect on earlier actions or predict what their current actions might imply for future action. If, on the other hand, the program requires joint planning and reviewing of ideas, there will be pressure on the children to talk about their ideas. The task is not framed by the software alone, however, otherwise it would be impossible to account for the different responses across groups; the language climate and the learning context are also implicated. A program which is potentially about sharing ideas can be subverted by a classroom context that has previously placed greater emphasis on action rather than reflection. Similarly, a program which looks as though it might lead to slavish progress through a series of very nearly discrete activities may give rise to a well-structured discussion about the environment in a classroom context where children are encouraged habitually to question the taken-for-granted.

SLANT bears out several of the things previously suggested about the learning culture. Where a classroom culture has habituated 'getting on with the job in hand', children were more inclined to respond to the instruction which most closely reflected that view. Where it had habituated 'standing back to reflect', that was what the children did most often. In the former case discussion was exclusively about the immediate action needed to further the task progress. It was often commentary on what was going on, or imperatives for action, rarely speculation about other possibilities or the consequences of alternative outcomes. In the latter case the group discussions were lively and interesting to the observer because they made evident much of the children's understanding, and demonstrated that they were busy thinking things through. These discussions often took place away from the computer itself, either before the activity began, or at a suitable 'thinking point' associated with the discovery of a problem. At other times it happened at the computer, with the children turning physically away from the screen to address one another. All in all, the classroom culture had a significant influence on the way in which the children interpreted the task before them, and this in turn affected the nature of the small group talk that ran alongside that task.

THE IMPLICATIONS FOR TALKING AND LEARNING IN SMALL GROUPS

What has been said so far is the longest preamble on record to a list of ten proposals for ensuring the continuing use of small group talk in the primary school. The list is predicated on the belief that the educative (or communicative) function of group discussion is its best claim to preservation.

- Activities carried out in small groups should be demonstrably better served by small group discussion than by either class teaching or individual reading and writing.[2]
- Group talk should have a real (action) outcome; it should not just be 'talking shop'. The discussion should, however, wherever possible, take place away from any mechanical activity as this is likely to inhibit planning, hypothesising and reflection.
- Attention to the linguistic ground rules of small group talk should be played down. With practice the children will learn them just as they learn the skills of dyadic conversation by 'doing' talk. Many of our judgements about the appropriateness of certain behaviours for small group talk are ill-informed anyway, being made by comparing them with tightly controlled class lessons instead of with group talk from a whole range of contexts, including those outside school.
- The cognitive ground rules for each group discussion should be clearly spelt out. Although this will not obliterate what children have learned from the learning culture over time, by being made explicit it will gradually become part of that culture.
- Discussion to collect information through brainstorming should always be a means to an end. The group is an ideal place for 'trying on' new information, playing with it imaginatively and exploring it through 'what if . . .' activities. The primary purpose of discussion should not be to collect information, but to make sense of it.
- Group talk should be framed in a way that invites a 'critical discourse'. Critical discourse sets out to interrogate the taken-for-granted, and to ask questions, speculate and hypothesise about the possible. 'Facts' are taken-for-granted hypotheses; they can be reflected upon in small group discussion, unpacked and turned into amazing new ideas.
- When setting up small group discussions, teachers should bear in mind that the task is framed by their instructions. They should choose their words carefully to ensure that the children know exactly what is required of them.

- The language used in the classroom should be a focus for study and analysis. There should be regular discussion about the metalanguage of talk, and of small group talk in particular.
- Teachers should model strategies for inquisitiveness, themselves challenging the taken-for-granted and playing with ideas. Class lessons should help children to see that it is all right to examine alternatives, so that when they take part in a group discussion they do not begin from scratch.
- The learning culture of the whole classroom should be one of excitement, curiosity and challenge. Framing the question should often be more important than finding the answer.

Small group talk in the primary school is too valuable to squander.

NOTES

1   A classic example of resistance to the notion of communication-as-act-of-knowledge-creation is found in the selective responses to Douglas Barnes' early work, in which he found that children not only took less part in lessons than teachers did, but were obliged when they did contribute to take part for a limited range of purposes (Barnes and Shemilt, 1974). For those determined to take a transmissive view of communication, it was possible to look at what Barnes said about closed questions (questions to which there was only one answer, an answer already known to the teacher who put the question) as a comment on the need to be a more effective transmitter. Barnes, however, not only pointed out that closed questions dictate the topic of a lesson and prevent any deviation from it, but also that the children who could not 'relate' to the topic had no way into it; that they were, in fact, unable to interpret what it was the lesson was really about. In short, Barnes had suggested that children failed to learn from the transmission process, not because teachers' questions were closed, but because any attempt to communicate transmissively is based upon an unsound underlying theory of what takes place when people talk together. In classrooms where they neglect to help children develop their natural roles as interpreters of the world, active creators of their own meanings, for most of the time, teachers are being unfair if they expect a group to behave differently just because they are a group.
2   An alternative to class lessons is independent working. There is an argument which suggests that writing used epistemically, i.e. to develop thinking through externalising it, is educationally more valuable than group discussion. There is certainly much to recommend the 'discussion in the head' of which Vygotsky speaks (Vygotsky, 1978). So, when sustained individual writing offers such a convenient means for individuals to increase their understanding and develop their ideas, why is there a need for the harder-to-organise group discussion? The answer is that, because discourse in the head is a dialogue mediated through a single mind, it is less likely to involve criticality. Criticality depends upon reflexiveness, to adopt a different stance from your own. If a critique is to be offered and evidence to be triangulated, other minds are needed.

REFERENCES

Barnes, D. (1976) *From Communication to Curriculum*. Harmondsworth: Penguin.
Barnes, D. and Shemilt, D. (1974) 'Transmission and interpretation', *Educational Review*, Vol. 26, No. 3.

Bellack, A., Kliebard, H., Hyman, R. and Smith, F. (1966) *The Language of the Classroom*. New York: Teachers' College Press.

Bergum, V. (1991) 'Being a phenomenological researcher', in Morse, J. (ed.) *Qualitative Nursing Research: A Contemporary Dialogue*. London: Sage.

Brazil, D., Coulthard, M. and Johns, C. (1980) *Discourse Intonation and Language Teaching*. London: Longman.

Butler, C. (1985) *Systemic Linguistics: Theory and Application*. London: Batsford.

Edwards, D. and Mercer, N. (1987) *Common Knowledge: The Development of Joint Understanding in the Classroom*. London: Methuen.

Fisher, E. (1992) *Characteristics of Children's Talk at the Computer and Its Relationship to the Computing Software*. SLANT Working Paper 5. University of East Anglia/Open University.

Flanders, N. (1970) *Analyzing Teacher Behavior*. Reading, Mass: Addison-Wesley.

Gergen, K. (1985) 'The social constructionist movement in modern psychology', *American Psychologist*, Vol. 40.

Gregory, M. and Carroll, S. (1978) *Language and Situation: Language Varieties and Their Social Context*. London: Routledge & Kegan Paul.

Grice, P. (1963) 'Logic and conversation', in Cole, P. and Morgan, J. (eds) (1975) *Syntax and Semantics 3: Speech Acts*. New York: Academic Press.

Habermas, J. (1985) *The Theory of Communicative Action*. Cambridge: Polity Press.

Halliday, M. (1970) 'Intonation and meaning', in Kress, G. (ed.) *Halliday: System and Function*. London: Oxford University Press.

Halliday, M. (1978) *Language as Social Semiotic: The Social Interpretation of Language*. London: Edward Arnold.

Halliday, M. (1985) *An Introduction to Functional Grammar*. London: Edward Arnold.

Halliday, M. and Hasan, R. (1985) *Language, Context and Text: A Social-semiotic Perspective*. Victoria: Deakin University Press.

Keller, E. (1981) 'Gambits: conversational strategy signals', in Coulmas, F. (ed.) *Conversational Routines*. The Hague: Mouton.

Kress, G. (1985) *Linguistic Processes in Sociocultural Practice*. Victoria: Deakin University Press.

MacLure, M. and French, P. (1981) 'A comparison of talk at home and at school', in Wells, G. (ed.) *Learning Through Interaction*. Cambridge: Cambridge University Press.

Martin, J.R. (1984) 'Language, resister, and genre', in Christie, F. (ed.) *Children Writing*. Victoria: Deakin University Press.

Penman, R. (1988) 'Communication reconstructed', *Journal for the Theory of Social Behaviour*, Vol. 18, No. 4.

Phillips, T. (1986) *The Analysis of Style in the Discourse of Middle School Children Working in Small, Teacherless Groups*. Unpublished M.Phil. thesis, University of East Anglia.

Phillips, T. (1987) 'Beyond lip-service: discourse development after the age of nine', in Mayor, M. and Pugh, A. (eds) *Language, Communication and Education*. London: Croom Helm.

Phillips, T. (1988) 'On a related matter: why successful small group talk depends upon *not* keeping to the point', in MacLure, M., Phillips, T. and Wilkinson, A. (eds) *Oracy Matters*. Milton Keynes: Open University Press.

Phillips, T. (1991) 'Creating contexts for exploratory talk', in Wray, D. (ed.) *Talking and Listening*. Leamington Spa: Scholastic.

Phillips, T. (1992) 'Why?: the neglected question in curriculum planning for small group talk', in Norman, K. (ed.) *Thinking Voices*. London: Hodder & Stoughton.

Phillips, T. and Scrimshaw, P. (1992) *Playing by the Rules: The Development of Expectations about Working and Computers in the Primary Classroom*. SLANT Working Paper 3. School of Education, University of East Anglia.

Reid, J., Forrestal, P. and Cook, J. (1989) *Small Group Learning in the Classroom*. Scarborough: PETA/Chalkface Press.

Sacks, H., Schegloff, E. and Jefferson, G. (1974) 'A simple systematics for the organisation of turn-taking for conversation', *Language*, Vol. 50, pp. 696–735.

Shreeve, A. (1992) *Oracy: Making Groups Work*. Norwich: Norfolk Oracy Project (Norfolk County Council).

Sinclair, J. and Coulthard, M. (1975) *Towards an Analysis of Discourse: The English used by Teachers and Pupils*. London: Oxford University Press.

Sless, D. (1986) *In Search of Semiotics*. London: Croom Helm.

Swann, J. and Graddoll, D. (1988) 'Gender inequalities in classroom talk in English', *English in Education*, Vol. 22, No. 1.

Ventola, I. (1986) *Shopping Encounters: A Systemic Linguistic Analysis*. Unpublished Ph.D. thesis, Sydney University.

Vygotsky, L. (1978) *Mind in Society: The Development of Higher Psychological Processes*. Cambridge, Mass: Harvard University Press.

Wells, C.G. (1981) *Learning Through Interaction*. Cambridge: Cambridge University Press.

Willes, M. (1980) 'Learning to take part in classroom interaction', in French, P. and MacLure, M. (eds) *Adult–child Conversation: Studies in Structure and Process*. London: Croom Helm.

Chapter 3

The assessment of oral language

Greg Brooks

WHY SO MUCH INTEREST IN ASSESSING ORAL LANGUAGE?

For centuries, all tests and examinations were oral, but in Britain from the early nineteenth century written exams gradually ousted orals almost completely. Elsewhere in the world (e.g. Denmark and the former Soviet Union), the tradition of oral testing, i.e. of assessing subject knowledge orally, has survived much more. Here practically the only remaining relic of the days before all-encompassing written papers is the viva voce examination for research degrees. But the viva system reminds us that the old tradition focused on content, i.e. on testing *through* talk, whereas the current movement focuses on the use of language, i.e. on the testing *of* talk. The distinction between these two is, of course, not watertight and cannot be: it is a question of the relative emphasis given to content or form. The concern of this chapter is the assessment of oral language, i.e. of how effectively pupils communicate through speech.

And given this definition of the topic, the UK seems to be leading the world in the amount of attention given to it. CSE English included a compulsory oral from the outset in 1965. The 23 years of the CSE oral up to 1987 were almost certainly the largest continuous system of oracy assessment yet seen in the world, since by the 1980s over 90% of each cohort of half a million pupils were entered for it. GCSE and Scottish O Grade have continued to include compulsory oral elements in exams for 16-year-olds and the various National Curricula in England and Wales, Scotland and Northern Ireland have extended this require-ment to younger pupils of various ages.

Surveys of the speaking and listening abilities in English of 11- and 15-year-old pupils in England, Wales and Northern Ireland were carried out in 1982, 1983 and 1988 by the Assessment of Performance Unit's (APU's) Language Monitoring Project based at the NFER (Brooks, 1987; Gorman *et al.*, 1984a, 1984b, 1988, 1991; MacLure and Hargreaves, 1986). Surveys of primary and secondary school pupils' speaking and listening abilities in Welsh as a first and second language were conducted on several occasions from 1979 onwards by the NFER's Welsh Unit based in Swansea, along similar lines to the APU surveys. A survey of the speaking and listening abilities in English of 9-, 11- and 14-year-old pupils in Scotland was carried out in 1984 (Neville, 1988). Though different in organisation and materials, it was based on the same principles as the APU surveys in the rest of the UK. A second such survey in Scotland was carried out in 1989. Research into the oracy abilities in Scots Gaelic of Gaelic-speaking pupils in the Hebrides formed part of a project based at the University of Stirling from 1984 to 1986.

The Standard Assessment Tasks for Year 2 pupils in England and Wales in 1991 included a substantial assessment of oral language (in 1992 this element was moved from the tests to teacher assessment). The 1991 oracy tests for 7-year-olds were the first large-scale assessment of oracy anywhere in the world for children aged under 9.

The only other countries which seem to have carried out national oracy surveys are Australia and the Netherlands, so why have the three 'autochthonous' languages of the UK received such comprehensive scrutiny in recent years?

There seem to have been several strands to the answer. There was the feeling that some, perhaps many, pupils had greater skills in spoken language than in reading and writing: if their oral language was not assessed their abilities would be underrated. This definitely seems to have been the major reason for the inclusion of the compulsory oral in CSE English.

In making the oral compulsory, the devisers of CSE English were also making conscious use of the backwash effect: they knew that if oracy were not included in formal examinations or assessments, it would continue to be neglected in school curricula.

However, the model of oracy included in CSE English conformed very much to what has been called the 'social accomplishment' view of talk: in this it reflected (rather distantly in practice, it must be conceded) the 'public speaking' tradition.

But in the late 1970s and the 1980s, this view of talk came to seem inadequate and was replaced by two other, overlapping, models, which have been called the 'communicative competence' and 'language for learning' models. These emphasised the value of talk both as a tool for learning in school, and as the most important means of communication in the world generally.

All these influences converged to produce the upsurge of interest in assessing oral language in the UK in the 1980s. This led in turn to the inclusion of oracy assessment in GCSE and Scottish O Grade already mentioned, to attempts to define a wider range of varieties of talk to be included in the curriculum, and to the permeation of this interest from large-scale systems of assessment into assessment of oral language in classrooms.

But still, why assess oral language at primary level? Not just because it is required in national assessments: that is to put the assessment cart before the curriculum horse.

The educational reason is the one already given: not to assess speaking and listening, when writing and reading are assessed, is to neglect at least half of pupils' language abilities. The curriculum should give them the chance to develop skill in a range of uses of language, and assessment practices should reflect that range.

Moreover, the point about possible disparity between oracy and literacy skills applies with particular force at primary level: some pupils, especially in Years 1 and 2, will have much greater abilities in speech than in writing: these will simply not show up if all assessment of language capabilities is based on writing and reading.

Whatever the fate of the UK's various National Curricula, of the assessment arrangements associated with them and of the weighting within those assessments of oracy versus reading and writing, the desirability of assessing oral language will remain valid.

PRINCIPLES FOR THE ASSESSMENT OF ORAL LANGUAGE

Any defensible method of oral language assessment should observe the following principles:

1 Talk is used for a wide range of communicative, social and cognitive purposes – see the next section.
2 Different purposes require different types of talk; therefore, the appropriateness of the talk used in a given situation is an important criterion of assessment.
3 Listening should not be artificially separated from speaking. Though there are some frequent and important non-reciprocal speaking–listening situations (e.g. listening to the radio), in normal circumstances we are never faced with an 'aural comprehension' on what we have heard. Listening is best assessed implicitly, by pupils' responses in some following speaking task, or by their involvement in interactive talk.
4 Because one main function of talk is to communicate, i.e. to give people information they previously did not have, tasks which require pupils to repeat back information to someone who already possesses it should be avoided.
5 Despite the greater difficulty of assessing interaction, both monologue (one-way) and interactive talk must be assessed, since to omit interaction is to omit the more important form of talk.
6 Oral communication is important across the whole curriculum as a powerful tool for learning, and the content of oracy assessments should therefore not be confined to the literary, personal growth or social issues content typical of many first-language syllabuses, or to designated 'language' lessons. APU oracy tests included geographical, mathematical and scientific content.
7 Children's oral language is developing very rapidly during the primary years. Assessment of it should therefore be based on sound knowledge of language development.

PURPOSES FOR TALK

But what types of talk should be assessed? The range of types of talk is potentially huge, since the purposes for which people communicate are indefinitely large in number.

To get a handle on the range of purposes for language use that the curriculum should cover and assessment should sample, a valuable exercise in in-service sessions on oracy is as follows (N.B. You will need an overhead projector and at least one blank transparency):

- Get the participants to spend two minutes writing down, individually and in silence, their own lists of the 10–12 most important purposes for which spoken language is used.
- Then ask them to compare and contrast their lists, in pairs. They should start by reading each other's lists. Allow three minutes for this.
- Then spend a few minutes collecting two ideas from each pair on to an overhead projector transparency.
- Next, combine pairs into groups of four, and ask them to look for groupings or categories within the ideas they have generated. For instance, can the types of talk be classified according to size of group or of audience? Are there groupings such as communicative/cognitive/affective/social? (But try not to give away too many answers.) Are some purposes for talk not worth including in the curriculum? Which? Among those that are worth including, are some more important than others? Which? Are some varieties of language under-emphasised in the curriculum? If so, what should be done about this? Which of the various types of language use should be assessed and how?

The APU's answer to the first part of the last question is illustrated in Table 3.1 which lists the general purposes for language use which were assessed in APU oracy surveys, together with short descriptions of the tasks used to assess those types of language.

Table 3.1 APU language monitoring: examples of tasks used

General purpose	*Specific task*
Describing and specifying	Description of observed object to permit identification Description of a place and explanation of interest Description of sequence of pictures Evaluating features of household object
Informing/Expounding	Interpretation of account of process (with diagram) Exposition of gist of account to others Interpretation of account of experiment Exposition of process to others Putting case to simulated meeting Presenting findings from researching printed materials or videotape Explaining principle of mathematical problem
Instructing/Directing	Practical interpretation of rules of game Instructing another pupil to play the game Constructing paper model following sequence of instructions

	Instructing another pupil how to carry out experiment Instructing other pupils to play a mathematical problem-solving game
Reporting	Report of something learnt and explanation of interest Report of a favourite book and explanation of interest Report of agreement reached through discussion Report of results of experiment Report of evaluation of household object Report of meeting whether consensus reached or not
Narrating	Interpretation of story (heard on audiotape or seen on video) and retelling to others Interpretation of anecdote and narrating personal experience Telling story based on sequence of pictures Telling story to explain pictured scene Telling story with specified elements and suitable for younger children
Arguing/Persuading	Explanation of choice of career – argument/justification of point of view Interpretation of opposing arguments
Structured discussion/Collaboration	Interpretation and discussion of evidence to decide on proposed action Interpretation and discussion of arguments to reach consensus Interpretation and discussion of evidence to reach agreement Interpretation and discussion of printed texts or videotaped sequences to locate and recast information Discussion of mathematical problem to discover underlying principle Discussion to agree on a storyline
Speculating/Advancing hypotheses	Speculating on reasons for experimental finding Speculating on characteristics of hidden object and producing diagram Speculating on features of household object Speculating on features of pictured scene to provide explanation Speculating on how storyline might continue from pictured scene

The list, it should be noted, is not meant to be either final or exhaustive: it evolved alongside the designing of tasks for surveys, and is open to constant revision in the light of new demands and insights.

FINDINGS

The national surveys of oracy performance have provided a body of findings on the speaking and listening abilities of pupils aged 8 to 12. Those from the APU surveys of pupils aged 11 in England, Wales and Northern Ireland are summarised, in very abbreviated form, in Table 3.2.

Table 3.2 The 11-year-old language user: findings from APU surveys

Speaking and listening tasks on which a high (70%+), medium (50%–70%) or low (<50%) percentage of 11-year-olds achieved a score of 4 or better on a 1–7 scale:

High
Following instructions to produce a model
Instructing a friend to play a board game
Instructing another pupil to carry out an experiment
Speculating on the reasons for a finding
Reporting the results of an experiment
Retelling a story heard on tape
Answering questions on a story or anecdote heard on tape
Narrating a personal anecdote
Describing pictures
Telling a story based on a sequence of pictures
Summarising the plot of a book

Medium
From a spoken description, identifying an object among a set of similar objects
Relaying simple information heard on tape
Describing a job
Arguing to justify a point of view
Describing objects for identification
Summarising written information
Discussing to reach agreement
Describing experimental procedures and observations
Appraising technological gadgets
Reporting conclusions on appraising technological gadgets
Inventing a scenario for an imaginary crime or an unusual pictured scene
Predicting events or the continuation of a plot
Reporting reasons for agreed or disputed conclusions
While listening to a tape, making notes for relaying
Explaining use of technical devices in video

Low
Discussing a technological problem
Discussing reasons for scientific problems
Presenting a point of view based on written notes
Reaching agreement on sequence of pictures for story

Source: Gorman *et al.* (1988: 19, Table 2.5), supplemented from Gorman *et al.* (1991: 49–50). Both reports should be consulted for further detail.

With a few exceptions, the tasks in the three categories in Table 3.2 seem to fall into levels of difficulty. Most of those in the 'High' (= easiest) group require either relatively straightforward responses to simple listening, or speaking from directly relevant personal experience. Most of those in the 'Medium' group require either listening to more complex information or recasting experience or information in some way. And those in the 'Low' (= most difficult) group are probably unusual in most primary pupils' experience, either of life or of the classroom.

While performing the tasks, most pupils were also able to:

- organise what they wanted to say clearly;
- avoid undue hesitation and pausing;
- employ appropriate vocabulary and syntax;
- adopt standard English usage and a widely intelligible accent (Gorman *et al.*, 1988: 19).

Table 3.3 presents an (also highly abbreviated) list of the listening and speaking abilities of Scottish pupils aged 8/9 and 11/12, as deduced from Neville (1988).

Table 3.3 Research findings on spoken language development between the ages of 8/9 and 11/12 reported in Neville (1988)

In a national assessment of performance in English in Scotland in 1984, pupils in Primary 7 (aged 11/12) performed significantly better than those in Primary 4 (aged 8/9) in the following tasks:

	page
A. Listening	
Free and probed spoken recall of a narrative text	46–48
Free (but not probed) spoken recall of an informative text	46–48
Written responses to aural cloze tests on narrative and informative texts	49–51
On these cloze tests, P7 pupils used more sophisticated vocabulary and handled text structure better	52
(But on same tests P4 pupils made fewer careless responses than P7 pupils)	52
Multiple-choice identification of word in sentence or in isolation	55–56
Following directions, following an explanation, interpreting a description and distinguishing fact from opinion	58–60
B. Speaking	
Recounting narrative and informative texts	130–131
Giving spoken directions	145–146
Giving spoken explanations	152–154
Stating and justifying an opinion	160–161

One other finding from Neville's survey can be inferred from her report, though she does not state it. She gives many pages of transcriptions of the pupils' responses. Within them, the amount of recognisably Scots dialect is remarkably small: almost all the sentences would be identical in syntax and vocabulary if spoken anywhere in Britain. Whatever their accents, then, it seems reasonable to infer that by the age of 11/12 and even 8/9 the vast majority of Scots children can speak Standard English when they perceive the situation as requiring it: these relatively formal test situations were evidently so perceived. For age 11 (and indeed age 15), this finding can, as already implied, be generalised to the rest of the UK from APU evidence (Brooks, 1990: 5).

COMMON OBJECTIONS TO ASSESSING ORAL LANGUAGE

1 'Isn't achievement in oral language dependent on: (a) personality, (b) intelligence, and (c) prior knowledge?'

Well yes, it is dependent on all these things. But it is logically impossible to produce an assessment of speaking (or of any other aspect of language or of any other subject) that would be free of such influences. When speaking and listening are assessed, what is assessed is how effectively pupils use oral language, *given* their personality, intellectual capacity and prior knowledge.

The positive way to consider these factors is this. Since a fair method of assessing oral language must give pupils the chance to show what they can do across a range of purposes for language use, no pupil must ever be assessed on one task or on a single occasion. Assessment across a range of situations and on a number of occasions makes it less likely that pupils will be unfairly affected by lack of prior knowledge or by diffidence and more likely that they will be able to show a level of performance that truly reflects their intelligence.

2 'Isn't the assessment of oral language inherently subjective and therefore unreliable?'

No, in both cases. For one thing, the distinction between 'objective' tests such as multiple-choice, true/false, etc., on the one hand, and 'subjective' assessments involving markers' judgements on the other is not as clear-cut as is commonly supposed.

Moreover, the assessment of oral language need not be unreliable. In APU surveys, high levels of inter-marker agreement were achieved. This was done by a system in which markers first assessed a common set of examples recorded on audiotape. They did this in isolation from each other, and with minimal guidance on what to look for in good or poor performances. No detailed criteria were given; merely the instruction to score the performances on their communicative effectiveness, given the requirements of the task.

Even with this minimal guidance, markers achieved very satisfactory levels of agreement and were always impressed (and relieved) at those levels when they came to the NFER for their training meeting and were presented with the grid of the scores they and their fellow-markers had given. They were then confident that they would mark to common standards when assessing separately from each other on the spot during the surveys.

But the assessors' reliability was not just taken on trust. While they were out on the surveys they were asked not just to administer the tasks and to give marks, but also to audio-record all the performances. Later, all the audiotapes were marked, twice, by a separate panel of teachers, who were trained to assess in the same way as the on-the-spot assessors. So the APU team then had three impression marks for each performance and were able to calculate the amount of agreement between them.

The results showed satisfactory levels of agreement between the two tape markings: but also just as much agreement between each of the two tape markings and the on-the-spot assessments. The APU team could therefore be confident not only that the on-the-spot assessors and the tape markers were marking consistently among themselves, but also that the two panels were in broad agreement.

3 'Won't oracy testing discriminate against female students, and/or those from ethnic or linguistic minorities?'

Though research into this aspect of oracy testing is in its infancy, a few helpful findings have emerged. In APU surveys, girls and boys did not differ overall in their performance in oracy (though there were minor differences on a few tasks). And though in APU surveys second-language speakers of English in England did receive significantly lower mean scores than native speakers, a research project at the London Institute of Education found very little evidence to support the idea that assessment of oracy in GCSE English was biased against ethnic minority candidates.

4 'When pupils are being assessed orally in pairs, won't some pupils' performances be dragged down by their partners'?'

There is evidence that this is not the case. In some APU oracy surveys, modifications of tasks originally developed by the APU Science Monitoring Project were used. The science versions were always done by individual pupils working alone, the language ones always by pairs working together. Where it was possible to compare performance on different versions of the tasks, there was a strong tendency for performance on the oracy version to be better in scientific terms than on the science version.

5 'That may work for pairs, but what do you do when you are assessing groups of, say, four pupils and one of them doesn't say anything?'

There are three strategies for dealing with this:

- give group rather than individual marks, and give the group mark to all members of the group, regardless of individual contributions;
- give every pupil a mark for 'orientation to listeners/partners': then even pupils who say very little or nothing can gain marks for being attentive and supportive listeners;
- in the last resort, pupils who say nothing and don't even seem to be attentive should be excluded from the assessment of that task. Note: *not given a zero*, but simply not assessed at all. There will always be other tasks on which these pupils can show what they can do.

IMPLICATIONS

Any system of assessment of oral language depends totally on the informed professional judgements of experienced teachers. The reliability with which many panels of teachers have carried out such assessment in national surveys implies that

- with appropriate training teachers can assess oracy just as capably as writing or reading;
- as experienced professionals, teachers in fact know a great deal more about what is valuable in talk than they commonly realise.

But how can this latent knowledge be tapped for the purposes of assessing oral language in the classroom? All such assessment must rely on observation of the pupils, as they use talk to decide, discuss, plan, argue, persuade, etc., in the course of classroom group activity.

Hard-pressed primary teachers would be totally justified in objecting at this point, however, that they have all the subjects of the National Curriculum (whichever version applies to their pupils) to teach: when can they possibly find the time to get round all their pupils to assess each one on oracy, as well as everything else? The answer to this has to be in several parts.

First, oracy need not be, in fact should not be, assessed in isolation. Whenever talk is occurring, and the teacher is observing for the purpose of assessing the content or outcome of what is going on, the assessment of oral language can be going on in parallel. Attention can be switched, in other words, between the form and the content of the activity.

Second, there seems no reason why teachers should have to carry out all the assessment of oral language (or of content, for that matter) all by themselves. A few pioneering schemes have suggested that a significant element of pupil peer and self-assessment can be developed, and can take a large share of the burden off teachers. Children are very astute at knowing who is good at what and why: with some training, they can be induced to turn these intuitive judgements into written statements, or ticks against criteria, that the teacher can then use. Pupils can be asked to make judgements against characteristics of effective discussion: 'Did we allow everybody to have their say and give their ideas? Did anybody talk too much? Did we add ideas together and not just grab the first one anyone suggested?' The teacher can act as moderator to the pupils' judgements on themselves and each other, just as (ideally) teachers in a school will moderate each other and be moderated from outside, when the full panoply of national assessment is in good working order.

Third, before they attempt to train their pupils in oral language assessment, teachers need such training themselves. Given the wide range of subjects and skills that will need to be assessed by primary teachers, specific training on oracy may be very long in coming from outside. But schools can give themselves a headstart by:

- buying at least one good audio-cassette recorder and a supply of tapes;
- setting up a system of recording a sample of their pupils' oral work;
- doing their own in-service on oracy assessment by using the recordings they have made as an agreement set: i.e. all the members of a group of interested teachers would have to mark the recordings independently, collate their marks, and then meet to discuss their results and sort out any discrepancies. A detailed suggestion for doing this is given in Brooks (1987: 56–58).

It may seem a mammoth task, but giving all pupils the chance to develop skill at types and purposes of talk, of as wide a range as possible, is surely part of their 'entitlement'. Not only that, but it holds the promise of paying off handsomely in terms of the entire curriculum, as pupils learn to use talk more effectively for learning and collaboration.

REFERENCES

Brooks, G. (1987) *Speaking and Listening: Assessment at Age 15.* Windsor: NFER-Nelson.

Brooks, G. (1990) 'Assessing oracy', *TOPIC* 3, item 2.

Gorman, T., White, J. and Brooks, G. (1984a) *Language Performance in Schools: 1982 Secondary Survey Report.* London: DES.

Gorman, T., White, J., Brooks, G. and English, F. (1991) *Language Learning: A Summary Report on the 1988 APU Language Surveys.* London: HMSO for SEAC.

Gorman, T., White, J., Brooks, G., MacLure, M. and Kispal, A. (1988) *Language Performance in Schools: A Review of APU Language Monitoring 1979–83.* London: DES.

Gorman, T., White, J., Hargreaves, M., MacLure, M. and Tate, A. (1984b) *Language Performance in Schools: 1982 Primary Survey Report.* London: DES.

MacLure, M. and Hargreaves, M. (1986) *Speaking and Listening: Assessment at Age 11.* Windsor: NFER-Nelson.

Neville, M. (1988) *Assessing and Teaching Language: Literacy and Oracy in Schools.* Basingstoke: Macmillan.

Part II

Reading

Editors' introduction

There can be little doubt that reading has been, and still is, the most controversial of the three Profile Components which make up the National Curriculum for English. Arguments about standards have spilled over into some quite bitter debates about teaching methods. Unfortunately, controversy has tended to lead to side-taking with a consequent polarisation in both theoretical and practical positions. Others have taken up fence-sitting, arguing somewhat blandly that if the full picture is to be found at neither pole the truth must lie somewhere in the middle, with 'balance' or 'eclecticism'. This is characterised by the advice about the National Curriculum English Orders given to the Secretary of State for Education by the National Curriculum Council (NCC, 1992) in which it is argued that 'It is also important that the Order is balanced in the emphasis which it gives to different methods of teaching children to read. This will ensure that all teachers develop *a properly eclectic approach* to this crucial area' (our italics). The problem with this argument is that it fails to give adequate recognition to the need for a properly worked out and reasoned theoretical position with regard to the reading process and its teaching. Such a position must take into account what is currently known about the nature of reading, how it works, what influences it, what makes it easier or harder and how children learn such a complex mental operation. The truth is that this knowledge is now substantial and there can be little excuse for simplistic approaches to teaching reading. We gave a review of some of the key knowledge about reading in Chapter 6 of *Literacy and Language in the Primary Years*, especially in terms of underlying theoretical models of the process. We went on to outline some teaching approaches stemming from particular versions of such models. The first two chapters in this part of the present volume present further discussion of these matters.

First, David Wray discusses the issues underlying the 'debate' about reading. He examines the research evidence used and the arguments put forward by advocates of code-centred and meaning-centred approaches to teaching reading. A synthesis of this range of research is used to suggest that a unifying theory of teaching reading is actually possible, based on the concept of reading as an interaction, or transaction, with text. Wray concludes by pulling out some practical implications of such a theory. If his case is correct, it suggests that the 'reading debate' may, in fact, now have been resolved theoretically.

This chapter is followed by Colin Mills' review of the extremely important field of children's literature with special emphasis on the ways in which, it has become clear, the texts which children are offered and choose to read influence fundamentally the nature of these children's learning about reading. Mills' chapter covers a wide range of theoretical perspectives, embracing insights from literary theory, sociolinguistics, critical theory and so on. In so doing, it provides an essential corrective to the heavily psychological orientation of most research on reading and learning to read. Reading is not, according to Mills, simply a psychological process but is rooted in its origins as social and cultural practice. It cannot therefore be fully understood without taking these perspectives into account.

There is a further aspect to reading, specified in the National Curriculum Orders but rather neglected in primary school teaching; that is, the development of 'information-retrieval strategies'. Consideration of this aspect is part of general thought about the ways in which literacy, particularly reading, contributes to learning. In Chapter 9 of *Literacy and Language in the Primary Years* we presented an analysis of what information skills might consist of and put forward some suggestions as to appropriate contexts for their development in the classroom. David Wray here elaborates on the importance of the ability to handle information effectively in any definition of literacy. He argues that, as literacy embodies autonomy of action, the teaching of it must stress its autonomous operation. In terms of information-handling the key components are purpose-setting and evaluation, both of which require that teachers permit children opportunities to decide issues for themselves.

As with other parts in this volume, the issue of assessment needs to be dealt with in a clear and thorough manner. Denis Vincent's chapter examines the philosophies and practices surrounding the use of standardised testing procedures for the assessment of reading. Somewhat unfashionably in view of the current emphasis in advice to professionals on the importance of formative, observation-based assessment procedures, he suggests that there may be more of a place for standardised tests than has hitherto been thought. However, he also argues strongly that a great deal of new and careful research and thought is needed to develop appropriate forms of these tests. Vincent puts forward a powerful case for the enhanced involvement of teachers in this process of development if they are to seize back the assessment initiative from those outside the classroom.

REFERENCE

National Curriculum Council (1992) *National Curriculum English: The Case for Revising the Order*. York: NCC.

Chapter 4

Reviewing the reading debate

David Wray

INTRODUCTION

Over 20 years ago, Jeanne Chall (1967) coined the phrase 'the great debate' with reference to contemporary controversies about the teaching of reading. By this phrase she referred to the debate between those who at the time advocated an approach to teaching reading which emphasised sound–symbol correspondences and those who argued in favour of what were termed 'meaning-based' approaches but which tended, in fact, to involve an emphasis on the recognition of whole words. Arguments about the relative merits of 'phonics' and 'look-and-say' have raged over the intervening 20 years, and, indeed, these terms are still regularly used as slogans in what seems a perennial battle. More recently, however, the terms of the debate have shifted and new controversies have arisen, fuelled by an apparent decline in the standards of reading achievement by 7-year-olds (although it must be admitted that the nature, extent and very existence of such a decline are in themselves controversial issues). The current 'great debate' concerns the relative efficacy of teaching approaches which are based upon radically different psychological and philosophical positions. On the one side there are those who argue that the teaching of reading should proceed according to 'bottom-up' principles, with children being taught first to decipher words or parts of words and then to put these words together to make meaning. On the other side there are those who advocate a 'top-down' approach in which children begin with meaningful units of language, either sentences arising from their spoken language or whole stories, and only later have their attention focused on the individual elements of these units. Both phonics and look-and-say are essentially 'bottom-up' approaches, in that they focus first on the building blocks of meaning: letters, sounds and words. The new element in the debate about reading is the growth in adherence to 'top-down' approaches. The 'great debate' is, therefore, rather old-fashioned in its terms of reference, and there is a need to shift the emphasis in discussions about reading teaching and also a need to question the polarisation of attitudes which the very terms of the debate seem to exacerbate.

This chapter will describe some of the major contributions of recent years to the new debate, from both sides. It should be said at this point, though, that the initial teaching of reading is badly in need of fresh empirical research into programme implementation in order to evaluate the theoretically, and sometimes polemically, based developments of recent years. It is hoped that this review may prove useful to teachers and others as they respond to the new developments in the reading field but what will become apparent is that there are problems with the evidence and arguments put forward by both sides in this debate. Many practitioners have, of course, already realised this but their response has often been a rather unreasoned eclecticism. 'If neither side has the complete answer', goes the argument, 'then the best course is to make sure that teaching approaches include a bit of both.' This 'balanced' view makes some political sense in an era in which teachers are under almost continual attack from outsiders for alleged 'trendy' or 'cranky' methods but, if it does not itself rest upon a well-worked out understanding of the reading process, its expression risks damaging the very notion of teacher professional knowledge which is under attack. The conclusion to the chapter will put forward an alternative interpretation of the theory behind reading which may give teachers a more secure basis upon which to plan teaching strategies.

MEANING-BASED APPROACHES: THEORIES AND PRACTICES

The major impetus towards a revision of many traditional ideas about reading came from the field of psycholinguistics, with its emphasis upon the ways in which humans make sense of their world through the use of language. Frank Smith and Kenneth Goodman in the 1970s and early 1980s popularised many of the key theories of this relatively new science and, each in their separate ways, has had a major influence upon a great many teachers. Smith's work (1978) is characterised by its unrelenting attacks on the teaching of phonics which, Smith claims, is unhelpful to the learning of reading, because of its unreliability as a word-decoding system and its intrinsic lack of emphasis upon meaning. Smith characterises reading as essentially a meaning-getting process and claims the essential ingredients for success in learning to do it are access to materials that a learner will consider worth reading, and help from an expert reader whose role is to make the process easy for the learner. This idea of the role of the expert foreshadows the so-called apprenticeship approach which has more recently been described by Waterland (1985) and Smith's attention to worthwhile reading materials also presages the focus of 'real books' advocates upon the quality of the texts used in teaching.

Goodman has argued from a wide range of empirical evidence to a general theory of the role of anticipation and guessing in the reading process (Gollasch, 1982) and the development of an influential model of the reading process (Goodman, 1975). From an analysis of children's reading errors (which he prefers to call 'miscues') he and his colleagues produced evidence that children almost instinctively try to make sense of what they are doing when they read. He sees miscues as a window on the reading process and characterises this process as, in a much-quoted phrase, a 'psycholinguistic guessing game' (Goodman, 1967). Although, for Goodman, the graphic and phonic cueing systems have a role in reading, they are seen as subordinate to prediction based upon cues from syntax and meaning.

Both Goodman and Smith argue for what Cambourne (1979) has called an 'inside-out' theory of the reading process. This, broadly speaking, views the act of reading as beginning inside the reader's head with a series of expectations about what will be perceived. The reader approaches the text to test out these expectations by sampling enough of it to confirm or reject them. On the basis of this sampling fresh expectations are engendered, and the process proceeds in this interactive way. This theory is contrasted by Cambourne with more traditional, 'outside-in' theories which see meaning as residing purely on the page, and the reader's task as to decode the symbols which contain this meaning into spoken language. It is important to realise that the inside-out theory thus developed does allow for other than a strict top-down model. Reading is seen as an interaction between reader and text (in Goodman's terms, a transaction [Goodman, 1979]), and this accords with the more recent inter-active models of reading suggested by psychologists (Rumelhart, 1985) and also with the emphasis in literary theory on transactions between text and reader (Rosenblatt, 1985). This point will be returned to later as it is the key to a theoretically based approach to teaching reading.

The psycholinguistic emphasis on reading as a meaning-getting, predictive and interactive process led naturally to an awareness that this kind of approach makes more sense if reading is taught using materials which are meaningful to children. This awareness has caused what is perhaps the most noticeable develop-ment in terms of the materials produced for reading instruction. Now even strictly structured reading programmes make strenuous efforts to ensure that the texts children are given to read are written in as natural sounding language as possible. 'Reading schemese' is nowhere near as common as once it was.

Psycholinguistic insights have also led to a good deal of writing about parti-cular teaching techniques. One widely discussed technique, used in fact for some time before the popularisation of psycholinguistics, is known as the language experience approach (Goddard, 1974). Ashton-Warner (1963) describes this method when she tells how she taught reading to young Maori children by using their spoken language as a basis. The approach, whether carried out in the informal manner described by Ashton-Warner or more formally by the use of materials such as 'Breakthrough to Literacy', is characterised by its beginning with language which, because it comes from the child as an accompaniment to experience, is inevitably meaningful. Attention to its surface manifestation as words to be read and written comes afterwards.

Other techniques are more recent. Holdaway (1979) describes an approach which has found a good deal of favour with educational publishers: that of the 'shared book'. This involves the use of 'big books', through the sharing of which teachers can eventually lead children towards attention to words and sentences. An important part of work with big books is the modelling by the teacher of reading behaviour, so that children are not only taught by exhortation but also by example. Modelling is an important element of the apprenticeship approach to teaching which has gained currency in several curriculum areas following the rediscovery of the social learning theories of Vygotsky (Wertsch, 1985).

Holdaway recommends the following up of the shared book experience with an approach known as 'individualised reading', which itself has a respectable history, from Veatch (1959) to Moon and Moon (1986), in which children read from books which are at a level appropriate to their developing expertise, but in the choice of which they have a great deal of say. It would be fair to say, however, that current trends tend to eschew the grading of books which this approach implies. Moon himself has recently seemed to move away from the grading recommendations of his extremely influential individualised reading pamphlets to a more unstructured approach (Moon, 1985), and it is more common now for structure in reading instruction to be described more in terms of the level of support given by teachers to children in their interactions with books than in terms of textual difficulty (Wray, 1992).

Moyle (1982) describes an approach to teaching reading he calls story method which sets the teaching of reading skills within a context of meaning. In its beginning stages it involves children being read stories until they are sufficiently familiar that the children can read them independently with every expectation of success. Subsequent focus upon the constituent parts of the stories may help them to develop generalisations which they can apply to other books and then to other reading tasks. Waterland (1985) recommends that children who cannot read for themselves can be helped to do it alongside a competent, sympathetic adult. This apprenticeship approach seems a natural corollary of story method, but Waterland goes one step further in recommending the use of so-called 'real' books instead of a reading scheme. The 'real books' movement has certainly received a great deal of attention, especially through such widely read writers as Jill Bennett (1979) and Margaret Meek (1982), although one of the most notable features of Cliff Moon's early work on individualised reading (Moon and Moon, 1986) was its inclusion of 'real' books among the books used to teach reading.

The movement towards meaning-based approaches has also coincided with the growth of programmes for the involvement of parents in reading instruction (Topping and Wolfendale, 1985). Both movements have influenced each other and a shift in emphasis has taken place in terms of the techniques recommended for parental programmes (Bloom, 1987). From early recommendations to parents to be simply 'a listening ear' the most common advice now seen is for parents to be fully involved in sharing books with their children (Branston and Provis, 1986) and many schools have accompanied this advice with extended development work with parents in school, volunteer reading helpers (Stierer, 1985) and home visiting.

Approaches to reading instruction which emphasise meaning are often considered as part of a much wider theoretical and practical movement. In the 'whole language' approach (Goodman, 1986) all the language arts including reading and writing are treated as one and developed together in meaningful situations. The approach is the antithesis of the hierarchical, skill-based model often employed as a guide for language arts teaching. As Wells (1987) demonstrates, the most meaningful language situations for many children seem to involve stories. The whole language approach is characterised therefore by its insistence on immersing children in stories (Newman, 1985) and literature-based programmes have begun to have a great deal of influence (Cullinan, 1987).

ALTERNATIVE VIEWS

The approaches to the teaching of reading just described have not been without critics. The more vociferous of these have tended to come from advocates of phonics approaches, although more balanced commentators have also noted weaknesses in extreme versions of the 'real books' movement. Prominent among the phonics advocates has been Dr Joyce Morris who, in a series of articles, has consistently attacked the idea implicit within meaning-based approaches that reading is 'a natural process' (Morris, 1979). Morris has argued that 'anti-phonic' theories have been accepted uncritically by teachers and educationalists (Morris, 1983), largely because of misunderstandings as to the true nature and use of phonic knowledge. She puts forward what she describes as a 'linguistics-informed type of phonics' (Morris, 1984) around which her 'Language in Action' reading scheme was designed (Morris, 1974). She does, however, tend to contrast phonics approaches with whole-word approaches, claiming that 'the so-called Chinese method of look-and-say continues to be dominant in English-speaking countries and, no doubt, contributes to the problem of functional illiteracy among their respective populations' (Morris, 1984: 13). This argument, as was suggested earlier, is rather out of date, but tends to resurface in the writing of several defenders of phonics methods.

Stott (1981), in a rather vitriolic attack on what he terms 'the psycholinguistic invasion', argues that the over-stressing of the context as a cueing system for reading is, in fact, unhelpful for beginning readers who do not have the wide background understanding and word knowledge of fluent readers. He argues that readers should be taught to apply both phonic knowledge and understanding of context to the reading task. He also suggests, in a similar way to Morris, that the chief reason for the mistrust of phonic methods is an assumption that phonics must be taught through drills and rules. He defends the teaching of phonics and claims that, 'intelligently done, it is a matter of guiding the child's "self-induction" of the phonic correspondences' (p. 24). Attacks on the efficacy of the whole language approach have also come from Jeanne Chall herself, who is quoted as calling the movement 'shocking' (*Times Educational Supplement*, 16 January 1987).

Research-based evidence is also beginning to suggest that skilful readers are not as context-reliant as Frank Smith suggested and in fact use a variety of cues operating in parallel in order to recognise words and meanings (Oakhill and Garnham, 1988). This, coupled with the now very robust evidence that an awareness of letter sounds is strongly linked with reading success in children

(Goswami and Bryant, 1990), suggests that there may be more of a place for the teaching of phonics in a balanced reading programme than whole language adherents have perhaps allowed in the past.

TOWARDS A SYNTHESISING THEORY

It is regretful in many ways that the debate about teaching reading has become so polarised, with polemic often substituting for evidence and argument on both sides (Lewis, 1990). Evidence currently available suggests in fact that there is merit in both sides. A recent, comprehensive review of research evidence on the beginnings of reading (Adams, 1990) recommends that instruction in spelling–sound correspondences should be an essential part of all reading programmes, but should be closely embedded in a meaningful context. Studies of the initiations into literacy of very young children (Harste *et al.*, 1984; Ferreiro and Teberovsky, 1983) highlight the intuitive search for phonic regularity which children show in their early writing, but also the primacy of function over form in children's literacy development. The meaning and method of print both seem to have an important place in reading and reading instruction. Approaches which nurture both these aspects seem to be a priority for future development. What kind of theory might underlie such approaches?

The most promising line of development has been that which has emphasised the multi-directional nature of a reader's approach to print. Research has suggested that, while context, word shape and letter sounds do play an important part in recognising words and hence reading, they are each, for adults, only one cue system among many (Zola, 1984). Adults seem to be able to process several sources of information at once (e.g. knowledge about language, knowledge about the world, grammar, letters, sounds, meaning etc.) to make very rapid decisions about words on the page and also which words to attend to and which virtually to ignore. This extremely complex 'parallel' processing takes place almost without conscious thought and is best described as an interaction between reader and text. Rumelhart (1985) has used such research to develop his *interactive* model of reading. He argues that bottom-up models cannot in themselves explain how certain items are read. A good example of this is the case of handwriting, in which it is common for readers to be able to identify individual letters only *after* they have identified words or longer stretches of text. Rumelhart, however, goes on to doubt the viability of top-down models also. Pure forms of these models certainly cannot explain how expectations about meanings are triggered by encounters with letters and words. It seems that fluent reading combines elements of both bottom-up and top-down processing and Rumelhart puts forward an interactive model which has at its heart a 'message centre' that deals with the input from the senses. This is constantly scanned by a number of 'knowledge sources' which contain specialised knowledge about, for example, the structure of stories and other text types, language patterns, sound–symbol relationships and the world in general. Each knowledge source scans the message centre for hypotheses relevant to that source, evaluates them and confirms or rejects them. This kind of model, in which readers employ a number of cue systems in parallel, is one which would now be accepted by many researchers and commentators on reading.

Kenneth Goodman himself (1985) has moved beyond a top-down approach to what he calls a 'transactional' model of reading. He borrows the term from the work of Louise Rosenblatt, the literary theorist (Rosenblatt, 1985). The essence of this model is the view of reading as a constructive process in which both reader and text are transformed. The reader is transformed as new knowledge and insights are assimilated: the text is transformed as the reader constructs in the course of reading a parallel text, related to but not identical to the published text. It is this parallel text which is comprehended and to which the reader responds. This model, like that of Rumelhart, does not deny the importance of textual features. Goodman's point here is that what really matters is what the reader does with the textual features.

Thus from a range of very different starting points a model seems to be emerging which does meet the demand for a 'balanced' approach to teaching reading, yet which is firmly based upon research and theoretical insights into the reading process. From this model conclusions about reading instruction might be drawn which would command wide acceptance among researchers.

1 Reading is an extremely complex process. This means that 'simple' approaches to teaching children to read will probably have little chance of success. The approach of 'put children in a room full of wonderful books and they will learn to read' is just as simplistic as that of 'teach children to recognise and pronounce letters and they will thereby learn to read' and neither is likely to be successful.
2 Teaching reading needs to build upon what children do well (look for meaning, attend first and foremost to functional aspects of print, learn through stories) before introducing aspects which they find more difficult (apply a range of cues simultaneously, respond to text without relying upon its physical context to give them its meaning).
3 Children need to be taught the technicalities of reading, but these must be set into a context of meaning. As Adams (1990: 422) puts it in the most comprehensive recent review of research into beginning reading, 'In both fluent reading and its acquisition, the reader's knowledge must be aroused interactively and in parallel. Neither understanding nor learning can proceed hierarchically from the bottom up. Phonological awareness, letter recognition facility, familiarity with spelling patterns, spelling–sound relationships and individual words must be developed in concert with real reading and real writing and with deliberate reflection on the forms, functions and meanings of texts.'

Such conclusions are anything but 'cranky' or polemical and do, in fact, suggest some very practical ways forward in terms of devising appropriate and effective teaching programmes.

REFERENCES

Adams, M. (1990) *Beginning to Read*. Cambridge, MA: MIT Press.

Ashton-Warner, S. (1963) *Teacher*. London: Secker & Warburg.

Bennett, J. (1979) *Learning to Read Through Picture Books*. Stroud: Thimble Press.

Bloom, W. (1987) *Partnership with Parents in Reading*. Sevenoaks: Hodder & Stoughton.

Branston, P. and Provis, M. (1986) *Children and Parents Enjoying Reading*. London: Hodder & Stoughton.

Cambourne, B. (1979) 'How important is theory to the reading teacher?', *Australian Journal of Reading*, Vol. 2, No. 2.

Chall, J. (1967) *Learning to Read – The Great Debate*. New York: McGraw-Hill

Cullinan, B. (ed.) (1987) *Children's Literature in the Reading Program*. Newark, Delaware: International Reading Association.

Ferreiro, E. and Teberosky, A. (1983) *Literacy before Schooling*. London: Heinemann.

Goddard, N. (1974) *Literacy: Language-Experience Approaches*. London: Macmillan.

Gollasch, F. (ed.) (1982) *Language and Literacy: The Selected Writings of Kenneth S. Goodman*. 2 Vols. Boston: Routledge & Kegan Paul.

Goodman, K. (1967) 'Reading: a psycholinguistic guessing game', *Journal of the Reading Specialist*, Vol. 6, No. 4, pp. 126–135.

Goodman, K. (1975) 'The reading process', in Gollasch, F. (ed.) (1982) *Language and Literacy: The Selected Writings of Kenneth S. Goodman, Vol. 1*. Boston: Routledge & Kegan Paul.

Goodman, K. (1979) 'The know-more and the know-nothing movements in reading', in Gollasch, F. (ed.) (1982) *Language and Literacy: The Selected Writings of Kenneth S. Goodman, Vol. 2*. Boston: Routledge & Kegan Paul.

Goodman, K. (1985) 'Unity in reading', in Singer, H. and Ruddell, R. (eds) *Theoretical Models and Processes of Reading*. Newark, Delaware: International Reading Association.

Goodman, K. (1986) *What's Whole in Whole Language?* Ontario: Scholastic.

Goswami, U. and Bryant, P. (1990) *Phonological Skills and Learning to Read*. Hove: Lawrence Erlbaum.

Harste, J., Woodward, V. and Burke, C. (1984) *Language Stories and Literacy Lessons*. Portsmouth, New Hampshire: Heinemann.

Holdaway, D. (1979) *The Foundations of Literacy*. Sydney: Ashton Scholastic.

Lewis, G. (1990) 'My problems with real reading', in Potter, F. (ed.) *Reading, Learning and Media Education*. Oxford: Blackwell.

Meek, M. (1982) *Learning to Read*. London: Bodley Head.

Moon, B. and Moon, C. (1986) *Individualised Reading* (17th edition). Reading and Language Information Centre, University of Reading.

Moon, C. (1985) (ed.) *Practical Ways to Teach Reading*. London: Ward Lock.

Morris, J. (1974) *Language in Action*. London: Macmillan.

Morris, J. (1979) 'New phonics for old', in Thackray, D. (ed.) *Growth in Reading*. London: Ward Lock Educational.

Morris, J. (1983) 'Focus on phonics: background to the perennial debate', *Reading*, Vol. 17, No. 3.

Morris, J. (1984) 'Children like Frank, deprived of literacy unless . . . ', in Dennis, D. (ed.) *Reading: Meeting Children's Special Needs*. London: Heinemann Educational.

Moyle, D. (1982) *Children's Words*. London: Grant McIntyre.

Newman, J. (ed.) (1985) *Whole Language: Theory in Use*. Portsmouth, New Hampshire: Heinemann Educational.

Oakhill, J. and Garnham, A. (1988) *Becoming a Skilled Reader*. Oxford: Blackwell.

Rosenblatt, L. (1985) 'The transactional theory of the literary work: implications for research', in Cooper, C. (ed.) *Researching Response to Literature and the Teaching of Literature*, Norwood, New Jersey: Ablex.

Rumelhart, D. (1985) 'Toward an interactive model of reading', in Singer, H. and Ruddell, R. (eds) *Theoretical Models and Processes of Reading*. Newark, Delaware: International Reading Association.

Smith, F. (1978) *Reading*. Cambridge: Cambridge University Press.

Stierer, B. (1985) 'School reading volunteers: results of a postal survey of primary school headteachers in England', in *Journal of Research in Reading*, Vol. 8 (1), pp. 21–31.

Stott, D. (1981) 'Teaching reading: the psycholinguistic invasion', *Reading*, Vol. 15, No. 3.

Times Educational Supplement (1987) 'When a house can be as good as a home', 16 January.

Topping, K. and Wolfendale, S. (eds) (1985) *Parental Involvement in Children's Reading*. London: Croom Helm.

Veatch, J. (1959) *Individualizing Your Reading Program*. New York: Putman's Sons.

Waterland, L. (1985) *Read With Me*. Stroud: Thimble Press.

Wells, G. (1987) *The Meaning Makers*. London: Hodder & Stoughton.

Wertsch, J. (ed.) (1985) *Culture, Communication and Cognition: Vygotskian Perspectives*. Cambridge: Cambridge University Press.

Wray, D. (1992) 'Professional knowledge in teaching reading', *Reading*, Vol. 26 (2).

Zola, D. (1984) 'Redundancy and word perception during reading', *Perception and Psychophysics*, Vol. 36.

xts that teach

Colin Mills

The interest of researchers and practitioners in the role played by texts in children's growth as readers is focused upon the way in which, in a literary text, 'the whole fabric of illusory events takes its appearance and emotional value from the way the sentences flow, stop, repeat, stand alone' (Langer, 1953: 44). The attention to the texts we give to children, especially in the early stages of reading, builds upon two assumptions. First, that texts do teach important lessons about reading. Second, that there is a developmental perspective to the interactions between readers and texts. These assumptions have given rise to shifts both in our theories of reading and in pedagogy. The serious consideration of texts has given rise to radical reconsiderations of what reading actually involves and how it connects with children's lives.

The concern with the centrality of what exists to be read in our discussion and assessment of children's reading has involved some exciting raids upon other disciplines: psychology, linguistics, cultural studies, structuralism and sociology. The aim of this chapter is to illustrate some of the work done by theorists, researchers and teachers. An attempt will be made to draw out key strands, to focus upon the significance of particular writers and teachers and to indicate some priorities for our further enquiries. Some of the work considered is theoretical in nature, some of it speculative. But given the highly charged political nature of any debate about children's reading, it is important that the discussions lead to direct or indirect applications to the kinds of practical actions teachers take in classrooms.

'BOOK PEOPLE' OR 'READING PEOPLE'?

It is important to point out the relatively recent attention given to the relationships between the study of children's reading, on the one hand, and books for children, on the other. The academic and critical study of children's literature has a long history (see Townsend, 1990 for a comprehensive and updated account). The 'canon' of classic and prize-winning texts and its readership was thought to be unproblematic. Much conventional critical discussion of children's books assumed a development from, say, Peter Rabbit through the classics of early and middle childhood to sophisticated adult books for readers like the critics themselves. These critics applied the high standards of sensitivity they derived from their own reading and assumed that the texts worked universally.

This resulted in a fine tradition of critical work (see Hunt, 1990 for the best historical survey of this). It also meant that consideration of 'the best' and of 'quality' in children's books often excluded its potential and emergent readers. Those concerned with bringing children and books together (librarians, teachers, parents) had to work hard at finding a voice within the debates about quality. Moss' account (1986) is a fascinating autobiographical example of a teacher, parent, librarian's view of the duality concerned.

KEY THEORISTS

Two critics, both of whom were educationalists, have had an influence on the conjunction of critical/literary and educational concerns. The work and writing of Aidan Chambers and Margaret Meek is worth discussion at this stage, as they influence, between them, much of the research and theory which follows.

Chambers' early writing for teachers, both as a critic, editor and writer of books for 'reluctant' readers, found a large audience among teachers (Chambers, 1969, 1973). The journal *Signal*, which he co-edited with his wife, Nancy, has been influential. An article of his on 'The Reader in the Book', first published in the journal in 1977, is an important reference point for our discussion here. Drawing upon the response or reception theories of critics such as Barthes (1975) and Iser (1978), it makes available to a wider audience concepts such as 'the implied reader'. By contrasting a short story by Roald Dahl with an extract from one of his children's books (*Danny, the Champion of the World*), Chambers illuminates the manner in which a writer adjusts style, voice and viewpoint to draw his young readers in and along.

Chambers illustrates the 'tell-tale gaps' in the work of writers whom he admires and the manner in which they lead children on to literary competence. He uses potent insights from literary and postmodernist theory to clarify and extend the deep reading of children's books. His discussion of writers' 'voices' and of the relationships that are established between writers and readers is important in that it gave a fresh charge to the kind of critical writing that had been prevalent up to the late 1970s. The focus before then had been upon the surface features of texts for children: plot, action, characterisation. Whereas objection to the work of Enid Blyton, for instance, had been put down to racism, sexism, class-based attitudes, Chambers' shifting to concepts such as 'side-taking' gave a new edge to the criticism of children's books.

Here is Chambers on Blyton:

There is about her stories a sense of secrets being told in whispers just out of earshot of the grown ups, a subversive charm made all the more potent for being couched in a narrative style that sounds no more disturbing than the voice of a polite maiden aunt telling a bedtime story over cocoa and biscuits. Ultimately Blyton so allies herself with her desired readers that she fails them because she never takes them further than they are. She is a female Peter Pan, the kind of suffocating adult who prefers children never to grow up, because then she can enjoy their petty foibles and dominate them by her adult superiority.

(Chambers, 1985: 45)

Texts for children, then, are not always innocent. Chambers played an important part in establishing the structure of feeling that brought together critical concerns and children's reading. (Chambers, 1985 is an excellent and well-annotated collection of his 'occasional' writing.)

Margaret Meek had a good and lengthy track record as a reviewer and a critic when, in 1977, she co-edited *The Cool Web*, which came to be seen as a seminal text in the study of the links between literature and literacy (Meek *et al.*, 1977). The central concern of the book, an eclectic collection of readings from psychology, literary criticism and other disciplines, was to mark out narrative as 'a primary act of mind'. Barbara Hardy's essay on narrative was included early in the collection. The essays and articles in the collection cohered to make an important thesis linking literature to 'our universal human tendency to tell stories'. The collection firmly linked literacy to this 'storying' and countered theories of reading which assumed that children came to reading as a new, discrete form of linguistic behaviour. The collection is still worth reading as a model of the patterning of a central idea from a variety of sources.

The themes within *The Cool Web* reverberated in subsequent work by other researchers and theorists, many of them Meek's students or colleagues. One particularly potent insight was that which stated that as children first encounter literary texts, they see (or hear) in art form the narrative competences that link to those they have acquired as they learned oral language.

Carol Fox's work is especially significant in linking the concept of narrative with children's competence as readers (Fox, 1983, 1988). She analysed the oral storytelling of young children aged from 3 to 6 years and traced the influences that written stories had on their own spontaneous productions. She found that these early narratives display sophisticated organisational devices, as complex, she claimed, as the Proustian strategies analysed by literary theorists (Genette, 1980). What Fox termed 'the discourse of storytelling' provides children with their culture's 'mirrors' or 'metaphors' which they learn as rules for structuring and telling stories.

LITERATURE AND LEARNING TO READ

In 1983, Meek co-edited a book which was a record of a longitudinal study of adolescents learning to read (Meek *et al.*, 1983). With colleagues, most of them English teachers in London comprehensive schools, she worked with pupils with a history of failure as readers. In addition to fascinating insights into the nature of collaborative development among teachers, the study afforded novel ideas on the literature–literacy relationship and on what the writers called 'the untaught reading lessons'. Drawing again upon an understanding of the power of narrative, the authors offered portrayals of reading development which were extended to early reading in a later book on learning to read (Meek, 1984). Here, the authors of *Achieving Literacy* reflect on the interactive nature of the writer–reader relationship:

> Children who learn to read without the help of adults discover first how a story works . . . The invitation to us to enter into the story (a lesson that has to be learned but is never taught) establishes a quasi-social relationship that all good readers understand and inexperienced readers scarcely glimpse.
>
> (Meek *et al.*, 1983: 214)

One of the most significant lessons for the teachers was that expert readers (and a revealing dichotomy is set up within the study of 'expert readers' and 'reading experts') 'are competent by virtue of what we were never taught in lessons' (Meek *et al.*, 1983: 222).

In subsequent work (Meek, 1987a, 1988, 1992) attention was refocused upon younger children. A priority was 'to discover how children come to understand, and to use, the language of books that are written for them to read' (Meek, 1987a: 1). This enquiry was allied to a grasp of the distinctiveness of the texts of children's books and of the modes by which the telling of a story shapes the novice reader's understanding of it.

A good example of one of these 'modes of telling' is the manner in which writers use intertextuality: the way in which texts draw from and rely upon other texts or other literary forms from within the literate world. Meek's sensitive reading of Janet and Allan Ahlberg's *The Jolly Postman* shows how that story's combination of letters, folk and fairy stories, postcards and invitations is a superb example of how authors and artists assume a 'shared cultural understanding' and also teach reading transactions as pleasurable (see Meek, 1987b for a sustained and more academic discussion of links between literary theorising and texts for children).

Although the work of Chambers and of Meek has been seminal, other researchers and practitioners, from Britain, the USA and Australia, have contributed to our understanding. Some of the key concepts from their work will now be drawn out.

PLAY AND PLEASURE

Much work has emphasised the sense of pleasurable play that interaction with texts teaches children about reading, especially where book reading, life experience and social relationships combine. Dorothy White's classic study of the role of books in very young children's lives is now nearly 40 years old, but well worth rereading for the insights afforded into the connections between lived and literary experience: 'The experience makes the book richer and the book enriches the personal experience even at this level. I am astonished at the early age this backward and forward flow between book and life takes place' (White, 1956: 13).

Dorothy Butler's study (1979) also gives revealing insights into the connections between reading, children's early cognitive development and the literary competences that children acquire. Shirley Payton's more recent British study follows in this tradition of fine-grained analysis of young children's early experience with texts (Payton, 1984). Gordon Wells' classic study of the language acquisition of a large group of young children shows numerous examples of early experiences with books offering alternative worlds for consideration and reflection (Wells, 1987).

Henrietta Dombey's work (1986) is significant in that she illuminates the precise nature of this pleasure in the shared story and draws out implications for the role of the adult and, in later work, the pedagogy of classrooms. Through detailed analysis of the child being read to by her mother, Dombey displays, with the tools of sociolinguistics, how 'children take on simultaneously new ways of organising discourse, new meanings, new words and new syntactic forms' (Dombey, 1983: 42).

A ROLE FOR THE TEACHER

In later work (1988a, 1988b), drawing upon observation and analysis of story-telling sessions in nursery classrooms, Dombey shows how the young can be helped to 'focus on the meaning' of a story being shared. Children learn the mechanics of how literary texts work in an interactive way. After careful interpretation of a teacher reading Leo Lionni's *Fish is Fish* with a class, Dombey shows how a teacher can, through words and action:

> model for the children how a reader sets about this business. She presents not a carefully rehearsed recitation of the text followed by an interrogation of the children, but an interrogation of the text, conducted out loud with invitations to the children to join her in this enterprise.
>
> (Dombey, 1988a: 80)

This view of the teacher as one who models intelligent, deep reading of texts and the kinds of active literary competences that children need to use themselves is also exemplified in the work of an American researcher, Hade, whose work on modes of teaching which foster literary understanding contains some fascinating case studies (Hade, 1991). British writers such as Fry (1985), Timson (1988), Martin (1989) and Marum (1991) also provide illuminative classroom-based studies which build upon Dombey's analysis of young children and their teachers at work.

Martin's work is of particular significance in that it builds upon an honoured tradition in English teaching of giving voice to children's perceptions and responses to their reading. Moreover, it links that tradition to the struggles and emerging competences of those whom we used to call 'reluctant' or 'slow readers'. Work such as Martin's is important in that it brings the concerns of the 'book people' and the 'reading people' so much closer. We see in that work how children's genuine engagement with real texts, and the reflections upon that engagement, are an important part of the process of becoming a reader (see Bloom *et al.*, 1988 for details of Martin's and colleagues' practical applications).

DEVELOPMENTAL APPROACHES

Other research aims to discern developmental patterns in this engagement and in children's responses to texts. Again, there is a long tradition in this approach to research. Jenkinson's thorough study is a classic still worth reading (Jenkinson, 1940). The approach tends to identify sequences of response to genres, events in stories, roles of characters and literary worlds. The classic work in this area is still Tucker's (1981). Those interested in following up this branch of study should also see Appleyard's (1990) work. The danger with that approach to under-standing the child–text relationship is that the kinds of interaction are regarded as stages to be worked through and discarded chronologically according to age and maturity. Interesting recent approaches to such developmental studies are those of Crago (1985) and Crago and Crago (1983) and Lowe (1991). Crago's in-depth study of his own child's development and his approaches to criticism (Crago, 1979) are innovative and stimulating. Lowe's work places 'developmental' enquiry in a classroom context and shows once more how teachers can foster more sensitive reading.

Other research has probed the development of children's grasp of the sorts of textual devices that children's writers and artists use. A study of an 8-year-old's reading of one of his first 'extended' texts – Leila Berg's *A Box for Benny* – showed how a comprehension of the swapping rituals and exchanges within the story built upon the child's prior reading of picture books with clear patterns and cycles (Mills, 1984). Close, detailed study of a 6-year-old reading Faith Jacques' story *Tilly's House* showed how a young reader builds upon her previous under-standings of the manner in which stories 'work'. Those are 'learned' behaviours, in which, as Dombey showed in relation to very young children, teachers of older children play an important part (Mills, 1985a, 1985b, 1988).

There is no doubt that we need further and finer models of the developments that can be seen and patterned in children's interactions with texts. We need also to see more clearly how children's engagement with particular writers and artists shows clear paths of growing understanding. Mills (1987, 1989, 1992) attempts to discern these paths in the work of authors such as Chris Powling and Mary Rayner. Sarland (1985) links Enid Blyton's texts to children's cognitive growth. Elaine Moss' study of picture book artists shows us a model of interpreting how children develop competence in their understanding of how stories in picture books 'work' (Moss, 1992).

NEW THEORETICAL PERSPECTIVES

Perspectives from literary theory, cultural studies, feminism and the kinds of analysis used in the study of adult fiction have all been productively used to study how children's texts teach them to read. In an interview published in 1986, Aidan Chambers described his application of literary theorists such as Barthes and Iser to children's reading and the changes that resulted in how he then talked with children about their reading: 'So the first base for me in talking with children is "let's tell what we want to tell of the story of our reading"' (ILEA, 1986).

Those interested in pursuing what insights from critical theory have to offer, and how these can be translated into classroom action, should see 'The post structuralist always reads twice', also in the influential ILEA English Centre house journal, *The English Magazine* (ILEA, 1985). Hunt's (1990) is an excellent collection which shows how ideas from various disciplines assist our grasp of children's literary reading. It is an international collection with seminal essays by Crago, Chambers and Meek (on 'What counts as evidence in theories of children's literature'). There is also an up-to-date review of the contemporary critical scene by the editor.

David Lewis' work shows how critical insights derived from postmodernism, critical practice and structuralist accounts can be employed in the criticism of picture books and in the analysis of how those texts 'teach'. His relation of features of adult fiction (e.g. excess, indeterminacy and boundary-breaking) to the evaluation of such artists as John Burningham, Shirley Hughes and Anthony Brown shows the potentially important new directions that critical understanding could take (Lewis, 1990). Australian research by Williams (1988) also shows how close, critical analysis of texts for young children can aid our understanding both of how narrative conventions are learned and what they teach.

A strong thrust in much of this work is that children's learning to read literary texts is an essentially interactive enterprise. It involves interplay between text, reader and those who help to bring the two together. When children learn to read the lively, fecund picture books that David Lewis considers, they have to explore possibilities, try out alternatives, infer what is not said. All this happens within social settings (homes, classrooms) and within particular social and cultural contexts.

Work which derives from feminism or theories of subjectivity shows how the processes of interpretation described above have strong gender-based implications. Reading is different, and differentiated, for boys and for girls. An account of how learning to read was woven into socialisation into bravura masculinity (Jackson, 1990) is well counterpointed by Carolyn Steedman's remarkable study of how her 8-year-old pupils (and she) learned powerful messages about femininity from the texts they read and constructed (Steedman, 1984, 1986). Gilbert and Rowe, in an Australian study of the role of the school in the construction of gender differences in children's reading, express a central thesis of this body of work well:

> to read and write is a cultural practice and inseparable from other cultural practices which work to construct people in gender specific ways. The basic

and unchangeable cultural difference between boys and girls is the hidden agenda of the classroom.

(Gilbert and Rowe, 1989: 39)

The work of Paul (1987) and Miller (1986, 1990) gives powerful indications of the potential of feminist theory and concepts in understanding the sometimes subversive things that texts teach children.

Literary forms are not arbitrary, but are continuous with social practices and with the ways in which culture is mediated to children. Different social groups encounter texts in different ways. Shirley Brice Heath's work uncovers the literacy learning in contrasting communities in North America. Children's texts, she argues, are part of the texture of subtle, intricate social patterns, connected with power, prestige and cultural imperatives. Texts that children read (and hear) are their 'ways of taking meaning from a culture' (Heath, 1984).

What children learn from texts is often implicit: officially sanctioned versions of themselves, 'school-endorsed discourses through which children are to interpret and explain their everyday lives' (Baker and Freebody, 1989: 1). The books that we give to children show them our versions of rationality and order (Rose, 1984). Baker and Freebody's study of 'primers' (early reading books) prevalent in Australian schools shows how such texts can counter the very rationality that educators claim to be the richest offering of the written word. These insights are important ones in that they counter and inhibit discussions of children's literacy which assume that it is the same for everyone, that it is neutral, technological, unrelated to wider cultural concerns.

TEXTS AND CLASSROOMS

A last but important strand in the discussion is the contribution of good practitioners to our understandings. Cliff Moon was one of the first practising teachers to show the value and the practical applications of quality texts in the classroom (see Moon, 1988). The work of Jill Bennett and Liz Waterland made significant contributions to knowledge and also provided teachers with practical strategies for seeing 'development'. The *Signal* stable of booklists was important in the dissemination of their work (Bennett, 1991; Waterland, 1988; see also Chambers, 1987).

Their participation, as classroom practitioners, is an important thread in the cultural tapestry. In the discourse about the teaching of reading there were, for a long time, significant gaps and omissions. One related to the power and primacy of individual teachers who have frames of reference for interpreting children's growth as readers and act accordingly. Another gap, more pertinent to this chapter, is the role within the whole process of learning what exists to be read.

Historical, social and cultural shifts are such that the National Curriculum programmes of study, based as they are on the well-informed and eclectic discussion of reading and literature within the report prepared by Professor Cox (DES, 1989), enshrine the principle that texts count and are powerful in teaching.

At the heart of the National Curriculum provision is the right of each reader to 'read an increasingly wide range and variety of texts, thereby becoming more experienced readers' (NCC, 1989). One role of those who help children to do this is to be constantly refining and redefining the literary competences that texts enable. Our own reading, and our reflection upon it, is as good a starting point as any. We now have available significant models of how we can apply these literary competences into classroom action and the assessment of quality learning (Barrs and Thomas, 1991).

Texts for children are constantly shifting and being reshaped. They both absorb the culture from which they come and feed back into that culture. Look closely at how new books for children build upon the discourses of television and video storytelling techniques. The strategies that children bring to their reading are also constantly changing and in a state of transition (Meek, 1992). David Lewis says that both young children's reading behaviours and the picture books created for them are 'in a perpetual state of becoming' (Lewis, 1990: 143). For these reasons, we cannot set in concrete, or have final vocabularies about, how, or what, texts teach children. We need to observe, listen to and pattern what children see and tell us.

REFERENCES

Appleyard, J.A. (1990) *Becoming a Reader: The Experience of Fiction from Childhood to Adulthood.* Cambridge: Cambridge University Press.

Baker, C. and Freebody, P. (1989) *Children's First School Books.* London: Blackwell.

Barrs, M. and Thomas, A. (1991) *The Reading Book.* London: Centre for Language in Primary Education.

Barthes, R. (1975) *The Pleasure of the Text.* New York: Hill and Wang.

Bennett, J. (1991) *Learning to Read with Picture Books* (4th edition). Stroud: Thimble Press.

Bloom, W., Martin, T. and Waters, M. (1988) *Managing to Read.* London: Mary Glasgow.

Butler, D. (1979) *Cushla and Her Books.* Sevenoaks: Hodder & Stoughton.

Chambers, A. (1969) *The Reluctant Reader.* Oxford: Pergamon.

Chambers, A. (1973) *Introducing Books to Children.* London: Heinemann.

Chambers, A. (1977) 'The reader in the book', *Signal* 23.

Chambers, A. (1985) *Booktalk.* London: Bodley Head.

Chambers, N. (ed.) (1987) *Fiction 6–9.* Stroud: Thimble Press.

Crago, H. (1979) 'Cultural categories and the criticism of children's literature', *Signal* 30.

Crago, H. (1985) 'The roots of response', *Children's Literature Association Quarterly*, Vol. 10, No. 3.

Crago, M. and Crago, H. (1983) *Prelude to Literacy: A Pre-school Child's Encounter with Picture and Story.* Carbondale: Southern Illinois University Press.

DES (1989) *English for Ages 5–16.* London: HMSO.

Dombey, H. (1983) 'Learning the language of books', in Meek, M. (ed.) *Opening Moves.* Bedford Way Paper 17, Institute of Education, University of London.

Dombey, H. (1986) *Aural Experience of the Language of Written Narrative in Some Pre-school Children and Its Relevance in Learning to Read.* Unpublished Ph.D. thesis, University of London.

Dombey, H. (1988a) 'Stories at home and in school', in Lightfoot, M. and Martin, N. (eds) *The Word for Teaching is Learning: Essays for James Britton.* London: Heinemann.

Dombey, H. (1988b) 'Partners in the telling', in Meek, M. and Mills, C. (eds) *Language and Literacy in the Primary School*. Lewes: Falmer Press.

Fox, C. (1983) 'Talking like a book', in Meek, M. (ed.) *Opening Moves*. Bedford Way Paper 17, Institute of Education, University of London.

Fox, C. (1988) 'Poppies will make them grant', in Meek, M. and Mills, C. (eds) *Language and Literacy in the Primary School*. Lewes: Falmer Press.

Fry, D. (1985) *Children Talk about Books*. Milton Keynes: Open University Press.

Genette, G. (1980) *Narrative Discourse*. Oxford: Basil Blackwell.

Gilbert, P. and Rowe, K. (1989) *Gender, Literacy and the Classroom*. Carlton: Australian Reading Association.

Hade, D. (1991) 'Being literary in a literature-based classroom', *Children's Literature in Education*, Vol. 22, No. 1.

Heath, S.B. (1984) *Ways with Words: Language, Life and Work in Communities and Classrooms*. Cambridge: Cambridge University Press.

Hunt, P. (1990) *Children's Literature: The Development of Criticism*. London: Routledge.

ILEA (1985) *The English Magazine*, 10. London: English Centre.

ILEA (1986) *The English Magazine*, 17. London: English Centre.

Iser, W. (1978) *The Act of Reading*. London: Routledge & Kegan Paul.

Jackson, D. (1990) *Unmasking Masculinity*. London: Unwin Hyman.

Jenkinson, A.J. (1940) *What do Boys and Girls Read?* London: Methuen.

Langer, S. (1953) *Feeling and Form*. London: Routledge & Kegan Paul.

Lewis, D. (1990) 'The constructedness of texts: picture books and the metafictive', *Signal* 62.

Lowe, V. (1991) 'Stop! You didn't read who wrote it!: The concept of author', *Children's Literature in Education*, Vol. 22, No. 2.

Martin, T. (1989) *The Strugglers*. Milton Keynes: Open University Press.

Marum, E. (1991) 'And the ground gives way: looking again at *Stig of the Dump* and the National Curriculum', *Children's Literature in Education*, Vol. 22, No. 3.

Meek, M. (ed.) (1983) *Opening Moves*. Bedford Way Paper 17, Institute of Education, University of London.

Meek, M. (1984) *Learning to Read*. London: Bodley Head.

Meek, M. (1987a) 'Playing the texts', *Language Matters*. London: Centre for Language in Primary Education.

Meek, M. (1987b) 'Symbolic outlining: the academic study of children's literature', *Signal* 53.

Meek, M. (1988) *How Texts Teach What Readers Learn*. Stroud: Thimble Press.

Meek, M. (1992) 'Transitions: the notion of change in writing for children', *Signal* 67.

Meek, M. and Mills, C. (eds) (1988) *Language and Literacy in the Primary School*. Lewes: Falmer Press.

Meek, M., Warlow, A. and Barton, G. (eds) (1977) *The Cool Web: The Pattern of Children's Reading*. London: Bodley Head.

Meek, M., Armstrong, S., Austerfield, V., Graham, J. and Plackett, E. (eds) (1983) *Achieving Literacy*. London: Routledge & Kegan Paul.

Miller, J. (1986) *Women Writing about Men*. London: Virago.

Miller, J. (1990) *Seductions: Studies in Reading and Culture*. London: Virago.

Mills, C. (1984) 'But I'm the reader, not the book', *School Librarian*, Vol. 32, No. 4.

Mills, C. (1985a) 'The making of readers', *Books for Keeps*, 31.

Mills, C. (1985b) 'Readers, books and classrooms', *Books for Keeps*, 34.

Mills, C. (1987) Essays in Chambers, N. (ed.) *Fiction 6–9*. Stroud: Thimble Press.

Mills, C. (1988) 'Making sense of reading', in Meek, M. and Mills, C. (eds) *Language and Literacy in the Primary School*. Lewes: Falmer Press.

Mills, C. (1989) 'Essays on Mary Rayner and Chris Powling', in Chevalier, T. (ed.) *Twentieth-Century Children's Writers*. London: St James Press.

Mills, C. (1992) 'Authorgraph: Chris Powling', *Books for Keeps*, 75.

Mills, C. and Timson, L. (eds) (1988) *Looking at Language in the Primary School*. Sheffield: NATE.

Moon, C. (1988) 'Reading: where are we now?', in Meek, M. and Mills, C. (eds) *Language and Literacy in the Primary School*. Lewes: Falmer Press.

Moss, E. (1986) *Part of the Pattern*. London: Bodley Head.

Moss, E. (1992) *Picture Books for Young People: 9–13* (2nd edition). Stroud: Thimble Press.

National Curriculum Council (1989) *English 5–11 in the National Curriculum*. York: NCC.

Paul, L. (1987) 'Enigma variations: what feminist theory knows about children's literature', *Signal* 54.

Payton, S. (1984) *Developing Awareness of Print. A Young Child's First Steps Towards Literacy*. Educational Review Offset Publication No. 2, University of Birmingham.

Rose, J. (1984) *The Case of Peter Pan, or the Impossibility of Children's Fiction*. London: Macmillan.

Sarland, C. (1985) 'Piaget, Blyton and story: children's play and the reading process', *Children's Literature in Education*, Vol. 16, No. 2.

Steedman, C. (1984) *The Tidy House*. London: Virago.

Steedman, C. (1986) *Landscape for a Good Woman*. London: Virago.

Timson, L. (1988) '"A living through": literature in the classroom', in Mills, C. and Timson, L. (eds) *Looking at Language in the Primary School*. Sheffield: NATE.

Townsend, J.R. (1990) *Written for Children* (5th edition). London: Bodley Head.

Tucker, N. (1981) *The Child and the Book*. Cambridge: Cambridge University Press.

Waterland, L. (1988) *Read with Me* (2nd edition). Stroud: Thimble Press.

Wells, G. (1987) *The Meaning Makers: Children Learning Language and Using Language to Learn*. Sevenoaks: Hodder & Stoughton.

White, D. (1956) *Books Before Five*. New Zealand Council for Educational Research.

Williams, G. (1988) 'Naive and serious questions: the role of text criticism in primary education', in Meek, M. and Mills, C. (eds) *Language and Literacy in the Primary School*. Lewes: Falmer Press.

Chapter 6

Information handling
An important dimension to literacy

David Wray

INFORMATION HANDLING: AN ESSENTIAL SKILL

Imagine yourself at a busy railway station. You have just alighted from a train and know you have to catch a connecting train in a few minutes' time. What do you do? Do you make straight for the prominently displayed timetable and, using a sound knowledge of this format, swiftly locate the desired information before confidently boarding the correct train? Or do you, like many adults, ignore written sources of information and instead look for someone official to ask? To do the former implies a thorough confidence in your information-retrieval and interpretation strategies in this context, whereas to do the latter suggests the opposite.

The inability to deal efficiently and confidently with sources of information such as this is not, perhaps, so remarkable. Everyone has problems with things like train timetables, don't they? What it means though is that, at best, we are often dependent on someone else to do the task for us and, at worst, we fail at the task. Both these events have major consequences, some obvious, some not and they apply equally to other information-handling tasks.

INFORMATION-HANDLING ABILITIES

Before examining these consequences in more detail, let us look at some of the evidence concerning general levels of information-handling ability in sections of the population. Most of the work done in this area has involved students at various institutions of further and higher education and their ability to use information in their studying. While this is not the only aspect of information handling which teachers need to consider, or even, arguably, the most important, work done in this area does have important implications for an evaluation of approaches to teaching. Most investigations have found that students, even the most academically gifted, are not generally very proficient at such things as using libraries and books to locate and extract the information they require (Blake, 1956; Irving and Snape, 1979). In the most quoted of these investigations, Perry (1959) managed to find some students at one of the most prestigious universities in the US who, when asked to determine what a particular chapter in a book was roughly about, simply began at the first word and ploughed through a mass of not particularly useful details until they reached the end. When the possibility of reading the chapter in a more circumspect way was pointed out to them their response was, 'Lord, how many times have I been told!' It was not that they did not know about these reading strategies, but rather that they were not aware of when they should apply them. This is a phenomenon often found in studies of information handling, from primary school up to adult level (Lunzer and Gardner, 1979; Neville and Pugh, 1982). Perry calls the performance of these students 'a demonstration of obedient purposelessness'. This is a phrase to which I shall return.

If we go on to look at the abilities of adults to handle and act on information, we find a similarly bleak picture. The most renowned work here is that done by Murphy (1973) who investigated the abilities of 8000 American adults to respond to tasks based on everyday reading material. Some of his results make alarming reading. He found, for example, that 15% of his sample could not adequately respond to a task based on the reading of a traffic sign. Sixty-two per cent of the sample had trouble with a magazine subscription form and a staggering 74% were unable to deal correctly with an income tax form. We may feel that this last finding tells us more about the design of the form than it does about the abilities of these adults but we must consider, of course, the consequences of getting the task wrong, which in all these cases can be significant. Every time we are unable to handle information efficiently there is a worst case consequence of this nature. We pay too much money, we miss trains, we fail to order the goods we want, etc. Almost all adults do something like this at least once in their lives.

These are the obvious consequences of mishandling information. Often, of course, the results are not that drastic. People usually succeed more or less at information-handling tasks, but the price of inefficiency shows itself in increased time and effort. When the task is recognised to be of extreme importance, many people, of course, are not prepared to take the risk of getting it wrong and this leads them to ask for assistance in the task. People with complicated tax affairs employ accountants, people who are nervous of their own abilities ask for other opinions. This is a common response to a lack of confidence in one's ability to handle information which has equally important, if more subtle, consequences. By passing on responsibility for the task to someone else, we are in effect putting part of our lives into the control of other people. We have to trust these other people to get the task right and in an important sense we lose personal autonomy.

This is crucial because any definition of literacy must include reference to the ability to function autonomously in a literate environment. Literacy is more than simply being able to read the words around us, but it includes knowing when it is appropriate to act upon these words and then being able to decide how to act. Handling information is therefore an essential aspect of literacy and also of personal autonomy. In a real sense, being able to locate, evaluate and act upon information is linked to having power over our own lives. The phrase 'information is power' is well known to agencies that seek to control our lives. There are many institutions in our society that seek to preserve their power by monopolising sources of information. As individuals we are rarely in a position to do much about this. Several areas of our lives are so complex that it is unreasonable to expect lay people to have sufficient command of the specialised information necessary to deal with problems themselves. The accountant may be the only person who can deal with complex tax affairs, the solicitor may be the only person who can deal with the complexities of house purchase. However, there are still many areas of our lives which ought to be under our control and which, as literate people, we ought to be able to deal with effectively ourselves. And usually this means being able to locate and use the relevant information.

THE INFORMATION PROCESS

Having established that becoming literate involves becoming able to handle information, let us move on to examine more closely what the process of 'handling information' involves.

One useful formulation is that which divides the process into six stages (Winkworth 1977), each of which has some part to play in any information-handling task. Let us define these stages a little more closely with reference to a particular information task, i.e. consulting a train timetable.

Stage 1. Define subject and purpose. Obviously when we go to the timetable we have a fairly clear idea of what we want to achieve. We want to find out when the next train leaves to our destination, which platform it leaves from and perhaps what time it will eventually get us there.

It would be quite unusual for anyone to browse through a timetable. Almost always they will have a clearly defined purpose – a fact which applies to most information tasks. A little later we will look at how this is reflected in the experience that many children have of information handling in school contexts.

Stage 2. Locate information. Obviously before we use information we have first to find it. In our particular example this involves finding where the timetable is and then finding particular pieces of information on it. Usually there are particular techniques we can use to speed this up. If we are looking in a book timetable, it will help if we can use the index to find the places that we are interested in. At the very least a knowledge of alphabetical order will speed up our search.

Stage 3. Select information. Once we have found the information, we then have to pick out the precise items that we require, in this case the times of particular trains. We have to evaluate and to be aware of a range of possible limiting factors. It is not much use, for example, if we pick out a train to catch, but fail to notice that it only runs on Saturdays.

Stage 4. Organise information. In simple information tasks there may not be much organisation to be done. Sometimes, for example, all we require is one train time and there are no snags. Often, though, it is more complex. We might have to change trains and we then have to synchronise several pieces of information. This involves re-arranging information into one coherent package and some method of organisation has to be employed. Some people will be able to do this in their heads but others will need to resort to pen and paper and take notes. Writing is the basic organisational tool at our disposal.

Stage 5. Evaluate information. The example of the train timetable is not a very good one to illustrate evaluation as it should not be necessary in this case. Misprints are possible, but generally we have to trust to the accuracy of the information on the timetable. There are, however, many information tasks in which evaluation is much more important as we shall see later.

Stage 6. Communicate results. Most information tasks involve some kind of communication as we relay what we have found to others. Communication may also lead to action as we respond to what we find. In this example we catch our train, either by ourselves, or with others whose knowledge of what they are doing is dependent upon our efficiency.

This, then, is the process of handling information and in each information task we engage in we follow, more or less, these six stages. We cannot, therefore, really be called literate unless we can perform these stages effectively.

However, although all six stages are essential components of the information process, it can be argued that, in fact, two of them are more important in the sense of underlying an extended view of literacy, in which personal autonomy plays a crucial role. This point can be illustrated by considering briefly the impact of new technologies on definitions of literacy. It is clear that access to a computer can simplify a number of information tasks for us. Processing information is what computers are good at. They can deal with millions of bits of information at very rapid speeds and, in certain areas, are far more efficient information handlers than we are. So perhaps all this emphasis on people being able to handle information has come too late. Maybe we should just let the computers do it for us, since they are so much more efficient.

This, however, will never be a complete answer. To see why, let us look at our six stages and assess how a computer can perform at each one of them. There is no doubt that a computer can locate information very efficiently indeed. By tapping my requirements into a computer terminal I can often have access to the precise information I require within seconds. Similarly a computer can select between vast quantities of information and present me with exactly the discrete two or three pieces I require. It can pull together information and organise it into a coherent whole and it can also, if I tell it, communicate its work to anywhere in the world.

So stages 2, 3, 4 and 6 can be done by computers, usually far more efficiently and quickly than any human could manage. But, of course, the computer can do these things only if it is given precise instructions. What it cannot do is determine a purpose for itself. A computer is a tool and is not capable of more than a limited autonomy. The ability to define our purpose for information seeking is one of the things which sets humans apart from machines in terms of literacy.

The second thing which sets us apart is our ability to evaluate what we read. The computer is good at finding information but poor at evaluating it. This explains why we used to hear tales of people getting bills for £0 or £1 million. These were unfairly put down to computer error, but in fact they were errors made by humans. The computer was only doing what it had been told to do, but was not capable of recognising that a mistake had been made. This fact still very much applies. Computers cannot themselves evaluate the information they locate and handle. Yet the ability to evaluate information is crucial to any real operation of literacy. If we cannot evaluate information, we are at the mercy of what anyone tells us. Again our autonomy is threatened.

INFORMATION HANDLING IN SCHOOL

Let us now relate these two crucial elements in information handling to the kind of teaching that may go on in school to develop information skills.

I argued earlier that adults rarely enter into information-handling situations without having clearly defined their purpose. It is possible for people to use sources of information in a purposeless way as in, say, browsing through a magazine while in a dentist's waiting room. Nevertheless, in comparison with the myriad information-finding tasks performed by the typical adult this purpose-less approach is of minor importance. The vast majority of times that adults get information from whatever source, they went there with a specific purpose in mind. If this purposefulness tends to characterise adult information handling we ought to expect it to be reflected in the experiences that children have of using information in school. Yet unfortunately much of children's information handling is characterised by the 'obedient purposelessness' that Perry found in his Harvard students.

The activity in schools in which children do most of their information handling is some form of project work. There is evidence which suggests that their dominant activity in this work is copying out sections from reference books (DES, 1978; Maxwell, 1977). When asked what they are doing they will often say something like, 'I'm finding out about birds, cars etc.' If asked why, they may ultimately respond with, 'Because teacher told me to.'

There are two points here. The first concerns the difference between the precise purpose an adult will have in seeking information and the vague and haphazard purpose all too often used by the child. What does 'finding out about' mean? What it often means is that once children have a topic such as cars, dinosaurs etc. they then have to collect every piece of information they can about it and write it down. It does not really matter whether they understand the information they find – since it is about the topic it must be relevant. But, of course, this is an impossible task. Finding out about cars could mean finding out everything there is to know about cars. Small wonder that children are so overwhelmed by the task that they simply copy down what the book says. The task is also imprecise since it does not specify what kind of information is required. Everything is relevant, so everything must be written down. This is in contrast to the precise purpose setting that children will need to do when they enter the adult world of information finding. No adult will go to a train timetable saying, 'I want to find out about train times' and then proceed to copy them down. Teachers need to move children on from the vague to the precise in terms of purpose setting in project work. It should not be too hard to ask children, 'What exactly do you want to find out about cars, trains etc.?' In other words, encourage them to ask specific questions which can then be used as a guide during their information search. These questions will demand that they search and sift through a great deal of information before locating the answers.

The second point to make about children's purposes for engaging in information tasks concerns their origins. For many children their real reason for doing certain activities is because the teacher told them to. Again we have to contrast this with the purposes of adults in pursuing information. Adults will rarely look for information because somebody else has told them to, without seeing the need themselves. Adults have to formulate their own purposes for finding information and cannot rely on someone else doing it for them. There is a need for children to be capable of formulating their own purposes for getting information if they are to be fully literate. In other words it will not be sufficient to encourage them to be more precise in their purpose setting if teachers actually do this for them. There is a danger of this happening in materials such as project work cards. Work cards asking children to find specific bits of information avoid the problem of vagueness in setting purposes but at the same time make the task less real to the children by doing the purpose setting for them.

I have argued elsewhere (Wray, 1985) that the answer to this problem lies in some kind of sharing between teacher and children. Teachers and children need to negotiate to formulate purposes for finding information. In negotiation each of the participants has his or her special contribution to make. The children contribute a desire to 'find out' and an existing body of knowledge within which new information can be interpreted, while teachers contribute the ability to make purposes more precise and capable of being satisfied. This negotiation can be the key to getting the best of both worlds from the process of purpose setting. Children can be gradually led towards becoming more precise, but they need never feel that they are not following their interests but their teacher's.

The second crucial element in information handling mentioned earlier is the ability to evaluate information. This we need to be able to do to be classed as fully literate, since if we cannot evaluate information we lose our autonomy. There are many occasions in our lives when we are confronted with propaganda, be it blatant or subtle. Blatant propaganda tends to be political and we are at least at an advantage in our country over some others in that we can choose the propaganda we read. When propaganda is blatant, as in political newspapers, we tend to read it either already sharing its views or with our critical faculties on the alert, ready to disbelieve what we read. With more subtle propaganda, however, we need continually to remind ourselves to evaluate the information we are given. One form of this is that found in the publicity material that confronts us daily. This often masquerades as information when it is really designed to be persuasive and we need, as literate people, to be able to recognise when we are being led to believe and act in certain ways, so that we can assess whether we really want to behave as the publicity is trying to make us. Of course, most of us at times are not good at this and the whole of the advertising industry is founded upon this fact. There would be no point in spending millions of pounds advertising a brand of toothpaste if no extra people bought it afterwards. We do respond to such publicity even if, on the surface, we can recognise the partiality and unreliability of the claim that this toothpaste will lead to 20% fewer fillings and give us a smile with sex appeal.

It is certainly true that we need to sharpen our own critical approach to such information and even more apparent that we need to give attention to developing such an approach in the children we teach – to make them more able to evaluate the information they come across (Zimet, 1976). Children are perhaps even more inclined than adults to believe that 'if it says it in print it must be true.' How can we get them beyond this and how, indeed, can we compensate for the dire effects that propaganda, subtle or otherwise, may have upon them?

One approach to this which has some adherents is that of removing biased materials from the children's reach (Jeffcoate, 1982). This leads many teachers to ban books like *Little Black Sambo* or *Dr Dolittle* from their classrooms on the grounds that they propagate racial stereotypes and so lead to racism. Many teachers similarly will not want to use books in which gender roles are portrayed in a traditional male-centred way. Other teachers will ban books because they portray family life as something completely removed from that of the children they teach. Nobody responsible for getting books to children can fail to be aware of the growing emphasis on providing non-racist, non-sexist or non-classist books. It is, of course, difficult not to sympathise with the motives of those who take this approach and simply remove the offending books from classrooms, presumably replacing them with books which give desirable messages. This is clearly done with the very best of intentions. It is possible, however, to argue that this approach misses the point. After all, when children leave school they will be confronted with books and other information sources with the same faults of sexism, racism etc. Some of the classic books in our culture suffer from these faults – *Robinson Crusoe* certainly portrays a view of racial superiority, *The Merchant of Venice* is anti-semitic and many books can be accused of being sexist in their portrayal of gender roles. The same is true of other sources of information. A brochure from the South African Tourist Board shows only one black face – a Zulu chieftain in traditional costume. Holiday brochures regularly use scantily clad young ladies as a lure to people to take their holidays in particular resorts. It would be inconceivable for us to prevent all this material from being read and used. The point is that when we read this material we need to be alert for the bias and we need to have ways of dealing with it. Children, of course, cannot develop these ways unless they have had practice in applying them.

An alternative response to this problem is the exact opposite of the protective approach taken by those who would ban biased materials from schools. It is possible to argue that what children need is to be confronted with bias, as much as possible, of all different kinds and then to have the bias brought out into the open. By this means they may begin to realise that much of the information they read is there to persuade them to a certain point of view and then be able to approach it critically.

CONCLUSION

This chapter began by arguing that any real definition of literacy has to take account of the need for people to deal effectively with a whole range of sources of information. 'Dealing with information' was defined and two crucial stages in the process of information handling were isolated – that of defining for ourselves a precise purpose for seeking information and that of evaluating the information we do find. Finally, some points were made about our approach to developing these two things in the children we teach.

Throughout the chapter, one point continually stressed has been the need for literacy to involve autonomy on the part of the literate person and for children to be led towards this autonomy from the earliest possible stages of the development of their literacy. This may involve a major re-evaluation of the respective roles of teachers and pupils, but the goal of creating independent literates seems to justify the effort involved.

REFERENCES

Blake, W. (1956) 'Do probationary freshmen benefit from compulsory study skills and reading training?', *Journal of Experimental Education*, 25, September, pp. 91–93.
Department of Education and Science (1978) *Primary Education in England*. London: HMSO.
Irving, A. and Snape, W. (1979) *Educating Library Users in Secondary Schools*. Boston Spa: British Library Research and Development Department.
Jeffcoate, R. (1982) 'Social values in children's books', in *Children, Language and Literature*. Milton Keynes: Open University Press.
Lunzer, E. and Gardner, K. (1979) *The Effective Use of Reading*. London: Heinemann.
Maxwell, J. (1977) *Reading Progress from 8 to 15*. Windsor: NFER.
Murphy, R. (1973) *Adult Functional Reading Study, Project 1*. Washington: United States Office of Education.
Neville, M. and Pugh, A. (1982) *Towards Independent Reading*. London: Heinemann.
Perry, W. (1959) 'Students' use and misuse of reading skills: a report to a faculty', *Harvard Educational Review*, 29, III.
Winkworth, E. (1977) *User Education in Schools*. Boston Spa: British Library Research and Development Department.
Wray, D. (1985) *Teaching Information Skills through Project Work*. Sevenoaks: Hodder & Stoughton.
Zimet, S. (1976) *Print and Prejudice*. Sevenoaks: Hodder & Stoughton.

Chapter 7

The assessment of reading

Denis Vincent

The argument of this chapter is simple: aversion to assessment, testing and measurement has not served the teaching of reading well. Behind this professional distrust of formalised assessment lies a confusion between the managerial and pragmatic role which assessment can, indeed must, fill and its pedagogic role as a classroom tool and a guide or support in working with individual readers.

MANAGEMENT VERSUS TEACHING?

Reading teachers have tended to dismiss assessment for management because it does not 'help them do their job in the classroom'. This is to take a restricted view of teaching. Classrooms and individual learning need management just as much as schools or school systems. They are also subject to the same imperatives to self-monitor, self-evaluate and to be accountable. The main purpose of this chapter is to rehabilitate such criteria and to lay the foundations for the case that formal methods of reading assessment, including standardised tests, are a potentially constructive resource in the teaching of reading.

As a preliminary, the unhelpfulness of many of the common criticisms of the testing and measurement of reading needs to be recognised. This critical rhetoric notwithstanding, the rearguard resistance to assessment has failed and has probably contributed to the imposition of an external national curriculum testing system. In the case of reading, it appears that, so far, this system is flawed.

As a first positive step primary teachers will have to regain the initiative in assessment. This involves more than willingness to live with testing. It requires the adoption and use of methods and assessment materials more credible than those imposed by central government.

READING: ASSESSMENT ... TESTING ... MEASUREMENT

The focus of this chapter is on standardised reading tests. To pre-empt subsequent confusion it would be as well to locate these within the assessment of reading generally.

'Assess', 'test' and 'measure' are commonly used as if they were inter-changeable. It is more accurate and helpful to treat them as a series of increasingly specific categories.

Assessment subsumes various ways of judging, appraising or evaluating readers. Assessments vary in precision and formality. Some reading assessments can be made and recorded in the reader's absence on the basis of the teacher's accumulated knowledge of the learner. The assessment may focus on reading activities experienced and the reader's interests and attitudes rather than matters of 'how well' he or she can read. Increasingly, such assessments have been made in the context of a cumulative recording system. The *Primary Language Record* developed originally by the Inner London Education Authority is the best-known example of such an approach although many other Local Education Authorities (LEAs) have devised similar guidelines for local use.

Testing is a special sub-category of assessment which requires readers to attempt set tasks designed to elicit observable or permanent evidence of their reading ability. The most widespread forms of testing are with commercially published examples. Some of these may be administered individually and require the reader to read texts aloud and then answer comprehension questions on the text (e.g. the *New Macmillan Reading Analysis*; the *Neale Analysis of Reading Ability*). Even more popular have been silent group reading tests to be taken by groups or whole classes at the same time. Typically, these consist of lists of (unrelated) incomplete sentences to be completed by selecting the correct word from a multiple-choice set of four or five alternatives. The most widely used version at present is Young's *Group Reading Tests*.

On reflection, completing lists of unrelated sentences, each with a word missing, seems a bizarre way of defining reading. 'Real' texts simply do not look like this! Yet, since the 1950s more published reading tests have taken this form than any other – the most recent addition to this genre, the *Macmillan Group Reading Test*, was published in 1990. There have been attempts to provide teachers with more plausible alternatives based on the comprehension of continuous prose passages (e.g. the *Edinburgh Reading Test* series) or on longer complete texts (e.g. the *Effective Reading Tests*). Use has also been made of 'cloze' procedure involving deleting a number of words from a continuous prose passage and instructing the reader to supply the missing words, e.g. the *GAP Reading Comprehension Test* and the *Group Literacy Assessment*. Nevertheless, sentence-completion tests have continued to command a majority share of the United Kingdom testing 'market'. The next section suggests reasons for this preference for tests which offer such a dismal vision of what reading is.

Just as testing is a sub-category of assessment, so, in turn, measurement is a sub-category of testing. Tests may be said to measure reading when they express the outcome quantitatively, relating a reader's ability to some form of scale. Most of the examples cited above meet this criterion by relating reading ability to a norm such as a percentile or reading 'age'. 'Homegrown' teacher-devised tests do not demonstrate this property – although they may have the potential to do so (e.g. Potter, 1986).

Also, there are testing procedures which concentrate on making a tally or completing a checklist of readers' capabilities/attributes, such as the *Bangor Dyslexia Test* or *Get Reading Right*. These do not, strictly speaking, 'measure' reading but permit the accumulation of separate pieces of evidence about a reader. There are also diagnostic/analytic procedures such as 'miscue analysis' which use testing to obtain qualitative data rather than measurements.

The distinction between tests which measure reading and those which do not, or at least place less emphasis on measurement, is easily overlooked in the controversy over the testing of reading.

In fact, much of the debate is really concerned with the role of tests as indicators, i.e. measures, of reading 'standards'. The problem which now faces teachers of reading is that they do not participate in the debate about standards of reading on an equal basis with their critics because it is these critics who largely define, manage and control the measurement process. The next section considers the causes of this.

READING TESTS IN THE UK SINCE 1958

In 1958 two tests were published in the UK – Daniels and Diack's *Standard Reading Tests* and Marie Neale's *Neale Analysis of Reading Ability*. Both continued in wide use over the next 30 years. This is perhaps indicative of the conservatism and inertia which characterise the testing of reading. Their publication date is thus a useful starting point for tracing developments in reading testing into the 1990s. Since the 1960s the history of the testing of reading in the UK has been characterised by the following:

1 LEAs increasingly made widespread use of standardised reading tests but the quality of a test's content and model of reading was of less priority than cost and ease of marking. The latter priority reflects the professional resistance that LEAs encountered in introducing testing programmes.
2 While LEAs persisted in conducting annual LEA-wide testing of age cohorts of children for the next 30 years it is now evident (e.g. Gipps *et al.*, 1983; Cato and Whetton, 1990) that little direct use of the results was made.
3 Many primary schools had policies of standardised reading testing, especially in the later primary years. Reading tests were also sometimes used for intake-screening in secondary schools and some secondary remedial/special needs teachers tested reading.
4 As in LEAs, priorities of cost and time tended to dominate choice and use of tests in many schools. Re-usable tests requiring 'once-only' purchase were preferred to those requiring written responses in a disposable answer booklet. This in part accounts for the continued popularity of the *Standard Reading Tests* and the Neale test as well as the notorious *Schonell Graded Word Reading Test*.
5 Both in LEAs and schools there was great reluctance to change once a test had been adopted, so the same tests often remained in use for many years.

6 A further group of schools regarded testing suspiciously or rejected it on grounds of policy/educational philosophy.

7 As central support teacher teams were established in LEAs some of these also found it necessary to use tests – either for individual diagnostic assessment or to identify children with genuine reading difficulties as opposed to, say, behavioural problems.

8 Neither initial nor in-service teacher trainers were enthusiastic about testing. Published professional/academic work in the field of reading tended to ignore issues of reading assessment or to be critical of testing.

9 A number of test-based national surveys of reading standards were conducted and reading tests featured in a number of important major research studies. As a result of a possible decline in standards detected in a survey reported in 1971 the Bullock Committee of Enquiry was set up. Its report (DES, 1975) was the first to raise the issue of test quality.

10 In 1974 the Department of Education and Science established its Assessment of Performance Unit (APU). The APU commissioned a series of six surveys of national reading standards at 11 and 15 years between 1979 and 1988. The reading tests specially developed for this used sustained and coherent texts and sought to test a range of reading skills.

While both 7 and 10 above refer to reasonably constructive trends, on balance the story of reading tests has been a depressing one and there are two features of this period which bear directly on reading assessment in the National Curriculum. First, it was a time of lost opportunities. The managerial and pragmatic uses which testing could and should have served were overlooked. Because LEAs (to some extent) and schools (to a greater extent) chose not to take full – if any – control of the assessment process a partial vacuum existed which central government filled with a mandatory assessment and testing system. It can be argued that shortcomings in assessment practices were less acute in the case of reading than most other areas of the primary curriculum. At least the history of reading teaching since the late 1950s included serious attempts to assess, test and measure the skill on a scale much greater than for any other subject. The fact remains that what schools and LEAs were doing to assess reading was not sufficiently thorough or credible to protect their independent position.

The second feature is the rhetoric of anti-testing which evolved. Testing remained ideologically unpopular throughout the period. The measurement principles employed in reading tests was similar to that used in testing children in the annual competition for places in selective secondary schools. Reading tests were thus associated by many teachers and educational theorists with competition, selection, labelling and streaming at a time when philosophies of cooperation, comprehensive education, mixed-ability teaching and individual growth were becoming increasingly important.

It was significant, too, that testing found little favour with proponents of the 'real books' approach to teaching reading which became increasingly influential in the 1980s. Tests were perhaps equated with the 'mechanism' of the despised reading scheme.

A persuasive anti-test rhetoric thus evolved (e.g. Rosen, 1982). Added impetus came from secondary English teaching (e.g. Stibbs, 1979). Here resistance to any external assessment of the subject was intensified because of the implications for public examinations.

The status of testing was not helped by its failure – especially in LEAs – to be seen to be of direct benefit by teachers ('a waste of time ... '). The increasing age and poor quality of the content of some of the most widely used tests also provided an easy target for criticism.

READING ASSESSMENT IN THE NATIONAL CURRICULUM

The distrust of testing discussed above had its ramifications in the National Curriculum for English, notably the statements of attainment for reading, En2. Their drafting seems to have been haunted by the spectre of the standardised group comprehension test. The statements emphasise assessing reading through (a) talk and (b) familiar texts. These conditions preclude using silent group written tests based on texts specifically selected or devised for assessment purposes.

A further constraint is imposed by a concern with range and variety in reading material experienced. Taken literally, this makes formal testing impracticable. Yet, the problem for testing is one which has been contrived by confusing statements about the nature of the reading curriculum (namely, breadth and variety in texts experienced) with statements about the nature of reading skill.

The resulting model of reading is far from coherent – although the agencies originally commissioned to develop the National Curriculum assessment for English at key stage 1 (5–7 years) and key stage 3 (12–14 years) were able to build on the curriculum idealism of the statements of attainment to produce reasonably coherent models of assessment: the original 'standard assessment tasks' (SATs) developed for National Curriculum assessment required teachers to carry out searching and structured assessments working closely with individuals or small groups.

However, in 1991 the Secretary of State for Education instructed the Schools Examinations and Assessment Council (SEAC) – the statutory body responsible for overseeing National Curriculum assessment – that assessment should primarily take the form of objective timed tests.

Yet, as we have noted, reading in the National Curriculum is defined so as to be incompatible with this format. This is a formula for bad tests and inadequate assessment of reading, i.e. a repeat of the pattern exhibited in many LEAs since 1960.

The position is not only due to ministerial insensitivity or excessive defensiveness by curriculum planners. Professional complaint during the piloting and first annual administration of the key stage 1 SATs in 1990 and 1991 was much publicised and surely influenced political decisions to abandon the curriculum idealism of the early SATs in favour of much more dubious testing proposals.

It seems that reading in fact presented teachers with fewer problems than other key stage 1 assessments. Moreover, no such outcry was encountered in response to early trials of the key stage 3 SATs, but by then the damage was done.

THE RHETORIC EXAMINED

Given that this outcry was so counterproductive, resulting not in the abolition of National Curriculum assessment but the imposition of a curriculum minimalist model, it is worth examining some of the central and recurring shibboleths. What is striking about them collectively is that (a) they are not new but were expressed recurringly over the previous 30 years and (b) they are often mutually contradictory (e.g. 1 and 2). They are analysed individually below.

1 Teachers are too busy teaching to assess (or give tests)
To allege that testing or other forms of assessment intrude or encroach on teaching time is to assume that the methods and purposes of assessment are inherently alien to those of good teaching – surely an ultimately untenable position? (Even quite elaborate assessment procedures occupy only a small proportion of learning time in the course of a year or term.)

2 Teachers don't need formal tests – they're assessing all the time, anyway
Too little is known about the teacher as assessor and opinions remain divided concerning the claims for teacher assessment. The Task Group on Assessment and Testing (TGAT) which was established to advise on National Curriculum assessment (DES, 1987) observed: 'A great deal of effective assessment is already carried out, often in an informal manner within the individual classroom' (p. 7). Yet subsequently the same report says: 'This process is not sharply focused, yields a diversity of information and tends to be only loosely related to purpose. Consequently it may not be clear how it relates to particular decisions about a pupil's education programme' (p. 41). More charitably, the Kingman Report (DES, 1988) notes: 'Such assessment is informal and often impressionistic and intuitive and none the worse for that *if impressions and intuitions are well informed*' (p. 58) (original italics). Yet, however excellent such internal teacher assessment may be, its strengths are pedagogic rather than pragmatic. Moreover, while it remains invisible to the external world its claim to make more formalised assessment redundant will lack credibility. The onus is upon teachers, and perhaps also researchers, to open up and make explicit this body of professional practice, rather as Campbell (1988) does for the practice of hearing children read.

3 Tests are very limited in what they can measure
This criticism is to be applauded for taking the premiss of a broad and rich model of reading. However, it is too often used misleadingly to argue that because tests cannot tell everything they tell the teacher nothing. It is true that tests cannot encompass all that reading may be. This should not exclude their use as indicators

alongside a range of other evidence which thoughtful teachers would be prepared to consider. Indeed, tests may well have certain strengths (e.g. psychometric properties such as known reliability and objectivity of scoring) not shared by other criteria.

4 Testing damages children

It is possible to imagine damaging ways in which tests could be applied . . . but they are imaginary. The possible dangers of testing are so widely and frequently referred to – notably the danger of 'labelling' children – that it is hard to believe that there are any teachers who are unaware of them or incapable of ensuring they do not happen.

The government's proposals for National Curriculum assessment at key stage 1 provoked numerous claims that children were 'too young' to be assessed/tested at 7 years of age. As regards reading, there is little reputable evidence to support this and much evidence to contradict it. For example, in 1987 the Effective Reading Test, Level 0 was administered to a national sample of 7-year-olds in a standardisation survey to establish 'norms' for the test. The test consists of an illustrated reading booklet containing two full-length stories and a separate booklet containing 35 objective questions testing comprehension of the stories. During the standardisation little evidence was found of children for whom such a task was in principle inappropriate or excessively stressful. A number of other published reading tests have been developed for this age range. None of their constructors reports problems connected with testing such young children.

5 Tests only tell teachers what they know already

This frequently made remark often refers to a correspondence between reading test scores and the teacher's own notional rank ordering: known weaker readers performed least well on the test . . . children regarded as good readers did better. However, few teachers will be so certain of their own judgement that they would not be prepared to allow an 'honest second look' using an external and possibly objective criterion. Moreover, there are many situations in which teachers have to make decisions or provide information about learners of whom they do not have adequate first-hand knowledge. Here test results can contribute usefully to the assessment data which will have to be assembled.

Teachers are not the only audience for test results. Tests can help to tell parents and public what it is that teachers 'know already'. Parents respect the work and professional judgement of teachers more than is assumed by the popular press and politicians. That they may prefer evidence about progress and attainment in reading to be a combination of teacher judgement and external/ objective assessment does not diminish this respect.

6 You're no further on once you've given the test

There is an abundance of introductory 'how to' texts on the productive use of assessment and testing in schools (e.g. Satterly, 1989; Shipman, 1983; Vincent, 1985). Yet in practice tests are not always used to good purpose. It is often a case of poor tests used badly.

In many such cases the decision to introduce an assessment and testing programme is implemented with insufficient commitment of resources and energy. The result, at least within the LEAs, has been typified by the findings of a recent survey (Cato and Whetton, 1990) which found that, while 59 out of 116 LEAs in England and Wales carried out LEA-wide testing of 7-year-olds, the tests used were outdated, tended to be poor technically and did not 'match modern conceptions of reading' (p. 70). Moreover, the research calls into question whether any practical use was made of the results: 'Even those LEAs which do collect data do not necessarily analyse it. Those who do, generally show very little statistical sophistication' (p. 64). The researchers re-analysed some of the LEA survey data: 'in two instances trends not discerned by LEA were revealed' (p. 64) . . . Teachers obliged to administer such tests might with justification complain that the exercise had been unproductive.

Nevertheless, the luxury of dismissing tests or other assessments as a pointless exercise which 'they' at the Education Offices or the DFE have imposed from outside can no longer be afforded. Much of the resentment arises from confusion between the pragmatic/managerial uses of testing and the pedagogic uses. Teachers have been required to carry out assessment for the former purpose – on behalf of administrators – without being either sufficiently informed or involved to feel that it has any value. Yet many of the burdens and concerns of adminis-trators are now in the process of being transferred to schools. Tests still may not 'tell teachers how to teach better', but their purpose and necessity are likely to become better recognised and accepted as the need to gather intelligence about the 'way the system is functioning' and to communicate this to a clientele becomes a priority for schools and teachers themselves.

TRENDS IN THE ASSESSMENT OF READING

Trends in practice and use

When the National Curriculum was first proposed in the late 1980s it seemed likely to replace existing patterns of assessment in the primary school and eliminate the commercial test market – in which reading tests were a major – perhaps the largest – component. The TGAT (DES, 1987) proposed that the National Curriculum should be largely assessed by annually developed SATs at the end of key stages 1–3. The TGAT also suggested that SATs developed for previous years could be used for purposes other than statutory end-of-key-stage assessment, such as further probing of SAT results or assessment in intermediate years of the key stage when SATs were not mandatory.

SATs have only been used on a national scale at key stage 1 for two successive years. It remains to be seen whether they will suit this extended role. So far, there have been only a few 'spin-offs' from the official work on developing National Curriculum assessment. Of these by far the most interesting is Bartlett *et al.*'s

(1991) *Formative Assessment in the National Curriculum: Reading*. This is a key stage 1 SAT for use in teacher assessment, although there is much to recommend it as a replacement for the official materials devised for mandatory assessment. It is far more sensible. All children are assessed using the same specially devised text. This would permit much greater comparability of assessment across the country than the bizarre arrangement for National Curriculum assessment in 1990 and 1991 whereby the teacher selected any one of a number of possible texts from a list of set books. In any case, there are pressures for the assessment of reading in school in forms beyond those provided for National Curriculum assessment. The most important of these are for internal evaluation, monitoring of progress and diagnostic assessment.

As Murphy (1991: 145) points out, it will not be sufficient to restrict assessment to the compulsory reporting requirements of end-of-key-stage assessment for key stages 1 and 2 – 'the fact that they will only be revealed at two age points during the years of primary schooling will restrict their usefulness for teachers in terms of day-to-day progress within the classroom'. Murphy predicts a continued role for standardised tests, as part of teacher assessment required by the National Curriculum as well as for the various screening, diagnosing and monitoring purposes for which tests have always been designed.

Evaluation in school

Proponents of educational measurement have long extolled tests as a means of evaluating changes in curriculum, organisation, and teaching methods and materials. Contemporary theories of evaluation define the enterprise more broadly and some reject testing altogether; nevertheless, test data continue to be used as a criterion in many published reports of evaluation studies in education.

A strong motive for the commissioning, sponsoring or initiation of evaluation studies has been the need for evidence concerning the effectiveness of spending money in a particular way. In the period since 1958 discussed previously this concern was largely confined to extra-school agencies. However, the introduction of local management arrangements in schools (LMS) creates a new local tier of 'clients' for evaluation studies within schools themselves. If, for example, money is to be spent providing additional resources for helping backward readers, school governors will need evidence that this has been beneficial. The inclusion of test data in this may provide essential reassurance about the rigour of the evidence – even if the tests only confirm the conclusions of the teachers themselves.

The current policy that end-of-key-stage assessment results should be published in school league tables presents an unwelcome challenge to schools. Although it remains to be seen how the policy will work in practice it is not too early to start considering strategies that schools might develop in response to it.

Self-monitoring should be central. It would be prudent to establish an early warning system involving efficient screening and monitoring of reading progress. Tests should be included; they would have to be of better quality than those so far produced for end-of-key-stage assessment. This is important not only for accuracy of assessment – essential if the early warning system is to be efficient – but also for regaining control over the assessment process.

In the past screening, monitoring and evaluation were LEA prerogatives. It remains to be seen whether LEA-wide reading surveys will continue now that legislation gives schools greater economic and managerial autonomy. This opens the way for schools to take greater internal initiatives with a greater institutional will to assess productively than under LEA arrangements. A new generation of textbooks has begun to appear (e.g. Connor, 1991) which presuppose considerable energy and commitment within schools to assess fully and thoughtfully. In fact, useful models have existed for some time. Shipman (1983) outlined an approach to assessment within the framework of in-school evaluation. His model included testing and measurement but extended to broader tools of evaluation research. It also dealt with both the pedagogical function of assessment (pupil evaluation) and its pragmatic and organisational functions (in-school/curriculum evaluation).

Shipman's model deserved to have been more widely adopted. It is not too late. His guidance remains eminently practical and can usefully be read alongside Connor (1991).

Diagnostic assessment

Public controversy over supposedly declining reading standards and/or methods/ policies for teaching reading is cyclical. At the time of writing this chapter there is a particularly acute alarm in Britain which will add further force to the pressures noted above.

Most of this chapter has been concerned with standardised testing and its role as a tool of management. Yet one of the ramifications of public concern over the standards and teaching of reading is the need for teachers in classrooms to identify, further diagnose and assist the backward readers who – whether their numbers are on the increase or not – are certainly an important feature of the controversy. This has long been routine for teachers, based either in schools or in LEA advisory and support teams, with special responsibility for reading, language or learning difficulties. Tests have contributed to this work, especially for appraising the severity of a reader's problem and for obtaining further qualitative data. Individually administered tests which combine these normative and diagnostic functions, such as the *Neale Analysis of Reading Ability*, the *Standard Reading Tests* and the *New Macmillan Reading Analysis*, continue to be popular in this context. However, surprisingly little is known about how, precisely, teachers use them diagnostically.

Diagnostic testing is, perhaps, less ideologically suspect than normative attainment testing. As well as published materials there are a number of techniques such as miscue analysis (e.g. Arnold, 1982 and 1992), cloze procedure (e.g. Mulholland, 1986) and the informal reading inventory (see Pumfrey, 1985). In the 1970s and 1980s these appeared as promising methods for better understanding individual readers' strengths, weaknesses and needs. In spite of this interest it is questionable whether they have fulfilled their promise. In a survey in 1987 Tobias (1992) found that many primary teachers were ignorant of these methods of assessment. Of those teachers who did claim to use miscue analysis, relatively few appeared to define it in forms consistent with the intentions of its originator, Kenneth Goodman (e.g. Gollasch, 1982; Goodman, 1970), or of writers such as Arnold (1982) who further developed miscue analysis for classroom uses.

Yet the need for competent diagnostic assessment of reading difficulty is as pressing as ever. Reappraisal of what this involves and a review of materials, methods and techniques are overdue.

The TGAT made a number of recommendations for greater provision of diagnostic materials and tests for assessing learners with special educational needs. However, national funding agencies have yet to show an interest in supporting such initiatives. Meanwhile, reading teachers need to consider anew for themselves what constitutes effective diagnostic reading assessment. Much can be done by identifying, clarifying and (above all) making explicit one's own practice.

There will be no ready-made panaceas. Attempts to devise free-standing comprehensive 'kits' have had limited success. A number of researchers, educational psychologists and teachers have developed diagnostic/remedial packages, e.g. the *Aston Index*, the *Macmillan Diagnostic Reading Pack* and *Quest*, which impressively structured the process of assessment for the teacher. However, the model of teaching that they imply – even if unintentionally – is that of the teacher as technician – technocrat even.

Many teachers probably feel uneasy cast in this role. However, in times of alarm about the teaching of reading there is an understandable tendency to seek the security and certainty which such diagnostic materials represent. Such ready-made procedures and algorithms for sorting out a reader's difficulties make diagnosis unproblematic and closed.

There is thus a danger of a revival of unreconstructed quasi-technical models of diagnostic assessment. Certainly, there is room for tests and structured assessment procedures – including published materials – in the diagnostic teaching of reading. However, it is essential that they are part of a continuum which includes the development of clinical, reflective and analytical skills in individual teachers. For example, Glazer *et al.* (1988) present concrete examples (from US contributors) of diagnostic assessments using various qualitative methodologies which do not lack rigour or coherent structure but do not rely on packages or standardised tests; for instance, using 'think aloud' protocols to evaluate comprehension strategies. Sceptics may argue that 'this is the sort of thing we're doing all the time, anyway'. But these examples are significant for their visibility to others (practitioners and parents) and their potential for becoming part of a shared body of professional practice.

A CONCLUDING ANXIETY

Reading, as attainment target En2, is but one of five attainment targets in but one of three core subjects assessed and reported in the National Curriculum. It may lose its traditional 'privilege' as the most tested area in the primary curriculum. Yet, if all attainment targets are to be assessed equally, all may be tested superficially. Assessment in primary schools may become a matter of finding out too little about too much. The debate about (a) priorities among subjects and attainment targets and (b) how far assessment should dwell on that which can be tested (here reading scores highly) must continue.

ACKNOWLEDGEMENT

The author is grateful to Georgina Dineen and John Aldridge for comments on earlier drafts of this chapter.

REFERENCES

Arnold, H. (1982) *Listening to Children Reading*. Sevenoaks: Hodder & Stoughton.
Arnold, H. (1992) *Diagnostic Reading Record*. Sevenoaks: Hodder & Stoughton.
Campbell, C. (1988) *Hearing Children Read*. London: Routledge.
Cato, V. and Whetton, C. (1990) *An Enquiry into LEA Evidence on Standards of Reading of Seven Year Old Children. A Report by the National Foundation for Educational Research*. London: Department of Education and Science.
Connor, C. (1991) *Assessment and Testing in the Primary School*. Basingstoke: Falmer Press.
DES (1975) *A Language for Life* (The Bullock Report). London: HMSO.
DES (1987) *Task Group on Assessment and Testing: A Report*. London: Department of Education and Science.
DES (1988) *Report of the Committee of Inquiry into the Teaching of English Language* (The Kingman Report). London: HMSO.
Gipps, C., Steadman, S., Blackstone, T. and Stierer, B. (1983) *Testing Children*. London: Heinemann.
Glazer, S.M., Searfoss, L.W. and Gentile, L.M. (1988) *Re-Examining Reading Diagnosis: New Trends and Procedures*. Newark, Delaware: International Reading Association.
Gollasch, F.V. (ed.) (1982) *Language and Literacy: The Selected Writings of Kenneth S. Goodman, Vol. 1*. Boston: Routledge & Kegan Paul.
Goodman, Y. (1970) 'Using children's reading miscues for new teaching strategies', *The Reading Teacher*, 23, 5, pp. 455–459.
Mulholland, H. (1986) 'Cloze procedure in the diagnostic assessment of silent reading', in Vincent, D., Pugh, A.K. and Brooks, G. (eds) *Assessing Reading*. Basingstoke: Macmillan.
Murphy, R. (1991) 'National developments in primary school assessment', in Harding, L. and Beech, J. (eds) *Educational Assessment of the Primary School Child*. Windsor: NFER-Nelson.
Potter, F. (1986) 'Teacher-devised tests: improving their validity and reliability', in Vincent, D., Pugh, A.K. and Brooks, G. (eds) *Assessing Reading*. Basingstoke: Macmillan.

Pumfrey, P. (1985) *Reading: Tests and Assessment Techniques*. Sevenoaks: Hodder & Stoughton.

Rosen, H. (1982) *The Language Monitors*. Bedford Way Paper 11, Institute of Education, University of London.

Satterly, D. (1989) *Assessment in Schools*. Oxford: Blackwell.

Shipman, M. (1983) *Assessment in Primary and Middle Schools*. London: Croom Helm.

Stibbs, A. (1979) *Assessing Children's Language*. London: Ward Lock Educational in conjunction with NATE.

Tobias, A.B. (1992) *Teachers' Knowledge of Miscue Analysis*. Unpublished M.Phil. thesis, Polytechnic of East London.

Vincent, D. (1985) *Reading Tests in the Classroom: An Introduction*. Windsor: NFER-Nelson.

TEST REFERENCES

Aston Index, M. J. Newton and M. E. Thomson, 1976, Wisbech: LDA.

Bangor Dyslexia Test, T. R. Miles, 1982, Wisbech: LDA.

Edinburgh Reading Test Series, Stages 1–4, 1977, 1980, 1981, 1977, Sevenoaks: Hodder & Stoughton.

Effective Reading Tests, Level 0, D. Vincent and M. de la Mare, 1989, Windsor: NFER-Nelson.

Formative Assessment in the National Curriculum: Reading, Levels 1–3, D. Bartlett, G. Johnson and C. Lutrario, 1991, Sevenoaks: Hodder & Stoughton.

GAP Reading Comprehension Test, J. McLeod, 1970, London: Heinemann.

Get Reading Right, S. Jackson, 1971, Glasgow: Robert Gibson.

Group Literacy Assessment, F. Spooncer, 1982, Sevenoaks: Hodder & Stoughton.

Group Reading Tests, D. Young, 1980, Sevenoaks: Hodder & Stoughton.

Macmillan Diagnostic Reading Pack, T. Ames, 1980, Windsor: NFER-Nelson.

Macmillan Group Reading Test, 1990, Windsor: NFER-Nelson.

Neale Analysis of Reading Ability, M. Neale, 1958, Basingstoke: Macmillan.

Neale Analysis of Reading Ability, Revised British edition, M. Neale, 1989, Windsor: NFER-Nelson.

New Macmillan Reading Analysis, D. Vincent and M. de la Mare (1985), Windsor: NFER-Nelson.

Quest Screening, Diagnostic and Remediation Kit, 1983, Leeds: Arnold-Wheaton Publishing.

Schonell Graded Word Reading Test, F. J. Schonell, 1955, London: Oliver & Boyd.

Standard Reading Tests, J.C. Daniels and H. Diack, 1958, St Albans: Hart-Davis Educational.

Part III

Writing

Editors' introduction

Writing and its teaching has certainly been the subject of some radical rethinking over the last ten or so years, with the work of Donald Graves and his colleagues having had immense impact. The National Writing Project acted as a significant catalyst for changes in teaching practice and it is now common to hear primary teachers talk about, and see them make classroom provision for, writing for a range of purposes and audiences. This, perhaps, has helped to prevent in the United Kingdom the often acrimonious debate which has raged in Australia between advocates of a Gravesian 'process writing' approach and those claiming the need for more specific teaching of written genre structures. In British schools, broadening the range of genres with which children gain experience of working has become almost synonymous with, and not contradictory of, a process approach to writing. It was for this reason that the major part of Chapter 7 in *Literacy and Language in the Primary Years* was concerned with the range of purposes and forms of writing with which primary children might engage.

In another chapter (Chapter 4) we also dealt with the other major influence upon theory and practice in teaching writing: that stemming from an emergent literacy perspective. This perspective allows us to look at the writing of young children for evidence of what it is they *know* about literacy and print, rather than what they do not know, and changing the view in this way has produced a major revision in our understanding of the processes by which children become literate and creators of text. We now place much more emphasis upon the role of teacher modelling, or providing demonstrations, of the process of writing and we also see children's early attempts to write as successively closer approximations to accepted adult forms. In Chapter 5 of *Literacy and Language in the Primary Years* we examined some of the classroom implications of this changing view.

In his chapter in this volume, Roger Beard examines in further depth the extent of our current knowledge about aspects of the writing process. He draws particular attention to the work of the Canadians, Carl Bereiter and Marlene Scardamalia, whose extremely revealing research into the composition process remains less well known in the United Kingdom than it deserves to be. Beard goes on to examine other aspects of the process, notably transcription and suggests that we need to bear continually in mind the wholeness of writing, each part of the process being inevitably closely linked with the others.

Jane Medwell takes up this holistic approach in her chapter as she reports on her studies of the contexts for writing apparently provided in primary classrooms. Context is clearly an important issue for teachers of writing but, Medwell argues, our ways of describing and, from there, affecting classroom contexts for the better are limited by a lack of sophistication in the theoretical frameworks used. Her studies clearly reveal that creating a context to help children's writing is not simply a matter of ensuring the presence of a list of desirable factors. Context, rather, is the product of a complex developing relationship between the perceptions of the various participants in the process and is thus better construed as subjective and mental than as objective and external to those involved in it. This view has important implications both for classroom action to do with the teaching of writing and for research into it.

An example of how the simple provision of a new 'factor' in the writing environment has not led to radical changes in practice or perceptions is given by Frank Potter in his chapter on the role of the word processor. Potter reviews research into the impact of word processors on children's writing and concludes that this has generally not been as positive as early experiences had led us to expect. Potter suggests that one of the reasons for this might be that the word processor has been given an inappropriate classroom role in terms of writing. It is not, he claims, a suitable tool for all forms of writing engaged in by primary children. He goes on to argue that careful thought needs to be given as to the kinds of computer most likely to be useful in encouraging a drafting approach to writing and also to the classroom management of such computers. It may be that the advent of cheap, powerful and *portable* computers will prove to be the most significant advance in this area.

Finally in this part Richard Fox discusses the assessment issue and provides a fascinating account of a multi-layered approach to the assessment of children's writing. The progression from his 'simple' to more complex assessment strategies is accompanied, it is clear, by a significant increase in the amount of information gained about the 'developing writer' and, thus, the usefulness of the assessment from the point of view of helping the child to develop further. Fox is aware of the implications of this for teacher time, yet argues that we need to develop our own capacity as teachers to make 'professional responses' to children's writing. It is important to note that the model of writing underlying Fox's assessment approach fits well with the holistic model earlier discussed by Roger Beard.

Chapter 8

The writing process

Roger Beard

The field of primary school children's writing has been influenced by some innovative thinking for some years. The 1960s, in particular, saw some striking publications on the creative possibilities of children's poetry and 'vivid prose' encouraged by teacher stimulation and the appropriate use of the environment (e.g. Clegg, 1964; Maybury, 1967). Greater differentiation was encouraged by the Bullock Report's adoption of James Britton's (1975) poetic – expressive – transactional model of language functions. At the time of writing my own *Children's Writing in the Primary School* (Beard, 1984), I was aware of a new interest in the process of writing itself, particularly in Canada (Bereiter and Scardamalia, 1987) and in 'conferencing' and 'drafting' in New Hampshire in the United States of America (Graves, 1983). Since that time, interest in the writing process has increased further, partly through the initiatives of the Schools Curriculum Development Committee National Writing Project and the continuing influence of Donald Graves, but the Canadian work remains less well known.

In discussing the writing process, it is necessary to consider not a single phenomenon, but the integration of several 'components'. In addition, it can be illuminating and entertaining to refer to reports of how well-known professional writers go about their work. Finally, in considering the process, we should not lose sight of the different types of writing which children need to undertake to help them to become independent and adaptable writers in subjects across the curriculum and in different contexts in the real world.

PERSPECTIVES ON THE PROCESS AS A WHOLE

In the past decade there has been increased interest in how conscious planning and reviewing contribute to the print on the page or screen. Such activities are difficult to model reliably, but one of the most influential diagrammatic versions of what is involved has come from Hayes and Flower (1980). (See Figure 8.1.) Each of the three main components, 'planning', 'translating' and 'reviewing', has been subjected to specialised investigations in the succeeding years, albeit under a variety of labels: major research into planning has been undertaken in Ontario

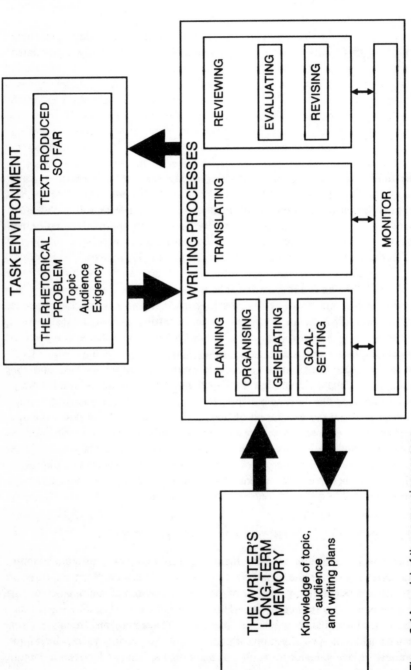

Figure 8.1 A model of the composing process

under the label of 'composing' (Bereiter and Scardamalia, 1987); discussions about 'translating' have tended to come under the labels of 'transcribing' (Smith, 1982) or 'secretarial skills' (Graves, 1983).

Together, these studies provide a helpful framework for considering teaching and learning in schools, although their interactions need continually to be related to the other aspects of the model, the writer's memory and the circumstances in which the writing is done. In addition, and as will be seen below, their synthesis may not quite do justice to the highly variable and idiosyncratic ways in which professional writers go about their work. In order to deal thoroughly with 'the state of the art', this chapter will discuss the different components of the writing process and will note any promising possibilities for teaching children how to communicate more successfully. Studies of the 'in the head' components of composing and reviewing are relatively new and inevitably speculative, compared with the 'on the page/screen' components of transcribing. It therefore seems appropriate to deal with these new studies particularly critically. This may help to prevent certain plausible possibilities being prematurely given the status of 'good practice' before systematic research has indicated their effectiveness.

COMPOSING THE TEXT

Underlying the 120 different studies in the Ontario research led by Bereiter and Scardamalia is a recognition of the psychological demands of writing compared to talking. The research has recognised that, in shifting from 'conversation to composition', young writers have to deal with three important adjustments: first, from using sounds in the air to using marks on the page or screen; second, from communicating 'here and now' to communicating over time and space; and third, from interacting with a conversational partner to producing language alone. Bereiter and Scardamalia have concentrated on the third of these adjustments. Their work has drawn attention to the demand on young writers, not only in getting the print on the page but also in prompting themselves as they struggle to compose the text. These prompts can be of two main kinds: one to call up from memory the necessary content knowledge and the other to structure the text in the light of the appropriate discourse knowledge, organising the text into a story, a poem, an information sheet or whatever is required. The researchers have investigated a number of 'procedures' which young writers can use in facilitating the composing process. The procedures have included listing words, brainstorming, setting out the main points of a report or argument and deciding on an ending sentence very early on in a story (which otherwise can drift without a clear sense of direction). The value of these procedures will obviously vary according to a whole range of circumstances, but children can be assisted by the way composing procedures relieve the pressure to produce a text, even a rough first draft, until they have assembled the support which they need. A double-page spread can be helpful in allowing the composing/planning to be set out on the left-hand page and the main text to be written on the right. Although adults might anticipate the usefulness of quite elaborate diagrams and schemes, many primary school children can benefit just from being encouraged to assemble a list of words which they feel they are likely to need. They seem to gain in confidence from having these 'resources for writing' accessed and available for use.

It is, of course, misleading to separate the composing of the text and its gradual translation or transcription on to the page or screen. These two components provide mutual support for each other, but it is the writer's discourse knowledge which will be the main influence in refining the overall shape of the text and its likely effectiveness. Bereiter and Scardamalia make a distinction between 'knowledge-telling', in which the writer churns out a relatively unstructured text, and 'knowledge-transforming', in which the writer grapples with the text and structures it according to the writer's discourse knowledge of different types of text organisation: registers, modes or genres. There is limited evidence on how this knowledge grows in children but specific teaching approaches which encourage 'reading with a writer's alertness to technique' seem likely to be influential (Beard, 1991).

The Ontario research is still not well known in the United Kingdom, although reviews of the main publication have been favourable, Colin Harrison (1990) agreeing with the views of Walter Kinsch that the book represented a 'high point of reading research'. However, criticisms can be made. The Ontario work is not accessible, being written in ascetic psychological language, and it is preoccupied with understanding the writing process, rather than with directly informing classroom practice. Much of the reported work is experimental and, although carefully controlled, it lacks the conviction of reports of children's writing in classrooms and homes. The other side of this is that the researchers are very cautious about their findings and the implications. When appropriate, they reveal a welcome frankness in reporting inconclusive findings and in admitting honest doubt about what their investigations indicate. In general, though, the Ontario research deserves far greater dissemination and discussion than has hitherto been the case in this country.

TRANSCRIBING THE TEXT

Transcribing has been likened to a 'tapestry' (Smith, 1982), involving as it does decisions on word choice, spelling and grammatical arrangement, as well as the application of handwriting or typing skills. It is important to note that words, spelling and grammar represent the main structures of a number of linguistic models of English (e.g. Crystal, 1987; see Figure 8.2).

This provides a reminder of the need to see the transcription skills not as a single activity but as the integration of several dimensions of language development. Hayes and Flower (1980) suggest that the writer is like a busy switchboard operator and that, if difficulties occur, there is a clear need to partition the problem, without losing sight of the underlying communicative purpose. Crystal's basic model divides language into meaning, pronunciation and grammar; applied to writing, it draws our attention to how the tapestry of

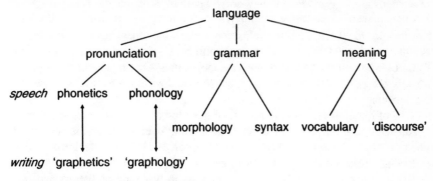

Figure 8.2 A linguistic model of English

transcription involves deciding upon the right words, spelling them correctly and placing them in the appropriate word order.

The tapestry of transcription is at the heart of the writing process and it is important to bear in mind the links with the other components. First, for example, Crystal's model subdivides meaning between words and discourse, thus linking with the use of 'discourse knowledge' in the composing of texts. Second, the finer aspects of transcription include the use of appropriate punctuation and, ideally, the near-automatic use of handwriting or typing skills, so that maximum attention can be devoted to what appears on the page or screen and how it might be shaped, rather than to a preoccupation with how it gets there. Third, integrating all the aspects of transcription can be an intimidating task for young writers, so that it would seem unlikely that a text could fulfil a writer's potential at a first attempt. It seems only reasonable not to leave it there, but to review it and consider the possibilities for editing and redrafting it in some way. Before dealing with reviewing in greater detail, though, more needs to be said about each main aspect of transcription.

Over some years, children's vocabulary has consistently been found to correlate with a range of indices of attainment in language use. One of the most illuminating studies on how limited vocabulary inhibits fluency, range and development in young people's writing was made by Shaughnessy (1977). In one of the finest books on the teaching of writing, frank, analytical and enriched with many examples, she concludes that 'vocabulary looms as perhaps the most formidable and discouraging obstacle' in the development of advanced literacy (p. 210). Recent publications have not always seemed to reflect this recognition, being preoccupied with the 'busyness' of writing – different tasks, collaboration, drafting and publishing, for example (e.g. Hansen *et al.*, 1985). Such a 'process orientated' curriculum model may not always adequately reflect the teacher's influence in capitalising upon classroom activity. Major studies of the effectiveness of primary schools (e.g. Galton *et al.*, 1980; Mortimore *et al.*, 1988) indicate how children can benefit from teachers encouraging them to reflect upon the use of written language and how their work in a certain 'semantic field' can be linked to other lexical possibilities. Children's own writing can be a very influential resource in this sharing of, and reflection upon, what others have written. Frank Smith's notion of a 'literacy club' is helpful here – drawing attention to how a sense of common purpose can motivate individuals – but intensive and systematically compiled reports of effective teaching and writing are curiously few and far between.

One of the most convincing reports of this kind came some years ago from a headteacher and university lecturer collaborating over work on the writing of poetry in one primary school (Hourd and Cooper, 1971). It is not surprising that poetry has featured in such publications, because 'the best words in the best order' has long been a predominant emphasis in this kind of literary writing. Similar studies are needed of the role of vocabulary in curriculum areas where informational literacy and technical vocabulary make specific demands, in both new words and familiar words with unfamiliar meanings (Perera, 1984). We should also note the nature of the challenge facing teachers in helping children to acquire these building blocks of the writing process. However 'real' and motivating the tasks which are provided, Shaughnessy's research indicates that 'there appear to be stubborn (and doubtless individually different) limits to the pace at which words can enter our active vocabularies' (Shaughnessy, 1977: 224).

Research into spelling provides a little more encouragement for teachers intent on significantly boosting children's attainment. It is now well established that most children will not 'catch' spelling unless they have their attention systematically drawn to the patterns of English orthography. Although verbal ability seems, not surprisingly, to be related to success in spelling in primary school children, visual perception of word form and carefulness seem also to be influential (see Peters, 1985 for a very readable review of the considerable body of research on spelling). There are two double-edged practical implications for primary teachers. First, it needs to be recognised that the sooner children can make spelling unconscious and automatic for a large number of words, the more attention can be devoted to the shaping of the structure of the text and its effective communication. Second, though, there is a need for constructive strategies to allow for approximations to spelling and for diagnostic and 'needs-related' teaching. Here again, there is an indication of the value in making *reviewing* an integral part of any model of the writing process, so that spelling uncertainties can be 'partitioned' and considered separately. Publications on 'invented spelling' have developed interest in this aspect of writing (Clarke, 1990), although it seems likely that teacher education will need to include considerably more on the structure of English orthography and the diagnostic implications across ranges of misspellings (such as those set out by Peters and Smith, 1993) before invented spelling is likely to be confidently encouraged on a large scale. Meanwhile, teachers can continue to draw inspiration from the findings of Margaret Peters' own systematic study of 1000 children: that it is what teachers do which seems to contribute more to children's success in spelling by the end of the primary years than any other factor.

Teachers can only exert a more subtle influence on the development of the grammatical aspects of children's writing. The patterns of word order are infinite; the patterns of the spelling system are conventionally structured. Studies of children's written syntax have included large-scale studies of collections of children's writing (e.g. Wilkinson *et al.*, 1980) and detailed analyses of samples of children talking and writing (e.g. Perera, 1986). Wilkinson's study traced the growth of syntax from simple, literal, affirmative sentences, through the development of more elaborate syntax and cohesion. The study also indicated the influence of 'task on text'. Clauses of condition, modal verbs ('could', 'should') and expressions of tentativeness were found in the writing of persuasive arguments, whereas they did not appear in earlier studies of children of similar ages, whose writing was mostly factual or 'creative' (Harpin, 1976). Perera goes on to show that children's writing is not so close to their speech as is sometimes suggested. She draws attention to the gains from reading a range of text types aloud to children throughout the primary years, so that they can internalise their distinctive features. Like Bereiter and Scardamalia, she also encourages the writing of continuous passages from an early age, so that children can grapple with the coherent structuring of texts.

A number of clear practical suggestions can be drawn from studies of the syntactic aspects of the writing process. First, teachers need to ensure that children undertake a range of writing tasks, where different syntactic structures are needed – diaries, letters, imaginative stories, poems, reports, information sheets, arguments and so on.

Second, teachers need to diagnose features of non-standard dialect and to promote discussions of syntactic alternatives. One of the few findings to support the use of discrete exercises in English has come from sentence-combining activities, where two simple sentences are combined into compound or complex ones (Smith, 1982: 229). If this work is based on children's writing or well-known texts, sentence combining could help to support the grammatical dexterity on which the tapestry of transcription depends.

Third, links between grammar and punctuation can be exploited. Unfortunately, the teaching of punctuation has rarely figured in recent educational publications on the writing process. In fact, it is interesting to note that one of the few recent books to discuss punctuation carefully has come from one of the professional writers who were members of the Kingman Committee (DES, 1988). Keith Waterhouse may have been driven to write *English Our English* by a sense of frustration that educational writers were not addressing the teaching of grammar with the conviction that he felt was needed (Waterhouse, 1991).

Of the various features and uses of punctuation, children will benefit early on in their school lives from orthodox use of the full stop in signalling sentence boundaries. This may involve, in itself, a major change in children's language development. As Kress (1982) has shown, we do not talk in sentences but rather chains of clauses. The formal structure of sentences is part of written language (we can easily detect someone reading aloud on the radio). This is a further indication of how children's early writing development is inspired by their learning to read with an alertness to the 'how' as well as the 'why' and 'what' of texts, including how the full stop indicates an abbreviation.

Beyond the full stop, some writers argue that the question mark and exclamation mark are especially important for young writers to understand because they indicate significant changes of 'tone'. Of the two, is not the use of the question mark absolutely essential if the asking of the question is to be confirmed? The need for an exclamation mark is a more open question; there are other ways of indicating the change of tone! For instance, at the end of a sentence, letters can be written in CAPITALS. Frank Smith (1982: 159) declares a relative dislike of exclamation marks – but admits to a relative indulgence in dashes. According to Keith Waterhouse, dashes have become less common as hyphenated words have been increasingly re-written as compound words, like 'rewritten'.

Paragraph boundaries are other instances of where 'variations in necessity' exist in some aspects of punctuation, whereas it is difficult to deny the old slogan that 'speech marks are essential to show exactly what someone has said'. The use of the comma can be more subjective, although it seems to be frequently misused for linking two simple sentences when no conjunction is present. In contrast, the semicolon seems to be under-used in the writing of children and students; it can be helpful in contrasting two simple sentences. The uses of the colon also seem under-valued: in setting out the advance organisers of a long text; in grouping the items within a long list; and as an alternative to a comma immediately before direct speech. Primary schools need to have a firm policy for deciding when and how these conventions are to be explained to children, in the context of their own writing and in developing children's reading with an eye on authors' techniques in using punctuation (including apostrophes, underlining and brackets) accurately and creatively when opportunities allow.

All the above depends on getting the print on to the page. There is now increased interest in handwriting because of the decision to set a separate attainment target for it in the National Curriculum. This is another of the inter-relationships in any model of the writing process. Research indicates a close link between the development of a swift, well-formed style of handwriting and success in spelling. The kinaesthetic experiences of the recurrent letter strings may help to familiarise the spelling patterns of English in the mind's eye. It hardly needs saying that having a swift, well-formed style of handwriting will often bring with it an increased self-concept. This can be exploited by the teaching of calligraphy: the writing of 'illuminated manuscripts' has been established practice in some primary schools for many years.

In reviewing this area, a number of clear practical suggestions arise: establish correct letter formation early; ensure a clear and consistent school policy for handwriting; maintain opportunities for regular practice. At the same time, there can be a tension with children's early scribbles and letter play which are associated with 'emergent literacy' (Clay, 1975). Marie Clay's insightful book gives pointers on some of the learning which can go on when young children experiment with marks on paper; for instance, taking stock of what they can do or making lines of text by repeating favoured shapes. Clay's work has inspired a great deal of interest in early writing development (e.g. Temple, 1988) and publication of a number of case studies (e.g. Hall, 1989). Such books provide helpful examples and seem to testify to what children's 'developmental writing' can bring. But they often fall short of describing in temporal detail what the teacher has done to guide the child and to consider the difficulties which may need to be diagnosed along the dimension from scribble to text, especially when whole cohorts of children are considered.

One of our most eminent authorities on handwriting (Sassoon, 1990) stresses that handwriting is a taught skill, the visible trace of hand movement; nothing is natural about it. Moreover, she warns, in order to lay the foundations for swift, automatic writing, the strokes of the basic letters must start at the correct point and move in the right direction; relearning is not easy once wrong hand movements have become automatic.This dilemma has cropped up in the pilot evaluation of the implementation of the National Curriculum. This suggests that the gap between levels 1 and 2 may be too wide and that the statements of attainment may need to be revised or additional Non-statutory Guidance may need to be published to reflect more adequately the progression between the two.

There seems to be little research on the typing skills which children need to develop in order to make fast and effective use of word processing. In fact, British and American studies indicate that word processing itself does not make children write better, prompt them to revise more or teach them new writing strategies (Cochran-Smith, 1991). Instead, word processing seems to help create new social contexts for teachers and children to work together. In these contexts, children may learn new strategies and, more particularly, greater efficiency in using the strategies they already have. Curiously, though, there has been little discussion of how and when to develop 'ten finger', as opposed to two finger, typing skills in children and young people and the way this could make transcription more efficient. (For further discussion of the teaching of 'keyboarding skills' see Frank Potter's chapter in this volume [Chapter 10].)

REVIEWING THE TEXT

The major influence on the reviewing and redrafting aspects of writing has been Donald Graves (1983). Graves' work has promoted a journalistic model of the writing process, sometimes referred to as 'process writing'. It embraces writing with a real audience in mind, drafting and redrafting, seeking 'child-centred' advice from the teacher and from peers and eventual publication. Through extended experience of this process, it is suggested that children find a 'voice' and a sense of 'ownership' in what they have produced. The collaboration which this brings can invigorate and enliven the 'communicative contexts' of classrooms. Indeed, because of the uncritical adoption of his framework within the National Writing Project, writing has become almost synonymous in some schools with drafting and redrafting, sometimes without due regard to the different aims and contexts of children's writing.

Nevertheless, interest has now centred firmly on the reviewing of what children have written far more than in the past and on the use of a draft as a resource for teaching and learning. There can be a number of valuable benefits from using the Graves model: children will be encouraged to look back over their work in the light of what they intended; they will be able to harness the feedback from other children on the sound, form and meaning of what they have written; conferencing can promote detailed discussion of the range and possibilities of texts; children can be helped to adopt editorial checks and to use some of the basic proof-reading marks (Chapter 7 in *Literacy and Language in the Primary Years* gives some examples of how these have been introduced to children); publication will provide a particular sense of satisfaction and reward. These refined insights and increased sensitivity have apparently met a major professional need, because of the speed and scope of Donald Graves' influence – across continents.

At the same time, there are some uncertainties about Graves' work and influence, particularly its 'research base', its application and some of its underlying assumptions. Remarkably, for a project of such influence, the research base is very limited and very vague. Some critics have suggested that his work is more evangelical 'reportage' than research. Graves' doctoral thesis was based on the study of four classes of children in a middle-class community (Graves, 1975). In a review of 11 subsequent papers by Graves and his colleagues, Smagorinsky (1987) notes that only 30 children are referred to: one child (Andrea) is referred to on 41 pages: only one other child is referred to on more than ten (Sarah, on 15 pages). Given the case study framework of Graves' work, questions arise about the significance of what is reported and what is not reported – there are hardly any mentions of where the model was found not to be valid and no mention of the influence of teacher enthusiasm (the so-called 'Hawthorne effect'). There seem to be special doubts about whether teachers tacitly signal what they really want from 'child-centred' conferences and whether extensive redrafting does lead to major restructuring of texts by young children. As Barrs points out:

> nowhere in Graves' book is there an example in all its successive drafts. Despite an insistent emphasis on the value of revision throughout the book, hardly any evidence is given of the writing process which Graves and his team were said to be studying . . . indeed, very little children's writing is quoted at all in this book.

> (Barrs, 1983: 23)

It is striking to note how cautious Bereiter and Scardamalia are about primary children redrafting their writing. They note that children find their first drafts 'highly salient' and that exhortations to redraft can lead to superficial tinkering which may threaten to diminish the overall effectiveness of the text.

Other uncertainties arise about the extent to which 'process writing' can be adopted in different contexts. Michael Rosen (1989) argues that 'process writing' can erode the 'feeling' from children's original words and that the subsequent redrafted and conferenced texts can lack authentic individual expression. Graves' journalistic model may be more applicable to the production of a classroom newspaper or information books for other children. (In fact, 'process writing' seems to assume whole class writing lessons.) It may not be so applicable to the 'emotion recalled in tranquillity' which can distinguish individual children's poetry, rather than the collaborative enterprise which Graves espouses. Similarly, it is difficult to accommodate conferencing and redrafting within the more personal kinds of 'expressive writing' to which James Britton and the Bullock Committee drew attention (Britton, 1975; DES, 1975), initially involving a search for meaning within the self rather than 'publication' within the school (see Beard, 1984, Chapter 7 for a number of personal and touching examples).

Nevertheless, Graves' work has drawn a healthy attention to how children can benefit from looking back over what they have written and has broadened understanding of the repertoire to which young writers can resort.

Finally, it is also worth asking questions about the basic assumptions underlying the Graves work and several of the other publications reviewed above, assumptions about how professional writers go about their work. References are sometimes obliquely made to 'real writing' and how 'real writers' write. However, generalisations are not easy from the published accounts of writers at work, some of which shed a dubious light on any nebulous notion of what 'the writing process' comprises which Graves and some of his colleagues assume. Lucy Calkins (1983), for example, refers in several publications to William Faulkner's description of the way he writes a novel as an illustration of the way most professional writers work: taking a character and letting the story develop spontaneously – 'all I do is trot along behind him (*sic*) with pencil and paper, trying to keep up.' Rosemary Harthill's (1989) collection, *Writers Revealed*, shows how unrepresentative this kind of generalisation can be. Iris Murdoch writes nothing until she knows how the story will develop ('I plan in enormous detail down to the last conversation before I write the first sentence. So it takes a long time to invent it.'). Piers Paul Read outlines the plot of each book on a single page. Brian Moore may rewrite the opening two or three pages of his books 'maybe forty, fifty times'. There are similarly huge contrasts in other aspects of how professional writers write: Tom Sharpe and Jeffrey Archer apparently swear by their word processors; Iris Murdoch prefers having the whole script to hand 'apt and ready for the eye: easily accessible' (Walsh, 1985). Given the current impasse over the teaching of language awareness and grammatical reference, an uncomfortable number of writers speak favourably about being taught grammar formally at school and of the teachers who showed them how the language worked as a system. The Poet Laureate, Ted Hughes, and the editor of *The Times*, Simon Jenkins, are recent examples (Hughes, 1987). There is also a tension between the unhurried 'busyness' which is sometimes equated with 'good primary practice' and the preference of many writers for quiet and solitude (e.g. Roald Dahl in Powling, 1985) and the admissions that there is no spur like a deadline (e.g. Douglas Adams in Walsh, 1985). Overall, then, it could be said that the writing process of professional writers is as variable as the products which result from their efforts.

CONCLUSION

The 1980s saw a great increase in interest in the writing process and this has led to much more attention as to how children write as well as why and what they write. In all this concern with the process, though, it is important not to overlook the variety of writing types which children need to undertake in order to develop the well-rounded and flexible competence which the world may require of them. This means not only following developments in our understanding of the process, but also keeping in mind the range and quality of the finished texts which the children actually produce.

REFERENCES

Barrs, M. (1983) 'Born again teachers' (Review of Graves, D.H., *Writing: Teachers and Children at Work*), *The Times Educational Supplement*, 24 June, p. 23.

Beard, R. (1984) *Children's Writing in the Primary School*. Sevenoaks: Hodder & Stoughton Educational.

Beard, R. (1991) 'Learning to read like a writer', *Educational Review*, 14, 1, pp. 17–24.

Beard, R. (ed.) (1993) *Teaching Literacy: Balancing Perspectives*. Sevenoaks: Hodder & Stoughton.

Bereiter, C. and Scardamalia, M. (1987) *The Psychology of Written Composition*. Hillsdale, New Jersey: Lawrence Erlbaum.

Britton, J., Burgess, T., Martin, N., McLeod, A. and Rosen, H. (1975) *The Development of Writing Abilities (11–18)*. Basingstoke: Macmillan.

Calkins, L.M. (1983) *Lessons From a Child*. Exeter, New Hampshire: Heinemann Educational.

Clarke, L.K. 'Encouraging invented spelling in first graders' writing: effects on learning to spell and read', cited in Adams, M.J. (1990) *Beginning to Read*. Cambridge, Mass.: MIT Press.

Clay, M.M. (1975) *What Did I Write?* Auckland, NZ: Heinemann.

Clegg, A. (ed.) (1964) *The Excitement of Writing*. London: Chatto & Windus.

Cochran-Smith, M. (1991) *Learning to Write Differently*. Hove: Ablex Publishing Company.

Crystal, D. (1987) *Child Language, Learning and Linguistics* (2nd edition). London: Edward Arnold.

DES (1975) *A Language for Life* (The Bullock Report). London: HMSO.

DES (1988) *Report of the Committee of Inquiry into the Teaching of English Language* (The Kingman Report). London: HMSO.

Galton, M., Simon, B. and Croll, P. (1980) *Inside the Primary Classroom*. London: Routledge & Kegan Paul.

Graves, D.H. (1975) 'An examination of the writing processes of seven-year-old children', *Research in the Teaching of English*, 9, pp. 227–241.

Graves, D.H. (1983) *Writing: Teachers and Children at Work*. Exeter, New Hampshire: Heinemann Educational.

Hall, N. (1989) *Writing With Reason*. Sevenoaks: Hodder & Stoughton.

Hansen, J., Newkirk, T. and Graves, D. (eds) (1985) *Breaking Ground*. Exeter, New Hampshire: Heinemann Educational.

Harpin, W. (1976) *The Second R*. London: Allen & Unwin.

Harrison, C. (1990) 'Review of Bereiter, C. and Scardamalia, M., *The Psychology of Written Composition*', *Journal of Research in Reading*, 13, 2, p. 151.

Harthill, R. (1989) *Writers Revealed*. London: BBC Books.

Hayes, J.R. and Flower, L.S. (1980) 'Writing as problem solving', *Visible Language*, 14, 4, pp. 388–399.

Hourd, M.L. and Cooper, G.E. (1971) *Coming Into Their Own*. London: Heinemann.

Hughes, T. (1987) 'To parse or not to parse: the poet's answer', *The Sunday Times*, 22 November.

Kress, G. (1982) *Learning to Write*. London: Routledge & Kegan Paul.

Maybury, B. (1967) *Creative Writing for Juniors*. London: Batsford.

Mortimore, P., Sammons, P., Stoll, L., Lewis, D. and Ecob, R. (1988) *School Matters: The Junior Years*. London: Open Books.

Perera, K. (1984) *Children's Writing and Reading*. Oxford: Basil Blackwell.

Perera, K. (1986) 'Grammatical differentiation between speech and writing in children aged 8 to 12', in Wilkinson A. (ed.) *The Writing of Writing*. Milton Keynes: Open University Press.

Peters, M.L. (1985) *Spelling: Caught or Taught? A New Look*. London: Routledge & Kegan and Paul.

Peters, M. and Smith, B. (1993) *Spelling in the Context of Writing: Learners and Teachers*. Slough: NFER-Nelson.

Powling, C. (1985) *Roald Dahl*. Harmondsworth: Penguin (Puffin) Books.

Rosen, M. (1989) *Did I Hear You Write?* London: André Deutsch.

Sassoon, R. (1990) *Handwriting: A New Perspective*. Cheltenham: Stanley Thornes (Publishers) Ltd.

Shaughnessy, M. (1977) *Errors and Expectations*. New York: Oxford University Press.

Smagorinsky, P. (1987) 'Graves revisited: a look at the methods and conclusions of the New Hampshire study', *Written Communication*, 4, 4, pp. 331–342.

Smith, F. (1982) *Writing and Writer*. London: Heinemann Educational.

Temple, C., Nathan, R., Burris, N. and Temple, F. (1988) *The Beginnings of Writing*. Boston, Mass.: Allyn & Bacon.

Walsh, J. (1985) 'Monstrous regimens', *Books and Bookmen*, December, pp. 6–7.

Waterhouse, K. (1991) *English Our English*. Harmondsworth: Penguin Books.

Wilkinson, A., Barnsley, G., Hanna, P. and Swann, M. (1980) *Assessing Language Development*. Oxford: Oxford University Press.

Chapter 9

Contexts for writing

The social construction of written composition

Jane Medwell

THE IMPORTANCE OF CONTEXT

Current theories and practices of teaching writing place a great deal of emphasis upon the importance of providing an appropriate and enabling context for children's writing. Teachers are urged to become literate models for their pupils and to create a print rich classroom environment which replicates as closely as possible the literate environment of the real world. The National Writing Project has encouraged many teachers to develop an interest in the processes of writing and a key factor in this has been the provision of authentic purposes and audiences for children's work. The Project has also given teachers a set of stimulus points from which to consider the ways in which they might teach writing and the classroom conditions they might try to create. The National Curriculum has set out a range of skills which children should employ and specified that these should be used in a range of contexts.

One of the implications of recent work in the general field of literacy is that for teachers concerned with developing the literacy of their pupils the major task is to provide appropriate contexts for that development. The features of these contexts have been expressed in terms of a set of 'conditions for learning' (Cambourne, 1988), prominent among which are plentiful demonstrations of accomplished literate behaviour, the opportunity to learn through progressive approximations to this behaviour, all set into a responsive, 'scaffolded' environment. Applying these ideas to writing, it has begun to seem that the teaching of writing is largely about getting the context right. It is tempting to assume that if the optimum classroom context could be established, this would in itself lead to an improved product and process in children's writing.

However worthy this assumption, it still leaves the problem of determining just what the best context for writing is and the role that the context plays in the child's learning. Unfortunately, our theory of which factors in context are important is as yet an *ad hoc* one. It has tended to be assumed that such context-producing teaching strategies as conferencing, drafting, collaboration and revising have a beneficial effect upon the process and product of writing. We have yet to formalise a theory to explain why this should be true and just how, and indeed if, these factors help.

WHAT CONSTITUTES CONTEXT?

The first step towards developing any such theory must be to decide what constitutes the context of children's writing and only when this has been done can the ideas involved be investigated. The common-sense approach to this might be to list all the factors which seem to impinge upon the child writer as he/she works on a piece of writing in school. This listing might include such factors as:

- school and county policies on teaching writing;
- recent in-service work in the school, or undertaken by a particular teacher;
- the teacher's views about writing and the learning of writing;
- the setting in which writing takes place, including the social and physical organisation of the classroom;
- the range of writing that a child has experienced in the past;
- the nature and range of the audiences for which the child has written;
- the teacher's intended outcome for a specific piece of writing;
- the intended outcome for the child for that piece of writing;
- any intervention by the teacher in the form of task description and subsequent response to the outcome;
- the subject, genre, purpose and audience of each particular piece.

These factors can be classified into two distinct groups:

(a) global factors operating over a range of pieces of writing and a period of time, that is, fairly permanent influences;
(b) local contextual factors which might have influence upon the creation of a particular piece of writing. By their nature these would be more temporary in effect.

This provides a complex web of contextual factors which are interrelated and may be differentially perceived by the participants in the process, namely teachers and children.

THE OPERATION OF CONTEXTUAL FACTORS

In order to investigate the operation of this web of factors, a number of case studies were undertaken into the contexts provided for children's writing in primary classrooms. Each case study focused upon the work over a period of one term (approximately 12 weeks) of one lower junior classroom in South Wales. The schools were selected from a range of schools which had recently undertaken a school-based in-service programme on writing. The classes were run by teachers selected as successful in the teaching of writing by the headteacher of those schools. Each case involved study at several levels:

- The teachers were interviewed to ascertain their general approaches to writing in the class and to establish their aims and intentions for the particular writing tasks which they set or encouraged.

- Two children in each class were selected and interviewed to establish both their general views about writing and their perceptions about particular writing tasks.
- Copies of the writing of these two children, at various stages of development, were collected over the case study period.
- A range of writing sessions was observed (by tape-recording and extensive field notes) and discussed with the children.
- Parents were visited and interviewed about their children's experiences of writing and the children were asked to keep writing diaries to include home-based activities over a two-week period.

Each case study yielded vast amounts of data, including pieces of writing, transcripts of interviews and observation notes, and much of this remains to be analysed in detail. There is space here only to report some of the broad implications which have begun to emerge from the studies. This chapter will attempt to contrast some of the data from two of the classes in order to sketch some of the similarities and differences of context and the implications of these findings for the teaching of writing.

These two classes were studied during the second term of the children's fourth primary year. The schools were of a similar size (350 children) on large housing estates. Both schools had completed a term-long in-service education course about children's writing, led by a local advisory teacher. The schools had been recommended as successful in the teaching of writing and the teachers volunteered to take part in the research. The teachers involved were seen as successful, in that the children in these classes achieved high standards. However, the classes were very different. Class A (whose teacher I shall refer to as Mr Jones) can be termed a 'traditional' writing class, while class B (whose teacher I shall refer to as Mrs Evans) is an example of a 'process writing' class. The classroom organisation in these two classes can be contrasted from the brief summary in Table 9.1.

THE TRADITIONAL CLASS

The traditional class was described by its teacher as a secure environment for work, in which children knew what was expected and received praise for effort. The teacher was most concerned to match the work to the child's level of attainment and felt the writing tasks were ideal as 'they can be tackled at any level'. Mr Jones recognised that the children did some writing in a number of subjects, but said that it was essential to practise writing for itself, particularly if new skills such as drafting were to be mastered. He felt under pressure to introduce a drafting approach, but said that on the whole he already encouraged the children to check their spellings before submitting work for marking. He felt that the ability to reshape the content of the story was probably beyond the abilities of children of this age.

The school day consisted of assembly, mathematics before play and English after play. Other subjects were tackled at various times in the afternoons. There were clear

Table 9.1 Classroom organisation

	Class A *(Traditional class)*	Class B *(Process writing class)*
Reading	Scheme books read in spare time or to the teacher.	Range of trade and scheme books. Group reading to the teacher. Reading area in constant use.
Grouping	Ability grouping according to scheme level. Groups change for maths.	Broad ability grouping/ friendship groups.
Content of the day	Subject sessions; then topic work when subject work finished.	Almost all work topic related, integrated through the day with groups selecting the order of tasks. Story read to class at the end of the day.
Physical features	Groups of desks arranged to form tables. Each child assigned a place. Teacher works at desk in front of the class.	Groups of tables and work areas flexibly used. Teacher works at tables with children.
Display	Commercially produced information and displays from local museum. Pupil work displayed high on walls.	Teacher created displays about reading and writing. Commercial posters. Children's work displayed at child height and in big books.

rules for classroom activity. The main teacher needs were for a smooth-running, orderly day without obvious noise, and the provision of activities within the capabilities of all the children so that as little disruption as possible occurred. With the exception of maths all tasks were tackled by the whole class at the same time. Cooperation between pupils was not encouraged, but quiet talk not interrupted.

English tasks consisted mainly of short-answer or cloze-based scheme work with a creative writing session each week. The teacher would assign a title from a list of ideas which had been successfully used before. The children also retold a Bible story each week, wrote a report of a science lesson and did short-answer work for history and geography. The main allocations of time were as follows:

- *Work time* – children had to complete work as neatly as possible, work quietly and if in difficulties go to the teacher's desk.
- *Talking time* – characterised by the teacher talking to the class, introducing a topic and asking questions of the children.
- *Transition time* – children moved between activities, to and from their classroom. At this time books were collected in or given out.

There was a low hum of activity and children talked, mainly about work-centred issues. If the noise level rose the teacher would call out a name and the class would instantly become quiet. Work was collected by a named individual at the end of each session. The work was marked, mainly for transcription details, and returned, sometimes with a verbal or written comment.

The 26 children in the class were cooperative and responsible workers who were keen to participate in the teacher-led discussions and attempted to complete the work they were given. The teacher was at pains to anticipate the needs of the children before lessons and planned carefully to avoid confusion. This allowed little scope for child-initiated decisions. Most conversational exchanges before work started were to clarify directions for completing a task. The children in this class have an exceptionally positive, warm and humorous relationship with their teacher.

THE PROCESS WRITING CLASS

Mrs Evans described her class as 'a context for learning about the writing process, a garden of opportunities'. This teacher stated that she wanted her children to become independent learners and support each other in learning the craft of writing. She was very enthusiastic about the writing process and committed to giving the children every possible support in learning to revise and edit their work. She gave a high profile to literacy activities and had provided a comfortable, well-stocked reading area and plenty of teacher-made posters on the walls emphasising various aspects of literacy and children's individual achievements.

The school day started with assembly followed by a news time when individuals were given the opportunity to share important news. Almost all tasks for the week were given out to the groups on the Monday by the teacher, with a record sheet for each group which the children filled in as they completed the tasks. Typical tasks involved worksheets and scheme work or writing up experiences, stories or letters. The children worked as groups of six, and although most work was individual they were encouraged to cooperate and help each other. The groups were responsible for deciding the order in which they tackled the week's tasks, but in practice everyone knew that maths work was done until play, then tasks involving writing until lunch. Occasionally, the teacher would set aside a time for the whole class to have a session together where she would introduce a task to everyone. Writing tasks were usually related to topic work or literature and most writing was done into rough books to be re-copied later into the appropriate exercise book or on to paper. Most, but not all, drafted work reached a finished stage. The teacher allocated the tasks, although not all children did the same tasks. Children were keen to have their work chosen for 'publication' in class books and displays. The children in this class generally worked round their home table, but did not have fixed places and sat with friends. Privacy was available in areas, and the cloakroom, for those who preferred it.

During sessions the teacher would either work with a group, perhaps on their group reading task which was done as a whole group, or help individual children to complete tasks. This sort of intervention was often child-initiated and characterised by teacher instruction and questioning.

The main allocations of time were as follows:

- *Work time* – children completed tasks, helped each other or sought advice.
- *Sharing time* – children shared news or, when asked by the teacher, read out work completed or in progress.
- *Reading time* – all the children read their own, school or class published books.
- *Story time* – the teacher read daily to the class.
- *Transition time* – children moved activities, changed for games, put work away or on to the teacher's desk for marking.

There was a moderate level of noise in the class and generally one or more children moving around. If the teacher thought the noise too loud she would stand up wherever she was and say, 'Excuse me'.

CONTRASTS AND SIMILARITIES

During the course of the case studies it was already clear that there were striking differences between the contexts in both classes, and also unexpected similarities. The differences which were observed existed not only between classes, as might have been expected, but also on a number of other levels. There were, of course, examples from children in both classes of excellent writing, appropriate to its purpose and audience, and others which were obviously not so well thought out, but it was difficult to link this variation infallibly to particular elements of the context of either class.

Although both teachers had recently participated in prolonged in-service work about writing, with the same advisory teacher, they had each reached very different conclusions about the teaching of writing. They differed in the ways in which they talked about writing. For example, Mr Jones talked about writing as a skill learnt through practice and felt that the weekly 'creative writing' session was essential practice for becoming a mature writer. He expressed the belief that other types of writing should be taught, for example, letter writing, but that this could be satisfactorily dealt with through exercises. Mrs Evans also stressed that children needed to practise writing, but she emphasised that her children needed to practise a range of writing skills which could only be done through experience of a range of types of writing. The manner and degree to which these expressed beliefs were realised as classroom practice differed in each class. For example, on a number of occasions Mrs Evans expressed concern with audience and purpose, and specifically structured writing tasks to focus upon these aspects. However, her notions of audience and purpose were not shared by the children, who still seemed to feel that they were writing for the teacher but that the rules had changed slightly. This was clearly seen on one occasion when the children were asked to write thank-you letters to the local vicar who had shown them around his church. She gave a full introduction to the whole class, discussing the

purpose of the letter and the content and language which might be used. Talking
to the children during their writing of these letters, however, it became clear that
they were more concerned with 'what Miss told us to write' and whether they
would meet her criteria and criteria agreed among themselves about length and
spelling than with the needs of the vicar as a audience. In fact, a number did not
remember that the letters were intended for the vicar. Some were not sure
whether they would actually be sent at all. It is doubtful, therefore, whether in
cases such as this the intended audience and purpose were actually part of the
context for writing as perceived by the children.

The ways the children discussed the writing process also differed, but not directly
according to their situation or the teacher's instruction. Mr Jones placed a strong
emphasis upon neatness and accuracy and would mention these qualities in every
introduction to a writing task. Both the children studied in this class, however,
seemed, on occasion, to go beyond the emphases of their teacher and talked about the
writing process in terms of content, revision and audience as well as neatness and
accuracy. In one instance a girl in class A attributed to her teacher critical facilities
about writing with which he actually showed no evidence of being concerned. She
suggested that in writing, 'You have to have the right ideas and they have got to be
interesting. You can put stuff in to make it longer but that isn't really ideas and Sir'll
know.' Mr Jones was flattered, but agreed that the child was going 'beyond her
teaching' in the sense that he had never discussed these aspects.

The similarities between the two classes were also notable. In discussing the
features of writing products the children in the traditional class usually prioritised
neatness and accuracy. However, in the process writing class the children were
also very concerned about the length of writing and neatness of work, although
these were aspects that the teacher was keen to play down. Mrs Evans' continual
stress on rough work and disregard for correct spelling in preliminary drafts
seemed to have had little effect. Not surprisingly, this was a source of some
frustration to the teacher who felt that her children were bound to be used to
traditional school demands and it would take some time before her new demands
resulted in a change of perceptions.

Looking at a number of discussions with members of both classes, it seems
that there were clear rules for writing which were recognised by the children.
These show a surprisingly high degree of similarity from class to class. What is
clear, from even a cursory examination of the evidence provided by these two
case studies, is the immense complexity of the relationship between contextual
factors and writing processes and products.

CONTEXT AS INDIVIDUAL

These observations seem to call for a re-evaluation of the notion of context and a shift
in a theoretical conceptualisation of contexts for writing. It may be that the whole
idea of context as a set of identifiable factors acting upon the individual is inadequate
and it may be more helpful, in fact, to consider context as mental, that is, as not

having an external existence identifiable to an observer. The context of writing might be considered as a construct which has no existence outside of the feelings and perceptions of the participants in it. This is similar to the conclusion arrived at by Edwards and Mercer (1987) who studied the ways in which shared understandings were created through classroom discourse. Context is, according to Mercer (1990), 'everything that the participants know and understand (over and above that which is explicit in what they say) which they use to make sense of what is said and done' (p. 31). This is further elaborated by Mercer: 'What counts for context for learners, as for analytic linguists, is whatever they consider relevant' (Mercer, 1992: 31). If this is the case, the contextual factors described earlier do not exist in an objective sense. They are only given meaning to the extent to which they are perceived as important by the participants. It is clear that these perceptions of the participants are not simply derived from any current experiences, but are a product of these experiences and previous experiences, the effects of which continue to reverberate for a considerable time. Edwards and Mercer (1987) talk about 'continuity' as 'a characteristic of context, being context as it develops through time in the process of joint talk and action' (p. 161).

CONTEXT AS CULTURE

While the differences in context perceived by individuals may lead us to consider context as mental it is also worth noting the high level of similarity between the understandings of children in the same class, and in some cases between all the children. The tape transcripts, field notes and photographs reveal that each classroom had a unique culture – complete with values, norms, beliefs and organisational structures. This appears as a set of shared understandings to which none of the participants explicitly shows adherence, yet in the light of which each acts. An interesting example of this occurred in one case study when the teacher, after an initial stimulus and discussion about pirates (which, incidentally, was exciting and bloodthirsty and thoroughly enjoyed by the children), asked the class for 'a really exciting story about pirates'. While the children were writing, he wrote requested spellings on the blackboard and, when the stories were completed, he marked them, concentrating on spelling accuracy and making no response whatsoever to content. When asked what they thought the teacher wanted from this piece of writing, the children replied with variations on 'two pages with no spelling mistakes'! Excitement, although requested, was not a priority, and this knowledge guided the actual actions of everyone involved.

The children seemed able to incorporate new rules into this system. In the process writing class the teacher produced a range of notices for the walls of the classroom about the various stages of writing. Then children were given the opportunity to discuss which processes would be suitable for a particular task. The teacher was at pains to talk to the children about the stages. This was not, however, reflected in the children's discussions. They referred to the stages they had discussed as a rule system which applied to the writing they did in this class (but not in other classes and not at home). They did not consider that the writing task they engaged in should influence the stages they would use, although the teacher had explicitly told them that it might. It seemed as if one rule system had been substituted for another without any apparent increase in the children's levels of awareness about writing processes.

As mentioned above, Mrs Evans was most concerned to provide authentic audiences and purposes for her children so that they could be involved in 'real' writing. Their discussions, however, seemed to indicate that they continued to view these as school tasks, primarily done for the teacher. The question of ownership further supported this impression, as the children in the process class did not feel that the work was theirs, while on some occasions a child in the traditional class expressed strong ownership of stories that she had written.

Another revealing aspect to emerge in these case studies was a difference in the way writing was approached at school and at home. One child said she disliked writing. Her parents confirmed this and said she never wrote at home. However, in the course of the home visit it became clear that her home writing, although not regarded as such by her parents, actually showed signs of more mature writing processes than her work at school. For example, she had produced written 'rules' for a club she was running which had been carefully and obviously revised, yet revision was something to which she was very resistant at school.

Thus in both these classes there was a strong culture in the sense of a set of social norms, rituals, conduct rules and meaning systems, which was clearly a school culture. Within these classes the rules and meaning systems about writing were school rules and meanings about the activity of writing in school – a process seen as different from writing at home, and, as Neisser (1976) suggests, it is not unusual for children to 'leave their life situations at the door' in approaching school tasks. Moreover, the rules in both classes showed a high degree of similarity, despite the different conceptions of writing held by the teachers. The process writing teacher was keen to talk about this. She felt that she had done all the right things to change the way children wrote, but realised that they had not gained the insights into the writing processes that she had expected.

IMPLICATIONS

In a general sense it is obvious that the context of all writing is socially shaped. All writers write for socially significant audiences and purposes and the genres they use reflect relationships between individuals and socially agreed conventions of style. School writing, therefore, has particular features shaped by its social setting. The context of any piece of writing can be considered as whatever the individual perceives to be relevant to the task of producing it. In the classroom the major part of these perceptions stems from the rules, norms and accepted practices of writing which form part of the prevailing culture in that class. What is striking is the fact that in this study it seemed that children's perceptions of these features were broadly similar across classes, even where one teacher had deliberately tried to change the children's understandings about writing.

It seems that this teacher's attempted introduction of real purposes and audiences for the children in her class had not really changed her children's perceptions of the audiences for whom they were writing. Given this, therefore, it might be thought reasonable to expect that the children would apply the understandings of writing and the writing processes with which they were familiar. The rules about writing might have changed as the teacher tried to introduce a process writing model, but as the classroom culture was essentially unchanged, new understandings about writing did not need to be generated.

The key to the problem raised here may be to do with the concept of authenticity in classroom writing. Authentic audiences and purposes are not necessarily those provided by the teacher, however real the teacher may consider them to be. Authenticity of task needs to be recognised by an individual within the classroom culture. In assigning 'real' tasks to the children, teachers may unwittingly transform them into teacher-set tasks which are no more authentic than traditional imaginative writing exercises. In the classrooms examined in this study the audiences and purposes for writing were largely teacher-dominated because they originated in a teacher-controlled curriculum. An authentic task is, by definition, one whose purpose is defined by the author.

In trying to teach children about writing it may therefore be necessary to negotiate new perceptions about writing through renegotiation of the classroom culture. This cannot be done by simply changing one element of the rules. Perhaps what needs to be renegotiated, in order to offer authentic purposes and audiences, is not the rule system, but control of the writing curriculum itself. It may be that only in a situation where young writers are able to negotiate tasks for purposes which they can recognise and have some say in, can the classroom culture, and the perceptions and context of the individuals within it, significantly increase young children's understandings about writing. Authorship is, after all, about exercising control over a particular medium to meet specific social demands. The purposes of writing will be dictated by the culture that gives rise to them and the processes for writing will be those agreed as appropriate within that culture. In classrooms there will always be a social context for writing which is formed by, and gives rise to, individual contexts for specific writing experiences. Change in the writing demands in a class must be created and recognised by all concerned. It is not something which can be imposed.

REFERENCES

Cambourne, B. (1988) *The Whole Story*. Auckland, NZ: Ashton Scholastic.

Edwards, D. and Mercer, N. (1987) *Common Knowledge*. London: Methuen.

Mercer, N. (1990) 'Context, continuity and communication in learning', in Potter, F. (ed.) *Reading, Learning and Media Education*. Oxford: Basil Blackwell.

Mercer, N. (1992) 'Culture, context and the construction of knowledge in the classroom', in Light, P. and Butterworth, G. (eds) *Context and Cognition*. Hemel Hempstead: Harvester Wheatsheaf.

Neisser, U. (1976) 'General, academic and artificial intelligence', in Resnick, L. (ed.) *The Nature of Intelligence*. London: Chambers/Murray.

Chapter 10

Word processors, redrafting and the niche of the laptop

Frank Potter

In schools, despite its potential to focus attention on the process of writing and encourage a redrafting approach to writing, the use of the computer as a tool for writing has drawn attention even more to the written product. This chapter summarises the reasons why this has happened and suggests that the cheap 'low-tech' laptop computer might be the key to encouraging a redrafting approach in the primary classroom.

PRACTICAL CONSTRAINTS TO USING THE WORD PROCESSOR AS A REDRAFTING TOOL

In the 1980s a number of teachers and researchers commented that a crucial factor that seriously limited the value of word processing for revising and redrafting text was children's lack of familiarity with the keyboard and the word processor itself. Lowd (1982) suggested that because of children's inadequate keyboard skills 'So much time is taken by each student for composing/typing that little or none is left over for revision or even for editing. Another time killer is the slowness of beginners using the editing functions of the word processor itself' (p. 27). According to Robson (1986) 'The benefits do not manifest themselves until the children become more familiar with the keyboard' (p. 66) and 'It is only when they become competent at manipulating the text that they will get maximum benefit from using the processor' (p. 78).

Kleiman and Humphrey (1982) reported that, in their research, children's revising behaviour changed as they became familiar with the editing capabilities of the word processor. First, they began to be more careful to correct typing, spelling and punctuation errors, then later began to change words and sentences. Finally, they learnt to reorganize the material, moving, adding and deleting large sections of text. They no longer edited simply for details but also paid more attention to the meaning of ideas and the order of presentation (p. 98).

Daiute (1986) in the USA and Peacock (1988) in the UK found that children wrote about a quarter to a third as much again in a given time with a pen or pencil, as compared with a word processor. The students in Daiute's (1986) study not only revised less when using word processors, they also tended to make additions at the end rather than within the text. From Kleiman and Humphrey's research this would indicate that they were not familiar enough with word processors to make good use of them for redrafting, and this was after they had used a touch typing programme for one month at the beginning of the year and had used a word processor for an hour a week for six months.

In order for children to use the word processor effectively as a redrafting tool it seems that they need a fair amount of practice, more than is realistic with the limited access that exists in schools even now. In British primary schools at present it is common for about 30 children to have to share access to one computer, and even if this were used exclusively for word processing children would have less practice than Daiute's students.

WAYS OF WORKING WITHIN THESE CONSTRAINTS

Teachers, however, are used to working within constraints and they have been able to find effective ways of using word processors. Baskerville (1986), for example, has described how word processors can be used as a teaching tool to demonstrate the process of redrafting to 6- and 7-year-old children. Earl (1987) has reported how children of a similar age can learn how to revise using the word processor. The problem posed by the children's unfamiliarity with the keyboard was circumvented in the following manner. The children wrote their first draft by hand, the teacher typed the text into the word processor, and the children reviewed and revised the printouts before using the word processor to revise and redraft their writing. Malone (1987) used the word processor to extend the language experience approach with 5-year-old children. She typed the texts into the computer as the children composed them. They then gradually took on more responsibility for revising and composing the texts using the word processor.

One important feature of the word processor is its large screen display and this can undoubtedly emphasise the public communicative nature of writing to the children, thereby developing their sense of audience. Because of this public nature of the normal VDU, the computer quite naturally becomes a focus for collaborative writing and its value in this respect has been emphasised many times (e.g. Baskerville, 1986; Somekh, 1986; Trushell, 1986).

Another important feature is the printout, as this naturally leads to the publication of children's writing, which again emphasises the public communicative nature of writing and develops a sense of audience. This is especially true now that word processors are available with different fonts. Earl and Malone both saw this as an essential element of their use of the word processor. The end products in their examples were small books created by the children themselves.

The communicative nature of language is further emphasised by using word processors to send electronic mail (O'Neill, 1986). Maxted (1987) has combined the use of the electronic mail facility with the publishing aspect of word processors by initiating the TTNS (now renamed Campus 2000) 'Newsdays'.

Campus 2000 is an electronic network and on these 'Newsdays' real up-to-the-minute news is entered into the Network which can then be 'downloaded' via TTNS into the school's computer. This provides the raw material for a class newspaper, which is produced for publication at the end of the school day. The activity is therefore more than just a simulation – it involves a real outcome, produced for a real audience and to a real deadline.

The constraints mentioned above also led the author to recommend (see e.g. Potter, 1988, 1990) that the most appropriate niche for the word processor at present in schools is for the collaborative production of short, public, non-narrative texts.

Short texts are more appropriate because they require less time to compose (other things being equal) and therefore leave more time for the writer to concentrate on revising and editing.

The printout seems to lead naturally to the publication of children's writing, which emphasises the *public*, communicative nature of writing. This is especially true now that word processors for children in the early stages of literacy are available with a wide variety of fonts in which texts can be printed out.

Even children who have just started school tend to have a good idea of the structure of a story. They have been exposed to the narrative form from an early age, through bed-time stories, fairy tales, the television, etc. Even those children with poorly developed story schemata will experience frequent exposure to stories from their very first day at school. If the structures are well known the children are less likely to need to reorganise their composed texts. Other kinds of writing, however, are much less familiar – persuasive writing, instructions, reports, for example. It is these *non-narrative* kinds of writing which will need more reorganising and for which the word processor is so much more useful.

The large vertical screen is an important feature of the normal computer, which makes it easy for all the children in a group to read a text as it is being composed. Hence the computer quite naturally becomes a focus for *collaborative* writing and its value in this respect has been emphasised by many teachers.

If word processors are best used for these kinds of writing, this affects the use of pens and other, older writing tools – they in turn become more appropriate for individual, personal and narrative writing. Indeed, a desktop word processor is such a public medium that it might be thought completely inappropriate for intensively personal writing in a classroom setting. Some children have, for example, been known to choose *not* to use a word processor when asked to write about 'The first time in your life that you ever remember being frightened'.

Indirect evidence to support the above recommendations comes from the fact that one of the most popular uses of the word processor is for the production of school and class newspapers. A newspaper is one of the most *public* writing products; it contains *non-narrative* writing (reports, editorials, persuasive writing) which tends to be quite *short* (as space is at a premium) and these reports are often produced by children working *collaboratively*. The benefits of this context for writing have been discussed by Wray and Medwell (1989).

Some more direct evidence to support this recommendation comes from a study carried out by Traves (1989), who found that children tended to make more structural revisions to their persuasive writing.

CURRENT PRACTICE IN SCHOOLS

The above review of the evidence can be summarised as follows. Until children have substantially greater access to and more familiarity with word processors we cannot expect these to be useful as a general-purpose redrafting tool. Within these constraints, however, we can identify an appropriate and recommended niche for the word processor as a redrafting tool – namely, for the collaborative production of short, public, non-narrative texts.

While this may be the most effective way to use the word processor as a redrafting tool and the best way to focus children's attention on the process of writing, it certainly does not seem to reflect current practice in schools.

To date, the niche that schools have found for the word processor is one which concentrates on the written product. Text editors such as FOLIO and CAXTON, with their wide variety of fonts, are used to produce attractive displays of children's work. But these programs cannot truly be described as word processors because they lack the ability to move or copy blocks of text. To reposition text within FOLIO or CAXTON the child has to delete the block and then retype it in the new position. These programs are therefore unable to allow pupils to develop a redrafting approach to their writing, as they do not take them to the third stage that Kleiman and Humphrey (1982) describe in the development of children's revising behaviour, the point at which they learn to reorganize the material, moving, adding and deleting large sections of text, paying more attention to the meaning of ideas and the order of presentation (p. 98).

It also seems likely that this state of affairs will continue, even with the more powerful 16- and 32-bit computers in schools, because CAXTON (for the Nimbus computer) and PHASES (for the A3000) are both popular text editors and at the time of writing neither has the facility to move blocks of text. Furthermore, primary schools are starting to invest in colour printers, which will focus atten- tion even more on the written product, rather than on the process of writing.

It might be argued that this attention to the written product has the potential to draw children's attention to the communicative function of writing, as publishing their written work can lead pupils to take more care and pride in their work. But the high standard of presentation, especially with newspaper programs, may also create the *illusion of publishing*. We should be careful not to equate printing with publishing. It is a small but dangerous step to assume that, just because a sophisticated printout has been produced, the work has therefore been published. It is actually quite difficult to define what is meant by 'publishing', but it clearly involves making the work publicly available, an essential ingredient of which is a *real* audience. Many teachers will be familiar with the way in which children's writing can be transformed when they are writing for a real audience. It is knowing that the letter (or whatever) is going to a real audience that encourages care and attention to the writing, not the fact that it is going to be printed out attractively on the computer.

There is also the danger that children and teachers may judge the work by the standard of presentation, thus creating the *illusion of quality*. For example, Peacock (1988) found that teachers perceived word-processed transcriptions of pupils' essays as superior to the handwritten originals and it is not uncommon when text is entered into Front Page Extra or other newspaper programs for the appropriate genre to be ignored and for the text typed in to be a narrative rather than a report. Examples of this can be found in Eyre and Duffill (1988: 23).

The illusion of quality and the illusion of publishing may even discourage redrafting, so it is unlikely that the word processor is used to any significant degree as a redrafting tool in schools at present.

THE WAY FORWARD

If we are to promote successfully the word processor as a tool for redrafting we must acknowledge the realities of the situation and work within the constraints, while at the same time having a clear idea of how to progress. It is likely that the new 16- and 32-bit desktop computers in schools will increasingly be used not only for the presentation of children's work but also for other powerful applications, leaving less and less time for their use as general-purpose redrafting tools. We must therefore acknowledge this reality. However, as desktop computers are becoming more powerful, low-technology laptop word processors are falling in price and it will be argued here that using both in conjunction is the way to promote the word processor as a tool for redrafting.

THE NICHE OF THE DESKTOP

The computer is such a powerful tool for the presentation of children's work that it would be strange if it were not used for this purpose and the only likely change is that it will be used increasingly in this way. For example, the desktop publishing program NEWSPAPER for the Nimbus puts high quality colour production of newspaper pages etc. with high quality graphics within reach of even infant pupils.

In addition to being a powerful tool for the presentation of children's work there are also other powerful text-processing applications; for example, THINK-SHEET and CD-ROM technology.

THINKSHEET is a simple-to-learn and easy-to-use hypertext program. Imagine writing on a number of cards, laying them down on a table and re-arranging them. Then imagine being able to cut and join these cards easily and quickly. The result can be printed out as connected text. In this sense it is like a simple word processor. But the power of THINKSHEET is that there can be a 'door' from each card leading to another tabletop of cards (up to 48 levels of tabletops). THINK-

SHEET is perhaps best viewed as a tool for organising thinking. Hughes (1991) reports how THINKSHEET helped Ben, aged 11, to clarify his thinking.

His imaginary universe, peopled with dynasties of creatures of his own invention, was pushed into shape by features in-built in the program; one feature being the optimum size of a card. A card will grow longer, the print scrolling as it is typed in, but it will not grow longer than the screen. It would destroy its own helpfulness if it did; any statement of some 60 or 70 words must contain more than one idea and that plurality of ideas should stand in some kind of categorised relationship. Young Ben was irritated at first by the warning bleeps he was getting, as he tried to use the program like some kind of inconvenient word-processor. After about half-an-hour's use, however, he had discovered for himself the classificatory potential of the program. He set about organising his creation into a mock Old and New Testament, a witty perspective that arguably may have taken much longer to perceive (if ever), had not THINKSHEET nudged him into an hierarchical stance.

(Hughes, 1991: 93)

Hughes also describes how Mary, an 18-year-old student, planned to organise her notes on economics using THINKSHEET and then to use the product for her revision, but was delighted to discover that this last step was unnecessary. The making of the THINKSHEET was in itself revision. 'It's the links that make you remember things,' went her explanation, 'seeing the links and finding links where at first you thought it was disconnected' (pp. 93–4).

McKeown (1991) describes a project that is a multimedia development of the language experience approach, which starts from the interesting premiss that by selecting, collating and editing written material the student will learn to read it. The project uses interactive video, CD-ROM and desktop publishing. Lenny Henry and Dawn French act as the video guides. The student follows their instructions and makes choices using a mouse. For example, one choice is to write a magazine article from a list of topics: health, housing, unemployment, divorce or bereavement. They can choose a suitable photograph from a graphics library to illustrate the text. They hear and see opposing points of view and select sentences that they want to include. They can hear their text spoken as many times as they like as it builds up. Finally, they can present their article with all the facilities provided by the desktop publishing package.

This kind of approach is almost within reach of the average-sized primary school, as CD-ROM becomes affordable. A CD-ROM drive is now about the same price as a colour printer and the latter are already finding their way into primary schools.

Desktop computers should be, and probably will be, used increasingly for these powerful applications, thereby leaving less and less time for their use as general-purpose redrafting tools.

THE NICHE OF THE LAPTOP

Low-technology laptop word processors have fallen in price to such an extent that they are now realistic tools for promoting the word processor as a tool for redrafting. For the price of an A3000 or Nimbus desktop it is now possible to buy five or six Tandy WP-2 or Sinclair Z88 laptop word processors.

The Tandy WP-2 is a thin A4 size dedicated word processor with a full size typewriter keyboard. Once created, a word-processed document can be revised and formatted and printed out on a printer. The Tandy has not only the normal word-processing facilities, including tabs and the ability to centre, emphasise, underline and italicise text, but also a 200,000 word-spelling checker and 100,000 word thesaurus. When the laptop is switched off the back-up battery preserves any files in memory. It is also possible to save the text on an external tape or disc drive, or to transfer the files via a transfer cable to a desktop. Transferring the documents enables the final revisions and the final printing out to be done on a desktop, thus allowing the use of more sophisticated packages with their variety of fonts and even colour. This transfer is desirable for all but the shortest of texts as the Tandy's screen display is limited to eight lines of text. If all documents are transferred it also eliminates the need to save work directly from the laptop, as the Tandy can store about 3500 words in memory.

The use of the laptop and the desktop in this manner makes the best use of their distinctive strengths. The laptop takes up very little room and is portable, so it is useful for note-making and note-taking as well as composition. Early drafts can be printed out directly on a dot matrix printer and preliminary editing and revising can be done directly with the laptop. The document can then be transferred to a desktop for final revisions and formatting. It can then be saved on disc and printed out on a high quality printer (in colour if desired). I have been working in this manner for nearly five years, initially using an earlier version of the Tandy and a BBC and more recently using the Tandy WP-2 and a Macintosh Classic.

With five or six laptops in one junior class (for the price of one desktop) each pupil could have access to word-processing facilities for about one hour a day. One incidental advantage would be greatly increased keyboard practice, thus enabling children to make more efficient use of their (in any case longer) time on a word processor. Given that desktops are used for a variety of applications the addition of five or six laptops would increase the word-processing capacity by at least tenfold, for only double the cost.

Although there has recently been increased interest in laptops there is little research available as to their effectiveness. The results of one pilot project may at first seem discouraging, but it will be argued below that they should not be taken as such and that we should learn from experience.

THE PILOT PROJECT: PEACOCK AND BREESE (1990)

Twenty-two first-year secondary pupils were 'given' a Z88 laptop, which became their responsibility. The machines were taken to and from the pupils' homes and most battery-charging was done at home. The laptops were used as an integral part of every school day and used in English, maths and science lessons. The pupils were interviewed after two full terms using the technology. The results, however, do not seem encouraging. Peacock and Breese concluded: 'Handwriting remains popular and quicker for most classroom writing tasks; neither planning nor constructive reflection on language seems to be enhanced; pupils are convinced that they write more; typing speeds remain very slow; and repeated loss of work is a commonplace' (p. 41).

At least in the early stages, learning to manage the computer was extremely time-consuming:

Ben   'They're a pest sometimes. They're heavy and you have to carry them around in your bag.'

Andrew   'Especially on Tuesdays. You've got games kit as well. And with books and everything . . . '

The rechargeable batteries proved a problem and the loss of everything in memory was a recurrent irritation. Every child in the class lost work at one time or another and even after two full terms many of the pupils were still regularly losing their work. Handwriting remained the more popular choice except for those tasks involving at least a few hundred words, but Peacock and Breese conjecture that this balance might well alter in favour of the word processor if pupils became more fluent at entering text via the keyboard. They concluded that there was a strong case for some planned teaching of the basics of computer management – spread over a few minutes a day, perhaps. They also concluded that there was a strong case for some regular, planned typing tutoring, to help the pupils become quicker at entering text at the keyboard.

WHAT WE CAN LEARN FROM THIS PILOT PROJECT

First, we cannot expect children of this age or younger to manage laptops without some training, and having to carry them around is demotivating. But this is not what is being suggested here. The computers would stay in the junior classroom, which would avoid children having to carry them around. Concerning the loss of work, using a laptop with a back-up battery (such as the Tandy) should eliminate this problem. However, given that children may be less careful at times (and the possibility of sabotage by one child of another's work), the investment in one external disc drive would enable children to save their work directly as well as print it out or transfer it to a desktop.

Second, this pilot project was essentially a test to see how the laptop fared against handwriting. What is being suggested here is that the laptops would be a preliminary to using a desktop. The children would only use the desktop for publishing their work once they had composed on the laptop.

Third, concerning the children's keyboard skills, Peacock and Breese conjecture that the children's preference for handwriting might alter in favour of the word processor if pupils became more fluent at entering text via the keyboard. The advantage of handwriting over keyboard skills would not be as pronounced in the junior school and, if children had regular access to laptops on entry to the junior school, would be even less so.

Fourth, perhaps it is now time that we addressed the issue of helping children to improve their keyboard skills. Peacock and Breese concluded that there was a strong case for some regular, planned typing tutoring and this is echoed by Lillywhite (1991) and Stanley (1991).

Fifth, the Tandy laptops have the advantage of including good spelling checkers. It has always seemed a puzzle why so little use has been made of spelling checkers, even such a powerful one as Computer Concepts' SPELLMASTER for the BBC. I had always thought it must be the cost (the SPELLMASTER ROM for the BBC is about a third of the price of the complete Tandy laptop). But this is probably not the main reason, as a small-scale experiment of mine in a first year junior classroom showed. I located SPELLMASTER in the resident BBC computer and also left a FRANKLIN calculator type spelling checker in the classroom. During the year the SPELLMASTER was hardly used at all, but the FRANKLIN spelling checker was used extensively. The key seemed to be ease of use. The spelling checker needed to be available 'on demand'. The BBC was in constant use with programs that could not access the SPELLMASTER ROM directly, but the FRANKLIN spelling checker was always available, as the spelling checking facility with the Tandy WP-2 would be.

With the benefit of learning from Peacock and Breese's experiences, the laptop, as an addition to the information technology facilities in the junior classroom, could be the key to the development of a redrafting approach to writing and greater exploitation of the full potential of new technology in this important area.

REFERENCES

Baskerville, J. (1986) 'The language curriculum and the role of the word processor in developing written language in the primary school'. Paper presented at the NFER Symposium on Word Processing, October.

Daiute, C. (1986) 'Physical and cognitive factors in revising: insights from studies with computers', *Research in the Teaching of English*, 20, 2, pp. 141–159.

Earl, S. (1987) 'Let's make a book with "Writer"', *Micro-scope*, 21, pp. 3–7.

Eyre, R. and Duffill, S. (1988) 'A term with owls', *Micro-scope*, 24, pp. 19–24.

Hughes, M. (1991) 'The use of Hypertext for developing literacy skills', in Singleton, C. (ed.) *Computers and Literacy Skills*. Hull: The British Dyslexia Association Computer Resource Centre.

Kleiman, G. and Humphrey, M. (1982) 'Word processing in the classroom', *Compute*, 22, pp. 96–99.

Lillywhite, C. (1991) 'Computers and keyboard skills at Fairley House', in Singleton, C. (ed.) *Computers and Literacy Skills*. Hull: The British Dyslexia Association Computer Resource Centre.

Lowd, B. (1982) 'Word processing: how will it shape the student as a writer?', *Classroom Computer News*, November/December, p. 27.

McKeown, S. (1991) 'Computers and adult literacy work', in Singleton, C. (ed.) *Computers and Literacy Skills*. Hull: The British Dyslexia Association Computer Resource Centre.

Malone, B. (1987) 'Using a word processor to teach children to read'. Paper presented at the MAPE conference, April.

Maxted, D. (1987) 'Electronic publishing: MEDU newspaper days'. Paper presented at the MAPE conference, April.

O'Neill, B. (1986) 'In search of genuine audiences'. Paper presented at the NFER Symposium on Word Processing, October.

Peacock, G. (1988) 'Telling tales together on the word processor', *Micro-scope*, 24, pp. 8–10.

Peacock, M. and Breese, C. (1990) 'Pupils with portable writing machines', *Educational Review*, 42, pp. 41–56.

Potter, F.N. (1988) 'Ecriture et micro-informatique', in Fijalkow, J. (ed.) *Decrire l'ecrire*. Toulouse: Presses Universitaires du Mirail. Paper originally entitled 'The word processor: a new literacy tool' and presented at the European Community 'Summer University' on Writing and First Contacts with Written Language held at the University of Toulouse le Mirail, July.

Potter, F.N. (1990) 'Word processors and children's writing: evaluating the research evidence', in Wray, D. (ed.) *Emerging Partnerships: Current Research in Language and Literacy*. Clevedon, Avon: Multilingual Matters.

Robson, S. (1986) 'No-one can see the mistakes you've made', *Primary Teaching Studies*, 1, pp. 62–79.

Somekh, B. (1986) 'Exploring word processing with children'. Paper presented at the NFER Symposium on Word Processing, October.

Stanley, L. (1991) 'Use of computers in the Dyslexia Institute', in Singleton, C. (ed.) *Computers and Literacy Skills*. Hull: The British Dyslexia Association Computer Resource Centre.

Traves, L.J. (1989) *An Examination of the Revisions made by Ten and Eleven Year Olds to Chronological and Non-chronological Texts Using the Word Processor*. Unpublished M.A. dissertation, Edge Hill College of Higher Education.

Trushell, J. (1986) 'Llanfairpwyllgwyngyllgogerchwyrndrobwllllantisiliogogogoch redrafted: a study of the effects of word processors upon the editing skills of primary pupils'. Paper presented at the NFER Symposium on Word Processing, October.

Wray, D. and Medwell, J. (1989) 'Using desk-top publishing to develop literacy', *Reading*, Vol. 23, No. 2, pp. 62–68.

Chapter 11

Assessing developing writing and writers

Richard Fox

The establishment of a National Curriculum in England and Wales has, as never before, focused the minds of professionals in primary education on the matter of assessment. By itself, however, it will not necessarily improve the quality of their assessments. The present programmes of Study for English, and the Attainment Targets and Statements of Attainment associated with them, have, in general, been welcomed. Their approach to writing endorses many of the features of 'good practice' identified by the National Writing Project and specifically re-inforces some of the features of assessment recommended by the Bullock Report (cf. DES, 1989: 17.67) and by the ILEA Primary Language Record (Barrs *et al.*, 1988). It also, however, leaves the way open to the possible imposition of a relatively crude form of assessment of children as writers which would ignore much progress made in this field over the past decade or so.

Writing is split, for assessment purposes, into three separate attainment targets: one relating to the construction of meaning, one to spelling and one to handwriting. In any weighting of the resulting 'profile component' the first (meaning) is to count for 70%, spelling for 20% and handwriting for 10%. Provided that teachers follow the programmes of study this splitting of writing into components should not have an injurious effect upon teaching. The levels of attainment specified are clearly meant to reflect a developmental model of writing.

As they stand, the Statements of Attainment are useful and draw attention to many important aspects of writing development. They suffer from some draw-backs, however. Attainment Target 3, the construction of meaning, includes within its levels a strange mixture of statements concerning punctuation, struc-ture, style and process. Elements of style (e.g. 'shape chronological writing beginning to use a wider range of sentence connectives than "and" and "then"') sit side by side with rather vague statements about structure ('write more com-plex stories with detail beyond simple events and with a defined ending') and indeed punctuation ('produce . . . complete sentences, some of them demarcated with capital letters and full stops or question marks'). This makes the description of developing writing rather muddled, even incoherent, and thus difficult to remember or use.

Defining criteria of attainment is helpful, in so far as it makes clearer to all concerned the nature of what is to be learned and the way in which the process and products of writing are to be judged. In the case of AT 4: Spelling, however, the complex development of learning about the English spelling system simply does not split conveniently into levels and thus the levels provided are somewhat arbitrary and difficult to use. But there is a more important point. Criteria hide within them implicit 'norms' of good, indifferent and poor levels of performance at a particular age, and already the results of Standard Assessment Tasks (SATs) are being used in discussions and evaluations of rising and falling 'standards'. Yet children cannot realistically be said to 'be' at any particular level. Their writing will ebb and flow, improve or stagnate, depending on their own mental state and on the teaching opportunities and contexts with which they are provided. The quality of any particular piece of writing can be placed at a level, but that quality is relative to the context in which it was produced and there is no way of separating out the influence of factors pertaining to the child and those pertaining to the teaching. Responsibility is shared, as in all educational achievements, between teacher, taught and others who influence the learning process.

The working group set up to advise on appropriate aims and content for English in the National Curriculum (the Cox Committee) had this to say about quality in writing:

> The best writing is vigorous, committed, honest and interesting. We have not included these qualities in our statements of attainment because they cannot be mapped on to levels. Even so, all good classroom practice will be geared to encouraging and fostering these vital qualities.
>
> (DES, 1989: 17.31)

They thus posed one of the central problems of assessing children's writing. On the one hand, it is clear that assessment should not get in the way of good teaching, and good teaching should aim to encourage high quality in writing. On the other hand, high quality cannot be reduced to a series of levels of difficulty, or developmental stages of attainment. Yet assessment in terms of levels is a legal requirement of the National Curriculum. How, then, can the quality of children's writing be protected, and children's writing be assessed in terms of quality?

Barrs (1990) raises a number of doubts about proposed methods of assessment and Armstrong (1990) takes a still more radical view. Nevertheless, it does not seem impossible to respond to the individual qualities of meaning in a piece of writing by a child and yet also assess its status in terms of developing control of the system of writing. This chapter will expand on this view, as the dominant professional view of assessment, but will return briefly to doubts about its validity at the end.

The piece of writing in Figure 11.1 was produced by an 8-year-old boy (AF) during a class session in which the children could choose to do any kind of writing. It was a one-shot story produced without any pre-writing activities, drafting or conferencing. It is not in any way extraordinary, but will serve to

November 25th 1982
<u>Danger down under.</u>

We were ~ at a Halloween party when it
all happened. We were parading around
on some land in our costumes when
the soft ground fell in below me. There was
a tunnel so I went up it because
if I tried to climb out of the
hole it might cave in. Nobody
had seen me fall because it was
night. The tunnel looked as if it had
been made by a machine. At the end
of it there was a light shining
and three people talking. They saw
me and grabbed me and shoved
me in to a corner they started
talking again. They said "when the place
blows up my cousin will be King" and
the others said "okay". Next they turned
their attention to me and said "but
what shall we do with this Kid?
He must of heard every thing." Then

Figure 11.1 Danger down under

one   said " we will   put   him   in   the
plane ". The others   agreed   and   explained
sarcastically <u>sarcastickly</u>   that   a   bomb   will be
disguised   as   one   of   the   engines
of   a   plane   and   in   an   exibition
which   the   king   will   visit   and
then   the   bomb   will   blow up . First
they   had   to   dig   an   under ground
tunnel . They   had a machine   and   they
started   to   work .   Before   they had
done   much   I   head   a   yell .
the   drill   had broken   down   but
worse   still   gas! .   I   ran   holding
my   nose   and   mouth .   I   tripped and
pulled   a   stone   out   with   my   leg
That part of the tunnel gave   way   and   trapped the
gas   and   the conspiritors with   it .   some
people   out   side   had   found   the hole
and   I   saw   them   coming   down the tunnel and we
got   out .   We   were   just in time to
see   a   large   explosion .   That
was   the end   of   the conspirators. Not

$\frac{9}{10}$ one   escaped .

Good .   Read to the class

Figure 11.1 Continued

introduce a short survey of trends in the assessment of writing. At the bottom of the story the teacher has written: '9/10 Good. Read to the class.' In addition, the word 'sarcastically' has been written in the margin with the original error underlined in the text. This is clearly not a detailed assessment of the story and it would be easy to be critical of it. It is plain that the teacher approves of the writing but there is no feedback to the writer about either its qualities or its deficiencies. Nor does the comment provide an inspiring response by the reader to what is clearly intended to be an exciting adventure story. The criteria for marking, if there were any, remain obscure. Nor are we given any idea of the story's place in this child's developing journey as a writer. We should bear in mind, however, that this story was one of 25 or more, marked by the teacher in her own time at the end of a long day. In addition, it might be added that this piece was not unusual for the writer. It is one of a total of 26 quite similar stories produced by this pupil during one school year.

This sort of brief written comment, with corrections, represents a traditional approach to the assessment of writing which will be labelled here as a minimal assessment. Traditionally, teachers have referred to this sort of minimal assessment as 'marking' and indeed it is easy to come across cases of adults who feel that as pupils they were 'marked' for life as a result. In minimal assessment, then, a general comment, encouraging or admonishing, is accompanied by corrected spellings and punctuation and often a comment on neatness of presentation. At least in the example above there is also the suggestion that the story should reach a wider audience, though this may have been a largely routine reaction. Presumably the mark of 9 out of 10 represents a judgement about general attainment in relation to the whole class, while the comment 'good' perhaps relates to the teacher's judgement about individual effort. It may well be that the teacher wrote no more, and said no more, because she didn't know what else would be worth writing, or saying.

Teachers' awareness of the need for a more demanding level of response and assessment of writing was given considerable stimulus by the Bullock Report (DES, 1975). The Report devoted only one of its 26 chapters to written language, in both primary and secondary phases, but, despite this sparse coverage of the topic, some trenchant comments were included. The Committee argued that the assessment of writing should start from a consideration of writing as a means of communication, which arises out of a particular context. The appropriateness of the language used by a writer should be judged in relation to the specific purpose of, and audience for, the writing. The differentiation of language for different purposes and audiences would not be great to start with but would be a feature of children's gradual development as writers. The Report also addressed a long-standing uncertainty among teachers as to how far assessment should be directed towards the 'secretarial skills' of spelling, punctuation and handwriting, and how far it should centre on content or originality. Bullock (11.5) tried to resolve this worry by proposing that 'a writer's intention is prior to his need for techniques' and (11.10) that therefore 'the teacher's first response to a piece of writing should be personal and positive. Only after responding to *what* has been said is it reasonable to turn attention to *how*. Correction and revision are then of unquestionable value.'

The best approach, the Report continues, is for the teacher to 'go over the pupil's work with him' discussing its qualities rather than merely assigning a grade to every piece of writing. Such routine marking was likely to push the teacher towards correcting surface features of the writing and away from matters of style and content. In general, Bullock argued for a more detailed form of assessment, even if this meant that not every piece of a child's writing would be 'marked'.

Let us attempt to apply this type of assessment, which will be labelled a 'detailed assessment', to 'Danger down under' and speculate on the sorts of comment a teacher might make to the writer, following the approach recommended by Bullock. There are a number of possible lines which might be followed. In the first place we might convey to the child that we got the point of the story: 'Phew! I'm pleased that you escaped', we might write. Given time, we might then consider how far the story matches up to the general need for such a narrative to have a coherent and exciting plot. We might comment on the careful attempt to set the scene in the tunnel but add that the reader would want to know more about the thoughts and feelings of the hero when captured and, again at the end, after his escape. A little more detail about the tunnel caving in might also strengthen the impact of that scene.

Alternatively, we might comment on the appropriateness of some of the language. The opening sentence projects the reader swiftly and economically into the action, through the clause 'when it all happened'. The use of 'grabbed' and 'shoved' is just right to convey the roughness of the actions described. The final sentence: 'Not one escaped' is again appropriate in its economy and finality. To pick out two more features, the use of 'conspirators' and the phrase 'worse still' show that here is a writer who is beginning to use literary language to good effect, in the first instance to delineate the status of the villains and in the second to suggest a crisis. Note also the phrases: 'turned their attention to me' and 'but what shall we do . . . ?' Indeed, given these signs of maturity of language choice and the virtually error-free level of transcription, we might venture a little further and suggest that 'sarcastically' was a good try, but not quite right. 'Brutally', 'cynically' or 'coldly' might be preferable. At the same time we might give the correct spelling of 'sarcastically'. Another possible critical point might be that few adjectives or adverbs are used to heighten the visual images suggested or the manner in which actions and events occur.

Clearly, there is no one way in which one might respond to this story and no definitive list of what to comment on to the writer. These are merely suggestions, intended to fit the broad guidelines established by the Bullock Report. Such an approach has much to recommend it but we might still feel that it has some shortcomings. It has little to say about the way the writer went about producing the story; in other words about the writing process. The writer has not, so far, been invited to evaluate the story for himself. Feedback to the writer concentrates on the end product and not on how to get better at the process of story writing. Nor do such comments provide the teacher with a means of looking at the developmental status of such a story. Is this exceptional for an 8-year-old, or merely ordinary? How might it be compared with the author's previous work? What sorts of signs of development might a teacher be looking out for? Lastly, it does not address the question of the context in which the writing was produced.

If we imagine a third level of assessment, therefore, which will be labelled 'in depth', it would need to go into still more detail, either in terms of interpreting the story's meaning or in terms of looking at its use of language, or by relating the finished piece to context and process. It is important to state at this point that such an 'in-depth' analysis would not be conveyed in all its complexity to the child but would be meant primarily to help the teacher and heighten awareness. One such model, developed by the present author, will be outlined here. Called 'The Developing Writer', it sets out to categorise any piece of writing by a child in the primary years in terms of three broad levels of developing attainment and six dimensions of writing (Fox, 1990).

The beginnings of writing are described at the first level, under the title 'emergent writing', followed by a second very broad level of attainment typical of 7- to 11-year-olds, which is described as 'developing writing'. The third and final level is called 'fluent' writing and is meant to describe the writing of a child who, at the completion of primary education, has a degree of confidence in managing the writing process independently, and the main writing conventions, across a variety of writing tasks. Such a child is still in many respects a beginner as a writer, of course. A 'fluent' writer is thus fluent in terms of the expectations we could reasonably hold of, say, an able 11-year-old.

A simple summary of the whole scheme, 'The simple picture', is reproduced in Figure 11.2. It deliberately simplifies in order to provide a brief overview. Three of the dimensions of writing are concerned with composition, or the construction of meaning, while the other three are concerned with transcription, or the management of the conventions of writing. The 'detailed picture' (see Appendix) includes both more descriptive detail and some intermediate steps towards the main attainment 'bench marks'.

Clearly, it will take some time for a reader to find his or her way around this scheme. The best way of using it is probably to try to apply its categories to a piece of writing and to record, at the same time, reservations about its accuracy or relevance. To illustrate the scheme in use, it will be applied to our original story, 'Danger down under':

1 *Process*. Little can be said here, without further information about the context in which the writing was produced. Given that the story was written in one draft, at a single sitting, it is highly likely that the writer has had little experience of pre-writing, drafting or revision. Note that this tells us more about the context of learning than about the learner. A close examination of the original script adds something more, however. Three words or phrases are

	EMERGENT	DEVELOPING	FLUENT
Process:	engages in emergent writing and talks about it	uses pre-writing, drafting and reading/revising to make sense (with prompting)	can discuss and make independent use of – topic choice – pre-writing strategies – reading/revision – self-evaluation
Structure:	shows awareness of functions of writing; can make sense of own writing (same day)	can use story, list, letter, poem, report; organises mostly via list and chronology	can write well-structured stories and poems and writes – to inform, to persuade – to explain, to argue; some organisation beyond list/chron; e.g. classify and summarise
Style:	words mostly chosen from oral vocab; syntax mostly simple statements and questions	some use literary or technical vocab, compound sentences; some noun, adj and adv phrases/clauses	selective word choice: expressive, technical and/or literary; some complex sentences; variety of clauses and verb forms to refine meaning
Spelling:	from letter strings to phonic inventions; can name some letters	transitional speller; visual and phonic cues; some editing; recites alphabet	mostly conventional; can edit most errors; can use sp. dictionary; aware of sp. patterns
Handwriting:	from scribble to some letters and letter-like forms	differentiates upper/lower case; mostly legible; developing fluency; types with one finger	legible and fluent cursive script; uses broad nib pen; tries decorative lettering; types with two fingers
Graphics:	uses pictures and own graphic symbols	most caps and stops; some ? or !; lays out letter or story titles (with help); adds own expressive graphics	mostly conventional . ? ! " "; some commas; some capitalisation; some apostrophes; can plan and lay out page, table or book

Figure 11.2 'The developing writer' – the simple picture

added with a caret mark or arrow, indicating an omission rectified. In addition, three words have letters added as an afterthought. There is also evidence of 'rubbing out' and of some capital letters being added in correction. All this suggests that AF was at least at the 'developing' level, in terms of process.

2 *Structure and function*. Here something can be said about AF's handling of the narrative genre. In this story AF is operating mainly at level (iib): there are several characters but they are depicted from the protagonists' subjective point of view and are stereotyped 'goodies and baddies'. They interact mainly physically, although there is a little dialogue. The emphasis is on action and reaction. The predicament concerns an initial upset of normality, the fall into the tunnel, which is then meshed with the conspirators' plan to assassinate the king and followed by another 'upset', the escape of gas and the tunnel cave-in. The issues focus on material safety and physical welfare and the resolution is violent. The setting is briefly described and even, to a limited degree, elaborated. These all fit level (iib) of the scheme.

3 *Style*. Here features of level (ii) are mixed with some features of level (iii). Level (ii) seems appropriate for the vocabulary: some use is made of literary words (e.g. 'parading around', 'conspirators', 'worse still' etc.). In terms of syntax one might claim that AF is already operating at level (iii). The first four sentences are all complex ones, containing at least a main and a subordinate clause. In the second half of the story it is notable that AF uses a succession of fairly sophisticated temporal connectives: 'Next . . . Then . . . First they had to dig . . . they started to work . . . Before they had done much . . . We were just in time . . . ' This contributes significantly to the coherence of the piece and goes far beyond the common use of 'and . . . and then . . . and so'. Not many adjectives or adverbs are used (with the notable exception of 'sarcastickly') and this accounts partly for the rather 'flat' tone of the piece. The verb forms are quite varied and generally appropriate (although 'a bomb will be disguised' should perhaps read 'a bomb would be disguised'). We might conclude that AF is showing many of the signs of a fluent written style, though there is still plenty of room for further improvement.

4 *Spelling*. Here it is necessary once again to seek further information, in this case about whether or not this standard of independent spelling was produced without any support. Such evidence as exists suggests that AF at this time was already a fluent speller, with a wide repertoire of remembered spellings and a well-developed awareness of English spelling patterns. Certainly he made many careless 'slips of the pen' at this time and also asked his teacher for the occasional spelling ('conspiriters' becomes 'conspirators', for example) but he could manage such words as 'Halloween', 'happened', 'tunnel', 'cousin', 'disguised' and 'explosion' without help. He does make the odd error ('exibition', 'conspiriters') but he also finds and corrects some errors. Clearly, AF is already a 'fluent' speller, at level (iii).

5 *Handwriting*. Not AF's strong point, perhaps, but he produces a generally legible cursive script. The slant of the writing is irregular but there are no grossly deformed letters and joins ('ligatures') are made effectively. It is worth noticing that the early part of the story is more neatly written, and spaced, than the later part. Fatigue and an increased attention to meaning are the likely reasons for this. Given that this is in effect a first draft, though corrected, the handwriting is adequate, if not elegant. Again level (iii), fluency, has been achieved or almost achieved.

6 *Graphics*. Punctuation and layout are mostly at level (iii). The story is given a title, underlined, though without two possible upper-case letters for 'down' and 'under'. Paragraphing has yet to be mastered (or probably taught). Punctuation is mostly correct, with sentences demarcated by full stops and capital letters. Speech marks are used correctly, as are a question mark and an exclamation mark, though the latter is mistakenly followed by a full stop. There is little to cavil at here, though some further sophistication will no doubt develop in time.

This rather exhaustive trawl through one story is carried out only for illustrative purposes. A practised reader would quickly focus on the salient points: AF is a fluent, or almost fluent, writer in terms of his mastery of the main conventions of spelling, handwriting and punctuation. He has a remarkably mature use of vocabulary and syntax for an 8-year-old, which strongly suggests that he reads widely. He is still developing his control of the narrative genre and thus his story has a number of typically immature features of structure and meaning, relating to the representation of character, predicament and environment. The plot is improbable and not very original but it is exciting and generally coherent. Its main weakness is its reliance on arbitrary accidents at crucial points. AF's control of the writing process shows promising signs of rereading and editing, but we may reasonably guess that the teaching he has received has not opened up the full power of the writing process to him.

One might well imagine that little more could be said of such a simple little story, but this would not be true. If we chose to switch to another sort of assessment, focused upon the interpretation of meaning, we would begin to notice, or at least speculate about, other features. For example, the story was written a few weeks after Guy Fawkes night, and is almost certainly an attempt to provide a contemporary parallel to the Gunpowder Plot, with which AF was familiar. Second, we might notice how the story plunges AF, as hero, almost arbitrarily into the world of terrorism, via an Alice-like fall into a hole in the ground, which is a device, or convention, which enables the writer to leave the normal, everyday world and enter temporarily into the world of fictional adventure where all sorts of improbable events may take place. Eight-year-olds have a liking for stories concerning violent conflict and adventure, but they almost always resolve fictional predicaments in a way which preserves the protagonist from all harm, restores normality and enables the forces of conventional authority to triumph over evil. Children thus use narrative, with which they are familiar, to rehearse an emerging sense of moral drama in the world and to explore the social world of interaction, conflict and relationships. AF cannot yet manage more than the beginnings of rounded individual characters who are able to think for themselves and have relationships with, and attitudes towards, one another. He does, however, make a real attempt to provide a rationale for the terrorists' actions and, at 8, this is a very promising sign. He also manages the dialogue between the conspirators well, in that it depends upon a realisation by them that 'the kid' has heard everything and thus poses a threat to their plans. In a similar way, the setting of the story is sketchy but contains signs of promise in the attempt to depict the original time and place and the nature of the tunnel. The mention of a 'king' leaves the time setting uncertain, although the machine-made tunnel and the mention of plane engines are contemporary enough. AF cannot quite get out of his predicament alone, but invokes benign adults ('some people out side') at the moment of crisis. This embedding of child heroes in adventures which have a framework of a more comforting normality, and in which the power of evil adults is overcome by the power of benign adult authority, is typical of writers in the age range 7 to 12.

AF cannot yet fully develop the inner mental world of his characters, and although his hero is purposeful and capable of intelligent action, his thoughts and feelings about his dreadful predicament have to be inferred, or ignored, by the reader. Thus information is carefully assembled for the reader to make sense of the outer events, but the horror, the fear and the relief of the hero remain implicit. In this context, 'sarcastickly' is a notable sign of things to come, showing as it does the writer's awareness that we 'read' significant clues about people's intentions from their tone of voice.

There are a number of difficulties connected with any relatively sophisticated assessment of children's writing. One has to do with the distinction between an assessment and a response to a text. A second concerns the level of inference that the reader is prepared to make about the writer's intended meanings. A third concerns the balance that is struck between assessing a given example of writing and assessing the writer. Something needs to be said about each.

Primary teachers are not teaching children to write with the expectation that they will become professional novelists or poets. It is rather that they aim to enable all children to be in possession of the powers of writing, so that they may use these in any ways they wish, for example in learning, communicating and recording. Given this, although teachers will of course want to respond to the aesthetic qualities of children's writing, they may nevertheless see it as a higher priority that all children become fluent writers, no matter what their imaginative powers may be. Thus teachers will naturally encourage all the good qualities of writing alluded to by Cox, and teachers, as readers, will respond to these qualities and talk to children about them. But when assessing the development of children as writers, it may well be sensible to leave aesthetic judgements on one side, while reviewing the underlying development of competence in terms of control over the essential processes of composition and transcription. To do this is to make a firm distinction between assessment and response.

The response of the teacher, as a reader, should be to the content and meaning of the piece, at least in the first place. It should also be a 'professional' response, in the sense that it should be constructive, encouraging and aimed at building up the writer's confidence. It will also be to some extent subjective, since any reader brings a particular view of the world to bear on a text. The teacher's assessment of the text, on the other hand, is to some degree separate and might, for example, involve judgements about the child's developing levels of control over the various dimensions of writing. Some of this assessment, but not necessarily all, will be shared with the child. The full details of it will become evidence to be used when reporting on, or recording, progress and achievement. Thus response and assessment are to some degree separate activities, each with their own criteria. It has to be admitted, however, that the neatness of such a distinction is clouded by the fact that writing is centrally to do with making meanings and no assessment of writing can afford to ignore the meanings made.

Another quandary has to do with the extent to which the assessment of writing should concentrate on meaning, or on language or on the writer's control of meaning via language. Language reflects our thoughts, indeed the act of authoring has been defined as 'the revision of inner speech' (Moffett, 1971). Wilkinson's Crediton Model of writing assessment (Wilkinson *et al.*, 1980) was intended to look first and foremost at meaning. It thus analyses writing, not in terms such as 'process' or 'structure and function' but in terms of psychological categories of developing thinking, emotional, social and moral awareness. This is to treat the writing as a means of investigating, or hypothesising about, the writer as a thinking, meaning-making being. There is no reason to reject such an analysis out of hand and it certainly produces particular kinds of insight into children as thinkers. It does mean, however, that the analysis goes beyond the child's progress as a writer in English and we might want to ask why teachers would want to do that. The answer would probably be that as teachers we are interested in our pupils as whole persons, not simply as writers. But in that case we need, again, to keep in mind the purposes of any assessment. Sometimes we may be interested in the children's progress in English, sometimes in their broader development as people.

Armstrong (1990, 1991) argues that assessment should be seen in the light of the question: 'How do we render an account of children's learning?' His answer leads him to consider that children's texts should be read and interpreted with the same degree of seriousness and care that we would devote to the work of any major adult author. Teachers should build up an 'archive' of each child's writing, to serve as a kind of intellectual autobiography. Although many teachers have gone some way towards this, few contemplate the kind of detailed analysis which Armstrong attempts. One danger here may be that if we over-interpret children's work we will eventually read into it significances which have more to do with ourselves as adult readers than with children as authors. Nevertheless, it is certainly possible to pursue the meaning in children's work beyond what arises in the course of the kind of analysis provided by a scheme such as 'The Developing Writer'. To do so, it may be helpful to ask the following questions, in succession, of any piece of writing:

- What kind of writing is this (i.e. what genre)?
- How appropriate is it to the genre?
- Whose meanings and whose voice do we recognise in it?
- What areas of meaning has the writer chosen to elaborate?
- What levels of awareness does this reveal about each topic?

Finally, it must be admitted that primary teachers are very busy and feel pressed to find time for any detailed observations of children's work, unless these are part and parcel of normal teaching. As a consequence, they are likely to continue to search for means of assessing and keeping records which are economical of time and effort. It seems pertinent to recall Bullock's warning that frequent 'routine' assessments of writing are likely to push teachers towards surface features of writing and away from style and content. More detailed analysis of occasional pieces of work may well pay better dividends in the long run. Teachers need in-service courses and time to digest the sorts of detailed and in-depth assessments of writing described above. Given these things, they may be able to bring a more detailed and powerful model of writing development to bear on their interactions with children and their reading of children's writing.

APPENDIX: THE DEVELOPING WRITER – THE DETAILED PICTURE

Composition

1 Process

This dimension refers to the writer's use and knowledge of the process of writing. The exact concepts and terminology used will vary according to the version of 'the writing process' that is taught. It is assumed that any version will make some reference to pre-writing strategies, drafting, reading, and revising and editing. (Generally, the term 'revision' is used here to refer to alterations in meaning and the term 'editing' to alterations in transcription.)

(i) Emergent writing

- scribbles.
- produces schematic drawings.
- produces letter-like forms and assigns meaning to them.
- writes own name correctly.
- talks about writing, in terms of intention to write, commentary while writing and explaining meaning of what has been written. This should show that the child clearly understands that writing communicates meaning.

(ii) Developing writing

(a)
- produces a sentence independently and can read it back to an adult.
- pre-writing: can use ideas from teacher and class discussion in own writing. Can use own picture(s) in relation to writing.
- drafting: can produce rough drafts independently. Shows by talk that he/she understands that changes can be made to this.
- revising: can make simple additions, with encouragement.
- awareness: talks about the process, conventions and meaning of writing in simple terms in discussion with the teacher and, occasionally, independently.

(b)
- produces sequence of related sentences which can be read by the teacher.
- topic choice: can choose own topics, with some help.
- pre-writing: can use brainstorming and simple diagrams to plan writing, when prompted by teacher.
- drafting: sometimes rereads while writing and makes occasional changes. Understands that appearance can be improved in a later draft.
- revising: can notice some omissions and repetitions that destroy sense. Can add to writing and will occasionally delete or substitute words, with encouragement.
- awareness: shows in talk some awareness of the need to plan or to collect material before writing; some awareness of the reader's needs; some awareness of the need to read through work and check its sense.
- evaluation: will make simple global judgements about own writing, which go beyond one word rejection or praise.

(iii) Fluent writing

- topic choice: can choose own topics or own interpretation of 'set' topics.
- pre-writing: can use a variety of pre-writing strategies, including brainstorming, diagrams or pictures, 'research reading' and note-taking.
- drafting: concentrates on meaning and intention while drafting; often rereads what has so far been written.
- revising: will independently return to a piece of work and redraft to improve meaning.
- awareness: can discuss how to go about planning or researching a piece of writing; shows awareness of need to select relevant material and to focus own intentions in writing; aware of reader's needs for information; can use appropriate terminology in discussing revisions (e.g. letter, word, sentence, paragraph, meaning, planning, drafting, revising, editing, publishing).
- evaluation: can discuss own work in relation to own intentions and point out some strengths and weaknesses. Can make sensible decisions about abandoning, continuing and/or publishing writing.

2 *The structure and functions of genres*

This dimension refers to the writer's experience of, and control over, the various types, or genres, of writing. It includes statements about the ability to use various genres and to understand their chief functions and also statements about the organisation of meaning, or discourse, within each genre.

(i) Emergent writing

- shows an awareness of the functions of writing either to record or to communicate meaning.

- shows an expectation that own writing should make some sense.
- attempts to use writing to communicate.

(ii) Developing writing

- has experience of writing in various forms, including story, list of recorded items, letter, poem and report of own experience.
- organises meaning mostly in terms of chronology and narrative, or by listing items. Attempts at argument or explanation tend to become assimilated to narrative. Reports tend to remain fragmented.
- stories: describes one or more characters faced with a predicament which is somehow resolved. At this age, stories tend to have the following sorts of characteristics:
  Characters tend to be represented from a single point of view, interact mainly at a physical level and are generally stereotyped.
  Predicaments either chronicle special social events or deal with a single disruption of normality. There is an emphasis on physical actions and reactions, on material safety, and on rewards and punishments.
  The environment, or settting, may be sketched but is not elaborated.
- describes attempts at writing in terms of genre, e.g. 'story', 'letter', 'recipe', 'list' or other genre name.
- has some knowledge of layout and form of a conventional letter.
- evaluation of writing may relate to the writing's function.
- shows some awareness of a need for coherence and clarity.

(iii) Fluent writing

- has experience of writing for a variety of purposes and audiences, including writing to inform, to record, to entertain, to persuade, to argue and to explain.
- organisation sometimes abandons the familiar ground of chronology and list, to attempt something such as: a presentation of contrasting points of view; a classification and summary of evidence; a generalisation with supporting facts; a longer piece organised in chapters or sections.
- shows some willingness to re-order or change material to improve clarity or coherence, with help.
- stories have at least some of the following characteristics:
  Characters not only think but communicate their thoughts; they may be realised as individuals with feelings and attitudes; they engage in social interaction and have an inner, mental, world.
  Predicaments are seen as problems to be solved, often via coordinated social planning and interaction. The psychological welfare of characters tends to be added, and eventually replaces simple material welfare.
  The environment is increasingly described, at first in terms of background to the main action and later as part of the realistic detailed setting or for the atmospheric effects it provides.
- can set out a conventional letter without help.
- beginning to control metre and form of poems (e.g. syllabic form, rhyme scheme).

3 Style

This dimension deals with language *per se*. It includes vocabulary, or word choice, and use of syntax. Thus, whereas 'structure' looks at the developing organisation of discourse on the larger scale, 'style' looks at organisation at the level of the sentence. Development will involve an increasing differentiation of syntax to refine meaning, the use of more complex and literary forms, and greater control over the choice of both words and constructions.

(i) Emergent writing

- choice of words differs little from the child's speech repertoire.
- syntax is mostly confined to simple sentences (a single main clause and associated phrases) made up of statements and occasional questions, though there may be rarer forms occasionally, modelled on speech.

(ii) Developing writing

- most words used are of common occurrence but some more specialised vocabulary is assimilated from reading and teaching. This may relate to expressive, literary or technical contexts.
- sentences make much use of compound forms (clauses joined by connectives such as 'and', 'then' etc.), as well as simple sentences expressing statements, questions and commands.
- some noun, adjectival and adverbial phrases and clauses appear, which refine meaning.

(iii) Fluent writing

- words are more deliberately chosen, more individual and more appropriate to context.
- words are regularly chosen from technical, literary or poetic vocabularies.
- words are regularly selected which are unusual, appropriate and influenced by reading.
- some complex sentences (main and subordinate clauses) are used (e.g. noun clause object, adverb clause of time), which differ from common speech forms.
- subordinators such as who, where, which, because, so, if, although, as etc. are more common.
- adjectives and adverbs are regularly used to refine meaning.
- a variety of verb forms, including passives and auxiliaries, are used to refine meaning.

Transcription

4 Spelling

This dimension covers various aspects of spelling development, including strategies used in inventing spellings, memory for conventional spellings, awareness of common spelling patterns, ability to edit writing for errors of transcription and use of the alphabet to locate spellings in dictionaries.

(i) Emergent writing

- invented spellings: pre-communicative: produces letters and letter-like forms, often repeating letters generated from a small set, often including letters from own name.
- semi-phonetic: some correspondence between symbols and letter names, or sounds; some remembered or copied spellings.
- can name some letters.

(ii) Developing writing

- invented spellings: phonetic; systematic attempt to match sounds and letters but often mistaking them; some remembered spellings.
- transitional: both phonic and visual patterns are attended to, producing a mixture of conventional and invented spellings.
- makes some successful attempts to 'proof-read' for spelling and other transcription errors.
- can recite the alphabet independently.
- can use the 'look-read-cover-write-check' routine to learn spellings.
- remembers many common spellings.

(iii) Fluent writing

- invented spellings: rare, now a conventional speller.
- can edit own and others' writing for common spelling errors and other errors of transcription.
- can use alphabetical order, e.g. when using a dictionary to look up words and spellings, using at least first two letters; can order a list alphabetically.
- shows awareness in talk and writing of many common spelling patterns in English.
- has a wide repertoire of remembered spellings.

5 Handwriting

This dimension includes both handwriting and some keyboard skills. The issue of teaching children either print script followed by cursive handwriting or a cursive style from the start is not addressed. Calligraphy is mentioned but not in detail; use of a broad-nibbed pen is considered an important experience as it involves the basic principle of varying the thickness of line.

(i) Emergent writing

- early stages: scribble in circular forms; simple schematic pictures; represents recognisable objects and events pictorially; imitates writing, using letter-like forms.
- draws fluently with some realism and detail.
- imitates letters and writes own name.
- can produce the basic strokes of handwriting: circles, diagonals, horizontals and verticals.
- begins to form lower-case letters correctly with help and in imitation.

(ii) Developing writing

(a)
- can independently form both upper- and lower-case letters and numbers, correctly in most cases.
- uses properly orientated and mainly legible print script (or cursive writing) differentiating lower- from upper-case letters correctly in most instances.

(b)
- developing some fluency which allows longer pieces of writing to be produced (e.g. more than a page).

- starting to produce cursive script with help.
- can type with a single finger, finding the keys on a qwerty keyboard with reasonable fluency.
- in final drafts can space letters and words correctly and can write neatly, using a line as a guide.

(iii) Fluent writing

- produces a legible and fluent cursive script, or print script, independently.
- differentiates between rough drafts and final 'published' work in terms of neatness and time devoted to appearance.
- can type using two fingers with some fluency.
- can use most functions on a familiar keyboard when word processing.
- has experience of using a broad-nibbed pen to produce decorative lettering and handwriting in specific styles (in imitation of models).

6 Punctuation and graphics

This dimension includes the developing use of punctuation marks and the skills of arranging and laying out texts.

(i) Emergent writing

- uses pictures and own graphic symbols.
- uses capital letter for own name.

(ii) Developing writing

(a)
- demarcates some sentences with capital letters and full stops.
- uses some question marks or exclamation marks.
- tends to add own graphic embellishments for expressive effect.
- can title work.
(b)
- demarcates most sentences correctly with capitals and full stops.
- uses capitalisation for most names.
- mostly uses question marks and exclamation marks correctly.
- attends to spacing of text on page with help.
- underlines and uses capitals for titles of stories etc.
- can lay out a conventional letter, with some help.

(iii) Fluent writing

- fluent user of capitals and full stops.
- uses full stops and capitals appropriately for some abbreviations (e.g. N.B.).
- can use speech marks (inverted commas) with some proficiency.
- beginning to use commas, e.g. in lists of items.
- can use apostrophes correctly some of the time to denote possession or contraction.
- can make some use of brackets, headings and asterisks.

- uses paragraphing in own work, with help.
- can plan and lay out a page with title headings, underlining and illustrations.
- can plan and lay out tables of data.
- has mastered some techniques for binding a home-made book.

REFERENCES

Armstrong, M. (1990) 'Another way of looking', *Forum* 33, 1, pp. 12–16.
Armstrong, M. (1991) 'On telling the story of learning'. Paper given at a conference on Assessment at Key Stage 1, University of Exeter, October.
Barrs, M. (1990) *Words Not Numbers: Assessment in English*. Exeter: NATE.
Barrs, M., Ellis, S., Hester, H. and Thomas, A. (1988) *The Primary Language Record: Handbook for Teachers*. London: Centre for Language in Primary Education, ILEA.
DES (1975) *A Language for Life* (The Bullock Report). London: HMSO.
DES (1989) *English for Ages 5–16*. London: HMSO.
Fox, R.M.H. (1990) *Language and Literacy: The Role of Writing* (Inset at a Distance: Module P47). Exeter: University of Exeter.
Moffett, J. (1971) *Coming on Centre: English Education in Evolution*. Montclair New Jersey: Boynton/Cook.
Wilkinson, A., Barnsley, G., Hanna, P. and Swan, M. (1980) *Assessing Language Development*. Oxford: Oxford University Press.

Part IV

Other themes and issues

Editors' introduction

There are, of course, many issues in the teaching of Primary English which cross the boundaries of language modes. As we pointed out in the general introduction to this book the major advance in our understanding of language and literacy processes has been the recognition of their holistic nature. Some of these cross-modal issues have achieved greater salience both through research and political developments. The chapters in this part of the book deal with three such issues.

In Chapter 12 Frank Potter provides an examination of the nature of media education and the niche it might be expected to come to fill in schooling in the future. Media education is defined as 'essentially about increasing children's critical understanding of the media' and it is made quite clear that 'media' includes print. This suggests a much broadened view of the nature of literacy and helps to explain why a study of media education should be located in the *English* curriculum. Potter suggests that media texts actually operate upon their 'readers' in similar ways to traditional print texts. The process of reading these texts is therefore amenable to study and to teaching using similar principles. In fact, the use of media texts in the classroom draws much needed attention to an aspect of print texts sometimes neglected by teachers: that is, that all texts are produced by someone for some purpose, and a conscious awareness of this purpose and the ways it shapes the text is an important aspect of a critical reading of the text.

This issue of awareness is taken up by Margaret Wallen in her chapter on knowledge about language. The area has been politically extremely contro-versial and Wallen's chapter provides useful background. After some discussion of just what the phrase 'knowledge about language' might mean, she spends some time outlining the Language in the National Curriculum Project, which is at the centre of the controversy. She goes on to outline several practical classroom activities which will be found useful by teachers wishing to introduce a more explicit focus on language into their classroom work. The nature of these activities makes it clear that sensitive work on knowledge about language is a long way from old-fashioned grammar exercises, but is best dealt with in the context of children's purposeful and meaningful engagements with language, a point which finds an echo in the following chapter of this book.

In the final chapter Bridie Raban and Ann Lewis provide an exhaustive review of research into the teaching of children with literacy difficulties. They place great emphasis upon the need to provide all children with a wealth of opportunities to engage purposefully and meaningfully with print in all forms, and go on to suggest that the problem with children who experience difficulties in literacy development may not lie so much in their deficiencies but in the impoverished 'special' teaching programmes designed to help them. Successful teaching, the chapter argues, is possible as long as this involves a close attention to the needs of individual learners. This makes a powerful argument for the role of teachers as action-researchers, constantly examining the effects and content of their own educational practice.

Chapter 12

Media education, literacy and schooling

Frank Potter

This chapter distinguishes media education from media studies and from multi-media approaches for teaching and learning and outlines how media education can be approached in the classroom. Following Bazalgette (1990) it is argued that media education encompasses both print literacy and audio-visual literacy and it is shown how this can provide a new perspective on print literacy. Finally, the implications are discussed for the role of schooling as a medium for education.

WHAT IS MEDIA EDUCATION?

What, then, is media education and why is it important? Perhaps these questions can best be answered by first considering what it is not.

First, media education is not about using TV (and other media) for instruction. It is not about schools' television, although this is often the association that is immediately made, both by teachers and by producers. For example, Lusted and Drummond (1985) comment:

> In both the BBC and ITV companies too often it was assumed that if teachers were interested in the educational impact of television then schools' pro-grammes must be their main concern . . . Producers often assumed that any discussion of the educational role of the programmes was an attempt to press them into taking a more didactic stance in their productions.
>
> (Lusted and Drummond, 1985: 67)

The way in which television and other media are used for instructional purposes is of course not only interesting and important, but also an area that should receive more attention. For example, in their First School Survey Report HMI (1982) observed that television 'programmes were often used as isolated experi-ences and there was seldom preparation or adequate follow up' (p. 13).

Greenfield (1984) concluded that television, used well, may be a more effi-cient way to convey information than print, and she recommended that television should therefore be used more in schools to communicate information, with the rider that it should be used with class discussion directed by the teacher. It has been found, for example, that children learn more when teachers make explanatory comments about the content of the programme (Corder-Bolz and O'Bryant, 1978) and when they reinforce the programme with a handout (Scarff, 1985).

We also need to consider, and take full advantage of, each medium's distinctive strengths and weaknesses for communication and learning. Greenfield (1984) has argued that print is the best medium for portraying thought, radio for stimulating the imagination and fostering creativity, and television for communicating feelings and promoting visual skills. We therefore need to find the most appropriate and efficient niche for each medium. This was not understood in the early days of instructional television, when directors simply sat a teacher before a stationary camera and filmed the lesson (Brown, 1986).

The increasing availability and affordability of CD-ROM technology is likely to focus our attention even more on the most appropriate way of communicating information, given that print, sound and visual images can all be stored and presented on the same physical medium.

Second, media education is not about teaching children to use different media technologies for communication, though this too is a matter that deserves more of our attention. Children are asked far too often to communicate in writing, even though audio and video presentations may be much more appropriate.

For example, one class of year 3 children with whom the author worked recently reported their 'water experiments' on video. Three groups presented the experiment they had undertaken. The general introduction, conclusion and links were made by one boy adopting a 'newsreader' style. Two children reported the first experiment, which demonstrated that a measured amount of cold water was heavier than the same amount of warm water. The second experiment was even more appropriate for video presentation. It showed how cold water, in the form of blue ice cubes, falls to the bottom of a tankful of warm water. The relevant portion of the transcript is:

We decided to do this experiment because we wanted to find out which way cold water moves.

To do this experiment you will need a plastic tank like this with hot water in it (it's over 50 degrees) and some coloured ice cubes.

Next you put the ice cubes into the warm water and watch what happens. You can see that the ice cubes are beginning to melt. Can you see the thin blue trail? Because the blue trail is sinking to the bottom of the tank it shows that cold water moves downwards.

Pinnington (1990) has commented on some appropriate uses of the audio recorder in schools. For example:

Historical events can be dramatised and recorded, bringing them to life. Pupils can turn historical events into radio news and current affairs programmes. Famous names from the past can be brought into the classroom to be interviewed. . . . Geography field trips are an excellent area in which to use audio recorders, to record material and observations at first hand before translating them back into the classroom.

(Pinnington, 1990: 23, 24)

The use of different media for communication is also part of the National Curriculum, as these extracts demonstrate:

Compile a news report or a news programme for younger children: perform a story or poem by means of improvisation, making use of video or audio recorders where appropriate.

(Attainment Target 1, level 5)

The range of opportunities should include the use, where appropriate, of audio and/or video recorders, radio, television, telephone and computer.

(Programme of Study, no. 7, supporting Attainment Target 1)

What is significant about the wording of the above extracts is the inclusion of the phrase 'where appropriate'. Not only do children have to be able to make use of the audio recorder, video recorder, word processor, teletext emulator and pen, but they also need to learn when it is appropriate to use which medium.

What, then, is media education about, if it is not about using TV (and other media) to help teaching and learning, or about teaching children to use different media technologies for communication? The answer is that media education is essentially about increasing children's critical understanding of the media – including print.

Media education presupposes a radically different attitude to the relationship between schooling, literacy and the media. In many people's minds print has a privileged position and it is the standard against which all other media are judged. Television, film and the newer electronic media are perceived as a threat to print (Greenfield, 1984). While 'being lost in a book' is considered an admirable state, being lost in a television programme lays children open to accusations of slack-jawed passivity (Bazalgette, 1989). The media are thought of as corrupting influences, rather than as agencies which inform and educate as well as entertain (Wollen, 1985).

By way of contrast, media education addresses all media, does not accord a privileged position to any one medium, but does stress the value of audio-visual media in order to persuade educators to acknowledge their importance. Along with audio-visual literacy, print literacy then becomes part of media education, just as linguistics can be regarded as part of the general science of semiology. The term semiology was coined by Ferdinand de Saussure (1915) and it is the term that he gave to the science which studies the life of signs within society and which teaches us what signs consist of and what laws govern them.

It would seem difficult to deny the importance of audio-visual literacy. The *Guardian* (1989) reported that in America there are now more video shops than bookstores and quoted Michael Green, the *Guardian* Young Businessman (*sic*) of that year, as saying: 'Forget books. This the age of video literacy.' According to Masterman (1985) it was estimated in the mid-1970s that children between the ages of 5 and 14 were spending 44% more time watching television than they were in lessons at school.

Yet it is this very exposure which seems to lead some teachers to conclude that the last thing we should be doing is letting the media into the classroom, thus increasing the exposure. However, this censorship has all the disadvantages of the practice of reading a difficult text *for* pupils rather than helping them to cope with the text's language demands – what Michael Marland has called 'circum-navigating print' (in Lunzer and Gardner, 1979: 279).

Another reason why it is sometimes thought unnecessary for teachers to concern themselves with audio-visual literacy is that it is claimed that we do not have to be taught to be audio-visually literate, that we all 'naturally' learn this. There is no doubt that children have a head start with the audio-visual media, partly because they are 'immersed' in television (would perhaps the same be true for print literacy if children were 'immersed' in reading to the same extent?). But even if it were true that we learn all the codes and conventions, we are not necessarily aware of them. For example, how many of us are aware that a television presenter filmed at an angle (in the three-quarter profile) is perceived as more sincere, more direct, more expert and generally presents a better set of connoted values, than one directly addressing the camera (Baggaley and Duck, 1976)?

Moreover, if the newer electronic media are perceived as a threat, as corrupt-ing influences, surely this is the best reason we can have for including media education in schools, for it is a school's task to educate children for life and that includes giving children the tools to understand the media critically, to shift their belief in the transparency of the media. In order to do this media texts have to be brought into the classroom and analysed, and children have to go through the process of constructing media texts for themselves. As Bazalgette (1988) argues, media education offers children the language and methods to make critical judgements, rather than simply offering them the critical judgements. In addition, media education also extends children's capacity to enjoy the media, a worth-while end in itself.

Before continuing, it is important to state that media education is not media studies. Media studies is a subject, but media education permeates the curri-culum. In other words, just as we have Language across the Curriculum and IT across the Curriculum, so we have Media Education across the Curriculum. Nowhere is it perhaps more important than in geography. For example, images of South Africa in some geography textbooks written for the 16+ age-group are 'rose-tinted', no doubt because 84% of them were provided by the South African Government Information Service and allied bodies (Masterman, 1985).

It should be clear from the above that media education is therefore not simply about producing media texts (although that is part of it). While some of what is done in schools, for example, the production of a class newspaper, may appear to be media education, it is often not, for similar reasons that not just any teaching involving the use of a book counts as literacy teaching.

How, then, should one approach media education in the primary classroom? This is a question which was addressed by the BFI/DES National Working Party for Primary Media Education (Bazalgette, 1989). They considered a number of possible approaches, including describing media education as sets of practices (things that children might do in the classroom), in terms of skills and media forms or technologies, but in the end concluded that the important elements were the conceptual elements – what children ought to know about and understand. From that would follow all the skills and practices and objects of study. The working group identified six areas and formulated signpost questions relating to each area:

Media agencies	*Who* is communicating and why?
	Who produces a text; roles in production process; media institutions; economics and ideology; intentions and results.
Media categories	*What type* of text is it?
	Different media (television, radio, cinema etc.); forms (documentary, advertising etc.); genres (science fiction, soap opera etc.); other ways of categorising texts; how categorisation relates to understanding.
Media technologies	*How* is it produced?
	What kinds of technologies are available to whom, how to use them; the differences they make to the production processes as well as the final product.
Media languages	*How* do we know what it means?
	How the media produce meanings; codes and conventions; narrative structures.
Media audiences	*Who* receives it and what sense do they make of it?
	How audiences are identified, constructed, addressed and reached; how audiences find, choose, consume and respond to texts.
Media representations	How does it *present* its subject?
	The relation between media texts and actual places, people, events, ideas; stereotyping and its consequences.

In their report (Bazalgette, 1989) the working party breaks down each area into 'Performance' and 'Knowledge and Understanding' attainment targets, providing a useful organised summary.

In order not only to help children understand media codes and conventions, but also to become aware of that knowledge, a crucial question for the teacher to ask is 'How do we know?', to discuss the clues which lead to the interpretation of a media text. This perspective can turn some activities already going on in schools into examples of media education.

For example, there is a picture-sequencing activity to be found in the BFI pack *Picture Stories* (Davies, 1986), a pack which not only includes a set of images for use in the classroom, but also explains how to study any images. One task is to select and order a number of photographs to form a narrative about a canal trip. At one level it is similar to sequencing activities commonly found in primary schools, but it differs in two main respects. First, there is not one fixed story. The number of photographs selected can vary, as can the order of events chosen, thus leading to a number of alternative narratives. Second, the main objective is to read and discuss the visual clues in individual images which can link one picture to the rest. Children will learn that, through different juxtapositions, different meanings can be emphasised in the same picture. To take a simple example, one of the photographs can be interpreted either as someone tying up a boat, or as someone untying a boat. The question 'How do we know they are tying up the boat?' draws the children's attention to the visual clues they are using to dis-ambiguate the visual image.

Another activity sometimes used to generate group discussion involves play-ing short video extracts of a programme without any sound and asking the children to say what they think is happening. The supplementary question 'How do we know?' again draws children's attention to the visual clues they are using to interpret the media text.

A MEDIA EDUCATION PERSPECTIVE ON PRINT LITERACY

A media education perspective can help us towards deeper understandings of print literacy. First, if media education subsumes print literacy (and audio-visual literacy) the six areas and 'signpost questions' should be just as relevant to print literacy. Originally, print literacy was mainly concerned with how meanings were produced (media languages), but we have recently seen more attention being paid to audience (media audiences), genre (media categories), and bias and stereotyping (representation). With the introduction of word processing and desktop publishing programs in schools there is more concern about how the text is produced (media technologies). Should we now be paying more attention to media agencies – to who is communicating and why?

Second, media education can also help us to appreciate the interaction between different media. Too often other media are regarded as subserving print. For example, the research on illustrations in reading books makes the assumption that the relevant question is whether illustrations help or hinder reading. How-ever, illustrations and writing complement each other, even in the narratives of 8-year-old children, as has been demonstrated by Browne (1990). She found that in children's illustrated stories the pictures and the writing worked together to produce a more comprehensive, detailed and clear story than would have been possible by the use of one medium alone. In one story about Thomas the Tank Engine, for example, such details as the weather and Thomas's feelings were incorporated into the story through the illustrations. Thomas's smiling face was replaced by a downturned mouth when he became derailed and smoke ceased to come out of his chimney. From a media education perspective this is unsurprising, and indeed children's early writing can be regarded as subservient to their pictures, merely providing captions for them (the function of a caption is to disambiguate the meaning of a picture or, to use the jargon, as visual images are polysemous, the caption enables the reader to fix, or anchor, the meaning of the image). However, although one would expect children's writing to complement their pictures, children in infant classes are often asked to write a sentence duplicating information they have already conveyed in their picture. As MacLure (1985) has pointed out, this must hinder children's appreciation of the communicative function of writing.

A third aspect concerns group prediction activities, which can be a media education exercise if the teacher makes a point of asking the question 'How do you know?' Masterman (1985) has recommended extending this activity with audio-visual texts, by asking the question 'What cannot happen?' For example:

> In *The Rockford Files* it is fairly clear that Jim Rockford cannot be killed, fail to solve the case, or act dishonourably. He is also unlikely either to settle down and get married or to renounce women entirely. Indeed, he can do nothing which will radically alter his circumstances.
>
> (Masterman, 1985: 177)

It is, of course, the series format which excludes so many narrative options and so this extension to the group prediction activity cannot be used with all texts – but it could be used with, for example, some reading schemes.

The commutation test is a standard technique used to deconstruct visual texts containing more than one unit in the grouping of images (and captions). The technique involves substituting one of the images and assessing the change in meaning that occurs. For example, try mentally substituting a man for the woman in a television advertisement for a washing detergent and note the change in meaning that occurs.

Applying the principle of the commutation test can lead to a new perspective on cloze procedure. Instead of asking children to consider which word is the most acceptable alternative, we can ask them how the meaning of the passage changes with each alternative. In other words, the emphasis is shifted from the effect of the context to the effect on the interpretation of the context. For example, there is a fairly dramatic effect depending upon whether one inserts *stockbroker* or *unemployed man* into the gap in the following text (from Bransford and Johnson, 1972: 415):

> The _____ stood before the mirror and combed his hair. He checked his face carefully for any places he might have missed shaving and then put on the conservative tie he had decided to wear. At breakfast, he studied the newspaper carefully and, over coffee, discussed the possibility of buying a new washing machine with his wife. Then he made several phone calls. As he was leaving the house he thought about the fact that his children would probably want to go to that private camp again this summer. When the car

didn't start, he got out, slammed the door and walked down to the bus stop in a very angry mood. Now he would be late.

Questions to ask could include:

1 Which page of the newspaper was he reading?
2 What was the nature of the discussion about the washing machine?
3 What make and model of car was it?
4 What kind of house was it? (e.g. small terraced house, three-bedroom semi-detached, detached, large country house set in ten acres with a paddock etc.)
5 Who was he telephoning?
6 Why did he decide to wear a conservative tie?

Media education, then, can provide a new perspective on print literacy. Indeed, perhaps it is only really possible to understand the functions and purposes of print literacy by understanding its role in relation to other media for, as each new medium comes to prominence, the preceding ones tend to take on new functions or become specialised in what they do best (Greenfield, 1984). Since television, radio has become specialised in music and the film newsreel (e.g. Pathe News) has disappeared. Or, as Marshall McLuhan (1964) phrased it, 'A new medium is never an addition to an old one, nor does it leave the old one in peace' (p. 186).

THE NICHE OF SCHOOLING AS A MEDIUM FOR EDUCATION

So far I have been arguing that media education has a valid place in the school curriculum, but now I should like to take this argument a step further and examine the possible future niche of schooling as a medium for education.

The disapproval voiced by 'education' of 'the media' is mutual. While teachers regard the media as having detrimental effects on the children they teach, the media, especially newspapers, take it upon themselves to reprimand schools for not doing their job properly. Whether it is increased violence, or supposedly falling standards, the fault lies with schools. This constant conflict between the media and schools can be explained by the fact that they are both competing for the right to define and transmit knowledge about the world, the right to be the main transmitter of culture in our society (Wollen, 1985).

Another reason for the hostility on the part of teachers is that children will voluntarily spend more time watching TV than they are compelled to spend at school. This, however, is not an argument for keeping other media out of the classroom, but for taking advantage of them, to help make learning experiences in school more attractive. Instead of competing with the media for the power to define and transmit knowledge (to educate), we should instead analyse our respective strengths and weaknesses and concentrate on finding a new niche for schooling.

Stonier and Conlin (1985) have described a vision of the future of schooling where the impact of microcomputers is so dramatic that much of the education system becomes home-based. Children will go to school because they need to play with other children, to acquire social skills, engage in sports, go on field trips, fiddle with machinery, perform experiments, dance, put on plays etc. In short, home will become the place to go to learn – school, where you go to play.

We have some way to go before this vision becomes a reality, as the National Curriculum emphasises information technology as a tool (e.g. for communicating information, handling information and for measurement and control). When it does, it is likely that television will play a major role, for why should 'educational' programmes not be made in such a way as to make them interesting and why should this not be part of children's homework, rather than using precious time in school for watching 'schools' programmes. The time released could then be used more profitably for teacher–pupil interaction and for media education, i.e. for analysing and creating audio-visual texts, rather than consuming them.

Now that we have a National Curriculum there is more incentive to invest in the production of materials (including videotapes and broadcast television programmes), as these materials are more likely to be used nationwide. It comes as no surprise, then, to learn that a major pet food manufacturer is giving away materials to help deliver the National Curriculum. As part of the National Curriculum in science the packs recommend feeding the pets with a certain brand of pet food! No surprise and perfectly understandable, but this does stress the importance of the signpost question *who* is communicating, and why?

Schools, in addition to being places where children go to play, will be places where they go to become literate, in all the media. A central role for schools will be media education, or as McLuhan (1964: 326) put it, 'Education will become recognised as civil defence against media fallout.'

REFERENCES

Baggaley, J. and Duck, S. (1976) *The Dynamics of Television*. Farnborough: Saxon House.

Bazalgette, C. (1988) '"They changed the picture in the middle of the fight . . . ": new kinds of literacy?', in Meek, M. and Mills, C. (eds) *Language and Literacy in the Primary School*. Lewes: Falmer Press.

Bazalgette, C. (ed.) (1989) *Primary Media Education*. London: British Film Institute.

Bazalgette, C. (1990) 'New developments in media education', in Potter, F. (ed.) *Reading, Learning and Media Education*. Oxford: Basil Blackwell.

Bransford, J.D. and Johnson, M.K. (1972) 'Considerations of some problems of comprehension', in Chase, W.G. (ed.) *Visual Information Processing*. New York: Academic Press.

Brown, L.K. (1986) *Taking Advantage of the Media*. London: Routledge & Kegan Paul.

Browne, A. (1990) 'Writers and readers: what do they know? An analysis of six stories written by and for children', in Potter, F. (ed.) *Reading, Learning and Media Education*. Oxford: Basil Blackwell.

Corder-Bolz, C.R. and O'Bryant, S.L. (1978) 'Can people affect television? Teacher vs. program', *Journal of Communication*, 28, pp. 97–103.

Davies, Y. (1986) *Picture Stories*. London: British Film Institute.

Greenfield, P.M. (1984) *Mind and Media*. London: Fontana.

Guardian (1989) *Green: Stand by for TV's Euro Explosion*. Friday, 7 April.

HMI (1982) *Education 5–9*. London: HMSO.

Lunzer, E. and Gardner, K. (eds) (1979) *The Effective Use of Reading*. London: Heinemann Educational.

Lusted, D. and Drummond, P. (eds) (1985) *TV and Schooling*. London: British Film Institute.

McLuhan, M. (1964) *Understanding Media*. London: Routledge & Kegan Paul.

MacLure, M. (1985) 'Early genres learned too well? Some comments on the first texts of beginning readers'. Paper presented at the International Writing Convention, held at the University of East Anglia, Norwich, April.

Masterman, L. (1985) *Teaching the Media*. London: Comedia.

Pinnington, P. (1990) *Oracy, Literacy and the Tape Recorder*. Wallasey: PP Communications.

de Saussure, F. (1974) (1st edition, 1915) *Course in General Linguistics*. London: Fontana.

Scarff, J. (1985) 'TV testing: an experiment to establish a more effective way of using television', *Times Educational Supplement*, 26 April, p. 63.

Stonier, T. and Conlin, C. (1985) *The Three Cs: Children, Computers and Communication*. Chichester: John Wiley & Sons.

Wollen, T. (1985) 'Television, media studies and schooling', in Lusted, D. and Drummond, P. (eds) *TV and Schooling*. London: British Film Institute.

Chapter 13

What is knowledge about language?

Margaret Wallen

It is only recently that the term 'knowledge about language' has become current and so there is still uncertainty in some quarters about which area it covers and what its relationship is to other aspects of English. It is sometimes assumed that it is just another name for the Latin-based 'grammar' taught in classrooms of the past. In fact, it goes far beyond this, uniting the traditionally separated 'language' and 'literature' by making all the ways in which human beings use language the legitimate subject of study. We are powerfully affected by the language of novels, plays and poems, but also by that of advertising, journalism and political speeches. There is thus some overlap of territory with media education. For example, a primary teacher using a picture sequence to help young pupils plan a story that they will write to fulfil one of the requirements of the National Curriculum for English is using the same technique that a secondary media education teacher calls 'storyboarding' and uses to help students make films. Both sets of pupils are making visual representations of the structure of a narrative and what they are doing is demonstrating 'knowledge about language', in this case at the level of whole texts.

Since the territory called 'knowledge about language' is potentially so wide, it may be helpful, before proceeding further, to attempt a visual map, using Figures 13.1 and 13.2. (In the rest of this chapter, at the risk of irritating those who abhor acronyms, I shall usually refer to KAL rather than endlessly repeating the phrase 'knowledge about language'.)

Figure 13.1 is intended to show that all human beings of normal development possess a store of implicit KAL which may be defined as the sum total of their experience to date of language use. This language use is their own and that of others. The acquisition of this store of implicit knowledge begins, quite literally, at birth and continues throughout life. It potentially covers all the countless ways in which human beings use language. In fact, each individual builds up a unique store which is the product of their personal language history, although, of course, many elements will be held in common with many other people.

In order to have arrived at such 'knowledge', the individual must have been engaged in some reflection on language at some level of consciousness,

Experience of reading

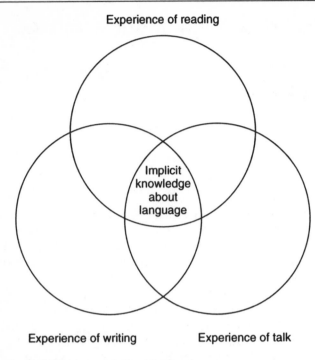

Experience of writing   Experience of talk

Figure 13.1 Implicit knowledge about language

generalising from many examples of paying specific attention to some aspect, and there will have been some explicit instruction by parent or teacher which helped this to occur. Nevertheless, the vast bulk of our stored, implicit KAL is never made explicit, although it is, of course, a resource on which we draw constantly as we use language ourselves and react to others' use of it.

KAL IN THE CLASSROOM: MAKING IT EXPLICIT

Figure 13.2 indicates the potential that exists for explicitness about what people know about language, and it is this as yet only partly explored territory that has come to be known as KAL in the classroom context. Many of the examples I shall use below to illustrate Figure 13.2 will be familiar to primary teachers, offering some reassurance that KAL has been going on in classrooms for some time without being labelled as such. Although my readership is specifically concerned with primary pupils, I have deliberately included references to pupils of different ages, in order to reiterate the important point that the acquisition of KAL occurs throughout the school years, despite the fact that the first reference to it in the statements of attainment in the National Curriculum for English appears only at Level 5. There should, in fact, be a continuity of experience in opportunities for explicitness about language which builds on those which already occur universally

Experience of reading

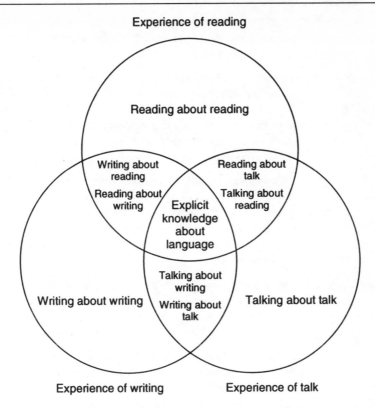

Reading about reading

Writing about
reading

Reading about
talk

Reading about
writing

Explicit
knowledge
about
language

Talking about
reading

Talking about
writing

Writing about writing

Writing about
talk

Talking about talk

Experience of writing   Experience of talk

Figure 13.2 Explicit knowledge about language

in reception classrooms as the early stages of reading and writing are taught, but which have tended to fade in importance in the junior years, to re-emerge partially later as 'Study Skills' or 'Language Awareness', in which guise they may no longer be the province of teachers of English. (Please note that, throughout, 'talk' refers to both speaking and listening.)

Here are some examples of classroom activities which illustrate Figure 13.2:

Talking about reading is already common, appearing as the reception class teacher helps her pupils to recognise individual letters, 10-year-olds recommend books to each other or as sixth-formers discuss *Hamlet*.

Talking about writing is becoming more common, because of the influence of the National Writing Project and the consequent inclusion in the National Curriculum for English of references to drafting and the shaping of writing to take account of real readers and purposes. A reception teacher might be seen 'scribing' for her pupils on a flip chart, pointing out to them that she has started writing at the top left-hand corner of the page, has left spaces between words and so on. Older primary pupils might be seen acting as 'response partners' for each other, commenting helpfully on writing in progress, while in secondary schools students might compare two pieces on the same topic by different writers and discuss the distinctive stylistic features.

Talking about talk is a more recent introduction to classrooms, but it is likely to be present in schools which have had some contact with the National Oracy Project. Here you might find pupils of all ages discussing what qualities are needed to be a helpful member of a group, using tape-recorders to enable them to assess their own performance as talkers, or discussing in which situations it is inappropriate to use slang in speech.

Writing about talk often happens in such classrooms, too; for example, when a class of 8-year-olds agrees a set of rules for group discussion and displays them on the wall, when 11-year-olds keep individual 'talk journals' to record the many purposes for which they talk, who they talk with and how well they are doing at it, or when older students collect and analyse examples of the vocabulary and syntactic features of regional dialects.

Writing about reading is more familiar territory, appearing in the traditional guise of book reviews, 'literary criticism' and 'comprehension' exercises as well as more recent introductions like writing in role as a character in a story or keeping a 'response journal' to record the reading of a novel or poem over time.

Writing about writing is not so frequently found when it refers to the pupils' own writing rather than to that of others encountered in reading. Nevertheless, one finds examples in the context of self-assessment sheets, 'learning logs' or 'port-folios' where pupils reflect on their own development as writers. Sometimes, too, a teacher will make a wall display of different drafts of a piece of writing and annotate them to point out the changes made at each stage, or she will devise a story-planning tool in visual or written form for pupils to fill in.

Reading about talk, Reading about writing and *Reading about reading* are done by teachers, but rarely by pupils below the sixth-form level, in the sense of reading academic texts about language. But they do occur with much younger children when the texts are other children's writing about these topics, such as those mentioned in the 'Writing about . . . ' sections above. A familiar example is reading each others' book reviews to find a 'good read'.

THE TEACHER'S ROLE

It will be seen from the examples given above that there is potential for classroom activities which enable pupils and teachers to make explicit their KAL in each section of Figure 13.2. In practice, however, some are exploited more fully than others. In some classrooms some sections of the diagram are not represented at all, while in others all are present but do not receive an equal emphasis. There is scope, therefore, for teachers of all age-groups to create more opportunities for explicitness about language, both by themselves and by their pupils. (In the course of classroom activities the focus may well tend to shift continuously across all three, talk, reading and writing, rather than remain on one alone, as Figure 13.2 may suggest.)

The teacher has at her disposal three means of helping her pupils to make their KAL explicit or of creating opportunities for doing so herself. The first, the one most universally used at present, by parents as well as teachers, is to seize opportunities as they present themselves to point out some feature of language in use. Almost without thinking about it, both will draw attention to a word in a book which they think children might not have met before. Teachers might also point out a letter string in a word with a tricky spelling or mention its derivation as they write it on the board. In this incidental and unplanned way, teachers already make explicit some of their own KAL to their pupils. It is desirable that they should continue to do so, since they may well be the nearest model their pupils have of an experienced and expert language user.

It is possible, though, to do this much more systematically, and to create opportunities for pupils to make explicit their KAL too, by adopting two other approaches. The first of these involves introducing into the classroom ways of working with pupils which necessarily involve explicitness by both teachers and pupils about language use. Examples of such approaches include 'conferencing', where teachers and individual pupils talk together about the pupils' writing while it is still in progress, rather than the teacher waiting until it is complete to make a response. If the writing is a story, and depending on the age of the pupil, the conversation might range over such areas of KAL as story structure, stereotyping of characters, sentence grammar, spelling of words, paragraphing and so on. This is not just an expert and novice situation, with the teacher doing all the talking, but an opportunity for pupils to show what they know too, and to make explicit what they are trying to do with a particular piece of writing.

Some of the other strategies which encourage explicitness have been mentioned above (the use of 'response partners', 'response journals' and 'learning logs', pupil self-assessment, scribing for pupils who cannot write independently and story-planning procedures). To these could be added: teachers 'modelling' other aspects of the process of writing such as redrafting, writing for real readers and purposes, collaborative writing, paired reading and transcribing talk.

In all these cases, the nature of the activity itself promotes discussion of what pupils are doing with language, whether it be reading, writing or talk. As such they are clearly useful additions to the repertoire of teaching and learning styles which a teacher has acquired. They are not, however, 'bolt-on' ideas for one-off lessons: they are ways of working which may take time to establish and time to perform. More important, they imply the view that effective learning depends on the active engagement of the learner and that reflection is a particularly helpful means of encouraging learning.

The second of the systematic means of creating opportunities for KAL to be made explicit is, to some extent, able to accommodate more formal and traditional teaching styles than the first. This is where some aspect of language itself is made the subject of study by pupils. This approach has been a feature of some secondary schools for a number of years and has involved units of work on such topics as 'The growth of the English language' or 'The language of advertising'. Consequently, commercially produced resources for KAL work with secondary students have been available for some time and the range has increased recently as the area has been highlighted in the National Curriculum for English.

WHY KAL NOW?

For many teachers, though, their first encounter with the phrase 'knowledge about language' may well have been via the National Curriculum, in the chapter of that name in *English for Ages 5–16* (DES, 1989). In fact, that document contains two other chapters which are also about KAL: 'Teaching Standard English' and 'Linguistic terminology'. But this is not the beginning of the story. The National Curriculum for English draws to some extent on an earlier non-statutory document known as the Kingman Report (DES, 1988), although the relationship between the two documents has always been unclear. The Kingman Report had aimed to create, with only partial success, a model of the English language which might serve both as definition of part of the curriculum to be taught and as instruction for teachers, who, it was recognised, had not all received adequate training in linguistics. It was found unsatisfactory by some linguists and not terribly helpful by some of the small minority of teachers who read it. It was, none the less, an important marker of the direction in which things were moving. In their paper, 'No common ground: Kingman, grammar and the nation', Cameron and Bourne (1988) offer an account of its genesis which places it in a broad linguistic and historical context and indicates just how complex were the political undercurrents which ran beneath its aims.

These undercurrents have become more visible recently, since the well-publicised non-appearance of the materials generated by the Language in the National Curriculum (LINC) Project. This project was set up in 1989 by the DES and funded for three years by Education Support Grants. It aimed to 'familiarise all primary school teachers and all secondary teachers of English with the model of the English language set out in the Kingman Committee Report'. Given the inadequacies of that model, this was a somewhat unrealistic aim. Equally unrealistic was the model of curriculum development initially envisaged, which involved the production of a 'central training package', followed by the appointment of 'expert trainers' in regional consortia of LEAs, who would themselves be trained using the package and then, in their turn, would train heads of English departments in secondary schools while the primary advisory teacher did likewise with language consultants in primary schools. Finally, these classroom teachers would train their own colleagues in school. All this was intended, in some unspecified way, to 'be closely related to parallel in-service training to promote general awareness, planning and implementation of the National Curriculum and subject-specific preparation'. (Quotations from

'Specification for preparation of central training package on Kingman model of English language'.)

It was apparent from the outset that this 'cascade' model of dissemination would be unworkable, both because of the short time-scale allowed and because of several erroneous assumptions. First, it placed faith in a 'top-down' style of INSET which had long been regarded by many INSET providers as ineffective. Second, it assumed that there existed an incontrovertible body of 'knowledge' in the form of facts about the English language and, third, that this could be written down succinctly in terms which could be understood by all teachers. Since it was clear from the outset that the Project as originally envisaged was unworkable, the 'expert trainers' sought to extend its scope and usefulness to teachers, and to try to clarify its relationship with the National Curriculum for English. They were renamed 'Consortium Coordinators', signalling a less hierarchical style of curriculum development, and they started work themselves on writing the 'training package', supported by some further instruction in linguistics, where necessary, by Professor Ronald Carter, the Project's National Coordinator.

The production of the 'training package' took far longer than the time that had been allocated. There was lengthy debate about its nature and about the detail of its contents. KAL, as I have already indicated, is a vast territory which impinges on many areas of human activity. The content of the package would inevitably have to be broader than those areas touched upon in the Kingman model if it was to give a comprehensive picture of the ways in which human beings use language. Treatment of such topics as the relationship between language and power and the social as well as linguistic dimensions of accent, dialect and Standard English would be unavoidable if an incomplete and distorted picture was not to emerge.

As soon as it became clear that such topics would be included, alarm bells sounded in the corridors of power and the draft materials were subjected to increasingly close scrutiny. Several redrafts were ordered of the most contentious sections and the resultant delays meant that the original time-scale and pattern of dissemination were abandoned. Finally, in 1991, some months before the official end of the Project, it was announced that the materials would not be published by HMSO and that crown copyright would be retained so that they could not be published elsewhere.

THE LINC MATERIALS

A predictable result of this publicity has been the creation of a demand by teachers and others to see the materials which caused all the fuss. The final version is prefaced by the words 'At the request of government ministers and of DES officials, LINC has agreed to state that these materials are for teacher training purposes only.' There is therefore no objection to their being used for the purpose for which they were intended, only to their official publication. The mechanism for their national distribution has been withdrawn, but this does not mean that they are unobtainable. Copies of 'Language in the National Curriculum Materials for Professional Development', as the materials are now known, are currently being reproduced and distributed by various means, within local education authorities, to many higher education institutions and even abroad. Anyone who wants to obtain a copy should be able to do so via an LEA LINC Primary Advisory Teacher or a LINC Consortium Coordinator.

It may be helpful to teachers to reiterate that the materials do not contain classroom materials for pupils but are intended as resources for developing teachers' understanding about language. (There has been some confusion on this point.) At 364 pages, they are a lengthy and, in some places, demanding read. It has to be said, too, that they vary in quality and potential for usefulness to teachers. Selective reading, following the guides to content provided, would be the most profitable approach. Nevertheless, they offer a useful resource for teachers without any background in linguistics.

There is an introductory section which outlines the reasons why both teachers and pupils can benefit from more understanding of language, states the theoretical assumptions implicit in the materials, describes their development and intended use, and relates them to other support materials. It also contains a table (pp. 7–8) which summarises the content and intended readership of each unit. Most are relevant to teachers of all key stages.

The units are:

Early Language
The Process of Reading
The Reading Repertoire
The Process of Writing
The Writing Repertoire
The Process of Talk
The Talk Repertoire
Spoken and Written Language
Accent, Dialect and Standard English
Multilingualism

The final sections are a 'Grammar and Glossary' (pp. 313–363) and an Appendix (p. 364) which summarises the relationships between the INSET activities contained in the units and each key stage of the National Curriculum for English.

Each unit is prefaced by a summary of its aims and an indication of how it relates both to the Kingman model of the English language and to the requirements of the National Curriculum for English. It consists of a series of INSET activities, most of which are followed by a commentary which contains linguistic information and analysis and often makes suggestions for further reading or classroom investigation.

In addition to the LINC materials there is also a collection of articles, written by Consortium Coordinators and others, which tends to focus on the 5–12 age range and covers both underlying issues and specific aspects of language in classrooms. This is *Knowledge about Language and the Curriculum: The LINC Reader* (Carter, 1990).

KAL IN THE PRIMARY SCHOOL

Primary teachers will be able to find much that is useful in these materials to supplement their own KAL. Unlike secondary teachers, however, they will find, as yet, very little in the way of commercially produced KAL resources for their pupils. This is because the 'language topic' has moved into primary schools only very recently, largely as the result of the work of the LINC primary advisory teachers. The nature and scope of their work has varied considerably owing to local circumstances and the absence until a late stage of the 'training package', but in general they have been actively exploring the extent to which KAL is of relevance to primary teachers and children and the forms it might take in this age range. At times their work has, understandably, been indistinguishable from general advisory work in English, but at others it has broken new ground by showing that even the youngest children in school are capable of focusing on language as a topic in its own right.

This is an exciting area of the primary curriculum where there is considerable scope for imaginative teachers to do innovative work. Unfortunately, it was never envisaged that the LINC Project would create mechanisms by which national publicity would be given to the work done by classroom teachers, as happened in the National Writing and Oracy Projects, via a systematic programme of dissemination by publications and other means. Relatively few accounts of KAL work in primary schools have so far appeared in print, but the remaining Consortium Coordinators are currently editing accounts of classroom work which teachers in all age groups have undertaken as a result of the Project. These may appear later in an as yet undecided form.

Given this gap in information at present, I have thought it useful to include some generalised examples of the kind of KAL topics or activities which have been found to be appropriate to the primary age range. They come from a variety of sources, including LINC primary advisory teachers and the teachers with whom they have worked in various parts of the country, and my own work. The necessarily brief descriptions are intended only to indicate possibilities. They would obviously need to be adapted to suit specific age groups within the primary years.

Examples of introductory activities to raise awareness about language

Language autobiographies

Pupils create a time-line showing significant events in their own development as language users, or write an account of that development. Parents are consulted about the early stages.

Language trails

Pupils record and categorise the language (written or spoken) to be found in a particular location. Variations involve a pupil pursuit through a lesson or a job-shadow of an adult in school.

Texts about your person

Pupils assemble a personal collection of written texts found in their pockets, on their clothing, in their bags and pencil cases and so on. They then categorise them according to readership, form and purpose.

Tub of texts

The teacher assembles a collection of single-page written texts in as great a variety as possible. Pupils take a 'lucky dip' and try to define the readership, form and purpose of the text they have received.

Examples of more specific topics

The Jolly Postman by J. and A. Ahlberg

This popular picture book and its sequel *The Jolly Christmas Postman* contain a range of types of text, written in role by characters from fairy tales etc. and presented in envelopes within the books. Pupils demonstrate their KAL by writing their own letters to extend the collection offered, using characters from a favourite story.

Mini-sagas

The challenge is to write a story which is complete in itself and exactly 50 words long, excluding the title. This simple and familiar idea can lead to discussion of such areas as the relationship between title and text, narrative structure, various features of sentence grammar and so on. Children like to present the sagas in suitably miniature books.

Variations on a theme

Some types of written information text (such as diagrams, instructions, maps) have a large number of variants. Pupils are challenged to collect as many examples as possible of one 'set' and then to categorise them in various ways, justifying each category by reference to features of the text or by readership and purpose.

Versions of stories and versions of pictures

It is well known that many folk tales or myths occur in variant forms across different times and cultures. As well as comparing the written versions, pupils also look at differences between the accompanying illustrations. This could include cartoon and film versions.

Greetings!

Greetings cards come in an ever-increasing variety of formats and their language ranges from the sentimental to the suggestive. A collection of different types from children's own homes offers opportunities to explore how language varies according to purpose, readership and format.

Names

Here is a very wide topic which could focus on any of the following: the names of boys and girls, historical and cultural differences, origins of family and place names, the names of pets, houses, boats, products, characters in stories, pop groups and so on.

Stories

Stories (which might include those told on television, in advertisements and cartoons as well as in books) offer scope for looking at narrative structure, openings and closings, characters' names, 'blurbs' on book jackets, the relationship between illustrations and text, spoken and body language in storytelling, and much else besides enjoyment of the story itself.

Rhymes

These occur in many contexts familiar to children, such as playground rhymes, nursery rhymes, poetry, songs and jingles, slogans in advertisements and product names (especially sweets, snacks and toys). They could collect examples and try to create their own.

The sweet alphabet

An idea with a lot of child-appeal: an alphabet book made by a whole class from the wrappers of sweets and snacks. The initial letter of the product name is used. (You may have to cheat with Extra Strong Mints for 'X'.)

Imaginative play

Finally, a more general idea: that the creation of a context in which imaginative play can occur allows opportunities to try out registers in spoken and written language which are not accessible to young children in real life. Home corner 'conversations' in shops, cafés, health centres, travel agents and so on are a useful starting point here. So are favourite stories, where children take on the role of a character.

Children in many parts of the country have enjoyed activities such as these. Through them they have been given an increased opportunity to make explicit what they already know about language and to reflect on its use. It is not unreasonable to assume that, in so doing, they might have become better at using it themselves.

REFERENCES

Cameron, D. and Bourne, J. (1988) 'No common ground: Kingman, grammar and the nation', *Language and Education*, Vol. 2, No. 3, pp. 147–160.

Carter, R. (ed.) (1990) *Knowledge about Language and the Curriculum: The LINC Reader*, London: Hodder & Stoughton.

DES (1988) *Report of the Committee of Inquiry into the Teaching of English Language* (The Kingman Report). London: HMSO.

DES (1989) *English for Ages 5–16*. London: HMSO.

Chapter 14

Children with literacy difficulties?

Bridie Raban and Ann Lewis

INTRODUCTION

In this chapter we review a wide range of recent studies relating to children with literacy difficulties. We have added a question mark after this phrase in the title to indicate an ambiguity in attributing responsibility for literacy difficulties. Are these difficulties only a characteristic of children or is it the case that some children present us with additional teaching challenges? In any classroom there will be a wide range of literacy ability among the children; there will be those who learn to read almost in spite of our teaching programme and there will be those who make much slower progress.

The likelihood that children will succeed in learning to read at school was reported by Raban (1984) to depend on how much they have already learned about reading before they get there (replicated by Wells *et al.*, 1984). This is also reflected in research findings from other countries by the work of Clay (1979a) and Ferreiro and Teberosky (1983). What we have learned from these observational studies is that all children pass through the same process of development in literacy learning and this is shown by Moon and Raban (1992). Some children pass through these developments faster than others and the varying rates of development have been shown to depend on the children's opportunities to make sense of the world of print around them.

During the last decade of reading research, one of the important methodological contributions to psychological investigations of reading and children with reading difficulties has been the work of Bryant and Bradley (1985). They have highlighted the importance of including chronological age and reading age controls in investigations if researchers are to make appropriate sense of their data. This additional concern for reading researchers has seen the replication of many previous studies which sought to distinguish between good and poor readers. What these replications are now showing is that poor readers are developmentally delayed rather than deficient in any way (see Raban, 1990 for a review of these studies). In this sense, those children referred to as 'poor readers' are not different from good readers, but they do take longer with their progress towards reading fluency, accuracy and understanding.

In the midst of the current debate concerning reading standards it is interesting to review the findings of Lake's study (1991) in Buckinghamshire. Reading test results of 1500 7–8-year-old children, tested every year at the same time on the same test for the previous 12 years, indicate that there was a significant increase in the proportion of slow starters with reading rather than any general deterioration in reading standards across the whole population being studied. Analysis of a variety of variables in this study points to some possible causes outside schools. Most important, changes in the characteristics of the catchment area were positively related to changes in reading scores. These characteristics were a measurable deterioration in the quality of background experiences which these children bring to school. In particular, their lack of experience of print through, for instance, bedtime stories and the general paucity of their life experiences. This has led to children arriving in school with very limited concepts and knowledge about print. A further related study of 257 children indicated that parental mediation and parental interest in young children's exploration of their world of things and ideas around them were generally decreasing.

In the case of children arriving in school with very limited experience of their world and of print, they can soon begin to experience failure as they encounter texts which are too difficult for them to read and understand. This results in their reading less than their peers. Lack of exposure to text and lack of practice will exacerbate their initial delay in learning to read. Results obtained by Allington (1984), for instance, in his sample of 6-year-olds, ranged from 16 words read in one week's school reading group by a poor reader, to 1933 words read by the most skilled reader. Because of this kind of discrepancy, Stanovich (1986) refers to a 'Matthew effect' whereby the rich get richer and the poor get poorer as educational and other supporting experiences both subtly and increasingly discriminate between children.

A study by Cox (1987) involved a group of 7½-year-old children who were selected for inclusion in his study because they obtained a reading age of 6.1 or less on the Burt (1954) Revised Word Reading Test. The same group were tested again at 15½ years using the Word Reading Scale of the British Ability Scales (Elliot et al., 1977). On the basis of this second test they were subdivided into three groups: long-term backward children, moderate progress children and slow starters. An analysis was then carried out to try to identify what features distinguished the long-term backward children from the slow starters. Cox acknowledges that correlation studies cannot establish causal links and he draws attention to the small size of the sample. He then reports that all variables, except reading scheme level reached and non-verbal reasoning, were associated with the pattern of slow reading development which led to long-term backwardness. He suggests that a lack of literary experiences in the home and a poor vocabulary result in poor concentration and low interest in the early stages of reading instruction.

One way in which schools are working to overcome this discrepancy among children is to involve parents in the early learning to read programme. Many different formats for this involvement have evolved and a few have been monitored and evaluated. HMI (DES, 1990) has indicated that those schools with high standards of reading also have home reading programmes and involve parents in their children's learning. Parents clearly welcome this involvement; however, they need systematic support and guidance if they are to be effective in their children's reading progress.

PARENTAL INVOLVEMENT

Goddard (1988) reports a study in which children's word recognition skills benefited from parents' involvement. Five children were tutored for one term using the technique of precision teaching as a method of instruction. However, it was not clear from the results whether the improvement was because of the parental involvement or the precision teaching method. Either way, for innovations like this to be successful, Goddard stresses that schools need to be committed and parents need to be provided with support meetings.

Rowe (1991), in a study involving over 5000 5–14-year-olds, found significant positive associations between reading at home and reading attainment. There was also an association between reading at home and attentiveness in school. These links were found to be independent of social class. Wheldall et al. (1987) describe the 'pause, prompt and praise' approach to tutoring children in reading and review research studies investigating its effectiveness. Both normal progress children and children with reading difficulties were involved in these projects. It was concluded that both parents and peers could be trained to use the strategies effectively. However, the procedure was not always found to be effective in producing reading gains.

A further study, conducted by Greening and Spenceley (1987), compares and contrasts shared reading with paired reading, the former being a modelling technique and the latter based on behavioural reinforcement schedules. Greening and Spenceley report results from three shared reading projects involving primary age children in Cleveland County. Improvements in attitude and fluency were observed even in children who made minimal reading age gains during the project. In addition, the authors maintain that shared reading, in contrast with paired reading, is a continuous process that maximises the advantages of modelling and enables the child to concentrate on the stories.

Paired reading has not always been found suitable for developing failing confidence, therefore a different technique was used in a study reported by Gaines (1989). He used a diary, kept and exchanged over a period of five weeks by the parents and teachers of 12 8–9-year-old poor readers. Six weeks between tests showed gains of six months in reading age. Along with these data, parental and child attitude changes were observed. The diary routine was made quite specific and knowing exactly what to do helped parents to keep these up to date. Importantly, the diaries acted as a record for evaluation that could be used by parents, teachers and children alike.

A follow-up study of the children in the Haringey Reading Project is reported by Hewison (1988). More than 80% of the children from the parental involvement groups and from those groups that experienced extra teacher help were available for this follow-up. Results of the borough screening test (ILEA, 1980) were used for these children at 11 years of age. This survey revealed that children who took part in the parental involvement exercise became and remained better readers. No statistically significant long-term effects were found from the 'extra teacher help' intervention. This finding is in contrast to that of Hannon (1987).

Hannon's study (1987) was a response to the Haringey Project, the findings of which suggested that parental involvement in school reading programmes can raise the reading ages of working-class children to, or above, the national average. His study involved 76 working-class children over a period of three years. The differences in reading attainment resulting from the project were marginal. This result stands in strong contrast to the Haringey Project findings and suggests that further assessment of the effect of parental involvement in reading programmes is needed.

In one small-scale study, Boland and Simmons (1987) evaluated the effects of the involvement of parents on the attitudes of 12 children aged from 7 to 9 years. They claim that the project demonstrated that the attitudes of parents and children, and the reading attainment of the children, were improved because of the parents' involvement and the use of real books which were related to the children's interests. In view of this they suggest that programmes including these elements are superior to conventional remedial reading sessions.

Robson and Whitley (1989) report on a regular book-borrowing service that was set up to encourage parents to read regularly to their pre-reception class children. This investigation included three groups of 20 children in different schools. The levels of parental and child interest were monitored throughout the study and the children's reading was assessed at the end of their first year in their infant schools (Brimer and Raban, 1979). No difference was found between the experimental school and children in the other two schools. However, the project revealed unexpectedly high levels of parental interest in orientating children towards literacy.

In a study involving parents, Wilson and Simmons (1989) worked with two families for three months in order to estimate the effect of parental involvement on children with specific learning difficulties. The project demonstrated that shared reading can bring the same benefits both to the parents of the children with learning difficulties and to the children themselves.

Loveday and Simmons (1988) asked the questions: Does it matter which method parents use? Is the reading tuition a key factor? Is the time spent together more important than the activity leading to recorded improvement? Does it matter what parents do as long as they do something? These authors report their work in three schools, engaging children and their parents in different activities. All the children in the three schools showed improvement in their reading (NFER Primary Test) after six weeks. This finding leads these authors to conclude that it does not matter what parents do in the sessions. However, like Goddard (1988), they note that all parents need initial counselling about working with their children and ongoing support from the school.

READING PROCESSES

The impact of illustrations on the reading performance of 19 children with reading difficulties drawn from the first-year classes of three comprehensive schools was examined by Beveridge and Griffiths (1987). Each child saw the same researcher on three occasions, reading two passages each time, one passage with illustrations and one without. The results suggested that at the lowest text difficulty level the children read faster, with less difficulty, making a higher percentage of omissions and insertions and a lower percentage of errors maintaining grammatical acceptability when the text was illustrated. At the highest difficulty level the results followed a directly contrasting pattern. It is claimed that the results show that children use different strategies according to the level of difficulty of the text, and that illustrations exercise some influence on the strategies chosen by the children.

In Simmons' (1987) study five boys from a reading clinic were each matched with two other boys, one a 'normal' reader of the same chronological age and the other a 'normal' reader with the same reading age (Bookbinder, 1976). The aim of the study was to compare the groups on their performance in a story-telling task. Analysis of these data revealed the highly individual nature of their control over story structure. Although the poorest readers showed little awareness of story structure, the same was true of some of the 'normal' readers. Similarly, two of the boys from the reading clinic used chaining devices (e.g. the frequent use of 'and') in a way more typical of younger children, but, at the same time, another reading clinic boy told the most sophisticated and syntactically complex story of all. Nevertheless, the author suggests that story-telling performance reflects the growth in control over language.

Pumfrey and Fletcher (1989) report the differences they found while investigating the reading strategies of 7–8-year-old children. Their sample of 60 children included high, average and low attainers (Burt, 1954). High reading attainers were found to make better quality syntactic, semantic and graphophonic miscues at lower levels of text difficulty. Passage complexity appeared to affect the ability of some children to make effective use of syntactic and semantic cues. Indeed, as the text difficulty increased, the miscue quality of high and average reading attainment groups deteriorated. High scores on the Burt test were significantly related to effective use of grapho-phonic miscues, but not syntactic or semantic ones in reading material from more demanding texts. High reading attainers in this age range were found to have mastered all three cueing systems while the average and below average readers had not.

In this study, when high attaining readers faced more difficult text, they were found to act like the average and low attainment groups. They fell back on inadequate use of grapho-phonic cues to decode words and to access the syntactic and semantic systems. Results from this study do not support a linear increase in the way developing readers access cueing systems. Low attainers were found to be able to make use of cues within texts. As texts became linguistically more complex, all readers were found to rely on grapho-phonic cues. The implications from this study suggest that the level of complexity of the text is crucially important for beginning readers. Also, pupils' background knowledge of a text's content is likely to be a key factor in effective use of different cue systems.

An instance of prior knowledge, in this case vocabulary, was found by McGregor (1989) to facilitate comprehension of stories. In this investigation of 545 Glasgow children aged 8–12 years, McGregor indicates that low frequency, or unfamiliar words in a story, may well hinder comprehension. A clear relationship was found between social deprivation and scores on a comprehension test and, while older children do better than younger ones, when they are younger, girls do better. The relationship that was found here was between world knowledge, influenced by sources of social deprivation, influencing in turn vocabulary and comprehension.

Investigating how children learn to read, Bridge (1990) was not able to distinguish between those taught through a traditional method employing reading schemes, flash cards and phonic skills, and those experiencing a story approach based on 'real' books chosen by pupils themselves in 'whole language' shared reading contexts. The findings from this study indicate that both approaches seemed to lead to children learning to read equally fast – or slow – in the early stages, but story approach learning provided the children with quality and variety of experience and expectation.

WORD RECOGNITION AND PHONOLOGICAL PROCESSING

Do poor readers have difficulty in generating phonological codes from print? Two experiments are reported by Johnston *et al.* (1987) which seek to investigate this question further. Forty 8–11-year-old poor readers of average and below average intelligence were compared with 40 reading age and chronological age controls on their performance in reading for meaning tasks. In comparing the performance of low and average IQ poor readers when reading for meaning, it was found that not only do these groups show phonological influences to the same degree, they also have similar overall levels of accuracy in these tasks. All the groups were found to show a phonological influence in carrying out these tasks.

Evidence is provided by Briggs and Underwood (1987) for Stanovich's (1980) interactive–compensatory model of reading as a way of reconciling inconsistent research findings on the comparison of good and poor readers' use of a phono-logical route for lexical access. Results of two tasks using 20 good and 20 poor young readers show that poor readers, like good readers, do use a phonological route to lexical access independent of task demand. They can use rules like those associated with spelling to sound, but perform badly when these rules are tested in isolation. Indeed, they perform badly when any of the subskills of reading are tested in isolation. Poor readers possibly demand more information prior to making a response to text.

Holligan and Johnston (1988) investigated the extent to which poor readers show evidence of impaired phonological processing in both memory and reading tasks. Using 8-year-old good and poor readers (Elliott *et al.*, 1977), along with age controls in four different experiments using letter and word-pair recognition tasks, they found that poor readers did not suffer from a global phonological dysfunction; rather, they performed appropriately for their stage of reading development, indicating that good and poor readers cannot be differentiated along this dimension. Poor readers appeared to be best described as developmentally delayed.

In research with similar findings, Fredman and Stevenson (1988) point out that it has been assumed that readers use two strategies: a whole word strategy for reading familiar words and irregular words which can be achieved with or without access to meaning, and a phonological strategy for unfamiliar words. Their project investigated whether severely retarded readers have an underlying phonological disability which differentiates them from normal and backward readers in their ability to read non-words and irregular words.

These researchers compared severely retarded readers and backward readers with each other and their IQ and IQ plus reading level controls (Neale, 1966). The severely retarded readers had more difficulty reading both words and non-words than backward readers when the effects of IQ were partialled out. However, when reading level was taken into account the groups did not differ. These authors claim, therefore, that reading ability accounted for much of the difference between the two groups. Fredman and Stevenson use these results to argue that retarded readers do not necessarily use different reading strategies from backward readers, and that reading level explains most of the differences between retarded and backward readers. Severely retarded readers and backward readers are not seen to be two distinct groups in terms of the reading process. Unexpectedly, for these authors, good and poor readers lie along a continuum.

The debate is continued by Johnston *et al.* (1988) who point out that it has been argued by others that poor readers are deficient in their use of phonological information when reading. The purpose of their study was to reassess the performance of good and poor readers on a lexical decision task employing non-words and pseudohomophones, matched for orthographic regularity and printed in lower-case letters, thus overcoming the weaknesses of earlier studies. Eight- and 11-year-old good and poor readers of average IQ were compared with their reading age controls (Elliott *et al.*, 1977), chronological age controls and a low IQ group. As with other studies, the poor readers in this research were found to perform very much like their reading age controls and it seems to these authors to be more appropriate to describe their difficulties in terms of delay, or even arrestment, in reading development.

The dilemma is resolved by Stuart and Coltheart (1988) who initially review three recent theories of reading development: Frith (1985), Marsh *et al.* (1981) and Seymour (Seymour and MacGregor, 1984). Each theory is outlined in turn, the commonalities and differences between them noted along with the problems they identify with each theory. These authors advance an alternative point of view and discuss the role played by phonological awareness and knowledge in the process of learning to read. The controversy as to the direction of causality in this relationship is also discussed. Data from their longitudinal study of 4–8-year-old children support their alternative viewpoint. They also ask the question: Is the ability to perform phonemic segmentation a necessary precursor to, or the result of, learning to read in an alphabet script?

In this study, children's phonological skills were tested before they began to learn to read in order to establish each child's pre-literate level of skill. It was suggested that children who are phonologically skilled before learning to read might use their phonological skills from the beginning of the process. On the other hand, children who are not phonologically skilled might initially treat reading as a visual memory task. Are there qualitative differences between phonologically skilled and unskilled children from the start of learning to read? Their findings indicated that children's pre-school phonological state, in conjunction with their letter–sound knowledge, was a significant predictor of later reading age (Elliott *et al.*, 1977; Young, 1976) even within the first year of schooling. These authors argue for an interactive relationship between phonology and orthographic analyses rather than one preceding the other in any causal relationship.

However, tutoring children's phonological skills in isolation has been shown by Hatcher *et al.* (1991) not to be an optimal method for improving literacy skills. In this study of poor readers, the group receiving an integrated programme of the teaching of phonology and reading skills made most progress. These researchers argue that the teaching of both these aspects in a reading programme is far more effective than working on either in isolation. They hypothesise a time lag between the development of phonological skills and novice readers' ability to make use of them in reading. They also ask the question: How can children's access to underlying phonological skills be facilitated in learning to read?

METALINGUISTIC AWARENESS

Children's abilities to think about their thinking processes (metacognition) have been shown to be closely associated with their learning. Metacognition has been defined by Borkowski *et al.* (1984) as 'an awareness of what you know about how you know'. However, Lloyd (1988) sees metacognition as more usually taken to include also the ability to act on this knowledge. These two aspects of metacognition have been labelled by Baker and Brown (1984) 'static knowledge' and 'strategic knowledge' respectively. So metacognition encompasses thinking about one's own learning processes as well as the ability to act on that information.

In relation to the task of reading, Babbs and Moe (1983: 423; cited in Spires, 1990) see metacognition as encompassing comprehension, critical reading and study skills because, 'They can be consciously invoked by the reader to aid in focusing on the important content in monitoring comprehension.' Presumably, there are other aspects of reading which can also be seen as requiring meta-cognitive skills; for example, conscious awareness of how to segment words when decoding.

Ashman and Conway (1989) and Wang (1990) have reviewed evidence concerning metacognition and children with learning difficulties. Children with reading difficulties have experienced reading failure and this influences what they subsequently notice and infer about themselves as readers. The research evidence shows that there is a strong and consistent relationship between pupils' metacognitive skills and achievement. For instance, Scruggs and Brigham (1990) found that poor readers are less successful at planning their learning (identifying, formulating and restructuring goals), monitoring their own learning (e.g. questioning, checking) or acting on this monitoring (e.g. seeking help at appropriate points, revising). Poor or immature readers need to understand that reading strategies should be modified according to the purpose of the task: skimming for information, for example, requires a different reading strategy from the reading of a poem.

Ashman and Conway (1989) report research evidence, as well as teachers' own reflections about children's learning, which suggests that personality interacts with metacognitive factors and this is particularly relevant when considering children with reading difficulties. Their attributions of failure invariably reflect perceived deficiencies in themselves, such as inherent lack of ability, while success is attributed to luck. Metacognitive training can help these children to perceive failure or success as linked instead with the need to use a particular reading strategy.

Training in metacognitive skills has been found to be effective in promoting reading attainment in poor readers. Paris and Winograd (1990) have focused mainly on the development of comprehension of texts. In their study four ways of developing metacognitive skills in poor readers have been identified. These approaches are metacognitive explanation, scaffolded instruction, cognitive coaching and cooperative learning. Effective programmes have involved teaching children both the usefulness of specific strategies (such as scanning) and how to monitor and evaluate their use of these strategies.

Winograd and Hare (1988) summarised the five key characteristics of metacognitive explanation as: stating the strategy, why it should be learned, how to use it, when and where to use it, and how to evaluate its use. The approach is illustrated in research by Duffy et al. (1986, 1987) in which teachers of 7- and 9-year-olds were trained to give metacognitive explanations. The approach seems to have been more successful with the teachers of the older children and, interestingly, Haller et al. (1988) claim that metacognitive training is particularly effective with upper (rather than lower) primary school children.

Scaffolded instruction involves a dialogue between teacher and pupil, highlighting metacognitive strategies. The approach is illustrated in work by Palincsar and Brown (1984) on reciprocal teaching. This involved the training of 11-year-old poor readers to use four particular strategies: summarising, questioning, clarifying and predicting. The approach operated rather like shared reading, with the teacher and pupil taking turns to lead a discussion on part of the text. The teacher began by modelling the various strategies in relation to one section, then the pupil did the same for the next part of the text.

Cognitive coaching encompasses features of both metacognitive explanation and scaffolded instruction. Paris and Jacobs (1984) see these as reflected in the development of 'informed strategies for learning'. Their work, with 8- and 10-year-olds, focused on teaching children when and why to use planning, regulation and evaluation strategies.

Cooperative learning has great potential as a strategy for developing meta-cognitive skills in children with reading difficulties. In cooperative learning children work together to complete tasks; there is a wide variation within co-operative learning in terms of the precise strategies used. Interestingly, the work of Webb (1982) shows that in cooperative learning both partners make gains in metacognitive and reading skills. There are strong parallels with work on peer tutoring reviewed by Ashman and Elkins (1990), and it is evident that when children work together on a task the situation can be designed so that the children are encouraged, either through a tutor role, or as part of the cooperative com-pletion of the activity, to articulate the thinking processes involved in success. However, much of this research has been carried out in experimental situations and cooperative learning needs careful monitoring in the classroom if meta-cognitive skills are to be developed.

Interestingly, Winograd and Hare (1988), Ashman and Conway (1989) and Spires (1990) have provided guidelines for teachers to help children develop metacognitive skills which will enable them to think about their thinking pro-cesses with respect to reading. Key teaching points include:

- providing a rationale for the importance of the reading strategy;
- explaining specifically how, when and why the strategy will be useful to pupils;
- modelling the use of the strategy;
- making sure that the pupils see that using the strategy leads to improved attainments;
- giving guidance about how pupils can monitor their own use of the strategy.

These guidelines are clearly important for all children but are particularly important for poor readers because, as noted earlier, their lack of these kinds of skills is frequently compounded with low academic self-esteem leading to a negative cycle of self-reinforcing failure.

WRITING AND SPELLING

Barr (1987) reports on a case study of a 12-year-old boy's development in spelling as a consequence of a programme of individual home tuition involving both spelling instruction and opportunities to write. The spelling tuition was basically the look/say/cover/write/check procedure. On each occasion the spelling lesson was followed by a ten-minute session of speed writing. The child's writing and spelling improved to a point where he was taken out of the remedial class and returned to the normal stream. The author places heavy stress on the close relationship between spelling

and writing and argues for the careful planning of spel,
be associated with regular opportunities to express ideas
of excessive correction of surface features.

Moore and Callias (1987) report an investigation
described as 'a severe underachiever' in spelling and re
instruction in both these areas over an 18-month period. Th
used was the Hayes Remedial Reading Scheme which cons
tured, phonic-based materials. It also uses token reinforc   ...ct
responses. Testing at the end of the programme showed that th   ...esult was
for words specifically taught. He showed a very limited ability to generalise to
words similar in structure to the learnt words. He did, however, show signs of
generalisation from the phonics taught in the reading programme. A follow-up
test after 14 months showed minimal improvement. The authors speculate that
different types of remedial programme might be appropriate for children with
different types of initial difficulty.

The three groups in Exley and Arnold's (1987) study were a group of profoundly
deaf 13-year-olds; a group of partially hearing 9½-year-olds; and a group of 7-year-
olds with normal hearing. The ability of the children in each of the groups to say,
write and understand the sentences in the sentence comprehension test was compared. A recognition test of spelling ability was also given to the children. Several
conclusions were drawn from the analysis of these data. First, it was found that all the
groups had more difficulty in writing sentences than in saying them. However, it
seems that hearing loss affects writing more than speaking. Next, it was found that
no significant differences existed in the ability of the three groups to understand the
written forms of the sentences. Finally, the spelling test results showed that the
hearing children made mainly phonic errors while the partially hearing made more
visual errors. The partially hearing, therefore, emerged as an intermediate group on
this test. The authors say that these results indicate that the hearing impaired
children's language skills are not unitary. Because they speak clearly it cannot be
assumed that they will have no difficulty in reading and writing.

Across evaluations of beginning reading programmes conducted by Aukerman
(1971) and by Evans and Carr (1985), emphasis on writing activities is repeatedly
shown to result in special gains in early reading achievement. The ability to read
does not emerge arbitrarily, but from regular and active engagement with print.
In Smith's study (1990), the language experience approach, where tutors scribe
what children say, was found to offer bridging texts in this respect. The children
know what the text is about because they have generated it, and so they do not
have to struggle for meaning. Moreover, Clark (1988) as well as Baron and
Treiman (1980) found that children who were allowed to write for themselves,
and use invented spellings based on their phonological coding, out-performed
others in traditional spelling groups. Adams (1990) points out that the challenges
of writing with invented spelling require children to think actively about print.
Other data, reported by Bond and Dykstra (1967), have indicated that exercise in
writing is a positive component of beginning reading instruction.

ING METHODS

opping (1988a) reviews research relating to peer tutoring and offers guidelines for those keen to set up the technique. In a further paper Topping (1988b) reviews ten projects which provide considerable evidence that peer-tutored paired reading has substantial promise. Both tutors and tutees appear to benefit.

Merrett (1988) reviews the 'pause, prompt, praise' technique which is developed from a firm theoretical base and used successfully by Reading Recovery teachers. It gives the child time to self-correct, it gives the child clues to meaning and praises appropriate behaviour. Studies from a variety of countries which give evidence of the effectiveness of the technique are cited in this review. Merrett stresses that even greater benefits emerge when the technique is used in conjunction with peer tutoring. Importantly, the technique requires training.

Pitchford and Story (1988) report a study where they used peer tutoring with special needs children across the curriculum. Sixteen 6–7-year-old failing readers (Neale, 1966) were included in an initial project. The use of group instruction and peer tutoring was found to combine many of the best features of mastery-based learning approaches while also giving children responsibility and status.

An evaluation of a corrective reading programme (SRA) is reported by Byron (1988). Ten 11-year-old pupils were included in the project and tested before and after the intervention, two months apart. Some gains in reading were reported. More important, using the materials captured the imagination of a demoralised special needs staff and this was suggested by Byron as probably more important than the reading gains of the children. This factor clearly cannot be ignored during innovations which involve and include teachers.

Several further studies have focused on peer tutoring. Atherley (1989) reports work with a group of 27 poor readers (France, 1979) with an average age of 10.9 years. A control group was included in this study which read independently for 15 minutes each day. The children in the experimental group were tutored for 12 weeks by other children who were trained in the 'pause, prompt, praise' technique and the children chose their partners. The experimental group made more gains than the control group and the tutors made more progress than the tutees! This study illustrates that not only do children learn from their peers, they also learn more from teaching their peers.

Medcalf (1989) also used the technique of peer tutoring in his study. Ten 9–10-year-old low progress readers were randomly assigned to two groups. One group received peer tutoring using the technique of 'pause, prompt, praise' and the other group received an individualised tape-assisted reading programme. The study continued for eight weeks. Substantial gains were reported for both groups of children, with gains being maintained and even increased at follow-up. While reading gains for the tutees on the peer-tutoring programme were similar to those of readers who were given the individualised programme, the greatest gains were made by the peer tutors.

Noting the unusual success of one school in the follow through programme in the USA, an analysis was undertaken by Meyer (1983) to see if there was anything particular that this school had done differently from the others in the programme – and there was. Specifically, it was found that pupils in this school had been frequently engaged in reading and interpreting stories from the very first day of entry to school. The single most important activity for building the knowledge and skills eventually required for successful reading is reported by Elley (1989) to be reading aloud to the children. Rather than reading a story straight through, however, Whitehurst *et al.* (1988) indicate that it seemed especially important to engage children's active involvement in the story.

It is not just reading to children that makes the difference, it is enjoying the books with them and reflecting on their form and content; it is developing and supporting children's curiosity about text and the meaning it conveys; it is encouraging them to examine print; it is starting and always inviting discussions of the meanings of words and the relationship between the text's ideas and the world beyond the book. A large body of research findings is now available from, for instance, Goldfield and Snow (1984), Johns (1984) and Teale (1984), which indicates that parents and others reading books with children are especially valuable in this respect.

Further evidence for the impact of teaching methods on children's reading ability is available from a recent study conducted by two research teams at Harvard University. Chall *et al.* (1990) followed the reading progress of children from low-income families, typically the group which are most at risk in learning-to-read programmes in US schools. Their study was characterised by statistical detail typical of the positivistic research tradition which Chall prefers. Their findings were corroborated by Snow *et al.* (1991) who studied the same group of children at the same time using an ethnographic paradigm.

Chall and Snow both observed children from low-income families in a longitudinal study. They investigated the children's abilities with respect to word recognition, reading comprehension and understanding of word meanings. The main characteristics of these children's school environment which were investigated included: the structure and organisation of their classrooms and the reading programme; how far activities focused on an understanding of what was read; the range of reading and related activities which extended the children's experience of their world; and the level of difficulty of the reading materials.

Data for these studies were collected through classroom observations, teacher questionnaires and interviews, as well as interviews with parents. As a result of their findings, Chall asked the question: What programme of reading instruction emphasis is best for this group of children? She concluded that a reading programme which is goal directed, structured and challenging, but which also provides for wide reading of 'real' books, was the kind of programme which was observed in their research to produce successful results.

For reading instruction, directed and guided by the teacher, the levels of difficulty of reading material should be challenging, neither too easy nor too hard. Fluency was found to be a critical underlying factor influencing effective reading, and wide reading was seen to be essential to its development. Importantly, it was found that time needed to be set aside in classrooms for reading; for instance, following taped stories, shared and paired reading etc. A low rate of vocabulary development was found to hinder later reading development and, in order to hasten the latter, children needed to hear challenging texts read aloud and discussed. However, this activity should not be at the expense of children's own reading time. Vocabulary development was also found to be assisted through children's own wide reading.

When contrasting approaches to reading between using reading schemes and 'real' books, Chall argues that either approach alone will not aid reading development. She presents evidence to support the view that children need access to the structure of a balanced reading programme, either published as a scheme or otherwise developed, along with the challenge and enrichment of wide reading coupled with experience of the world and opportunities for writing at length. Snow and her colleagues add that classrooms where solid gains were found in vocabulary development and reading comprehension were those with a rich variety of materials and activities used for literacy instruction.

In these combined studies challenge was a theme that recurred throughout these children's school experiences and was found to be most effective in facilitating many aspects of literacy. It was also important that teachers made time for children to read texts of some length. Not surprisingly, children who were required to write at some length became better writers and their reading comprehension improved. Therefore, Chall and Snow suggest that more instructional time needs to be given over to writing – children require opportunities to compose their own texts and to express their own ideas.

What is clear from both these studies is the account that school literacy programmes need to take of the varying amounts of literacy experience that all children bring with them into school. Where children who are perceived as having literacy difficulties differ is in their world knowledge and uses of literacy in extended contexts. If school notions of literacy ignored these differences, the children in these studies were seen to fail as their school experience progressed. The kinds of problem which these children encountered were related to reading longer connected texts, understanding new information from their reading, and writing paragraphs or stories.

READING RECOVERY

A significant contribution to our knowledge of best practice in recent years has been the emergence of Marie Clay's (1979b) Reading Recovery Programme. The impact of this programme in New Zealand has been reported by Clay (1987) and has captured the imagination of reading teachers all over the world. This prescription for teaching reading identifies children shortly after starting school who are at risk of making slow progress with learning to read. It begins with a diagnostic survey of letter-recognition abilities, knowledge of the structure and function of print, word-recognition abilities, passage comprehension and writing skills. Children are tutored individually and during the first two weeks of the programme the tutor explores what is already known by the child. The programme continues with a focus on the real reading and real writing of authentic texts. Reading takes place with texts that the child can read using the technique of rereading known stories. Writing is the principal means of developing word-analysis skills. A language experience approach to writing is used initially, although independent writing is encouraged as soon as possible. A wide variety of other literacy activities is engaged in by the tutor and the child; these include learning letter identities, clapping out syllables and segmenting words into phonemes, pointing to words while reading etc. All this takes place in a supportive, structured environment which is fine-tuned to the individual needs of each particular child.

The important feature of this programme is that it is implemented before children experience failure. Children are identified in their first year in school and the 'recovery' programme is aimed specifically at 6-year-old children. It is interesting to note that the features of the programme rest on research under-standings and current best practice. The teacher spends time identifying what each child already knows, reading and writing are developed together, children are supported in making developmental increments, and reading from books that the children can read and writing for a purpose provide material for practice.

In the USA, where Reading Recovery is attracting attention through the work of Pinnell (1989) in Ohio, there is a call for more research to determine its long-term effects, although it is acknowledged that the programme does have promise for helping large numbers of children. Pinnell argues that Reading Recovery itself is not as important as what educators can learn from it. The results reported from Ohio appear to support engaging at-risk children in reading stories and in writing stories and real messages. They support the idea that attention to detail can be effectively taught within the context of extended reading and writing. The key factor noted is the teacher's ability to make appropriate decisions based on observation of the child rather than on a list of arbitrary actions determined by a publisher.

Reading Recovery teachers, in their research, take on a stance which resembles that of learners rather than that of providers of knowledge as the teachers modify appropriately what they do with each individual child. Children are not passive recipients of instruction but active responders to teaching. If we want to know why and how children are 'failing' in reading, we have to find out what sense children are making of the task.

In Britain, Pluck (1989) reports Reading Recovery work with four 6-year-old children in Cumbria. This study found that all the tutored children had progressed well beyond the point of being the poorest readers in the class at the end of their programme, and were using much more independent strategies when reading and writing after the tutoring period was complete. More studies which document the progress of this innovation are needed, of course, but initial findings like these are encouraging. While Clay (1987) has pointed out that Reading Recovery is labour-intensive, it addresses effectively the issue of children failing to learn to read, an issue which has wide negative educational and social implications in terms of other resources if ignored at this early stage.

CONCLUSION

From all this accumulated evidence, some enduring trends are beginning to emerge. Clearly, the role of parents in their children's reading development is crucial. Schools have a responsibility here in defining this role and in supporting it with specific programmes. Children with literacy difficulties are left further and further behind their peers if schools do not take positive action early on to increase their literacy experiences in specific ways. The argument is not about whether or not to teach these children phonic strategies. What these children need is access to the wealth of experience which successful children bring with them into school, both of the world and of literacy in relation to their world.

Children with literacy difficulties are not necessarily any different from children who do not experience difficulties. However, this does not mean that they do not need, indeed demand, provision in school. What is implied from the research evidence reviewed here is much closer attention to the design and implementation of beginning reading programmes for these children. The responsibility is on teachers to identify these children as early as possible so that 'catch-up' or 'recovery' programmes can be put in place before this group of children contribute to the numbers of failing readers in our schools.

REFERENCES

Adams, M.J. (1990) *Beginning to Read: Thinking and Learning about Print*. Cambridge, MA: MIT Press.

Allington, R.L. (1984) 'Content coverage and contextual reading in reading groups', *Journal of Reading Behaviour*, 16, pp. 85–96.

Ashman, A.F. and Conway, R.N.F. (1989) *Cognitive Strategies for Special Education*. London: Routledge.

Ashman, A. and Elkins, J. (1990) 'Cooperative learning among special students', in Foot, H.C., Morgan, M. and Shute, R.H. (eds) *Children Helping Children*. Chichester: Wiley.

Atherley, C.A. (1989) '"Shared reading": an experiment in peer tutoring in the primary classroom', *Educational Studies*, 15, 1, pp. 145–153.

Aukerman, R.C. (1971) *Approaches to Beginning Reading*. New York: Wiley.

Baker, L. and Brown, A. (1984) 'Metacognitive skills in reading', in Pearson, D. (ed.) *Handbook of Reading Research*. New York: Longman.

Baron, J. and Treiman, R. (1980) 'Use of orthography in reading and learning to read', in Kavanagh, J. and Venezky, R. (eds) *Orthography, Reading and Dyslexia*. Baltimore, Maryland: University Park Press.

Barr, J. (1987) 'Spelling in writing: lessons from a case study', *Education 3–13*, 15 (2), pp. 44–50.

Beveridge, M. and Griffiths, V. (1987) 'The effect of pictures on the reading processes of less able readers: a miscue analysis approach', *Journal of Research in Reading*, 10 (1), pp. 29–42.

Boland, N. and Simmons, K. (1987) 'Attitudes to reading: a parental involvement project', *Education 3–13*, 15 (2), pp. 28–32.

Bond, G.L. and Dykstra, R. (1967) 'The cooperative research program in first-grade reading instruction', *Reading Research Quarterly*, 2, pp. 5–142.

Bookbinder, G. (1976) *Salford Sentence Reading Test*. Sevenoaks: Hodder & Stoughton.

Borkowski, J.G., Reid, M.K. and Kurtz, B.E. (1984) 'Metacognition and retardation: paradigmatic, theoretical and applied perspectives', in Brooks, P.H., Sperber, R. and McCauley, C. (eds) *Learning and Cognition in the Mentally Retarded*. Hillside, NJ: Lawrence Erlbaum.

Bridge, M. (1990) 'Learning to read – a two-year study of beginner readers', in Wade, B. (ed.) *Reading for Real*. Milton Keynes: Open University Press.

Briggs, P. and Underwood, G. (1987) 'The nature of reading ability differences in lexical access', *Journal of Research in Reading*, 10 (1), pp. 57–74.

Brimer, A. and Raban, B. (1979) *Infant Reading Test*. Newnham: Education Evaluation Enterprises.

Bryant, P. and Bradley, L. (1985) *Children's Reading Problems*. Oxford: Basil Blackwell.

Burt, C. (1954) *Graded Word Recognition Test*. London: Hodder & Stoughton.

Byron, D. (1988) 'Corrective reading in a comprehensive school: the Hartcliffe Project', *Educational and Child Psychology: Effective Learning*, 5, 4, pp. 35–41.

Chall, J.S., Jacobs, V.A. and Baldwin, L.E. (1990) *The Reading Crisis: Why Poor Children Fail*. Cambridge, MA: Harvard University Press.

Clark, M.M. (1988) 'New directions in the study of reading', in Anderson, C. (ed.) *Reading: The ABC and Beyond*. Basingstoke: Macmillan.

Clay, M.M. (1979a) *Reading: The Patterning of Complex Behaviour* (2nd edition). London: Heinemann.

Clay, M.M. (1979b) *The Early Detection of Reading Difficulties: A Diagnostic Survey with Recovery Procedures* (revised edition). London: Heinemann.

Clay, M.M. (1987) 'Implementing Reading Recovery: systematic adaptations to an educational innovation', *New Zealand Journal of Educational Studies*, 22, 1, pp. 35–58.

Cox, T. (1987) 'Slow starters versus long-term backward readers', *British Journal of Educational Psychology*, 57 (1), pp. 73–86.

DES (1990) *The Teaching and Learning of Reading in Primary Schools*. London: HMSO.

Duffy, G.D., Roehler, L.R., Meloth, M.S., Vavrus, L.G., Book, C., Putnam, J. and Wesselman, R. (1986) 'The relationship between explicit verbal explanations during reading skill instruction and student awareness and achievement; a study of reading teacher effects', *Reading Research Quarterly*, 21, 3, pp. 237–252.

Duffy, G.D., Roehler, L.R., Sivan, E., Rackliffe, G.N., Book, C., Meloth, M.S., Vavrus, L.G., Wesselman, R., Putnam, J. and Bassiri, D. (1987) 'Effects of explaining the reasoning associated with using strategies', *Reading Research Quarterly*, 22, pp. 347–368.

Elley, W.B. (1989) 'Vocabulary acquisition from listening to stories', *Reading Research Quarterly*, 24, 2, pp. 174–187.

Elliott, C.D., Murray, D.J. and Pearson, L.S. (1977) *The British Ability Scales*. Windsor: NFER.

Evans, M.A. and Carr, T.H. (1985) 'Cognitive abilities, conditions of learning and the early development of reading skill', *Reading Research Quarterly*, 20, 3, pp. 327–350.

Exley, S. and Arnold, P. (1987) 'Partially hearing and hearing children's speaking, writing and comprehension of sentences', *Journal of Communication Disorders*, 20, pp. 403–411.

Ferreiro, E. and Teberosky, A. (1983) *Literacy Before Schooling*. London: Heinemann.

France, N. (1979) *Primary Reading Test*. Windsor: NFER-Nelson.

Fredman, G. and Stevenson, J. (1988) 'Reading process in specific reading retarded and reading backward 13-year-olds', *British Journal of Experimental Psychology*, 6, pp. 97–108.

Frith, U. (1985) 'Beneath the surface of developmental dyslexia', in Patterson, K.E., Marshall, J.C. and Coltheart, M. (eds) *Surface Dyslexia: Neuro-psychological and Cognitive Studies of Phonological Reading*. London: Lawrence Erlbaum.

Gaines, K.F.S. (1989) 'The use of reading diaries as a short-term intervention strategy', *Reading* 23, 3, pp. 160–167.

Goddard, S.J. (1988) 'Parental involvement in precision teaching of reading', *Educational Psychology in Practice*, 4, 1, pp. 36–41.

Goldfield, B.A. and Snow, C.E. (1984) 'Reading books with children: the mechanics of parental influences on children's reading achievement', in Flood, J. (ed.) *Understanding Reading Comprehension*. Newark, Delaware: International Reading Association.

Greening, M. and Spenceley, J. (1987) 'Shared reading: support for the inexperienced readers', *Educational Psychology in Practice*, 3 (1), pp. 31–37.

Haller, E.P., Child, D.A. and Walberg, H.J. (1988) 'Can comprehension be taught? A quantitative synthesis of metacognitive studies', *Educational Researcher*, 17, pp. 5–8.

Hannon, P. (1987) 'A study of the effects of parental involvement in the teaching of reading on children's test performance', *British Journal of Educational Psychology*, 57, 1, pp. 56–72.

Hatcher, P., Hulme, C. and Ellis, A. (1991) *Overcoming Early Reading Failure by Integrating the Teaching of Reading and Phonological Skills: The Phonological Linkage Hypothesis*. Unpublished paper, University of York.

Hewison, J. (1988) 'The long-term effectiveness of parental involvement in reading: a follow-up to the Haringey Reading Project', *British Journal of Educational Psychology*, 58, 2, pp. 184–190.

Holligan, C. and Johnston, R.S. (1988) 'The use of phonological information by good and poor readers in memory and reading tasks', *Memory and Cognition*, 16, 6, pp. 522–532.

Inner London Education Authority (1980) *The London Reading Test*. Windsor: NFER.

Johns, J.L. (1984) 'Students' perceptions of reading: insights from research and pedagogical implications', in Downing, J. and Valtin, R. (eds) *Language Awareness and Learning to Read*. New York: Springer-Verlag.

Johnston, R.S., Rugg, M.D. and Scott, T. (1987) 'The influence of phonology on good and poor readers when reading for meaning', *Journal of Memory and Language*, 26 (1), pp. 57–68.

Johnston, R.S., Rugg, M.D. and Scott, T. (1988) 'Pseudohomophone effects in 8- and 11-year-old good and poor readers', *Journal of Research in Reading*, 11, 2, pp. 110–132.

Lake, M. (1991) 'Surveying all the factors: reading research', *Language and Learning*, 6, pp. 8–13.

Lloyd, J.W. (1988) 'Direct academic intervention in learning disabilities', in Wang, M.C., Reynolds, M.C. and Walberg, H.J. (eds) *Handbook of Special Education: Research and Practice, Vol. 2: Mildly Handicapping Conditions*. Oxford: Pergamon.

Loveday, E. and Simmons, K. (1988) 'Reading at home: does it matter what parents do?' *Reading*, 22, 2, pp. 84–88.

McGregor, A.K. (1989) 'The effect of word frequency and social class on children's reading comprehension', *Reading*, 23, 2, pp. 105–115.

Marsh, G., Friedman, M., Welch, V. and Desberg, P. (1981) 'A cognitive-developmental theory of reading acquisition', in MacKinnon, G.E. and Waller, T.G. (eds) *Reading Research: Advances in Theory and Practice, Vol.3*. New York: Academic Press.

Medcalf, J. (1989) 'Comparison of peer tutored remedial reading using the Pause, Prompt and Praise procedure with an individualised tape assisted reading programme', *Educational Psychology*, 9, 3, pp. 253–262.

Merrett, F. (1988) 'Peer tutoring and reading using the 'Pause, Prompt and Praise' techniques', *Educational and Child Psychology: Effective Learning*, 5, 4, pp. 17–23.

Meyer, L.A. (1983) 'Increased student achievement in reading: one district's strategies', *Research in Rural Education*, 45, 3, pp. 28–31.

Moon, C. and Raban, B. (1992) *A Question of Reading* (3rd edition). London: David Fulton.

Moore, V. and Callias, M. (1987) 'A systematic approach to teaching reading and spelling to a nine year old boy with severely impaired literacy skills', *Educational Psychology*, 7 (2), pp. 103–115.

Neale, M.D. (1966) *The Neale Analysis of Reading Ability*. London: Macmillan.

Palincsar, A.S. and Brown, A.L. (1984) 'Reciprocal teaching of comprehension-fostering and comprehension-monitoring activities', *Cognition and Instruction*, 1, pp. 117–125.

Paris, S.G. and Jacobs, J.E. (1984) 'The benefits of informed instruction for children's reading awareness and comprehension skills', *Child Development*, 55, pp. 2083–2093.

Paris, S.G. and Winograd, P. (1990) 'Promoting metacognition and motivation of exceptional children', *Remedial and Special Education*, 11, 6, pp. 7–15.

Pinnell, G.S. (1989) 'Reading Recovery: helping at-risk children learn to read', *The Elementary School Journal*, 90, 2, pp. 161–183.

Pitchford, M. and Story, R. (1988) 'Companion reading: group instruction, peer tutoring and in-service for teachers', *Educational and Child Psychology: Effective Learning*, 5, 4, pp. 29–34.

Pluck, M.L. (1989) 'Reading Recovery in a British infant school', *Educational Psychology*, 9, 4, pp. 347–358.

Pumfrey, P. and Fletcher, J. (1989) 'Differences in reading strategies among 7–8 year old children', *Journal of Research in Reading*, 12, 2, pp. 114–130.

Raban, B. (1984) *Observing Children Learning to Read*. Unpublished Ph.D. thesis, University of Reading.

Raban, B. (1989) 'Reading research in Great Britain in 1987', *Reading*, 23, 3, pp. 133–149.

Raban, B. (1990) 'Reading research in Great Britain in 1988', *Reading*, 24, 3, pp. 107–127.

Robson, C. and Whitley, S. (1989) 'Sharing stories: parents' involvement in reading with inner-city nursery children', *Reading*, 23, 1, pp. 23–27.

Rowe, K.L. (1991) 'The influence of reading activity at home on students' attitudes towards reading, classroom attentiveness and reading achievement: an application of structural equation modelling', *British Journal of Educational Psychology*, 61, 1, pp. 19–35.

Scruggs, T.E. and Brigham, F.J. (1990) 'The challenges of metacognitive instruction', *Remedial and Special Education*, 11, 6, pp. 16–18.

Seymour, P.H.K. and MacGregor, C.J. (1984) 'Developmental dyslexia: a cognitive experimental analysis of phonological, morphemic and visual impairments', *Cognitive Neuropsychology*, 1, 1, pp. 43–83.

Simmons, K. (1987) 'Children's story telling: what it can tell us about reading difficulties', *Reading*, 21 (1), pp. 43–52.

Smith, B. (1990) *Evaluating the Use of Dictated Stories as Reading Text for Poor Secondary Readers*. Unpublished Ph.D. thesis, Middlesex Polytechnic.

Snow, C.E., Barnes, W.S., Chandler, J., Goodman, I.F. and Hemphill, L. (1991) *Unfulfilled Expectations: Home and School Influences on Literacy*. Cambridge, MA: Harvard University Press.

Spires, H. (1990) 'Metacognition and reading: implications for instruction', *Reading*, 24, 3, pp. 151–165.

Stanovich, K.E. (1980) 'Towards an interactive–compensatory model of individual differences in the development of reading fluency', *Reading Research Quarterly*, 16, 1, pp. 32–71.

Stanovich, K.E. (1986) 'Matthew effects in reading: some consequences of individual differences in the acquisition of literacy', *Reading Research Quarterly*, 21, 4, pp. 360–406.

Stuart, M. and Coltheart, M. (1988) 'Does reading develop in a sequence of stages?', *Cognition*, 30, pp. 139–181.

Teale, W.H. (1984) 'Reading to young children: its significance for literacy development', in Goelman, H., Oberg, A. and Smith, F. (eds) *Awakening to Literacy*. London: Heinemann.

Topping, K. (1988a) 'An introduction to peer tutoring', *Educational and Child Psychology: Effective Learning*, 5, 4, pp. 6–16.

Topping, K. (1988b) 'Peer tutoring of reading using paired reading', *Educational and Child Psychology: Effective Learning*, 5, 4, pp. 24–28.

Wang, M.C. (1990) 'Learning characteristics of students with special needs and the provision of effective schooling', in Wang, M.C., Reynolds, M.C. and Walberg, H.J. *Special Education: Research and Practice*. Oxford: Pergamon.

Webb, N.M. (1982) 'Student interaction and learning in small groups', *Review of Educational Research*, 52, pp. 421–445.

Wells, G., Barnes, S. and Wells, J. (1984) *Linguistic Influences on Educational Attainment. Final Report to DES Home and School Influences on Educational Attainment Project*. University of Bristol.

Wheldall, K., Merrett, F. and Colmar, S. (1987) 'Pause, Prompt and Praise' for parents and peers: effective tutoring of low progress readers', *Support for Learning*, 21 (1), pp. 5–12.

Whitehurst, G.J., Falco, F., Lonigan, C.J., Fischal, J.E., De Baryshe, B.D., Valdez-Manchaca, M.C. and Caulfield, M. (1988) 'Accelerating language development through picture book reading', *Developmental Psychology*, 24, pp. 552–559.

Wilson, J. and Simmons, K. (1989) 'Right to read? Shared reading and children with severe learning difficulties', *Educational Psychology in Practice*, 5, 1, pp. 30–33.

Winograd, P. and Hare, V.C. (1988) 'Direct instruction of reading comprehension strategies: the nature of teacher explanation', in Goetz, E.T., Alexander, P. and Weinstein, C. (eds) *Learning and Study Strategies: Assessment, Instruction and Evaluation*. New York: Academic Press.

Young, D. (1976) *SPAR Spelling and Reading Tests*. London: Hodder & Stoughton.

Conclusion

The chapters in this book, of course, for all their breadth and the range of issues they cover, do not provide a complete analysis of the field encompassed by the term 'Primary English'. There are areas which have only been touched upon and others which have not received mention at all. These no doubt will be glaringly obvious to readers and we do not intend at this point to list them, or to apologise for their absence. A book can only do so much. Rather, we want to speculate a little on the future of this rapidly developing, and perennially controversial, field. If a similar volume to this were to be compiled ten years hence, what issues might still be regarded as 'state of the art'?

There can be little doubt that, unless things change in unforeseeable ways, the issue of assessment will still be engaging the minds of teachers and researchers for many years to come. This is so for two reasons. First, we have not yet come to an agreement about exactly what in the development of language and literacy it is important to assess. This is to say no more than that there is still considerable debate about the exact nature of these processes. One's view about what is crucial in an activity such as reading, for example, naturally determines what one prioritises for assessment. Second, there is always likely to be a tension between desirability and feasibility in assessment. As we argued in Chapter 11 of *Literacy and Language in the Primary Years*, assessment strategies are often required to serve too many purposes at once and teachers must be forgiven for questioning whether it is in fact possible for them to meet all the demands made by the range of interested parties they must appease. There is clearly a limit to what can be done in practical classroom situations if the assessment tail is not to wag too strongly the teaching dog. Assessment clearly must be an integral part of successful teaching, but achieving an appropriate balance of attention is extraordinarily difficult, and likely to remain so for some time.

Another issue likely to persist is that of the role of oral language in classroom learning. Of course, in theoretical terms, this is well established. Models of learning as an active, constructive and, perhaps above all, social enterprise place tremendous emphasis upon the place of talk. Talk between learners is seen as vital in the construction of shared knowledge, and talk between teachers and learners as crucial in the provision of the 'scaffolding' necessary to support and develop the understanding of these learners. Yet problems remain in the extent to which teachers are able to use these insights given the realities of classroom life. As Edwards and Westgate (1987) argue in their comprehensive review of research into talk in classrooms, it is difficult for teachers to foreground talk in the learning process in the way current learning theory would suggest for three main reasons. First, the sheer numbers of children they have to deal with forces a large proportion of classroom talk to be devoted to management rather than learning matters. Second, the curriculum they are required to teach, being largely content-based, militates in favour of a large proportion of 'transmission' talk and questioning. Third, many teachers also have 'a less than whole-hearted belief in the value that pupils' talk has for their learning' (Edwards and Westgate, 1987: 174). Of these three reasons, only the third has begun to change for the better by widespread current understandings such as those promulgated by the National Oracy Project (Norman, 1992). (The first two, indeed, may be getting worse.) The problems involved in the development of a more talk-based classroom ethos are therefore likely to occupy us for some considerable time. These problems will most likely be of implementation rather than of theoretical origin.

In parallel with the issue of talk in learning, that of the role of literacy in learning is also likely to remain of interest. The majority of research and professional attention has always tended to be given to the learning and teaching of the processes involved in literacy, rather than to the ways in which these processes function as media and mechanisms of learning. The last 10 to 15 years have seen an enormous amount of energy being put into developing an understanding of the emergence of literacy and it is now accepted that this process begins very early indeed in a child's life. A priority during the next ten years is almost certain to be to establish a more rounded theoretical and practical understanding of how reading and writing work and can best be developed as tools for learning. Such an understanding will need to be curriculum-wide and will need to give much greater attention to the structure and functions of text, particularly non-fiction text. As Christie (1990) has convincingly argued, the nature of literacy itself has changed considerably since the Second World War and these changes are likely only to accelerate. In order to prepare children for the literacy demands of the twenty-first century, schools need to place much greater emphasis on the awareness of textual structure and its relationship to purpose and social context. Such an approach offers a challenge to the narrative-dominated textual experience currently offered to most children in primary schools and in many ways assumes more explicit teaching of text structures and genres than might be currently fashionable. The EXEL Project, based at the University of Exeter, has begun to examine strategies for teaching children to use non-fiction texts more effectively. (See Wray, 1992 for some initial suggestions in this area.)

Whatever the issues which will dominate thinking about literacy and language over the next few years, one thing is, of course, guaranteed. Debate and discussion about this area will maintain its ferocity and its fascination. In the introduction of the National Curriculum in the United Kingdom, no area has caused such public debate as the requirements in English, and this picture has been repeated world-wide. The teaching of literacy and language has always been accompanied by argument and controversy, partly because it is recognisably such an important aspect of children's learning and partly because it is so interesting. This state of affairs is, thankfully, unlikely to change very much during the next decade and we can confidently predict further fascinating debates to come.

REFERENCES

Christie, F. (1990) *Literacy for a Changing World*. Victoria: Australian Council for Educational Research.

Edwards, A. and Westgate, D. (1987) *Investigating Classroom Talk*. Lewes: Falmer Press.

Norman, K. (ed.) (1992) *Thinking Voices*. Sevenoaks: Hodder & Stoughton.

Wray, D. (ed.) (1992) *Reading: Beyond the Story*. Widnes: United Kingdom Reading Association.

Name index

Subject index

Praise for *Everything Good Will Come*

"*Everything Good Will Come* is like listening to an old friend recounting and bringing up-to-date and to life the happenings in our beloved city of Lagos. From Ikoyi bordering the Marina, to the south nearing Yoruba towns, every part is reawakened and alive: red, throbbing, like the heartbeat of a healthy newborn.
I was sorry when I came to the end."
Buchi Emecheta

"There is wit, intelligence and a delicious irreverence in this book. But it is Sefi Atta's courage in choosing to look at her fictional world through fiercely feminist lenses that I most admired."
Chimamanda Ngozi Adichie

"Sefi Atta's first novel is a beautifully paced stroll in the shoes of a woman growing up in a country struggling to find its post-Independence identity. The main characters are well realized, and the supporting cast—campaigning journalist, put-upon mother-in-law, co-wives in a polygamous marriage, stroppy secretary—avoid caricature. The relaxed tempo of the narrative allows for proper character development. *Everything Good Will Come* depicts the struggles women face in a conservative society. This is convincing; more remarkable is what the novel has to say about the need to speak out when all around is falling apart."
The Times Literary Supplement

"*Everything Good Will Come* is an original, witty coming-of-age tale: *Tom Sawyer* meets *Jane Eyre*, with Nigerian girls. Reading *Everything Good…* you can feel the dust and the sun… an iridescent introduction to a fascinating nation."
The Observer

"A literary masterpiece… *Everything Good Will Come* put me into a spell from the first page to the very last… It portrays the complicated society and history of Nigeria through brilliant prose."
World Literature Today

"Skillful... impressive debut novel... Thematically, Atta's work is wide-ranging and yet powerfully focused, the different areas of concern drawn together so that they inform each other... Again and again her writing tugs at the heart, at the conscience. At the same time, reflecting the resilience of the Logosians whose lives she explores, humour is almost constant, effervescent, most often with a satirical slant... There are no delusions in Atta's novel, no romanticisation or overstating of a case. Her work stands as a paean to her central character's strengths and her determination to combat oppression."
The Sunday Independent

"Atta's distinctive coming-of-age novel... will appeal to all readers interested in contemporary women's stories and/or African culture. Recommended."
Choice

"This lively first novel breaks new ground with a close-up, honest story of a contemporary Yoruba woman's coming-of-age in Lagos. Nigerian-born author Atta now lives in the U.S., and she offers a hilarious if angry take on the Western view of dark, noble, savage Africa 'with snakes and vines and ooga-booga dialect'. Yet with all the fast talk, this is a heartfelt drama of family, friendship, and community, especially among women. Enitan Taiwo always knows how privileged she is in her lawyer father's home. She sees the poverty and knows about the brutal military dictatorship. But it is not until politics invades her own family that she defies her kind husband and moves from bystander to activist. Never reverential, Enitan's first-person narrative reveals the dynamic diversity within the city, the differences across class, generation, gender, faith, language, tradition, and individual character. Differences, yes, but sometimes connections, too."
Booklist

"[A] book of spirit and an inspiration for anyone who has ever been in opposition to societal or cultural norms."
Bloomsbury Review

Sefi Atta

EVERYTHING GOOD WILL COME

This edition first published in 2019 by
Myriad Editions
www.myriadeditions.com

Myriad Editions
An imprint of New Internationalist Publications
The Old Music Hall, 106–108 Cowley Rd, Oxford OX4 1JE

First printing
1 3 5 7 9 10 8 6 4 2

First published in 2005 by
Interlink Books, USA

A CIP catalogue record for this book
is available from the British Library

ISBN (pbk): 978-1-912408-52-8
ISBN (ebk): 978-1-912408-53-5

Printed and bound in Great Britain
by Clays Ltd, Elcograf S.p.A.

*For my dearest, Gboyega,
and our sweetest, Temi*

Also by Sefi Atta

1971

From the beginning I believed whatever I was told, downright lies even, about how best to behave, although I had my own inclinations. At an age when other Nigerian girls were masters at ten-ten, the game in which we stamped our feet in rhythm and tried to outwit partners with sudden knee jerks, my favorite moments were spent sitting on a jetty pre000g to fish. My worst was to hear my mother's shout from her kitchen window: "Enitan, come and help in here."

I'd run back to the house. We lived by Lagos Lagoon. Our yard stretched over an acre and was surrounded by a high wooden fence that could drive splinters into careless fingers. I played, carelessly, on the West side because the East side bordered the mangroves of Ikoyi Park and I'd once seen a water snake slither past. Hot, hot were the days as I remember them, with runny-egg sunshine and brief breezes. The early afternoons were for eat and sleep breaks: eat a heavy lunch, sleep like a drunk. The late afternoons, after homework, I spent on our jetty, a short wooden promenade I could walk in three steps, if I took long enough strides to strain the muscles between my thighs.

I would sit on its cockle-plastered edge and wait for the water to lap at my feet, fling my fishing rod, which was made from tree branch, string, and a cork from one of my father's discarded wine bottles. Sometimes fishermen came close, rowing in a rhythm that pleased me more than chewing on fried tripe; their skins charred, almost gray from sun-dried sea salt. They spoke in the warble of island people, yodeling across their canoes. I was never tempted to jump into the lagoon as they did. It gave off the smell of raw fish and was the kind of dirty brown I knew would taste like vinegar. Plus, everyone knew about the currents that could drag a person away. Bodies usually showed up days later, bloated, stiff and rotten. True.

It wasn't that I had big dreams of catching fish. They wriggled too much and I couldn't imagine watching another living being suffocate. But my parents had occupied everywhere else with their fallings out; their trespasses unforgivable. Walls could not save me from the shouting. A pillow, if I stuffed my head under it, could not save me. My hands could not, if I clamped them over my ears and stuffed my head under a pillow. So there it was, the jetty, my protectorate, until the day my mother decided it was to be demolished.

The priest in her church had a vision of fishermen breaking into our house: They would come at night, *labalaba*. They would come unarmed, *yimiyimi*. They would steal valuables, *tolotolo*.

The very next day, three workmen replaced our jetty with a barbed wire fence and my mother kept watch over them; the same way she watched our neighbors; the same way she checked our windows for evil spirits outside at night; the same way she glared at our front door long after my father had walked out. I knew he would be furious. He was away on a law conference and when he returned and saw her new fence, he ran outside shouting like a crazed man. Nothing, nothing, would stop my mother, he said, until she'd destroyed everything in our house, because of that church of hers. What kind of woman was she? What kind of selfish, uncaring, woman was she?

He enjoyed that view. Warm, breezy evenings on the veranda overlooking it is how I remember him, easy as the cane chair in which he sat. He was usually there in the dry season, which lasted most of the year; scarcely in the chilly harmattan, which straddled Christmas and New Year, and never in the swampy rainy season that made our veranda floor slippery over the summer vacation. I would sit on the steps and watch him and his two friends: Uncle Alex, a sculptor, who smoked a pipe that smelled like melted coconut, and Uncle Fatai, who made me laugh because his name fitted his roly-poly face. He too was a lawyer like my father and they had all been at Cambridge together. Three musketeers in the heart of darkness, they called themselves there; they stuck together and hardly anyone spoke to them. Sometimes they frightened me with their stories of western Nigeria (which my father called the Wild West), where people threw car tires over other people and set them on fire because they belonged to different political factions. Uncle Alex blamed the British for the fighting: "Them and their bloody empire. Come here and divide our country like one of their bloody tea cakes. Driving on the left side of the bloody road..."

The day the Civil War broke out, he delivered the news. Uncle Fatai arrived soon afterward and they bent heads as if in prayer to listen to the radio. Through the years, from their arguments about federalists, secessionists, and bloody British, I'd amassed as much knowledge about the events in my country as any seven-year-old could. I knew that our first Prime Minister was killed by a Major General, that the Major General was soon killed, and that we had another Major General heading our country. For a while the palaver had stopped, and now it seemed the Biafrans were trying to split our country in two.

Uncle Fatai broke the silence. "Hope our boys finish them off."

"What the hell are you talking about?" Uncle Alex asked.

"They want a fight," Uncle Fatai said. "We'll give them a fight."

Uncle Alex prodded his chest, almost toppling him over. "Can you fight? Can you?" My father tried to intervene but he warned, "Keep out of this, Sunny."

My father eventually asked Uncle Alex to leave. He patted my head as he left and we never saw him in our house again.

Over the next months, I would listen to radio bulletins on how our troops were faring against the Biafrans. I would hear the slogan: "To keep Nigeria one is a task that must be done." My father would ask me to hide under my bed whenever we had

4

bomb raid alerts. Sometimes I heard him talking about Uncle Alex; how he'd known beforehand there was going to be a civil war; how he'd joined the Biafrans and died fighting for them even though he hated guns.

I loved my uncle Alex; thought that if I had to marry a man, it would be a man like him, an artist, who cared too much or not at all.

He gave my father the nickname Sunny, though my father's real name was Bandele Sunday Taiwo. Now, everyone called my father Sunny, like they called my mother Mama Enitan, after me, though her real name was Arin. I was their first child, their only child now, since my brother died. He lived his life between sickle cell crises. My mother joined a church to cure him, renounced Anglicanism and herself, it seemed, because one day, my brother had another crisis and she took him there for healing. He died, three years old. I was five.

In my mother's church they wore white gowns. They walked around on bare feet, and danced to drums. They were baptized in a stream of holy water and drank from it to cleanse their spirits. They believed in spirits; evil ones sent by other people to wreak havoc, and reborn spirits, which would not stay long on earth. Their incantations, tireless worship and praise. I could bear even the sight of my mother throwing her hands up and acting as I'd never seen her act in an Anglican church. But I was sure that if the priest came before me and rolled his eyeballs back as he did when he was about to have a vision, that would be the end of me.

He had a bump on his forehead, an expression as if he were sniffing something bad. He pronounced his visions between chants that sounded like the Yoruba words for butterfly, dung beetle, and turkey: *labalaba, yimiyimi, tolotolo.* He smelled of incense. The day he stood before me, I kept my eyes on the hem of his cassock. I was a reborn spirit, he said, like my brother, and

5

my mother would have to bring me for cleansing. I was too young, she said. My time would soon come, he said. Turkey, turkey, turkey.

The rest of the day I walked around with the dignity of the aged and troubled, held my stomach in until I developed cramps. Death would hurt, I knew, and I did not want to see my brother like that, as a ghost. My father only had to ask how I was feeling, when I collapsed before him. "I'm going to die," I said.

He asked for an explanation.

"You're not going back there again," he said.

Sundays after that, I spent at home. My mother would go off to church, and my father would leave the house, too. Then Bisi, our house girl, would sneak next door to see Akanni, the driver who blared his juju music, or he'd come to see her and they would both go off to the servants' quarters, leaving me with Baba, our gardener, who worked on Sundays.

At least, during the Civil War, Bisi would sometimes invite me over to hear Akanni's stories about the war front far away. How Biafran soldiers stepped on land mines that blew up their legs like crushed tomatoes; how Biafran children ate lizard flesh to stay alive. The Black Scorpion was one of Nigeria's hero soldiers. He wore a string of charms around his neck and bullets ricocheted off his chest. I was old enough to listen to such tales without being frightened, but was still too young to be anything but thrilled by them. When the war ended three years later, I missed them.

Television in those days didn't come on until six o'clock in the evening. The first hour was news and I never watched the news, except that special day when the Apollo landed on the moon. After that, children in school said you could get Apollo, a form of conjunctivitis, by staring at an eclipse too long. Tarzan, Zorro, Little John, and the entire Cartwright family on *Bonanza* were there, with their sweet and righteous retaliations, to tell me any other fact I needed to know about the world. And oblivious to any biased messages I was receiving, I sympathized with Tarzan (those awful natives!), thought Indians were terrible people and memorized the happy jingles of foreign multi-national companies: "Mobil keeps your engine—Beep, beep, king of the road." If Alfred Hitchcock came on, I knew it was time to go to bed. Or if it was Doris Day. I couldn't bear her song, "Que Sera."

I approached adolescence with an extraordinary number of body aches, finished my final year of primary school, and began the long wait for secondary school. Secondary school didn't start until early October, so the summer vacation stretched longer than normal. The rains poured, dried up, and each day passed like the one before unless something special happened, like the afternoon Baba found iguana eggs, or the morning a rabid dog bit our night watchman, or the evening Bisi and Akanni fought. I heard them shouting and rushed to the servants' quarters to watch.

Akanni must have thought he was Muhammad Ali. He was shadow boxing around Bisi. "What's my name? What's my name?" Bisi lunged forward and slapped his face. He reached for her collar and ripped her blouse. "My bress? My bress?" She spat in his face and grabbed the gold chain around his neck. They both crashed into the dust and didn't stop kicking till Baba lay flat out on the ground. "No more," he said. "No more, I beg of you."

Most days were not that exciting. And I was beginning to get bored of the wait when, two weeks to the end of the vacation, everything changed. It was the third Sunday of September 1971, late in the afternoon. I was playing with my catapult when I mistakenly struck Baba as he was trimming the lawn. He chased after me with his machete and I ran into the barbed wire fence, snagging my sleeve. Yoruba tradition has us believe that Nature heralds the beginning of a person's transition: to life, adulthood, and death. A rooster's crow, sudden rainfall, a full moon, seasonal changes. I had no such salutations as I remember it.

"Serves you right," came a girl's voice.

A nose appeared between the wide gap in the fence, followed by a brown eye. I freed my sleeve from the barbed wire fence and rubbed my elbow.

"For running around like that," she said. "With no head or tail. It serves you right that you got chooked."

She looked nothing like the Bakare children who lived next door. I'd seen them through the wide gap in our fence and they were as dark as me; younger, too. Their father had two wives who organized outdoor cooking jamborees. They always looked pregnant, and so did he in his flowing robes. He was known as Engineer Bakare. He was Uncle Fatai's friend and Uncle Fatai called him Alhaji Bakare, because he'd been on pilgrimage to Mecca. To us he was Chief Bakare. He threw a huge party after his chieftancy ceremony last year and no one could sleep that night for the sound of his juju band badabooming through our walls. Typical Lagos people, my father said. They made merry till they dropped, or until their neighbors did.

"I'm Sheri," she said, as if I'd asked for her name.

"I've never seen you before," I said.

"So?"

She had a sharp mouth, I thought, as she burst into giggles.

"Can I come to your house?" she asked.

I glanced around the yard, because my mother didn't want me playing with the Bakare children.

"Come."

I was bored. I waited by the barbed wire fence, forgot about my torn sleeve, even about Baba who had chased me. He, apparently, had forgotten me too, because he was cutting

8

grass by the other fence. Minutes later, she walked in. Just as I thought, she was a half-caste. She wore a pink skirt and her white top ended just above her navel. With her short afro, her face looked like a sunflower. I noticed she wore

"How old are you?" I accused.

"Eleven," she said.

"Me too."

"Eh? Small girl like you?" she said.

At least I was a decent eleven-year-old. She barely reached my shoulders, even in her high heel shoes. I told her my birthday was next January, but she said I was still her junior. Her birthday was two months earlier, in November. "I'm older, I'm senior. Don't you know? That's how it is. My younger brothers and sisters call me Sister Sheri at home."

"I don't believe you."

"It's true," she said.

Breeze rustled through the hibiscus patch. She eyed me up and down.

"Did you see the executions on television last night?"

"What executions?"

"The armed robbers."

"No."

I was not allowed to watch; my father was against capital punishment.

She smiled. "Ah, it was good. They shot them on the beach. Tied them, covered their eyes. One, two, three."

"Dead?"

"*Pafuka*," she said and dropped her head to one side. I imagined the scene on the beach where public executions were held. The photographs usually showed up in the newspapers a day later.

"Where is your mother from?" I asked.

"England."

9

"Does she live there?"

"She's dead."

She spoke as if telling the time: three o'clock sharp, four o'clock dead. Didn't she care? I felt ashamed about my brother's death, as if I had a bad leg that people could tease me about.

"*Yei,*" she exclaimed. She'd spotted a circus of flying fish on the lagoon. I, too, watched them flipping over and diving in. They rarely surfaced from the water. They disappeared and the water was still again.

"Do you have brothers and sisters?" she asked.

"Nope."

"You must be spoiled rotten."

"No, I'm not."

"Yes, you are. Yes, you are. I can see it in your face."

She spun around and began to boast. She was the oldest of the Bakare children. She had seven brothers and sisters. She would be starting boarding school in two weeks, in another city, and she...

"I got into Royal College," I said, to shut her up.

"Eyack! It's all girls!"

"It's still the best school in Lagos."

"All girls is boring."

"Depends how you look at it," I said, quoting my father.

Through the fence we heard Akanni's juju music. Sheri stuck her bottom out and began to wriggle. She dived lower and wormed up.

"You like juju music?" I asked.

"Yep. Me and my grandma, we dance to it."

"You dance with your grandma?"

"I live with her."

The only grandparent I'd known was my father's mother, who was now dead, and she scared me because of the gray-ish-white films across her pupils. My mother said she got them

10

from her wickedness. The music stopped.

"These flowers are nice," Sheri said, contemplating them as she might an array of chocolates. She plucked one of them and planted it behind her ear.

"Is it pretty?"

I nodded. She looked for more and began to pick them one by one. Soon she had five hibiscus in her hair. She picked her sixth as we heard a cry from across the yard. Baba was charging toward us with his machete in the air. "You! Get away from there!"

Sheri caught sight of him and screamed. We ran round the side of the house and hobbled over the gravel on the "Who was that?" Sheri asked, rubbing her chest.

I took short breaths. "Our gardener."

"I'm afraid of him."

"Baba can't do anything. He likes to scare people."

She sucked her teeth. "Look at his legs crooked as crab's, his lips red as a monkey's bottom."

We rolled around the gravel. The hibiscus toppled out of Sheri's afro and she kicked her legs about, relishing her laughter and prolonging mine. She recovered first and wiped her eyes with her fingers.

"Do you have a best friend?" she asked.

"No."

"Then, I will be your best friend." She patted her chest. "Every day, until we go to school."

"I can only play on Sundays," I said.

My mother would drive her out if she ever saw her.

She shrugged. "Next Sunday then. Come to my house if you like."

"All right," I said.

Who would know? She was funny, and she was also rude, but that was probably because she had no home training.

She yelled from our gates. "I'll call you *aburo*, little sister, from now on. And I'll beat you at ten-ten, wait and see."

It's a stupid game, I was about to say, but she'd disappeared behind the cement column. Didn't anyone tell her she couldn't wear high heels? Lipstick? Any of that? Where was her respect for an old man like Baba? She was the spoiled one. Sharp mouth and all.

Baba was raking the grass when I returned to the back yard.

"I'm going to tell your mother about her," he said.

I stamped my foot in frustration. "But she's my friend."

"How can she be your friend? You've just met her, and your mother does not know her."

"She doesn't have to know her."

I'd known him all my life. How could he tell? He made a face as if the memory of Sheri had left a bad taste in his mouth. "Your mother will not like that one."

"Please, don't tell. Please."

I knelt and pressed my palms together. It was my best trick ever to wear him out.

"All right," he said. "But I must not see you or her anywhere near those flowers again."

"Never," I said, scrambling to my feet. "See? I'm going inside. You won't find me near them."

I walked backward into the house. Baba's legs really were like crab's, I thought, scurrying through the living room. Then I bumped my shin on the corner of a chair and hopped the rest of the way to my bedroom. God was already punishing me.

My suitcase was under my bed. It was a fake leather one, large enough to accommodate me if I curled up tight, but now it was full. I dragged it out. I had two weeks to go before leaving home, and had started packing the contents a month early: a mosquito net, bed sheets, flip-flops, a flashlight. The props for my make-believe television adverts: bathing soap, toothpaste, a bag of sanitary towels. I wondered what I would do with those.

As I stood before my mirror, I traced the grooves around my plaits. Sheri's afro was so fluffy, it moved as she talked. I grabbed a comb from my table and began to undo my plaits. My arms ached by the time I finished and my hair flopped over my face. From my top drawer, I took a red marker and painted my lips. At least my cheeks were smooth, unlike hers. She had a spray of rashes and was so fair-skinned. People her color got called "Yellow Pawpaw" or "Yellow Banana" in school.

In school you were teased for being yellow or fat; for being Moslem or for being dumb; for stuttering or wearing a bra and for being Igbo, because it meant that you were Biafran or knew people who were. I was painting my finger nails with the marker pen, recalling other teasable offenses, when my mother walked in. She was wearing her white church gown.

"You're here?" she said.

"Yes," I said.

In her church gowns I always thought my mother resembled a column. She stood tall and squared her shoulders, even as a child, she said. She would not play rough, or slump around, so why did I? Her question often prompted me to walk with my back straight until I forgot.

"I thought you would be outside," she said.

I patted my hair down. Her own hair was in two neat cornrows and she narrowed her eyes as if there were sunlight in my room.

"Ah-ah? What is this? You're wearing lipstick?"

I placed my pen down, more embarrassed than scared.

She beckoned. "Let me see."

Her voice softened when she saw the red ink. "You shouldn't be coloring your mouth at your age. I see you're also packing your suitcase again. Maybe you're ready to leave this house."

13

My gaze reached the ceiling.

"Where is your father?"

"I don't know."

"Did he say when he will be back?"

"No."

She surveyed the rest of my room. "Clean this place up."

"Yes, Mummy."

"And come and help me in the kitchen afterward. I want to speak to you later on tonight. Make sure you wash your mouth before you come."

I pretended to be preoccupied with the contents of my dressing table until she left. Using a pair of scissors, I scraped the red ink from my nails. What did she want to speak to me about? Baba couldn't have told.

My mother never had a conversation with me; she talked and knew that I was listening. I always was. The mere sound of her footsteps made me breathe faster. She hardly raised a hand to me, unlike most mothers I knew, who beat their children with tree branches, but she didn't have to. I'd been caned before, for daydreaming in class, with the side of a ruler, on my knuckles, and wondered if it wasn't an easier punishment than having my mother look at me as if she'd caught me playing with my own poop. Her looks were hard to forget. At least caning welts eventually disappeared.

Holy people had to be unhappy or strict, or a mixture of both, I'd decided. My mother and her church friends, their priest with his expression as if he was sniffing something bad. There wasn't a choir mistress I'd seen with a friendly face, and even in our old Anglican church people had generally looked miserable as they prayed. I'd come to terms with these people as I'd come to terms with my own natural sinfulness. How many mornings had I got up vowing to be holy, only to succumb to happiness by midday, laughing and running helter-skelter? I wanted to be holy; I just couldn't remember.

I was frying plantains in the kitchen with my mother that evening, when oil popped from the frying pan and struck my wrist.

"Watch what you're doing," she said.

"Sorry," Bisi said, peeping up from the pots she was washing.

Bisi often said sorry for no reason. I lifted the fried plantains from the pan and smacked them down with my spatula. Oil spitting, chopping knives. Onions. Kitchen work was ugly. When I was older I would starve myself so I wouldn't have to cook. That was my main plan.

A noise outside startled me. It was my father coming through the back door.

"I knock on my front door these days and no one will answer," he muttered.

The door creaked open and snapped shut behind him. Bisi rushed to take his briefcase and he shooed her away. I smiled at my father. He was always miserable after work, especially when he returned from court. He was skinny with a voice that cracked and I pitied him whenever he complained: "I'm working all day, to put clothes on your back, food in your stomach, pay your school fees. All I ask is for peace when I get home. Instead you give me *wahala*. Daddy can I buy ice-cream. Daddy can I buy Enid Blyton. Daddy my jeans are torn. Daddy, Daddy, Daddy. You want me dead?"

He loosened his tie. "I see your mother is making you understudy her again."

I took another plantain and sliced its belly open, hoping for more of his sympathy. My mother shook a pot of stew on the stove and lifted its lid to inspect the contents.

"It won't harm her to be in here," she said.

I eased the plantain out and began to slice it into circles.

My father opened the refrigerator and pulled out a bottle of beer. Again Bisi rushed to his aid, and this time he allowed her to open the bottle.

"You should tell her young girls don't do this anymore," he said.

"Who said?" my mother asked.

"And if she asks where you learned such nonsense, tell her from your father and he's for the liberation of women."

He stood at attention and saluted. My father was not a serious man, I thought.

"All women except your wife," my mother said.

Bisi handed him his glass of beer. I thought he hadn't heard because he began to drink. He lowered the glass. "I've never asked you to be in here cooking for me."

"Ah, well," she said, wiping her hands with a dish cloth. "But you never ask me not to either."

He nodded in agreement. "It is hard to compete with your quest for martyrdom."

My mother made a show of inspecting the fried plantains. She pointed to the pan and I emptied too many plantain pieces into it. The oil hissed and fumes filled the air.

Whenever my father spoke good English like that, I knew he was angry. I didn't understand what he meant most times. This time, he placed his empty glass on the table and grabbed his briefcase.

"Don't wait up for me."

My mother followed him. As they left the kitchen, I crept to the door to spy on them. Bisi turned off the tap to hear their conversation and I rounded on her with all the rage a whisper could manage: "Stop listening to people's private conversations! You're always listening to people's private conversations!"

She snapped her fingers at me, and I snapped mine back and edged toward the door hinge.

My parent's quarrels were becoming more senseless; not more frequent or more loud. One wrong word from my father could bring on my mother's rage. He was a wicked man. He had always been a wicked man. She would shout Bible passages at him. He would remain calm. At times like this, I could pity my mother, if only for my father's expression. It was the same as the boys in school who lifted your skirt and ran. They looked just as confused once the teacher got hold of their ears.

My mother rapped the dining table. "Sunny, whatever you're doing out there, God is watching you. You can walk out of that door, but you cannot escape His judgment."

My father fixed his gaze on the table. "I can't speak for Him, but I remember He will not be mocked. You want to use the Bible as a shield against everyone? Use it. One day we will both meet our maker. I will tell him all I have done. Then you can tell him what you have done."

He walked away in the direction of their bedroom. My mother returned to the kitchen. I thought she might scold me after she found my plantains burning, but she didn't. I hurried over and flipped them.

A frown may have chewed her face up, but one time my mother had smiled. I'd seen black and white photographs of her, her hair pressed and curled and her eyebrows penciled into arches. She was a chartered secretary and my father was in his final year of university when they met. Many men tried to chase her. Many, he said, until he wrote her one love letter. One, he boasted, and the rest didn't stand a chance. "Your mother was the best dancer around. The best dressed girl ever. The tiniest waist, I'm telling you. The tiniest. I could get my hand around it, like this, before you came along and spoiled it."

He would simulate how he struggled to hug her. My mother was not as big as he claimed. She was plump, in the way mothers

17

were plump; her arms shook like jelly. My father no longer told the joke and I was left to imagine that it was true that she had once showed him affection. If she didn't anymore it was because it was there in the Bible: God got jealous.

After dinner I went to their bedroom to wait. I still had no idea what my mother wanted to speak to me about. My father had left the air-conditioner on and it blew remnants of mosquito repellent and cologne into my face. Their mosquito net hung over me and I inspected my shin which had developed a bump since my collision with the sofa.

My mother walked in. Already I felt like crying. Could Baba have told? If so, he was responsible for the trouble I was in.

My mother sat opposite me. "Do you remember, when you used to come to church with me, that some of the sisters would miss church for a week?"

"Yes, Mummy."

"Do you know why they missed church?"

"No."

"Because they were unclean," she said.

Immediately I looked at the air-conditioner. My mother began to speak in Yoruba. She told me the most awful thing about blood and babies and why it was a secret.

"I will not marry," I said.

"You will," she said.

"I will not have children."

"Yes, you will. All women want children."

Sex was a filthy act, she said, and I must always wash myself afterward. Tears filled my eyes. The prospect of dying young seemed better now.

"Why are you crying?" she asked.

"I don't know."

"Come here," she said. "I have prayed for you and nothing bad will come your way."

She patted my back. I wanted to ask, what if the bleeding started during morning assembly? What if I needed to pee during sex? Before this, I'd had blurred images of a man lying on top of a woman. Now that the images had been brought into focus, I was no longer sure of what came in and went out of where. My mother grabbed my shoulders and stood me up.

"What are you thinking?" she asked.

"Nothing," I said.

"Go and wash your face," she said tapping me toward the door.

In the bathroom mirror I checked my face for changes. I tugged at the skin below my eyes, stretched my lips, stuck my tongue out. Nothing.

There was a time I couldn't wait to be grown because of my mother's wardrobe. She had buckled, strapped, and beaded shoes. I would slip my feet into them, hoping for the gap behind my heels to close, and run my hands through her dresses and wrappers of silver and gold embroidery. Caftans were fashionable, though they really were a slimmer version of the *agbadas* women in our country had been wearing for years. I liked one red velvet caftan she had in particular, with small circular mirrors that sparkled like chandeliers. The first time my mother wore it was on my father's birthday. I was heady that night from the smell of tobacco, whiskey, perfume, and curry. I carried a small silver tray of meat balls on sticks and served it to guests. I was wearing a pink polyester babushka. Uncle Alex had just shown me how to light a pipe. My mother was late getting changed because she was busy cooking. When she walked into the living room, everyone cheered. My father accepted congratulations for spoiling his wife. "My money goes to her," he said.

On nights like this I watched my mother style her hair from start to finish. She straightened it with a hot comb that crackled through her hair and sent up pomade fumes. She complained about the process. It took too long and hurt her arms. Sometimes, the hot comb burnt her scalp. She preferred to wear her hair in two cornrows, and on the days my brother fell ill, her hair could be just as it was when she woke up. "It's my house," she would say. "If anybody doesn't like it they can leave."

It was easy to tell she wanted to embarrass my father. People thought a child couldn't understand, but I'd quarreled with friends in school before, and I wouldn't speak to them until they apologized, or at least until I'd forgotten that they hadn't. I understood, well enough to protect my parent's vision of my innocence. My mother needed quiet, my father would say. "I know," I would say. My father was always out, my mother would complain. I wouldn't say a word.

All week I looked forward to going to Sheri's house. Sometimes I went to the hibiscus patch, hoping she would appear. I never stayed there long enough. I'd forgotten about sex, even about the bump on my shin which had flattened to a purple bruise. This week, my parents were arguing about particulars.

My father had lost his driver's license and car insurance certificate. He said my mother had hidden them. "I did not hide your particulars," she said. He asked if I'd seen them. I had not seen his particulars, I said. I finally joined in his search for the lost particulars and was beginning to imagine I was responsible for them when he found them. "Where I already looked," he said. "See?"

I was tired of them. Sunday morning, after my parents left, I visited the house next door for the first time—against my mother's orders, but it was worth knowing a girl my age in the neighborhood. The place was full of boys, four who lived across the road. They laughed whenever they saw me and pretended to vomit. Next to them was an English boy who played fetch games with his Alsatian, Ranger. Sometimes he had rowdy bicycle races with the four across the road; other times he sent Ranger after them when they teased him for being white and unable to stomach hot peppers: "*Oyinbo* pepper, if you eat-ee pepper, you go yellow more-more!" Two boys lived further down the road and their mother had filled half the teeth of my classmates. They were much older.

With boys there always had to be noise and trouble. They caught frogs and grasshoppers, threw stones at windows, set off fireworks. There was Bisi at home, who really was a girl, because she was not old enough to be married, but she was just as rough. She watched whenever Baba beheaded chickens for cooking, flattened the daddy-long-legs in my bathtub with slaps. She threatened me most days, with snapped fingers. Then she pretended in front of my mother, shaking and speaking in a high voice. I kicked a stone thinking of her. She was a pretender.

Most houses on our quiet residential road were similar to ours, with servants' quarters and lawns. We didn't have the uniformity of nearby government neighborhoods, built by the Public Works Department. Our house was a bungalow covered in golden trumpets and bougainvillea. The Bakare's was an enormous one-story with aquamarine glass shutters, so square-shaped, I thought it resembled a castle. Except for a low hedge of dried up pitanga cherries lining the driveway and a mango tree by the house, the entire yard was cement.

I walked down the driveway, conscious of my shoes crunching the gravel. One half-eaten mango on the tree caught my eye. Birds must have nibbled it and now ants were finishing it up. The way they scrambled over the orange flesh reminded me of a beggar I'd seen outside my mother's church, except his sore was pink and pus oozed out. No one would go near him, not even to give him money which they threw on a dirty potato sack before him.

A young woman with two pert facial marks on her cheeks answered the door.

"Yesch?"

"Is Sheri in?" I asked.

"Is schleeping."

In the living room, the curtains were drawn and the furniture sat around like mute shadows. The Bakares had the same chairs as most people I knew, fake Louis XIV, my father called them. There wasn't a sound and it was eleven o'clock in the morning. At first I thought the 'sch' woman was going to turn me away, then she stepped aside. I followed her up the narrow wooden stairway, through a quiet corridor, past two doors until we reached a third. "Scheree?" she called out.

Someone whined. I knew it was Sheri. She opened her door wearing a yellow night gown. The 'sch' woman dragged her feet down the corridor.

"Why are you still sleeping?" I asked Sheri.

In my house that would be considered laziness. She'd been out last night, at her uncle's fortieth birthday. She danced throughout. Her voice did not yet sound like hers. There were clothes on the floor: white lace blouses, colorful wrappers, and head ties. She'd been sleeping on a cloth spread over a bare mattress, and another cloth was what she used to cover herself at night. A picture of apples and pears hung above her bed and on her bedside table was a framed photograph of a woman in traditional dress. In the corner, some dusty shoes spilled out of a wooden cupboard. The door dropped from a broken hinge and the mirror inside was stained brown. A table fan perched on a desk worried the clothes on the floor from time to time.

"Is this your room?" I asked.

"Anyone's," she said, clearing her throat noisily. She drew the curtains and sunlight flooded the room. She pointed to a wad of notes stashed by the photograph: the total amount she received for dancing.

"I got the most in the family," she said.

"Where is everyone?" I asked.

She scratched her hair. "My stepmothers are sleeping. My brothers and sisters are still sleeping. My father, I don't know where he is."

She reached for her behind.

I screwed up my nose. "I think you'd better have a bath."

One o'clock and the entire house was awake. Sheri's stepmothers had prepared *akara*, fried bean cakes, for everyone to eat. We knelt before them to say good morning, they patted our heads in appreciation. "Both knees," one of them ordered. I found myself looking at two women who resembled each other, pretty with watery eyes and chiffon scarves wrapped around their heads. I noted the gold tooth in the smile of the one who had ordered me to kneel.

In the veranda, the other children sat on chairs with bowls of *akara* on their laps. The girls wore dresses; the boys were in short-sleeved shirts and shorts. Sheri had changed into a tangerine-colored maxi length dress and was strutting around ordering them to be quiet. "Stop fighting." "Gani, will you sit down?" "Didn't I tell you to wash your hands?" "Kudi? What is wrong with you this morning?" She separated a squabble here, wiped a dripping nose. I watched in amazement as they called her Sister Sheri. The women were called Mama Gani and Mama Kudi after their firstborns.

"How many children will you have?" Sheri asked, thrusting a baby boy into my arms. I kept my mouth still for fear of dropping him. He wriggled and felt as fragile as a crystal glass.

"One," I said.

"Why not half, if you like?" Sheri asked.

23

I was not offended. Her rudeness had been curtailed by nature. Whenever she sucked her teeth, her lips didn't quite curl, and her dirty looks flashed through lashes as thick as moth wings. She knew all the rude sayings: mouth like a duck, dumb as a zero with a dot in it. If I said "so?" she said, "Sew your button on your shirt." When I asked "why?" she answered, "Z your head to Zambia." But she was far too funny to be successfully surly. Her full name was Sherifat, but she didn't like it. "Am not fat," she explained, as we sat down to eat. I had already had breakfast, but seeing the *akara* made me hungry. I took a bite and the peppers inside made my eyes water. My legs trembled in appreciation. "When we finish," Sheri said. "I will take you to the balcony upstairs." She chewed with her mouth open and had enough on her plate to fill a man.

The balcony upstairs resembled an empty swimming pool. Past rains had left mildew in its corners. It was higher than my house and standing there, we could see the whole of her yard and mine. I pointed out the plants in my yard as Sheri walked toward the view of the lagoon.

"It leads to the Atlantic," she said.

"I know," I said, trying not to lose my concentration. "Bougainvillea, golden trumpets..."

"You know where that leads?"

"Yes. Almond tree, banana tree..."

"Paris," she said.

I gave up counting plants. Downstairs, two of the children ran through the washing lines. They were playing a Civil War game: Halt. Who goes there? Advance to be recognized. Boom! You're dead.

"I want to go to Paris," Sheri said.

"How will you get there?"

"My jet plane," she said.

I laughed. "How will you get a jet plane?"

"I'll be an actress," she said, turning to me. In the sunlight, her pupils were like the underside of mushrooms.

"Actor-ess," I said.

"Yes, and when I arrive, I'll be wearing a red negligée."

"Em, Paris is cold."

"Eh?"

"Paris is cold. My father told me. It's cold and it rains."

"I'll have a fur coat, then."

"What else?" I asked.

"High, high heels."

"And?"

"Dark sunglasses."

"What kind?"

"Cressun Door," she said, smiling.

I shut my eyes, imagining. "You'll need fans. All actresses have fans."

"Oh, they'll be there," she said. "And they'll be running around, shouting, 'Sheri. *Voulez-vous. Bonsoir. Mercredi.*' But I won't mind them."

"Why not?"

"Because I'll get into my car and drive away fast."

I opened my eyes. "What kind of car?"

"Sports," she said.

I sighed. "I want to be something like... like president."

"Eh? Women are not presidents."

"Why not?"

"Our men won't stand for it. Who will cook for your husband?"

"He will cook for himself."

"What if he refuses?"

"I'll drive him away."

"You can't," she said.

"Yes I can. Who wants to marry him anyway?"

"What if they kill you in a coup?"

"I'll kill them back."

"What kind of dream is that?"

"Mine." I smirked.

"Oh, women aren't presidents," she said.

Someone downstairs was calling her. We looked over the balcony to see Akanni. He was wearing heart-shaped sunshades, like mirrors.

"What?" Sheri answered.

Akanni looked up. "Isn't that my good friend, Enitan, from next door?"

"None of your business," Sheri said. "Now, what do you want from me?"

I smiled at Akanni. His sunshades were funny and his war stories were fantastic.

"My good friend," he said to me in Yoruba. "At least you're nice to me, unlike this trouble maker, Sheri. Where is my money, Sheri?"

"I don't have your money," she said.

"You promised we would share the proceeds from last night. I stayed up till five this morning, now you're trying to cheat me. Country is hard for a poor man, you know."

"Who asked you?"

Akanni snapped his fingers. "Next time you'll see who will drive you around."

"Fine," Sheri said, then she turned to me. "Oaf. Look at his face, flat as a church clock. Come on, let's go back inside. The sun is beating my head."

"Now?" I asked.

She pressed her hair down. "Can't you see I'm a half-caste?"

I didn't know whether to laugh or feel sorry for her.

"I don't mind," she said. "Only my ears I mind and I cover them up, because they're big like theirs."

"Whose?" I asked.

"White people's," she said. "Now, come on."

I followed her. She did have huge ears and her afro did not hide them.

"You know that foolish Akanni?" she asked as we ran down the stairs.

"He comes to our house."

"To do what?"

"Visit our house girl, Bisi."

Sheri began to laugh. "He's doing her!"

I covered my mouth.

"Sex," she said. "Banana into tomato. Don't you know about it?"

My hand dropped.

"Oh, close your mouth before a fly enters," she said.

I ran to catch up with her.

"My grandma told me," she said.

We were sitting on her bed. Sheri tucked her tangerine dress between her legs. I wondered if she knew more than me.

"When you... " I asked. "I mean, with your husband. Where does it go? Because I don't... " I was pointing everywhere, even at the ceiling.

Sheri's eyes were wide. "You haven't seen it? I've seen mine. Many times." She stood up and retrieved a cracked mirror from a drawer. "Look and see."

"I can't."

"Look," she said, handing me the mirror.

"Lock the door."

"Okay," she said, heading there.

I dragged my panties down, placed the mirror between my

legs. It looked like a big, fat slug. I squealed as Sheri began to laugh. We heard loud knocks on the door and I almost dropped the mirror. "Who's that?" I whispered.

"Me," she said.

I hobbled to her bed. "You horrible... "

She rocked back and forth. "You're so funny, *aburo!*"

"You horrible girl," I hissed.

She stopped laughing. "Why?"

"I don't think it's funny. What did you do that for?"

"I'm sorry."

"Well, sorry is not enough."

I pulled my panties up, wondering whether I was angry with her, or what I'd seen between my legs. Sheri barricaded the door. "You're not going anywhere."

At first I thought I'd push her aside and walk out, but the sight of her standing there like a star tickled me.

"All right," I said. "But this is your last chance, Sherifat, I'm warning you."

"Am not fat," she yelled.

I laughed until I thought my heart would pop. That was her insecurity: her full name, and her big ears.

"Don't go," she said. "I like you. You're very English. You know, high faluting."

The woman in the photograph by her bedside table was her grandmother.

"Alhaja," Sheri said. "She's beautiful."

Alhaja had an enormous gap between her front teeth and her cheeks were so plump her eyes were barely visible. There were many Alhajas in Lagos. This one wasn't the first woman to go on *hajj* to Mecca, but for women like her, who were powerful within their families and communities, the title became their name.

Sheri did not know her own mother. She died when Sheri

was a baby and Alhaja raised her from then on, even after her father remarried. She pressed the picture to her chest and told me of her life in downtown Lagos. She lived in a house opposite her Alhaja's fabric store. She went to a school where children didn't care to speak English. After school, she helped Alhaja in her store and knew how to measure cloth. I listened, mindful that my life didn't extend beyond Ikoyi Park. What would it be like to know downtown as Sheri did, haggle with customers, buy fried yams and roasted plantains from street hawkers, curse Area Boys and taxi cabs who drove too close to the curb.

My only trips downtown were to visit the large foreign-owned stores, like Kelwarams and Leventis, or the crowded markets with my mother. The streets were crammed with vehicles, and there were too many people: people buying food from street hawkers, bumping shoulders, quarreling and crossing streets. Sometimes masqueraders came out for Christmas or for some other festival, dancing in their raffia gowns and ghoulish masks. Sheri knew them all: the ones who stood on stilts, the ones who looked like stretched out accordions and flattened to pancakes. It was juju, she said, but she was not scared. Not even of the *eyo* who dressed in white sheets like spirits of the day and whipped women who didn't cover their heads.

Sheri was a Moslem and she didn't know much about Christianity, except that there was a book in the Bible and if you read it, you could go mad. I asked why Moslems didn't eat pork. "It's a filthy beast," she said, scratching her hair. I told her about my own life, how my brother died and my mother was strict.

"That church sounds scary," she said.

"I'm telling you, if my mother ever catches you in our house, she'll send you home."

"Why?"

I pointed at her pink mouth. "It's bad, you know."

She sucked her teeth. "It's not bad. Anyway, you think my

father allows me to wear lipstick? I wait until he's gone out and put it on."

"What happens when he comes back?"

"I rub it off. Simple. You want some?"

I didn't hesitate. As I rubbed the lipstick on my lips I mumbled, "Your stepmothers, won't they tell?"

"I kneel for them, help them in the kitchen. They won't tell."

"What about the one with the gold tooth?"

"She's wicked, but she's nice."

I showed her my lips. "Does it fit?"

"It fits," she said. "And guess what?"

"What?"

"You've just kissed me."

I slapped my forehead. She was forward, this girl, and the way she acted with the other children. She really didn't do much, except to make sure she was noticed. I was impressed by the way she'd conned Akanni into staying up late for her uncle's party. Sheri got away with whatever she did and said. Even when she insulted someone, her stepmothers would barely scold her. "Ah, this one. She's such a terrible one."

They summoned her to act as a disc jockey. She changed the records as if she was handling dirty plates: The Beatles, Sunny Adé, Jackson Five, James Brown. Most of the records were scratched. Akanni arrived during, "Say it loud, I'm black and proud." He skidded from one end of the room to the other and fell on the floor overcome as the real James Brown. We placed a hand towel on his back and coaxed him up. By the time "If I had the wings of a dove" came on, I was singing out loud myself, and was almost tearful from the words.

As a parting gift Sheri gave me a romance novel titled *Jacaranda Cove*. The picture was barely visible and most of the pages were dog-eared. "Take this and read," she said. I slipped it under my arm and wiped my lips clean. My one thought was to return home before my mother arrived. I'd disobeyed her too much. If she found out, I would be punished for life.

Our house seemed darker when I arrived, though the curtains in the living room were not drawn. My father once explained the darkness was due to the position of the windows to the sun. Our living room reminded me of an empty hotel lounge. The curtains were made of a gold damask, and the chairs were a deep red velvet. A piano stood by the sliding doors to the veranda.

The house was designed by two Englishmen with the help of an architect my father knew. They lived together for years, and everyone knew about them, he said. Then they moved to Nairobi and he bought the house from them. The two men living together; the Bakare house full of children; grandparents, parents, teachers, now Akanni, and of all people, Bisi. The whole world was full of sex, I thought, running away from my footsteps. In my bedroom, I read the first page of Sheri's book, then the last. It described a man and woman kissing and how their hearts beat faster. I read it again and searched the book for more passages like that, then I marked each of them to read later.

My father arrived soon afterward and challenged me to a game of *ayo*. He always won, but today he explained the secret of the game. "You'd better listen, because I'm tired of defeating you. First, you choose which bowl you want to land in. Then you choose which bowl will get you there."

He shook the beads in his fist and plopped them, one by one, into the six bowls carved into the wooden slate. I'd always thought the trick was to pick the fullest bowl.

"Work it out backward?" I asked.

"Exactly," he said, scooping beads from the bowl.

"Daddy," I said. "I wasn't watching."

He slapped the table. "Next time you will."

"Cheater."

We were on our fifth round when my mother returned from church. I waved to her as she walked through the front door. I didn't get up to greet her as I normally would. I was winning the game and thought that if I moved, I would lose my good fortune.

"Heh, heh, I'm beating you," I said, wriggling in my chair.

"Only because I let you," my father said.

I scooped the beads from a bowl and raised my hand. My mother walked through the veranda door.

"Enitan? Who gave this to you?"

She grabbed my ear and shoved Sheri's book under my nose. "Who? Answer me now."

"For God's sake," my father said.

Her fingers were like iron clamps. The *ayo* beads tumbled out of my hand, down to the floor. Sheri from next door, I said. My mother pulled me to my feet by my ear as I explained. Sheri handed it to me through the fence. The wide gap in the fence. Yes, it was wide enough. I had not read the book.

"Let me see," my father said.

My mother flung the book on the table. "I go to her suitcase, find this... this... If I ever catch you talking to that girl again, there will be trouble in this house, you hear me?"

She released my ear. I dropped back into my seat. My ear was hot, and heavy.

My father slammed the book down. "What is this? She can't make friends anymore?"

My mother rounded on him. "You continue to divide this child and me."

"You're her mother, not her juror."

"I am not raising a delinquent. You look for evil and you will find it."

My father shook his head. "Arin, you can quote the whole Bible if you want."

32

"I am not here to discuss myself."

"Sleep in that church of yours."

"I am not here to discuss myself."

"It will not give you peace of mind."

"Get up when I'm talking to you, Enitan," my mother said. "Up. Up."

"Sit," my father said.

"Up," my mother said.

"Sit," my father said.

My mother patted her chest. "She will listen to me."

I shut my eyes and imagined I was on the balcony with Sheri. We were laughing and the sun had warmed my ear. Their voices faded. I heard only one voice; it was my father's. "Don't mind her," he said. "It's that church of hers. They've turned her head."

He shook my shoulders. I kept my eyes shut. I was tired, enough to sleep.

"Come on," he said. "Let's play."

"No," I said.

"You're leading."

"I don't care."

Soon I heard his footsteps on the veranda. I stayed there until my ear stopped throbbing.

I spoke to neither parent for the rest of that evening. My father knocked on my door before I went to bed.

"You're still sulking?" he asked.

"I'm not sulking," I said.

"When I was a boy, I had no room to lock myself in."

"You had no door."

"Yes, I did. What are you saying?"

"You lived in a village."

"Town," he said.

I shrugged. It was village life outside Lagos, where he grew up. He got up early in the mornings to fetch water from a well, walked to school and studied by oil lamp. My father said his growth was stunted because food never got to him. If a Baptist priest hadn't converted his mother to Christianity and taken him as a ward, I would never have been born thinking the world owed me something.

He pointed. "Is this the famous suitcase?"

He was pretending that nothing had happened.

"Yes."

"I have something for it."

He retrieved a rectangular case from his pocket and handed it to me.

"A pen?"

"Yours."

It was a fat navy pen. I pulled the cap off.

"Thank you, Daddy."

My father reached into his pocket again. He pulled a watch out and dangled it. I collapsed. It was a Timex. My father promised he would never buy me another watch again, after I broke the first and lost the second. This one had a round face the width of my wrist. Red straps. I rocked it.

"Thank you," I said, strapping it on.

He was sitting on my bed. Both feet were on it, and he still had his socks on. I sat on the floor by them. He rubbed my shoulder.

"Looking forward to going to school?"

"Yes."

"You won't be sad when you get there."

"I'll make friends."

"Friends who make you laugh."

I thought of Sheri. I would have to avoid girls like her in school, otherwise I might end up expelled.

"Anyone who bullies you, beat them up," my father said.

I rolled my eyes. Who could I fight?

34

"And join the debating society, not the girl guides. Girl guides are nothing but kitchen martyrs in the making."

"What is that?"

"What you don't want to be. You want to be a lawyer?"

Going to work was too remote to contemplate.

He laughed. "Tell me now, so I can take back my gifts."

"I'm too young to know."

"Too young indeed. Who will run my practice when I'm gone. And another thing, these romance books you're reading. No chasing boys when you get there."

"I don't like boys."

"Good," he said. "Because you're not going there to study boy-ology."

"Daddy," I said.

He was the one I would miss. The one I would write to. I settled to write a poem after he left, using words that rhymed with sad: bad, dad, glad, had. I was on my third verse when I heard raps on my window. I peeped outside to find Sheri standing with a sheet of paper in her hand. Her face appeared like a tiny moon. She was crouching.

"Open up," she said.

"What are you doing here?" I whispered.

"I came to get your school address."

Wasn't she afraid? It was as dark as indigo outside.

"On your own?"

"With Akanni. He's in your quarters, with his girlfriend."

She pulled a pencil from her pocket. She was like an imp who had come to tempt me. I couldn't get rid of her.

"Eni-Tan," she spelled.

"Yes," I said.

"Your school address," she said. "Or are you deaf?"

1975

Had I listened to my mother, that would have been the end of Sheri and I, and the misfortune that would bind us. But my mother had more hope of squeezing me up her womb than stopping our friendship. Sheri had led me to the gap between parental consent and disapproval. I would learn how to bridge it with deception, wearing a face as pious as a church sister before my mother and altering steadily behind her. There was a name my mother had for children like Sheri. They were *omo-ita*, street children. If they had homes, they didn't like staying in them. What they liked, instead, was to go around fighting and cursing, and getting up to mischief.

Away from my own home, my days in boarding school were like a balm. I lived with five hundred other girls and shared a dormitory with about twenty. At night we let down our mosquito nets and during the day we patched them up if they got ripped. If a girl had malaria, we covered her with blankets to sweat out her fever. I held girls through asthma attacks, shoved a teaspoon down the mouth of a girl who was convulsing, burst boils. It was a wonder we survived the spirit of samaritanism, or communal living. The toilets stunk like sewers and sometimes excrement piled up days high. I had to cover my nose to use them and when girls were menstruating, they flung their soiled sanitary towels into open buckets. Still, I preferred boarding school to home.

Royal College girls came from mixed backgrounds. In our dormitory alone we had a farmer's daughter and a diplomat's daughter. The farmer's daughter had never been to a city before she came to Lagos; the diplomat's daughter had been to garden parties at Kensington palace. There were girls from homes like mine, girls from less privileged homes, so a boarder might come back from class to find her locker had been broken into. Since she knew she'd never see her missing belongings again, the next step was to put a hex on the thief by shouting out curses like,

"May you have everlasting diarrhea." "May you menstruate forever." If the thief were caught, she would be jostled down the hallways.

I met Moslem girls: Zeinat, Alima, Aisha who rose early to salute Mecca. Some covered their heads with scarves after school, and during Ramadan, they shunned food and water from dawn till dusk. I met Catholic girls: Grace, Agnes, Mary, who sported gray crosses on their foreheads on Ash Wednesday. There were Anglican girls, Methodist girls. One girl, Sangita, was Hindu and we loved to tug on her long plait. The daughter of our math teacher and the only foreign student in our school, she had such a resounding, "Leave me alone!" she sent the best of us running.

I met girls born with sickle cell anemia like my brother. Some were sick almost every other month, others hardly ever. We called them sicklers. They called themselves sicklers. One thought it excused her from all ills: untidiness, lateness, rudeness. I learned from her that I carried the sickle cell trait, which meant I would never be sick, but my child could be, if my husband also carried the trait.

I learned also about women in my country, from Zaria, Katsina, Kaduna who decorated their skin with henna dye and lived in *purdah*; women from Calabar who were fed and anointed in fattening houses before their weddings; women who were circumcised. I heard about towns in western Nigeria where every family had twins because the women ate a lot of yams, and other towns in northern Nigeria, where every other family had a crippled child because women married their first cousins. None of the women seemed real. They were like mammy-water, sirens of the Niger Delta who rose from the creeks to lure unsuspecting men to death by drowning.

Uncle Alex had always said our country was not meant to be one. The British had drawn a circle on the map of West Africa and called it a country. Now I understood what he meant. The girls I met at Royal College were so different. I could tell a girl's ethnicity even before she opened her mouth. Hausa girls had softer hair because of their Arab heritage. Yoruba girls like me usually had heart-shaped faces and many Igbo girls were fair-skinned; we called them Igbo Yellow. We spoke English, but our native tongues were as different as French and Chinese. So, we mispronounced names and spoke English with different accents. Some Hausa girls could not "fronounce" the letter P. Some Yoruba girls might call these girls "Ausas," and eggs might be "heggs." Then there was that business with the middle-belters who mixed up their L's and R's. If they said a word like lorry, there was no telling what my bowels would release, from laughing.

It all provided jokes. So did the stereotypes. Yoruba girls were considered quarrelsome; Hausa girls, pretty but dumb; Igbo girls, intelligent, but well, they were muscular. Most girls had parents of the same origin, but there was some intermingling and we had a few girls, like Sheri, who had one parent from a foreign country. Half-castes we called them, without malice or implications. Half because they claimed both sides of their heritage. There was no caste system in our country.

Often at Royal College, we shared family stories while fetching water from a tap in the yard. I learned that my mother's behavior wasn't typical. I also learned that every other girl had an odd family story to tell: Afi's grandmother was killed when a bicycle knocked her down in the village; Yemisi's mother worked till her water broke; Mfon's cousin smoked hemp and brought shame on the family; Ibinabo's father stripped her down, whipped her, and made her say "thank-you" afterward.

In the mornings, we congregated in the assembly hall to sing our national anthem and took a few minutes to appreciate Beethoven or some other European composer. At meal-times we packed into our dining hall and sang:

Some have food but cannot eat,
Some can eat but have no food,
We have food and we can eat,
Glory be to God, Amen.

After school, we drummed on our desks and sang. We sang a lot, through the transformations in our country; when we began to drive on the right side of the road; when we switched from pounds, shillings, and pence to naira and kobo. Outside our school walls, oil leaked from the drilling fields of the Niger Delta into people's Swiss bank accounts. There was bribery and corruption, but none of it concerned me, particularly in June 1975. It was as vague as the end of Vietnam. I was just glad our fourth-year exams were over. For those sleepless weeks, I joined my classmates, studying through the night and spreading bitter coffee granules on my tongue. In a class of thirty odd girls, I was neither a bright star Booker T. Washington or dim-wit Dundee United. I enjoyed history, English literature, Bible studies because of the parables. I enjoyed music lessons because of the songs our black American teacher taught us, spirituals and jazz melodies that haunted me until I began to dream about churches and smoky clubs I'd never seen. I was captain of our junior debating society, though I longed to be one of those girls chosen for our annual beauty pageants instead. But my arms were like twisted vines and my forehead like sandpaper. Those cranky nodules behind my nipples didn't amount to breasts and my calf muscles had refused to develop. The girls in my class called me *Panla*, after a dry, stinky fish imported from Norway. Girls overseas could starve themselves on leaves and salad oil if they wanted. In our country, women were hailed for having huge buttocks. I wanted to be fatter, fatter, fatter, with a pretty face, and I wanted boys to like me.

Damola Ajayi had spoken like an orator, as good as any I'd heard. He was skinny with big hands that punched the air as he spoke. Warm hands. We almost collided on the stairs leading to the stage and I held his hands to steady myself. I turned to the Concord Academy debating team as he joined them. Their entire bench sat upright with the same serious expression. They were dressed, like him, in white jackets and blue striped ties. On the bench, next to them, our team slumped forward in green pinafores and checked blouses. Behind them were Saint Catherine girls in their red skirts and white blouses. The hall was a show of uniforms from all the schools in Lagos.

Here, we played net ball and badminton games; staged plays and hosted beauty pageants. Sometimes we had films shows and school dances. We never used the gymnastic equipment because no one had explained what it was for. By the back wall, a few boys draped themselves over two pommel horses, studying girls. Debating was the only way to socialize during school terms and if students had strict parents, it was the only way to socialize all year. We came together for tournaments, bearing our different school identities. Concord was gentlemanly but boring. Saint Catherine's was snobbish and loose. Owen Memorial boys and girls belonged in juvenile detention homes and their worst students smoked hemp. We at Royal, we were smart, but our school was crowded and filthy.

"Thanks to our co-hosts," I said. "And thanks to everyone else for participating."

Few people clapped. The crowd was getting restless. Yawns spread across the rows and students keeled over. Our own team looked as if their mouths had dried up from talking. It was time to end my speech.

"I would like to invite questions, comments from the audience?"

A Saint Patrick's boy raised his hand.

"Yes sir, at the back?"

The boy stood up, and pulled his brown khaki jacket down. There was a low rumble from the crowd as he strained forward: "Mr. Chairman, s-s-sir. W-when c-can we start the social acker-acker-acker-tivities?"

The crowd roared as he took bows. I raised my arm to silence them, but no one paid attention. Soon the noise trickled to a few laughs. Someone switched on the stereo. I came down from the stage and people began to clear their chairs for the dance.

Our final debate had lasted longer than I expected. We lost to Concord's team because of their captain. Damola was one of the best in the league, and he delivered his "with all due respects" to cheers. I couldn't compete. He was also the lead singer of a band called the Stingrays, who had caused a stir by appearing on television one Christmas. Parents said they wouldn't pass their school certificate exams carrying on that way. We wondered how they could dare form a band, in this place, where parents only ever thought about passing exams. What kind of homes did they come from? A girl on our debating team had answers, at least about Damola: "Cousin lives on the same street as him. Parents allow him to do what he wants. Drives a car. Smokes."

His hand tapped my elbow. "Well done."

"You too," I said.

He already had traces of mustache on his upper lip, and his eyes were heavy with lashes. "You're a good debater," he said.

I smiled. Normally, I could not accept verbal defeat. Arguments sent my heart rate up, and blood rushing to my temples. Outside the debating society, I annoyed my friends with words they couldn't understand, gagged class bullies with retorts until their lips trembled. "You have a bad mouth, Enitan Taiwo," one recently said. "Just wait and see. It will catch up with you."

43

I had nothing to say to Damola. As captains of our teams we had to start the dance. We walked to the center of the hall. People flooded the floor, pushing us closer. Damola danced as if his jacket were tight and I avoided looking at his feet to keep my rhythm. We ended up under a ceiling fan and the lyrics of the song amused me after a while: rock the boat one minute, don't rock it the next.

The song ended and we found two empty chairs. Damola was not an enigma, I'd told my friends, who were searching for the right word for nobody-knows-what's-inside-his-mind. Enigmas would have more to hide than their shyness. I counted from ten down.

"I've heard your song," I said.

"Which one?"

"No time for a psalm."

I'd memorized the words from television. "I reach for a star, it pierces my palm, burns a hole through my life line... "

My father said it was teenage self-indulgence and the boys needed to learn to play their instruments properly. They did screech a little, but at least they attempted to express themselves. Who cared about what we thought at our age? Between childhood and adulthood there was no space to grow laterally, and whatever our natural instincts, our parents were determined to clip off any disobedience: "Stop moping around." "Face your studies." "You want to disgrace us?" At least the boys were saying something different.

"Who wrote it?" I asked.

I already knew. I crossed my legs to look casual, then uncrossed them, so as not to be typical.

"Me," he said.

"What is it about?"

"Disillusionment."

Damola had a slight hook nose and from the side he almost

44

resembled a bird. He wasn't one of the fine boys that girls talked about; the boring boys who ignored me.

"Are you disillusioned?" I asked.

"Sometimes."

"Me too," I said.

We would get married as soon as we finished school, I thought. From then on we would avoid other people. People our age clung together unnecessarily anyway. It was a sign of not thinking, like being constantly happy. Really, there was no need to reach as high as the stars. Around us was enough proof that optimism was dangerous, and some of us had discovered this before.

Outside it looked like it was about to rain. It was late afternoon but the sky was as dark as early evening because of the rainy season. Mosquitoes flew indoors. They buzzed around my legs and I bent to slap them. The stereo began to play a slow number, "That's the Way of the World" by Earth, Wind, and Fire. I hoped Damola would ask me to dance, but he didn't.

I tapped my foot under the end of that record. Afterward, our vice principal came into the hall to turn the stereo off. She thanked the boys and girls for coming and announced that their school buses were waiting outside. I'd spent most of the dance sitting next to Damola who nodded from time to time as though he were above it all. Together, we walked to the gates and I stopped by the last travelers palm beyond which boarders weren't allowed to pass.

"Have a nice summer," I said.

"You too," he said.

A group of classmates hurried over. They circled me and stuck their chins out: "What did he say?" "Do you like him?" "Does he like you?"

Normally, we were friends. We fetched water and bathed together; studied in pairs and shared scrapbooks details. Damola was another excuse for a group giggle. I wasn't going to tell them. One of them congratulated me on my wedding. I asked her not to be silly.

"What's scratching you?" she asked.

The others waited for an answer. I managed a smile to appease them, then I walked on. In the twilight, students shifted in groups back to the dormitory blocks.

The structure of our blocks, three adjacent buildings, each three floors high with long balconies, made me imagine I was living in a prison. Walking those balconies, I'd discovered they weren't straight. Some parts dipped and other parts rose a little and whenever I was anxious, because of an examination or a punishment, I dreamed they had turned to waves and I was trying to ride them. Sometimes I'd fall off the balconies in my dreams, fall, and never reach the bottom.

Friday after school, I received a letter from Sheri. I was sitting in class. It was raining again. Lightning flashed, followed by a crash of thunder. About thirty girls sat behind and on top of wooden desks indoors. School hour rules no longer applicable, we wore mufti and spoke vernacular freely. Outside, a group of girls scurried across the quadrangle with buckets over their heads. One placed hers on the ground to collect rain water. The wind changed direction. "Shut the windows," someone said. A few girls jumped up to secure them.

Over the years, Sheri and I exchanged letters, sharing our thoughts on sheets torn from exercise books, ending them "love and peace, your trusted friend." Sheri was always in trouble. Someone called her loose, someone punished her, someone tried to beat her up. It was always girls. She seemed to get along with boys. Occasionally I saw her when she came to stay with her father. She sneaked to my room, rapped on my window and frightened me almost to death. Her brows were plucked thin, her hair pulled back in a bun. She wore red lipstick and said *"Ciao."* She was way too advanced for me, but I enjoyed seeing her anyway.

She had had the best misadventures: parties that ended in brawls, cinemas where audiences talked back to the screen. Once, she hitched a ride from a friend who borrowed his parents' car. They pushed the car down the driveway, while his parents were sleeping, and an hour later they pushed it up again. She was a bold-face, unlike me. I worried about breaking school rules, failing exams. I even worried about being skinny, and for a while I worried that I might be a hermaphrodite, like an earthworm, because my periods hadn't started. Then they did and my mother killed a fowl to secure my fertility.

In her usual curvy writing, Sheri had written on the back of the envelope: *de-liver, de-letter, de-sooner, de-better.* And addressed it to: *Miss Enitan Taiwo Esquire, Royal College, Yaba, Lagos, Nigeria, West Africa, Africa, The Universe.* Her writing was overly curly, and her letter had been opened by my class teacher who checked our letters. If they came from boys she ripped them up.

June 27, 1975.

Aburo,

I'm sorry I haven't written for so long. I've been studying for my exams and I'm sure you have too. How were yours? This term has been tough for me. I've worked hard, but my father still says I'm not trying enough. He wants me to be a doctor. How can I be a doctor when I hate sciences? Now I have to stay with him over the summer and take lessons in Phi, Chem and Bi. I think I will go mad...

Someone switched the lights on as the sky darkened. The rain drummed faster on our roof and the girls began to sing a Yoruba folk song:

47

> The banana tree
> in my father's farm
> bears fruit every year.
> May I not be barren
> but be fruitful and blessed
> with the gift of children.

A fat mosquito landed on my ankle, heavy and slow. I slapped it off.

> I can't wait to get away and see your face. I don't want to stay in my father's house though. It's too crowded. Can I come and stay in yours? I'm sure your mother will love that—ha, ha...

Sheri was not afraid of my mother. If she sneaked to my window, who would find out? she asked. But I knew she would not last a day in my house, loving food as much as she did. On my last vacation food had become a weapon in our house. My mother cooked meals and locked them up in the freezer so my father couldn't eat when he returned from work. I had to eat with her, before he returned, whether or not I was hungry. One morning, she took the sugar cubes my father used for coffee and hid them. He threatened to stop her food allowance. The sugar cubes came out, the other food remained locked in the freezer. I could not tell anyone this was happening in our house.

As the rain turned to drizzle, I finished reading Sheri's letter. Girls opened the windows and the wind brought in the smell of wet grass. My classmates were singing another song now, this one a jazz standard and I joined them, thinking only of Damola.

> Always get that mood indigo
> Since my baby said goodbye...

Summer vacation began and the smell of wet grass was everywhere. I'd seen fifteen rainy seasons and was finding this one predictable: palm trees bowing and shivering shrubs. The sky darkened fast; the lagoon, too, and its surface looked like the water was scurrying from the wind. The rain advanced in a wall across the water and lightning ripped the sky in two: *Boom!* As a child, I clutched my chest and searched for the destruction outside. The thunder often caught me by my window, hands over my head and recoiling. These days I found the noise tedious, especially the frogs.

Sunday afternoon, when I hoped it had stopped raining for the day, Sheri appeared at my window, startling me so much, I accidentally banged my head on the wall.

"When did you arrive?" I asked, rubbing my sore spot.

"Yesterday," she said.

Her teeth were as small and white as milk teeth. She stuck her head inside.

"What are you doing inside, Mrs. Morose?"

"I'm not morose," I said.

"Yes, you are. You're always indoors."

I laughed. "That is not morose."

Outside the grass squeaked and wet my shoes; mud splattered on the back of my legs and dried. Inside, I had my own record player, albeit one with a nervous needle. I also had a small collection of Motown records, a Stevie Wonder poster on my wall, a library of books like *Little Women*. I enjoyed being on my own in my room. My parents, too, mistook my behavior for sulking.

This vacation I found them repentant. They did not argue, but they were hardly at home either and I was glad for the silence. My father stayed at work; my mother in her church. I thought of Damola. Once or twice, I crossed out the common letters in my name and his to find out what we would be: friends, lovers, enemies, married. We were lovers.

"This house is like a graveyard," Sheri said.

"My parents are out," I said.

"Ah-ah? Let's go then."

"Where?"

"Anywhere. I want to get out of here. I hate my lessons and I hate my lesson teacher. He spits."

"Tell your father."

"He won't listen. All he talks about is doctor this and doctor that. *Abi*, can you see me as a doctor?"

"No."

She would misdiagnose her patients and boss them around.

"Let's go," she said.

"Walk-about," I teased.

She flung her hand up. "You see? You're morose."

I thought she was going home so I ran to the front door to stop her. She said she wasn't angry, but why did I never want to do anything? I pushed her up the drive.

"I'll get into trouble, Sheri."

"If your parents find out."

"They'll find out."

"If you let them."

Sheri already had a boyfriend in school. They had kissed before and it was like chewing gum, but she wasn't serious because he wasn't. I told her about Damola.

"You sat there not talking?" she asked.

"We communicated by mind."

"What does that mean?"

"We didn't have to talk."

"You and your boyfriend, *sha*."

I poked her shoulder. "He is not my boyfriend."

She forced me to call him. I recited his number which we found in the telephone book and my heart thumped so hard it reached my temples. Sheri handed the receiver to me. "Hello?"

came a high-pitched voice, and I promptly gave the phone back to Sheri.

"Em, yes, helleu," she said, faking a poor English accent. "Is Damola in please?"

"What's she saying?" I whispered.

Sheri raised a finger to silence me. Unable to sustain her accent, she slammed the phone down.

"What happened?" I asked.

She clutched her belly.

"What did she say, Sheri?"

"He's not... in."

I snorted. That was it? My jaw locked watching her kick. She threatened to make another phone call, just to hear the woman's voice again. I told her if she did, I'd rip the phone from its socket. I too was laughing, from her silliness. My stomach ached. I thought I would suffocate.

"Stop."

"I can't."

"You have to go home, Sheri."

"Wh-why?"

"My mother hates you."

"S-so?"

We slapped each other's cheeks to stop.

"Don't worry," she said. "We won't phone your boyfriend again. You can communicate with him, unless his mind is otherwise occupied."

She went home with mascara tears and said it was my fault. The following Sunday, she appeared at my bedroom window again. This time, Baba was burning leaves and the smell nauseated me. I leaned over to shut my window and Sheri's head popped up: "*Aburo!*"

I jumped at least a foot high. "What is wrong with you?

51

Can't you use the door?"

"Oh, don't be so morose," she said.

"Sheri," I said. "I don't think you know the meaning of that word."

She was dressed in a black skirt and strapless top. Sheri was no longer a yellow banana. She could easily win any of the beauty contests in my school, but her demeanor needed to be toned down. She was *gragra*. Girls who won were demure.

"You look nice," I said.

She also had the latest fashions: Oliver Twist caps, wedge heels and flares. Her grandmother knew traders in Quayside by the Lagos Marina, who imported clothes and shoes from Europe.

She blinked through her mascara. "Are your parents in?"

"Out."

"They're always out."

"I prefer it."

"Let's go then."

"No. Where?"

"A picnic. At Ikoyi Park. Your boyfriend will be there."

I smiled. "What boyfriend, Sheri?"

"Your boyfriend, Damola. I found out he'll be there."

Tears filled my eyes. "You rotten little... "

I resisted the urge to hug her. As she tried to explain her connection to him, I lost track. I wore a black T-shirt and white dungarees. In the mirror, I checked my hair, which was pulled into two puffs and fingered the Fulani choker around my neck. I picked a ring from my dressing table and slipped it on my toe.

"Boogie on Reggae Woman," Stevie Wonder was singing. Sheri snapped her fingers and muddled up the lyrics between grunts and whines. I studied her leg movements. No one knew where this latest dance came from. America, a classmate had said, but where in that country, and how it crossed an ocean to reach ours, she couldn't explain. Six months later the dance would be as fashionable as our grandmothers. Then we would be learning another.

"Aren't you wearing makeup?" she asked.

"No," I said, letting my bangles tumble down my arm.

"You can't come looking like that," she said.

"Yes, I can."

"Morose."

I was, she insisted. I wore no makeup, didn't go out, and I had no boyfriend. I tried to retaliate. "Just because I'm not juvenile like the rest of you, following the crowd and getting infatuated with... "

"Oh hush, your grammar is too much," she said.

On the road to the park we kept to the sandy sidewalk. I planned to stay at the picnic until six-thirty if the rain didn't unleash. My mother was at a vigil, and my father wouldn't be back until late, he said. The sun was mild and a light breeze cooled our faces. Along the way, I noticed that a few drivers slowed as they passed us and kept my face down in case the next car was my father's. Sheri shouted out insults in Yoruba meanwhile: "What are you looking at? Yes you. Nothing good will come to you, too. Come on, come on. I'm waiting for you."

By the time we reached the park, my eyes were streaming with tears.

"That's enough," she ordered.

I bit my lips and straightened up. We were beautiful, powerful, and having more fun than anyone else in Lagos. The sun was above us and the grass, under our feet.

The grass became sea sand and I heard music playing. Ikoyi Park was an alternative spot for picnics. Unlike the open, crowded beaches, most of it was shaded by trees which gave it a secluded air. There were palm trees and casuarinas. I saw a group gathered behind a row of cars. I was so busy looking ahead I tripped over a twig. My sandal slipped off. Sheri carried on. She approached two boys who were standing by a white Volkswagen Kombi van. One of them was Damola, the other wore a black cap. A portly boy walked over and they circled her. I hurried to catch up with them as my heart seemed to punch through my chest wall.

"We had to walk," Sheri was saying.

"You walked?" Damola asked.

"Hello," I said.

Damola gave a quick smile, as if he had not recognized me. The other boys turned their backs on me. My heartbeat was now in my ears.

Sheri wiggled. "How come no one is dancing?"

"Would you like to?" Damola asked.

I hugged myself as they walked off, to make use of my arms. The rest of my body trembled.

"How long have you been here?" I asked the portly boy.

The boys glanced at each other as if they hadn't understood.

"I mean, at the party," I explained.

The portly boy reached for his breast pocket and pulled out a packet of cigarettes.

"Long enough," he said.

I moved away. These boys didn't look like they answered to their parents anyway. The portly one had plaits in his hair and the boy with the cap wasn't even wearing a shirt under his dungarees. Damola, too, looked different out of school uniform. He had cut-off sleeves and his arms dangled out of them. He was smaller than I'd dreamed; a little duller, but I'd given him light, enough to blind myself. I pretended to be intrigued by the table where a picnic had been laid. The egg sandwich tasted sweet and salty. I liked the combination and gobbled it up. Then I poured myself a glass from the punch bowl. I spat it back into the cup. It was full of alcohol.

The music stopped and started again. Sheri continued to

dance with Damola. Then with the boy in the cap, then with the portly boy. It was no wonder other girls didn't like her. She was not loyal. I was her only girl friend, she once wrote in a letter. Girls were nasty and they spread rumors about her, and pretended to be innocent. I watched her play wrestle with the portly boy after their dance. He grabbed her waist and the other two laughed as she struggled. If she preferred boys, she was free to. She would eventually learn. It was obvious, these days, that most of them preferred girls like Sheri. Whenever I noticed this, it bothered me. I was sure it would bother me even if I was on the receiving end of their admiration. Who were they to judge us by skin shades?

I walked toward the lagoon where the sand was moist and firm, and sat on a large tree root. Crabs dashed in and out of holes and mud-skippers flopped across the water. I searched for my home. The shore line curved for miles and from where I sat I could not see it.

"Hi," someone said.

He stood on the bank. His trouser legs were rolled up to his ankles and he wore bookish black rim glasses.

"Hello," I said.

"Why aren't you dancing?" he asked.

He was too short for me, and his voice wavered, as if he were on the verge of crying.

"I don't want to."

"So why come to a party if you don't want to dance?"

I resisted the urge to frown. That was the standard retort girls expected from boys and he hadn't given me the chance to turn him down.

He smiled. "Your friend Sheri seems to be enjoying herself. She's hanging around some wild characters over there."

That wasn't his business, I wanted to say.

He pushed his glasses back. "At least tell me your name."

"Enitan."

"I have a cousin called Enitan."

He would have to leave soon. He hadn't told me his own name.

"Would you like to dance?" he asked.

"No, thanks."

"Please," he said, placing his hands together.

I swished my feet around the water. I could and then go home.

"All right," I said.

I remembered that I sat on my sandals. Reaching underneath to pull them out, I noticed a red stain on my dungarees.

"What?" he asked.

"I'm sorry. I don't want to dance."

"Why not?"

"I just don't."

"But you said... "

"Not anymore."

He stood there. "That's the problem with you. All of you. You're not happy until someone treats you badly, then you complain."

He walked away with a lopsided gait and I knew he'd had polio. I considered calling after him. Then I wondered why I had needed to be asked to dance in the first place. I checked the stain on my dungarees instead.

It was blood. I was dead. From then on I watched people arrive and leave. More were dancing and their movements had become lively. Some stopped by the bank to look at me. I tried to reason that they would eventually leave. The day could not last forever. For a while a strange combination of rain and sunset occurred, and it seemed as if I was viewing the world through a yellow-stained glass. I imagined celestial beings descending and frightened myself into thinking that was about to happen today. My feet became wrinkled and swollen. I checked my watch; it was almost six o'clock. The music was still playing, and the picnic table had been cleared. Only Sheri, Damola, and his two friends remained. They stood by a Peugeot, saying goodbye to a group who were about to leave. I was planning exactly what to say to Sheri, constructing the exact words and facial expression to use, when she approached me.

"Why are you sitting here on your own?" she asked.

"Go back to your friends," I said.

She mimicked my expression and I noticed her eyes were red. She was barefooted and about to scramble up a tree, or fall face down on the bank; I wasn't sure which.

"Are you drunk?" I asked.

"What if I am?"

The air smelled sweet. I looked beyond her. The Peugeot had gone. Damola and his friends were huddled in a semi-circle by the Kombi van. Damola was in the middle, smoking what looked like an enormous cigarette. I'd never seen one before, never smelled the fumes, but I knew: it reddened your eyes, made you crazy. People who smoked it, their lives would amount to nothing.

"What are they doing?" I asked.

Sheri lifted her arms and her top plummeted.

"We have to go," I said.

She danced away and waved over her shoulder. When she reached the boys, she snatched the hemp from Damola. She coughed as she inhaled. The boys laughed. I stamped my feet in the water. I would give them ten minutes. If they hadn't gone, I would risk the disgrace and walk away. I heard Sheri cry out, but didn't bother to look.

I got up when I no longer heard voices, walked toward the van. From the angle I approached it, I could see nothing behind the windscreen. As I came closer, I spotted the head of the boy with a cap bent over by the window. I edged toward the side door. Sheri was lying on the seat. Her knees were spread apart. The boy in the cap was pinning her arms down. The portly boy was on top of her. His hands were clamped over her mouth. Damola was leaning against the door, in a daze. It was a silent moment; a peaceful moment. A funny moment, too. I didn't know why, except my mouth stretched into the semblance of a laugh before my hands came up, then tears filled my eyes.

The boy in the cap saw me first. He let go of Sheri's arms and she pushed the portly boy. He fell backward out of the van. Sheri screamed. I covered my ears. She ran toward me, clutching her top to her chest. There was lipstick across her mouth, black patches around her eyes. The portly boy fumbled with his trousers.

Sheri slammed into me. I shook her shoulders.

"Sheri!"

She buried her face in my dungarees. Spit dribbled out of her mouth. She beat the sand with her fists. Her arms were covered in sand and so were mine. I tried to hold her still, but she pushed me away and threw her head back as the van started.

"N-nm," she moaned.

I dressed her, saw the red bruises and scratches on her skin, her wrists, around her mouth, on her hips. She stunk of cigarettes, alcohol, sweat. There was blood on her pubic hairs, thick spit running down her legs. Semen. I used sand grains to clean her, pulled her panties up. We began to walk home. The palm trees shrunk to bamboo shoots, the headlights of oncoming cars were like fire-flies. Everything seemed that small. I wondered if the ground was firm enough to support us, or if our journey would last and never end.

She looked tiny. Tiny. There were red dots at the top of her back, pale lines along her lower back where fingers had tugged her skin. She hugged herself as I ran warm water into a bucket.

I helped her into my bathtub. I began to wash her back, then I poured a bowl of water over her. She winced.

"Too hot?" I asked.

"Cold," she said.

The water felt warm. I added hot water. The hot water trickled out reluctantly.

"My hair," she said.

I washed it with bathing soap. Her hair was tangled, but it turned curly and settled on her cheeks. I washed her arms, then her legs.

The water dribbling down the drain, I wanted it to be clear. Once it was clear, we would have survived. Instead it remained pink and grainy, with hair strands and soap suds. The sand grains settled and the scum stayed.

"You have to wash the rest," I said.

She shook her head. "No."

"You have to," I said.

She turned her face away. I could tell her chin was crumbling.

"Please," I said. "Just try."

I placed my book on the table. It was her fourth donut since we'd been sitting on the veranda and it was hard to concentrate with the gulping sounds she was making. Biscuits, coconut candy, now donuts. Sheri brought food to my house each time she visited and she had not said a word about what happened.

"Where are you going?" she asked when I stood up.

"Toilet," I snapped.

How could she eat so much? After I bathed her, I had to teach myself how to breathe again. Breathing out wasn't the problem, breathing in was. If I didn't prompt myself, I simply forgot. Then when I wasn't thinking, the rhythm came back. I realized I hadn't felt hungry in days. I didn't even feel thirsty. I imagined my stomach like a shriveled palm kernel. At night,

I had visions of fishermen breaking into my room. I dreamed of Sheri running toward me with her face made up like a masquerader. She slammed into me and I fell out of my bed. I held my head and sobbed.

I sat on the toilet and waited for the urge to pee. What I wished was for my parents to come home. Sheri was making me angry enough to punch walls. I came out without washing my hands. She was eating another donut.

"You're going to be sick," I said, grabbing my book.

"Why?" she asked.

"If you keep eating and eating like that."

She wiped grease from her mouth. "I don't eat that much."

I used the book to cover my face. "Eating and eating," I said to provoke her.

"I don't... "

She stood up and let out a cry. My book slid off my face, just as she lurched. Her vomit splattered over the table, hitting my face. I tasted it in on my tongue; it was sweet and slimy. She lunged forward and another mound of vomit plopped on the veranda floor. I managed to grab her shoulders.

"Sorry," I said. "You hear me?"

Tears ran down her face. I sat her in the chair and went to the kitchen to get a bucket and brush. The water gushed into the bucket and I wondered why I was so angry with her. Holding my breath, I delved deeper and the fist in my stomach exploded. Yes. I blamed her. If she hadn't smoked hemp it would never have happened. If she hadn't stayed as long as she did at the party, it would certainly not have happened. Bad girls got raped. We all knew. Loose girls, forward girls, raw, advanced girls. Laughing with boys, following them around, thinking she was one of them. Now, I could smell their semen on her, and it was making me sick. It was her fault.

The foam poured over the edge of the bucket. I struggled

with the handle. The water wet my dress as I hobbled through the living room. I remembered the moment Sheri came to my window. Why did we go? I could have said no. She wouldn't have gone without me. One word. I should have said no. Damola and his friends, they would suffer for what they did. They would remember us, our faces. They would never forget us.

I reached the veranda and she stood up.

"I'll do it," I said.

She shut her eyes. "Maybe I should go home."

"Yes," I said.

She'd eaten the last donut.

She didn't come back to my house, and I didn't visit her either because I hoped that if we pretended long enough the whole incident might vanish. As if the picnic hadn't done enough damage that summer, as if the rains hadn't added to our misery, there was a military coup. Our head of state was overthrown. I watched as our new ruler made his first announcement on television. "I, Brigadier... "

The rest of his words marched away. I was trying to imagine the vacation starting over, Sheri coming to my window. I would order her to go home.

My father fumed throughout the announcement. "What is happening? These army boys think they can pass us from one hand to the other. How long will this regime last before there's another?"

"Let us hear what the man is saying," my mother said.

The brigadier was retiring government officials with immediate effect. He was setting up councils to investigate corruption in the civil service. My father talked as if he were carrying on a personal argument with him.

"What qualification do you have to reorganize the government?"

"I beg you," my mother said. "Let us hear what he is saying."

I noticed how she smirked. My mother was always pleased when my father was angry.

"You fought on a battle front doesn't make you an administrator," he said. "What do you know about reorganizing the government?"

"Let us give him a chance," she said. "He might improve things."

My father turned to her. "They fight their wars and they retire to their barracks. That is what they do. The army have no place in government."

"Ah, well," she said. "Still let us hear."

They followed the latest news about the coup; I imagined the summer as I wished it had started. That was how it was in our house over the next few days. There was a dusk to dawn curfew in Lagos and I wanted it to end so I could have the house to myself. I was not interested in the political overhaul in our country. Any voices, most of all my parents' animated voices, jarred on my ears, so when Uncle Fatai came by a week later, I went to my bedroom to avoid hearing about the coup again.

I thought they would all talk for a while. Instead, my father knocked on my door moments later. "Enitan, will you come out?"

I'd been lying on my bed, staring at my ceiling. I dragged myself out. My mother was sitting in the living room. Uncle Fatai had gone.

"Yes, Daddy?"

"I want you to tell me the truth," my father said.

He touched my shoulder and I forgot how to breathe again. "Yes, Daddy... "

"Uncle Fatai tells us a friend of yours is in trouble."

My mother stood up. "Stop protecting her. You're always

protecting her. Don't take her to church, don't do this, don't do that. Now look."

"Your friend is in hospital," my father said.

"Your friend is pregnant," my mother said. "She stuck a hanger up herself and nearly killed herself. Now she's telling everyone she was raped. Telling everyone my daughter was involved in this." She patted her chest.

"Let me handle this," my father said. "Were you there?"

"I didn't do anything," I said, stepping back.

"Enitan, were you there?"

I fled to my room. My father followed me to the doorway and watched my shifting feet. "You were there, weren't you," he said.

I kept moving. If I stopped, I would confess.

"I didn't do anything."

"You knew this happened and yet you stayed in this house, saying nothing."

"I told her not to go."

"Look at you," he said, "involved in a mess like this. I won't punish you this time. It's your mother that will punish you. I guarantee."

He left. I shut my door quietly and climbed into bed.

She was at my window. It was night outside.

"Let's go."

Our yard was water. The water had no end.

"Let's go."

I struggled to pull her through my window. She was slipping into the water. I knew she was going to drown.

"They're waiting for you," I said. "At the bottom."

Three slaps aroused me. My mother was standing over me.

"Out of bed," she said. "And get yourself ready. We're going to church."

It was morning. I scrambled out of my bed. I had not been to my mother's church in years, but my memory of the place was clear: a white building with a dome. Behind it, there were banana and palm trees; behind them a stream. In the front yard there was red soil, and the walls of the building seemed to suck it up. People buried curses in that soil, tied their children to the palm trees and prayed for their spirits. They brought them in for cleansing. More than anything else, I was embarrassed my mother would belong to such a church—incense, white gowns, bare feet and drumming. People dipping themselves in a stream and drinking from it.

Along the way, road blocks had been set up, as they always were after a military coup. Cars slowed as they approached them and pedestrians moved quietly. A truck load of soldiers drove past, sounding a siren. The soldiers jeered and lashed at cars with horsewhips. We pulled over to let them pass. A driver pulled over too late. Half the soldiers jumped down from the truck and dragged him out of his car. They started slapping him. The driver's hands went up to plead for mercy. They flogged him with horsewhips and left him there, whimpering by the door of his car.

At first the shouting scared me. I flinched from the first few slaps to the driver's head, heard my mother whisper, "They're going to kill him." Then, I watched the beating feeling some assurance that our world was uniformly terrible. I remembered my own fate again, and Sheri's, and became cross-eyed from that moment on. The driver blended in with the rest of the landscape: a row of rusty-roofed houses; old people with sparrow-like eyes; barefooted children; mothers with flaccid breasts; a bill board saying "Keep Lagos clean." A breadfruit tree; a public tap; its base was embedded in a cement square.

I had no idea what part of the city we were in.

My mother's priest was quiet as she explained what had

64

happened. He had the same expression I remembered, his nose turned up as though he was sniffing something bad. She was to give me holy water to drink, since my father would not allow me to stay for cleansing. Then he produced a bottle of it, green and slimy. I recognized the spirogyra I'd seen in biology classes. I had to drink the water in the churchyard, and make myself sick afterward. None of it was to remain in me. Outside my mother handed the bottle to me. I gagged on every drop.

"Stick your finger down your throat," she said, when I finished.

Two attempts brought the entire contents of my stomach onto the ground, but I continued to retch. My eyes filled with tears. Some of the water had come through my nose.

"Good," my mother said.

I thought of stamping on her feet, squeezing her hand to regain my sense of balance.

"You should never have followed that girl," she said. "Look at me. If anything had happened to you, what would I have done? Look at me."

My gaze slipped from hers.

"The bottle," she said. "Give me the bottle, Enitan."

I handed it to her. It could have been a baton. My mother was hollow, I thought. There was nothing in her. Like a drum, she could seize my heart beat, but that was all. I would not say another word to her, only when I had to, and even then I would speak without feeling: "Good morning, good afternoon, good evening. Good night."

We arrived home and I walked to the back yard, by the fence where the scarlet hibiscus grew. Sheri had gotten pregnant from the rape. Didn't a womb know which baby to reject? And now that the baby had been forced out, how did it look? The color of the hibiscus? I placed one by my ear and listened.

1985

Muffled rage stalks like the wind, sudden and invisible. People don't fear the wind until it fells a tree. Then, they say it's too much.

The first person to tell me my virginity belonged to me was the boy who took it. Before this, I'd thought my virginity belonged to Jesus Christ, my mother, society at large. Anyone but me. My boyfriend, a first-year pharmacy student at London University, assured me that it was mine, to give to him. In those brief seconds between owning and giving up my virginity, he licked the walls of my mouth clean. After I thought he pierced my bowels, I burst into tears.

"What's wrong with you?" he asked.

"I'm sorry," I said. "I have to wash."

It was his semen. I couldn't bear the thought of it leaking out of me and rolling down my thighs. But each time I opened my mouth to tell him, about Sheri and me that awful summer, I thought my voice would blast my ribs apart, flatten him, flatten the bed, toss my sheets around like the wind, so I said nothing.

The next time around my boyfriend strummed me like a guitar. "I don't know what's going on," he said. "Maybe you're frigid." Frigidity was a form of mental illness, he said. We would eventually separate one night, when he complained that I was just like other Nigerian women in bed. "You just lie there," he said. "Like dead women."

I escorted him to my door.

I was in England for nine years, coming home only for vacations. My parents sent me to a boarding school there after that summer, as was the fashion in the seventies, and for the first time I would have to explain why I washed my hair once a week and put grease straight back in. My new school friends were surprised that I didn't live in a hut in Africa, that I'd never seen a lion except in the London zoo. Some confessed their parents didn't like black people. Only one had decided that she didn't either and I ignored her, the way I ignored another who said "hey man" and did all sorts of silly dances whenever she saw me.

I'd always thought English people didn't wash regularly. I expected them to behave like characters from an Enid Blyton book. My best friend, Robin, thought this was absolutely *wuh*-diculous. We became close because she, too, thought Bob Marley was a prophet, and she loved to abhor her parent's values. Dear Robin, she couldn't pronounce her R's. "Wound and wound the wound-about," the other girls teased her. "Wound and wound the wound-about the wabid wascal wan Wobin Wichardson."

Twagic. Altogether I thought it was easier being black in that school, but Robin wouldn't say the word: black. Her parents had taught her that it was rude. So, I was her friend with the afro, you know, The-Brown-One. I told her that black was what I was, not an insult. I wasn't even proud of it, because I'd never been ashamed of it, so there. I forced her to say it one night: Black. Bu-lack. Buh-lee-yack. She burst into tears and called me awogant. The day she finally plucked up the courage, I took offense. I didn't like the inflection in her voice. "Flipping heck," she said. "There's no pleasing you."

Robin was the laziest and smartest fourteen-year-old I knew, and she beat me in class tests every time. She was the first person to tell me that nothing a woman does justifies rape. "Some girls encourage it," I said. "Who taught you that cwap?" she asked. I couldn't remember, but bad girls got raped was all I'd heard before, and of the bad girls I knew, not one had taken her matter to court. For Sheri, justice came when Damola Ajayi was admitted into a mental institution where drug addicts in Lagos ended up: therapy included regular beatings. I wasn't even sure she knew about his demise. Her family moved out of our neighborhood and I lost contact with her. Robin assured me that justice was not much fairer in her country. The motto of the Old Bailey should read, "Pwotect the wich and punish the Iwish."

My parents separated while I was in school in England. My father delivered the news to me and I remember feeling like I'd mistakenly swallowed a worm in a glass of water; I wanted to throw up. I wondered if the trouble I'd caused hadn't divided them further. My father explained that my mother would take his duplex in another suburb of Lagos, and she would live in one unit while collecting rent from the next. There were no phone lines in the area, so I couldn't call her. I was to stay with him.

A squabble began between them, over ownership of property and over me. My mother vowed to have my father disbarred. Instead she developed hypertension and said my father had caused it. I spent vacations with her, and she spent most of them complaining about him; how he ignored her in public; how he insinuated something or the other. My mother clung to details while my father seemed confused: "I don't know what she's talking about. I haven't done anything to her." Soon I began to spend vacations in London, working as a shop assistant in department stores to supplement my allowance to avoid staying with either of them.

I studied law at London University and became part of the Nigerian student community, who, like the English community in Lagos, clung to each other, grappling with weather conditions and sharing news from home. We had had two military governments since the summer of 1975. The first ended with the assassination of our head of state; the second, in a transition to civilian rule. Still the news from home had not improved: "Ah, these civilians, they are worse than the military." "Ah, these politicians. Don't you know? They're nothing but thieves." I heard about Sheri again during this time. She had won the Miss Nigeria pageant, after taking her university title, and would be representing our country in the Miss World contest in England. I was curious to see her. I watched the contest that night with two fellow law students, Suzanne and Rola. Rola was Nigerian and Jamaican, and rooting for both Misses, Suzanne was from Hong Kong and rooting for no one. "I can't believe we're sitting here watching this," she kept mumbling. Rola, as usual, was ready to analyze. "I mean, she is pretty, but nothing special. Just pretty-pretty. I mean, she couldn't catwalk or anything. Maybe face model, but not even that. I mean, she definitely can't model-model... "

I was too busy smiling. It wasn't Paris, Sheri wasn't wearing a red negligee, but it was good enough. I regretted judging her; regretted my ignorance at age fourteen. Sheri didn't make it past the first round of the Miss World contest. None of our girls ever did. Later, I heard she'd become part of the sugar daddy circuit in Lagos, hanging around senators, and going on shopping sprees abroad. She was given all the titles that came with that.

1981, I graduated from university and joined a firm of solicitors in London. 1983, there was another military coup in my country. This time, I was recovering from a failed relationship, having discovered the boy I'd been dating half the year was dating someone else. It was out of respect for me that he lied to me, he said. He knew I wasn't the sort of girl to like two-timing. Still, he called to invite me to a vigil.

"Vigil for what?" I asked.

"Democracy," he said.

At the Nigerian High Commission. Would I come? I almost checked the ear-piece. When did he ever do such a thing? We called him Stringfellow, after the night club. And wasn't he the one who, whenever we passed the South African embassy in Trafalgar square, would say about the English people protesting against apartheid, "There they go again. Always fighting for blacks who live far away, never the blacks they have to live with."

I thought of standing on Fleet street where our High Commission was, in the cold, with a candle in my hand, all night long, for any cause. I thought of this boy who had lied from the minute I set eyes on him.

"Stringfellow," I said. "Never call me again."

People talked about the influence of Western culture as though Western culture were the same throughout the West, and never changed. But our parents had graduated in the dawn of sixties England, and we were to graduate in the material eighties. Like any generation defined by the economics of their childhood, we were children of the oil boom, and furthermore, we were the children who had benefited from the oil boom. Politics in England played out on a continuum from left to right wing. Politics in our country was a scuffle between the military and politicians. Both were conservative and so were we. Now our greatest contribution to our society was that we were more traditional than the people who had given birth to us.

A boy loved a girl and he called her his wife. A girl loved a boy and she stayed at home on weekends to cook for him, while he went out with some other girl. We were going out and staying in. Any talk of political protest was the talk of mad English people, or Nigerians who were trying to be like them. We didn't spare a thought for those who were finding it difficult to pay their school fees, now that the oil boom in our country had become a recession. We rebelled and used our pocket money to buy leather jackets, or unusual shoes. That was what we did.

I looked at the small stack of books in my room long after I hung up on Stringfellow. I'd acquired them after I stopped reading stories I could predict, or stories that had nothing to do with my life. Stringfellow would say they were written by women who really ought to straighten their dreadlocks and stop complaining.

"Bloody wolly," I said.

All lines to Lagos were busy. I didn't get through to my father until late the next evening and by then, had established my opinions. Our civilian government had begged for the coup. Never had there been a more debauched democracy: champagne parties, embezzlements. My father explained that our constitution had also been suspended, a development I couldn't fathom with my head full of English text-books. "Can they really do that?" I asked. "They can do whatever they want," he explained. "The power of a constitution comes from the respect people give it. If they don't, then it is words on paper. Nothing else."

He was wary of the new military government, and their promise to wage war against indiscipline. I thought that it wasn't such a bad idea, in a country where you still couldn't expect electricity for a full week. Then the reports started coming in: floggings for jumping bus queues; squats for government workers who came late to work; a compulsory sanitation day to stay home and dust; military tribunals for ex-politicians; Decree Two, under which persons suspected of acts prejudicial to state security could be detained without charge; Decree Four, under which journalists could be arrested and imprisoned for publishing any information about public officials. My father kept asking, but I told him I never wanted to go back.

I changed my mind one winter morning, while waiting for a double-decker bus to arrive. The wind popped my umbrella inside out, flipped my skirt almost to my waist. It ripped tears from my eyes and knocked my braids backward into my face. A braid scratched my eyeball. I stood there listening to the wind, whizzing in all directions, colliding with my thoughts, which were colliding with each other. I was thinking of men who were given to acts of cowardice, lying when they should be braver. I was thinking of a certain partner in my firm who stared at my braided hair as if it were a head full of serpents. I thought of partners who walked like they'd never passed wind. I remembered my phone bills. I was thinking that if I returned home, at least, at least I would be warm.

Summer of 1984, I returned home for law school. My father bought me a new car, a white Volkswagen Jetta, which I drove straight to my mother's house. "He spoils you," she said, dusting her hands in disapproval. The Jetta was less attractive to armed robbers than other imported models. When my father bought it, it was selling for six times my salary working for him as a newly qualified lawyer. A year later, a second-hand model would sell for twice that amount. He paid for it in cash. There was no such thing as a car loan, and I couldn't drive it on Tuesdays and Thursdays because during weekdays in Lagos, odd and even number vehicle plates were assigned separate days to ease the traffic flow. And, I would have to continue living with my father because rents in Lagos were paid two, three years in advance.

I was almost tempted to board a British Airways back. Then, one day, a lecturer stopped me along the corridors at law school.

"Yes sir?" I said, startled that he knew my last name.

"Is your father Sunny Taiwo?" he asked.

"Yes," I said.

"He is in the papers a lot these days."

He was.

"How is he?"

"Fine, sir."

"You were studying in England?"

Yes, I said.

"Welcome back," he said. "And give my regards to your father. We were at Baptist High together."

I realized I was glad to be back. There were partners in my old firm who may have been to Cambridge with my father. Heaven forbid they admitted that to me, or to themselves. Some of my law school peers from overseas would continue to complain about Lagos: the surly clerks, lazy air-conditioners, power cuts, traffic we called go-slow, water shortages, armed robbers, bribery. But I would embrace the nuisances of Lagos from then on; all of them, to be acknowledged at last.

My father had recently gained publicity for a case he won. His client, a newspaper columnist, Peter Mukoro, was arrested at a police check point earlier in the year. Peter Mukoro wrote articles criticizing the police. He claimed that they targeted him because of this, but they claimed he was indisciplined at the time of his arrest. My father argued that his arrest was unlawful anyhow and won the case.

Peter Mukoro had initially approached my father over a land dispute. He was nothing like my father's usual clients, wealthy property owners who wished to maintain a low profile. He was a man in his early forties, an unabashed dissident who courted publicity. I met him once and thought he drank too much and talked too loud. I suspected he was driven more by vanity than anything else, but my father was enjoying the publicity, holding press conferences with him, making statements about police harassment. I called him an old rebel, but secretly I was proud. As a child, this was how I'd envisioned a lawyer's work to be. Now all I could foresee was paper-work.

Law school ended the summer of 1985. Within a week of my graduation, there was another military coup and our constitution was further suspended. Days later, I registered for national service. My first month would be spent in military training; the remainder of the year, I would work for my father who had no obligation to pay me since, technically, I was employed by the government. Initially posted to a rural district, I begged the registration clerk to send me to another camp, when I saw signs warning campers not to walk around at night, because they might be abducted and used for human sacrifice. The alternative camp was based in a busier district, on the campus of a technical college that was closed for the summer vacation.

I drove there hoping that the new camp would be better than I was predicting, hoping even, that I might finally meet someone nice and honest.

An early morning mist hung over the race tracks of the College of Technology. Fifty odd platoons were lined up on the grass patch within it, awaiting roll call. The grass was heavily beaded with dew. I slid my combat boots along and pulled my cap down. It was too early for roll call, and too chilly for warm blood.

"Enitan Taiwo," our platoon leader called out.

"Yeah," I answered.

My platoon mates laughed as he checked my name on the rota.

"Mike Obi?"

"Yes," said the man in front of me. His voice was deep. I'd noticed him as I joined the platoon for roll call. He was standing with his hands in his pockets: wide back, uniform looking like it had been pressed over him. I would be taller than him if I wore heels. He dug his combat boots into the grass and lifted his cap and I saw that his head was shaved.

Our platoon leader blew his whistle. "Round the tracks!"

There were complaints all around. "See me, see trouble," the woman behind me said. "All this *wahala*," my neighbor said.

Mike Obi turned to me. "That's why they're calling us the pregnant platoon."

"Why?" I asked.

"Because we're the laziest, fattest platoon around."

"None of the above," I said.

He dimpled like side pockets. We began to jog along the race tracks.

"Are you one of the lawyers?" he asked, as we rounded the bend. I nodded in response. I was beginning to feel the stretch in my legs.

"How come you start camp later than everyone else?" he asked.

"Because we are better than everyone else."

He laughed. "I'm not so sure about that."

"Law school graduation ceremony," I said.

A group of joggers passed us, chanting an army song.

"You must have been here during the coup a week ago," I said.

"Yes."

"What was that like?"

"No one really cared. Soldiers go. Soldiers come. We had morning drill, went out during the curfew."

"That's a pity."

He stretched out his hand. "I'm Mike."

"Enitan," I said.

His hand felt coarse. I slowed and he slowed, too.

"What do you do, Mike?" I asked.

"Me? I'm an artist."

"I've never met an artist before."

He pulled his cap down. "Actually, I'm an architect, but I studied fine art for a year."

"Liar... "

"At Nsukka university."

"Liar," I said.

"I *am* an artist," he said. "You should see my mosaics."

"Mosaics? Talk true. What kind?"

"With beads. Very beautiful."

"I'm sure."

"And you?" he asked.

"I've just finished law school."

"You don't look that young to me."

I swiped his shoulder. It felt like wood.

"I'm sorry," he said. "But some of the graduates here look twenty-one. You and I don't."

"Speak for yourself."

"You should be proud of your age."

I smiled. "I am. I'm not a new graduate. I worked for three years after my degree."

"Where?"

"England."

"What made you come home?"

"It was cold. It was time. What made you give up on your art?"

"You know our people. Everyone told me I would starve and I believed them."

"Hm. Maybe you didn't believe in yourself."

"Maybe."

"You don't regret giving up?"

"I don't regret anything."

"And yet you still call yourself an artist."

"If necessary," he said.

"To do what?" I asked.

Impress, he said. We strolled back like old friends. Mike was wrong. Most women I knew would sprint from an artist. It meant that they might have to dabble with poverty and poverty always cleared people's eyes in Lagos. After morning drill, where I learned how to march and about-turn, we parted ways. He didn't know it, but I was ready to reach into his dimples and pluck out a gold coin.

I walked back to the women's halls located five minutes away from the race tracks. A poorly-lit building normally inhabited by the college's students during the academic year, the halls housed national service participants during military training. At the entrance, a group of women were arguing with the caretaker. "Why can't we have men inside?" one woman asked. "After all, we're not students, and some of us are married."

"Is not allowed," the caretaker said.

"Who said?" she asked.

"Jesus," he said.

The old man wasn't letting any men in. He sat by the entrance, flicking his horsewhip and waiting for those who dared. The day before he had lashed out at one graduate who had studied in the US, and still held his rights dear. "You have no rat!" this graduate screamed at him in a Nigerian-American accent. "You have no rat to whip me like that! Nobady has the rat to whip me like that!" The old man looked him up and down. "You want your rights, you go back to the country where you learned how to shout at an elder," he said. "Now, clear out of here, Johnny jus' come."

Baba, they called him. Every old man in my country was Baba, or Papa. This one was keeper of graduate vaginas.

Walking up the stairs, I smelled urine from the toilets and remembered my old school in Lagos. I was almost tempted to laugh: ten years later and still living in similar lodgings. My fear of inhaling the foul odor prevented me. I placed my palm over my nose and hurried past.

Inside the dormitory, I removed my T-shirt and lay on the bed. The shutters were open, but the air was flat and dry. The dormitory was like a prison cell: two iron spring beds and four walls sullied by the hand prints and head smears of previous inmates. My roommate, a graduate from the university of Lagos, refused to sleep in it. She shuttled from home, but home was far away for me and I wasn't sure I could wake up early enough to make roll call.

I rested a little, decided to buy mosquito coils from the hawker who sat under an almond tree by the parking lot. A few campers were there, chatting in groups. Visitors drove in all day to see friends and family, and sometimes camp felt like an everlasting party. At the hawkers stall, I selected a box of mosquito coils, a packet of Trebor mints and paid for them.

Contemplating another packet, I felt a tap on my shoulder. It was Mike. He bent to pick a box of mosquito coils.

"You, too?" he said.

"They're eating me alive," I said.

He paid the hawker and we began to walk toward the halls.

"What are you doing now?" he asked.

"Nothing," I said.

"Come and talk to me."

He pointed to the spectator stand by the race tracks. We walked there and sat on the bottom row. Mike removed one of the coils from the box and lit it. I was lulled by the sounds: crickets chattering and laughter from the parking lot. The mosquito coil turned a fluorescent amber and gray smoke rose from it. Mike caught me watching him.

"I'm afraid," he said. "The way you look at me, like I've stolen your money. Are you one of those women who can't trust somebody?"

"I'm one of those women who wants to trust somebody."

He lifted the mosquito coil and placed it between us.

"That's good," he said.

He spoke softly between pauses. I talked till I almost bit my tongue and delayed swallowing to slip in punch lines.

"You this girl," he kept saying. He rarely laughed.

Mike grew up near Enugu, a city in eastern Nigeria that was the heart o f Biafra. His parents were lecturers at the state university. His mother taught drama, and his father, history. During the Civil War, he was sent to a foster home in England and I teased him because years later, he still had traces of an English accent in addition to his Igbo one.

"Eni-ton," I corrected him, when I'd had enough of him mispronouncing my name.

"Eni-tan," he said.

"On! on! Do your mouth like this... on... on."

"An."

"For heaven's sake."

It was terrible that we'd had different experiences of the Civil War. In university, I finally acknowledged the holocaust that was Biafra, through memoirs and history books, and pictures of limbless people; children with their stomachs bloated from kwashiorkor and their rib cages as thin as leaf veins. Their parents were mostly dead. Executed. Macheted. Blown up. Beheaded. There were accounts of blood-drinking, flesh-eating, atrocities of the human spirit that only a civil war could generate, while in Lagos we had carried on as though it were happening in a different country. Our Head of State got married even. The timing of the truce, Mike said, came about because the warring troops wanted to watch Péle play football. Péle. Civil war. I hoped that he was joking.

A trip to Oshogbo in Western Nigeria gave him his love for art. He visited the art institutes and the groves of Yoruba gods. He loved football, played it, dreamed about it. Sometimes when he talked about it, I feared he might gag on joy. He told me about Brazil's Péle, Argentina's Maradona. Nigeria's striker, Thunder Balogun and goal keeper, Okala, his first hero. "Okala had mystical powers," he said. "I saw it with my two eyes."

"Bury your head in shame," I said.

Friday, we left camp for a meal at Mama Maria's, a food spot on Victoria Island. It was owned by a local madam and run by her prostitutes. I'd heard about it from friends at law school and thought it was the sort of place Mike might want to visit. We drove there in his car, an old white Citroen that he occasionally patted like a dog. I noticed a rusty hole in the floor, through which I could see the road below.

"What do you do when the rain comes?" I asked.

"I avoid puddles," he said.

"Doesn't it bother you? This big hole?"

He laughed. "No, neither do my headlights."

"What's wrong with them?"

"They're attached with masking tape."

"One day you'll be driving the steering wheel alone."

We were stopped at every police checkpoint. Some policemen even laughed as we pulled away. As we drove through the gates at Mama Maria's, a group of prostitutes mauled his car. They wiggled their tongues and pressed their breasts to the windscreen. They made shrill noises like huntsmen. Once they realized we were not a couple of white men, they abandoned us.

Walking in, we found the place full of pot-bellied expatriates. We never called them immigrants. I'd seen their faces before, working on construction sites overseas. One or two had prostitutes on their laps. The prostitutes eyed us as we headed for the view overlooking the lagoon. They were majestic, and they were ugly. A man was useless-ing me, they would say, for all my propriety and education, so what was I looking at? I noticed the airline stickers on the wall behind the drinks bar.

"Is that some sort of honor roll?"

Mike glanced at it. "More like a tombstone."

At first, I didn't know what he was talking about, then I remembered AIDS. I didn't know much about the disease, but I was sure that people would hide and ignore it, like the drug problem of the seventies, until it was out of control. So far, in Lagos, we blamed expatriates and prostitutes for AIDS.

One of the women approached us and we ordered two plates of food. She handed us beers and we began to drink. The street lights of Ikoyi shimmered down the lagoon. It was possible to believe that I could swim across with ease. My gaze dropped to the shoreline a few meters from Mama Maria's. There was a broken beer bottle to my right, a car tire to my left. A line of rotten seaweed joined them together.

"Filthy," Mike said.

I fingered the bottle of Gulder beer and wondered if it was the cold malt or his voice making me relax.

"You never talk about your mother," he said.

"I do," I said.

"No, you talk about your father, but never about your mother."

I took another swig of the beer and wiped my mouth clean. A daughter was not meant to be at odds with her mother. Especially an only child. Thinking of my mother made me feel like I'd left the door of a vault wide open for thieves.

"We hardly see each other. She belongs to a church, a cult, actually. One of those, take your money and give you fear. She's been a member for as long as I can remember. I think she was drawn in because of my brother. She thinks I idolize my father. But I've never had illusions about my father. You have to be friends with at least one of your parents. Don't you think?"

"Yes."

"Well, there it is, my mother."

There was a time that I would be more open about our relationship, but the responses I got were the same: "Well, my dear, she is your mother." "Only have one mother." "Shiece your mother! She suffered for you!"

"When was the last time you saw her?" Mike asked.

"I see her all the time."

"The last time was?"

"My graduation."

"You should try to see her soon."

"Should I? Why should I?"

"Because you should."

Our mothers were wonderful, mostly. They shielded us from the truths about our fathers, remained in bad marriages to give us a chance. But I'd seen, met, heard of daughters who admitted their mothers were vain, weak, bullying, sluttish, drunken. The difference between these daughters and I was that I did not know my own mother, and I had kept our lack of relationship hidden, often lied about it. How could I tell Mike about my graduation photograph, the one my mother had refused to pose in if my father were by my side? I asked her to let the day end without fighting, and she accused me of taking his side. My graduation day ended in silence. I posed separately with either parent, and then vowed that they would never involve me in their arguments again.

"Because you should," I repeated.

"Yes," Mike said.

"Everything is that simple?"

"Why stop at B, when you can go from A to Z?"

"Isn't that what life's about? The stops along the way, the unraveling?"

He shrugged. "When death knocks, who remembers the unraveling? Only the outcome is important, I believe."

"Then you might as well be born and die immediately."

"I'm sorry," he said.

"Don't be. I'm just saying, I don't think family ties are as simple as people like to say they are, over here. That's all I'm saying."

He reached for my hand. "Why are we fighting? You're too serious tonight. And this place is depressing anyway, for tourists. Next time I will take you somewhere better."

"Only you knows," I said, childishly.

He bothered me like a white sheet. I wanted to search for stains, hidden dirt.

It was Makossa night. The evening ended with us watching other people make fools of themselves, until Manu Dibango's "Soul Makossa" came on, then we made fools of ourselves.

On our way to camp we slowed through a night market. Fluorescent lights from the stalls lit up the street. The street was narrow and juju music blared from a battered cassette player perched on a wooden stool. Street hawkers sat around selling boxes of sugar, bathing sponges, tinned sardines, chewing sticks, cigarettes, and Bazooka Joe gum. A group of old men huddled together playing a board game. A kerosene lantern lit up their faces, casting huge shadows on a wall behind them. We came to a stop and I edged closer to the window to watch them moving their chips. The air was warm and the sky pitch-black. I heard a loud crack above the music. At first I thought it was fireworks, but it was the wrong time of the year, and since one military regime had banned them, they were scarce.

A man was running down my side of the street. His hands were up and he was shouting. The music drowned out what he was saying. I noticed people in the market stand up, heard another crack. The man was thrown forward. He crashed over the trunk of the car behind us. People in the market began to run. The old men disappeared from their table. Mike was looking in his rearview mirror. His hand went to the back of my neck. My head dropped to my knees. I found myself staring through the hole in his car. One moment I could see the road, the next, dirt. We were moving. I wondered how; there had been other cars in front of us. I heard car engines. Mike pressed on his horn and I covered my ears. We drove over a bump and my knee punched my chin. I no longer saw the hole. His hand touched my back.

"Armed robbers," he said.

I sat up. "They were coming from behind?"

We were now on an expressway with street lights.

"The car behind us drove through the market," he explained. "I followed him and everyone else followed us."

"The people in the market?"

"They scattered."

I was meant to feel something. I did not know what.

"I hear it is university students. Is it?"

"I don't know."

We didn't speak until we reached a police check point. Mike reported the raid, and the policeman asked for his driver's license. For the rest of the journey we were silent.

"How are you?" He asked as we drove into camp.

I'd been rubbing my chin.

"Fine," I said. "You?"

He patted my shoulder. We stopped by the women's halls in the college and I crept past Baba, the caretaker, who was asleep with his horsewhip in his lap. I knew I was meant to feel something; I still didn't know what. In my room I shut my door and leaned against it. It was what people in films did.

"It's you?" my mother said.

There was a crease across the bridge of her nose where her frown had set. Gray hair peeped from her hairline and time had cast shadows under her eyes. I knew that would be my fate.

"It's me," I said, forcing cheer into my voice.

"You're still plaiting your hair?" she said.

"Yes."

"You don't want to try something new?"

"No."

She walked to her chair. "You young girls and all these hair extensions."

My mother's house smelled of unused linen, shut cupboards, rusty valves, mothballs, candlewick, and incense for prayer. Her window panes were thick with dust and I was sure that if she'd employed someone, they would be clean; but every house help she had ran away. "How is camp?" she asked.

"Fine," I said.

"Only fine? You can't take that attitude. You must try to enjoy life more."

I almost laughed out loud. She who was always accounting

or predicting a bad event. If the sun were shining, rain might fall. If rain fell, piss might follow.

"How are you?" I asked.

"I'm all right, but my medicine, the price has gone up. And my tenants, they are late with their rent again."

"What is it this time?"

"They cannot pay. I will give them till the end of next week. If they don't pay by then, I will have them evicted."

Her tenants just didn't believe in paying on time. My father would send a letter to them, I promised her.

"This is Lagos," she said. "People don't move until they're forced. And your father anyway, what does he care? He keeps talking about human rights. The man still hasn't put my houses in my name. What about my rights?"

"He hasn't?"

"Maybe if you ask him, he will. You know you and your father. He thinks you're his lawyer." She patted her chest. "You didn't even ask after me during the coup. You could have at least come to check I was all right."

"We were not allowed out."

My mother calculated dates, situations, betrayals, and she looked at me long enough to summarize my life. She was still angry about my graduation, I knew. But I was angry too, and that didn't start on the day of my graduation. Grievances had set in her bones like cement and it was difficult to be around her.

"You want me to leave?" I finally asked.

"You met me here on my own," she said. "If you wish, you can leave."

Now, I said what I wanted: "All this over one photograph. Is this what you want? To ruin every good day in your life because of one man?"

"You can leave right now, if this is how you want to speak to me."

"He doesn't care. Can't you see?"

"Go back to that house where you learned to abuse your mother."

"You get angry and he forgets. It's all in the past to him."

"It is not past you're living in his house."

"I don't care who is right or wrong."

"It's not past he struts around like a man of conscience."

"I do not care."

"It's not past I'm living in a house that still doesn't belong to me."

I waved her words away.

"Always," she said. "You were too busy trailing in his footsteps."

"How?"

"You always were," she said. "He never gave you a chance."

"You remember things as you want."

"From the day you were born, feeding you ideas. Don't cook, this and that. Maybe you should have been born a son to satisfy him."

"What is it you won't forgive me for?" I asked. "That I like my own father?"

"He was no good."

"To me, he is."

"If he's no good to me, he's no good to you. The day you realize it, I'll be here waiting for you. The damage has been done already. You're still too blind to know."

I stood up. "You want to make me doubt myself? That is it?"

"Yes," she said. "Yes, you never want to hear it. Never about your father. Go on. Continue to deceive yourself."

I no longer believed her; hurt one moment, hurtful the next. She could recall what my father said ten years ago, and yet she misconstrued my entire childhood. She who took a child to church to heal him. She who swallowed pills regularly. She was like one of those mothers who put their children's feet in fire to stop them convulsing. Why didn't they put their own feet in, if they so believed in its healing powers?

"Go on," she said. "Who asked you to come with your trouble? Not one minute's peace did you give me as a child, now you want to criticize me. Asking me why I won't stand next to him in a photograph. Why should I stand next to him? For any reason? The man gave me nothing. Nothing, for all his education, he's as typical as they come. And I may not have paid your school fees, but remember I gave birth to you. Just remember that, while you're out there walking around with certificate, calling yourself a lawyer. Someone gave birth to you."

It took all my strength to shut her door gently. At her gate, I swore that I would never visit my mother's house again. Some people were happy by habit; others were not. It had nothing to do with me.

We were thirty minutes into our endurance test, a ten-mile run. I was hoping to make it to my old school, to see what had become of the place. Mike and other healthy people were in front. I had fallen behind. I took shorter breaths as my heart raced. I was trying to run with some dignity, unlike some of my platoon members who were using their hands to support their backs.

This part of Lagos was a shanty town. We passed a house with flaky yellow paint and a group of pot-bellied infants scurried out. One almost toppled into the gutter alongside the road and his mother yanked him out and boxed his ear. He began to howl. We passed a group of palm trees huddled together and a pink and white building with a sign post saying: "Hollywood Hair. Mannycure, Pennycure, Wash and Set. Fresh Eggs and Coca-Cola." A woman, the proprietor perhaps, sat on a stool with a cloth wrapped around her body. She was polishing her teeth with a chewing stick and paused to spit into the gutter. The entire area smelled of goat droppings and morning mist. I decided to head back to camp.

The soldiers on duty eyed me as I walked through the gates of the college. I remembered how I tried to bribe them to sneak out during the day as my roommate did. They waited while I fumbled with the money in my pocket. Mike later said, "You greet them every day, then you give them something to buy beer. That's how you do it. Not bringing out wads of *naira* notes. Where have you been?"

I could have swiped his head.

A car horn tooted. I turned to see a new Peugeot. Stepping on the side of the road, I waited for it to pass, but it came to a halt. The windscreen was tinted so I couldn't see the driver, but as soon as the windows came down, I knew.

"Sheri Bakare," I said.

It was like finding a pressed flower I'd long forgotten about. Her smile was less broad; her pink gums seemed to have disappeared.

"*Aburo*," she said. "Is this your face?"

"What are you doing here?"

She laughed. "I came to see my brother."

"Which one?"

"Gani."

"Gani's here? I'm too old. Far too old."

We were holding hands. She was wearing a yellow *agbada* with gold embroidery around the neckline, and her fingers were laden with gold rings.

"Can I give you a lift?" she asked.

Inside her car I smelled perfume and new leather seats. I sat up because I was wet with sweat. Sheri slowed over a speed bump.

"How come you're in national service?" she asked.

"I'm just out of law school."

"You're a lawyer?"

"Yes, and you?"

"I studied education."

"You're a teacher?"

"Me? No."

We drove past the race tracks and stopped by the women's halls. As we got out, Sheri wrapped her scarf around her head and leaned against the car. She moved with the rhythm of big women I admired; like a steady boat on choppy water. I noticed she was wearing black high heeled sandals with rhinestone buckles. It was ten thirty in the morning.

"You look well," I said.

"You too," she said. "You're still slim and don't even try to tell me I am."

I laughed. "I wasn't going to, Miss Nigeria."

"Ah, don't remind me," she said. "Those skinny girls. I still have a pretty face, *sha*."

"Beautiful," I said.

Even with her big ears. Her cheeks hollowed as she spoke.

"I hear you went to England that summer," she said. "I wish I could have gone, for university at least."

"Why didn't you?"

"My father died."

"I'm sorry to hear that. I only heard that you moved."

"He died," she said, scraping the ground with her shoe. "And we lost Alhaja, too. Not long afterward."

I watched her sandals cloud up with dust.

"You remember Kudi?" she asked.

"How can I forget her?"

"She's in her first year at Lagos University. I've just been to visit her. You should have seen her, all of them, nineteen-year-olds wearing the latest fashions. No wonder she keeps asking for money."

"Aren't they supposed to be studying?"

She sucked her teeth. "Their heads aren't in studying. They are looking for boys with cars. I told Kudi, 'If you want clothes, take some of mine.' But she said she didn't want any of mine."

"Why not?"

"She said I dress like an old mama. Can you believe it? She said that to me? Children of nowadays. No respect. We were never like this, I'm sure."

I laughed. "How is Kudi?"

It was as though I saw her a day ago. She continued to talk about her sister and I encouraged her, only because it was easy conversation to make. Before I left, I took her address and promised to visit her over the weekend. It was an apartment block not far from my father's house, and I knew she couldn't afford to live there without a sponsor. But Sheri was sugary, as we said in Lagos; she had a man, an older man, a man as old as my father even, and he would pay her rent.

"Make sure you come," she said. "I'm lonely there."

Saturday morning I drove into Lagos Island via the mainland bridge to see her. A few freighters were docked along the harbor of the marina. Descending the bridge, I caught a partial view of the commercial center I had come to know by driving. A mishmash of skyscrapers crowded the skylines, scattered between them were dull concrete one-story buildings with cor-rugated-iron roofs. They were mostly trading stores. Each bore a sign in need of painting. A web of electricity and telephone lines criss-crossed above them.

The Atlantic weaved its way around Lagos. Sometimes dull and muddy, other times strident and salty, bearing different names: Kuramo waters, Five Cowry Creek, Lagos Marina, Lagos Lagoon. It was the same water. Asphalt bridges connected the islands to the mainland and the sky always looked as sad as a person whose lover had lost interest. People rarely noticed it, even its amber sunsets. If the sun were going down, it meant there would be no light soon and Lagosians needed to see their way. Street lights here did not always function.

Millions lived in Lagos. Some were natives, but most had roots in the provinces. They fell in and out with the elements as though the weather were created to punish and reward: "Sun beat my head," "Breeze cooled me." Most days it felt like a billion people walking down the labyrinth of petty and main streets: beggar men, secretaries, government contractors (thieves, some would say), Area Boys, street children. You could tell how well they ate by the state of their shoes. Beggars, of course, went bare foot. If no one noticed the sky, it was because they were busy watching vehicles. There was a constant din of cars, popping exhaust pipes, and engines, commuters scrambling for canary-yellow buses and private transport vans we called *kabukabu* and *danfo*. They bore Bible epitaphs: Lion of Judah, God Saves. Their drivers drove devilishly, and added to the incongruity around: cattle grazing in a rubbish dump, a man crossing the highway in a wheel-chair, a street hawker with a Webster's dictionary in one hand and a toilet brush in the other.

There were countless billboards: Pepsi, Benson and Hedges, Daewoo, Indomie Instant Noodles, Drive Carefully, Fight Child Abuse. All smells joined hands in one: sweaty skin and fumes, and the heat was the kind that made your forehead crease, and crease, until you witnessed something that made you smile: a taxi driver making lurid remarks; people cursing themselves well and good; All right-Sirs, our urban praise singers or borderline beggars, who hailed any person for money. Chief! Professor! Excellency!

It was a hard city to love; a bedlam of trade. Trade thrived in the smallest of street corners; in stores; on the heads of hawkers; even in the suburbs where family homes were converted into finance houses and hair salons, according to the need. The outcome of this was dirt, piles of it, on the streets, in open gutters, and in the marketplaces, which were tributes to both dirt and trade. My favorite time was early morning, before people encroached, when the air was cool and all I could hear was the call from Central Mosque: *Allahu Akhbar, Allahu Akhbar.* All that crooning when the city was most quiet, it made sense.

By the Cathedral Church of Christ, I met a bottleneck and was cornered by a group of lepers. One rapped on my window and I rolled it down to put money into his tin cup. A group of refugee children from North Africa, noticing my gesture, scurried to my car. They rubbed my windows and pleaded with feigned expressions. I felt ashamed for wishing them off the streets. Passers-by trespassed the stairs of the Cathedral without regard. Once a monument along the marina, people could now buy fried yams, brassieres, and mosquito coils inches away from her ebony doors. The traffic gave way and I drove on.

I remembered my mother's medicine and made a detour into a market district to check their prices. The roads there were as tight as corridors and gutters dipped inches from my car tires. Crowded stalls blasted out bluish-light fluorescent lights. Their iron roofs collapsed into each other. I called out to a young man behind the counter at a pharmacy stall. "You have Propanolol?"

He nodded.

"Let me see it," I said.

He hurried over and held the bottle up. I noticed the expiration date.

"This has expired," I said.

He snatched it and walked away.

I drove fast until I approached a large round-about. A group of police wives sat within it, waiting for customers who came to braid their hair. Some had infants strapped to their backs, but they pursued my car. I recognized one who regularly braided my hair and waved to her. Lagos festered with people: drivers, sellers, shoppers, loiterers, beggars. Madmen. The latter some-times walked the streets with nothing but dust covering their private parts. I once saw a woman like that. She was pregnant.

When I reached Sheri's house my shoulders were as tight as springs. She opened her door wearing another colorful *agbada* and matching head tie. I sniffed.

"What are you cooking?"

"A little food," she said.

"For me?"

She prodded my shoulder as I walked in. Sheri's apartment was like an array of plastic flowers. Each piece of furniture had a flower motif on it; some in powdery pastels, others in strident reds and yellows. I almost expected to smell pungent potpourri instead of the onions and peppers simmering in her kitchen.

"Sit here while I finish," she said.

I sunk into a sofa of daffodils and noticed the miniature porcelain ornaments on her center table. There were kittens, a woman with an umbrella, and a house with the inscription "Home is where the heart is." The kittens were lined up. I was sure that if I moved one, she would notice. Her cushions were lined up the same way on the sofas, equally spaced.

Pepper smoke scratched the back of my throat. I heard a pot rocking over a hot plate. "I hope I'm going to eat some of that," I said.

"Eat what you want," she said. "Ibrahim doesn't eat much."

"Ibrahim?"

Her head appeared around the corner. "Hassan," she said. "The Brigadier. Have you heard of him?"

A tall, skinny man who played polo. He collected polo ponies and women as young as his daughters and was always in the papers during the Lagos tournament.

"He has a stomach ulcer," she said, and disappeared into her kitchen.

I stared at the spot where her face had been.

"Does he treat you well?"

She came out again, cleaning her hands with a dish towel. "I live here. I don't have to worry about money."

"Yes, but does he treat you well?"

She sat down. "Which one of our men really treats women well?"

"I don't know many."

"So," she said.

I inspected my nails. "Isn't he married, Sheri."

Polygamy was considered risqué. Women in our generation who opted for it ended up looking quite the opposite of traditional.

She nodded. "To two women, and he can marry two more if he wants. He's a Moslem."

"Is that what you want?"

She laughed. "Want? I beg you, don't talk to me about want. When my father died who remembered me? Chief Bakare done die, God Bless his family. We didn't even know where our next meal was coming from, and no one cared. Not even my uncle, who took all his money."

"But your father and uncle were close."

She shook her head. "Don't let anyone deceive you. Pray you're never in a situation to need them. It is then you will know what two plus two really makes. Listen, I take care of my family, I even take care of Ibrahim. Since morning I'm cooking. He may not show up, and this won't be the first time. So if I have to tie my head up when I go out... "

"You have to tie your head?"

"He's a strict Moslem."

I rolled my eyes. I knew strict Moslems. Uncle Fatai was one.

He was gentle and monogamous. His only vice was gluttony. His wife was a Lagos state judge and her head was covered because she wanted it to be.

"And if I can't go out once in a while," Sheri was saying.

"He stops you from going out? What's next? Purdah?"

She laughed.

"You think it's funny?" I said. "You're better than this, Sheri. Anyone you want, you can have."

"Who said? You remember what happened to me?"

I remembered only that she was the most powerful girl I knew, and then she wasn't anymore, and I became disappointed with her.

"Not that," she said. "You can say it. I did not rape them; they raped me, and if they see me they'd better cross the road."

"The border and hemisphere even," I mumbled.

"Yes," she said. "They can cross that too, because if I get my hands on them, there will be nothing left to cross with."

The boys were absurd in my mind, with their red eyes and hemp, and skinny bodies. I would have to exaggerate them to explain why they jinxed her life and why I still couldn't open my mouth to talk about them.

"I didn't know," I said apologetically. "I shouldn't have talked to you as if it was your fault."

"And me, myself," she said. "What did I know? Taking a hanger to myself, with all the biology I studied. I still thought I had a black hole inside me. So, which single man from a normal family would have a person like me?"

Better to be ugly, to be crippled, to be a thief even, than to be barren. We had both been raised to believe that our greatest days would be: the birth of our first child, our wedding and graduation days in that order. A woman may be forgiven for having a child out of wedlock if she had no hope of getting married, and she would be dissuaded from getting married if she didn't have a degree. Marriage could immediately wipe out a sluttish past, but angel or not, a woman had to have a child. For me, coming home to Nigeria was like moving back to the fifties in England.

"You are strong," I said.

"Have no choice," she said.

I'd been looking at my hands. I had feeble nails and they wouldn't grow past the tip of my fingers. I never bothered to paint them. Sheri's nails were varnished and sometimes she clicked them as she spoke. If she sounded cynical, I'd always found the cynical to be honest, like the mad: they could not be manipulated into pretending that it was good to ignore the bad things in life.

"Let's eat," she said.

Her stepmothers had kept their family together by buying and selling gold jewelry. Gold from Italy was the best, Sheri said. It was eighteen-carat, and the Italian traders were no different from Nigerians: they loved to shout and bargain. Saudi gold was also good. They had those twenty-four-carat pieces Lagos people wore for traditional functions. Sheri didn't care much for the gold from Hong Kong. It was too yellow, and didn't suit our skin color. Neither did the gold from India. She would never buy fourteen-carat gold, like the Americans, or nine, like the British. Never.

My mouth watered as she brought out one steaming Pyrex dish after another. Sheri had prepared food I hardly saw in my father's house: *jollof* rice; *egusi* stew with crushed melon seeds, and *eba*, a meal made from ground cassava. She cooked with enough pepper to tear the roof of my mouth off. I was crying and eating. Sheri meanwhile sprinkled dried pepper over her stew, because none of it was hot enough for her.

"I cook for a week," she explained. "Ibrahim sometimes shows up with friends, and there has to be food. I make his separately. He can't eat pepper because of his ulcer."

"That's nonsense."

"Why?"

"You are not his cook."

"You have that attitude?"

"Who has time to sit in a kitchen from morning to night?"

She shook her head. "You've been away too long. You've become a butter-eater."

"It's rude for him to behave that way, that's all."

She laughed until she spilled her water.

"Is this what you learned abroad, *aburo*?"

I waited for her to stop.

"You want to marry someday?"

"I might," I said.

She leaned forward. "Maybe you don't know this because you were raised by your father, but let me tell you now, to save you from unnecessary headache in the future. Forget that nonsense. Education cannot change what's inside a person's veins. Scream and shout, if you like, bang your head against this wall, you will end up in the kitchen. Period. Now, where I differ from most women is, if you lift your hand to beat me, I will kill you. God no go vex. Secondly, while I am there cooking for you, I won't be thinking of dropping some poison in because you've gone to eat another woman's stew."

"Because?"

"I'm getting what I want in return," she said.

"Love?"

"Please, my sister."

"Sex?"

She sucked on a bone. "I beg, which one of them can do."

"Money?"

She threw the bone on her plate.

"One day your eyes will open."

By the time I was ready to leave, I was bloated, but Sheri wouldn't hear of it. She served more *jollof* into a Tupperware container and handed it to me.

"You should start a catering business," I told her.

"I wish I could," she said.

"What's stopping you? You have property in a good location; your stepmothers can cook, and you trust them."

"I can't come and go as I like."

"I don't want to hear that, Sheri."

"I can't," she said.

I realized she was serious.

"Okay," I said. "My father sometimes entertains and his cook is terrible. I will mention you to him."

She patted me toward the door. "Thank you, *aburo*."

As I left her home, it occurred to me that I was glad I was not pretty. Prettiness could encourage people to treat a woman like a doll, to be played with, tossed around, fingered, dismembered, and discarded. Prettiness could also make a woman lazy, if she were congratulated for it too often and remunerated too long. Sheri was the Nigerian man's ideal: pretty, shapely, yellow to boot, with some regard for a woman's station. Now she was a kitchen martyr, and may well have forgotten how to flaunt her mind.

I took her *jollof* to my father; the Tupperware was still flexible and warm when I arrived. Over the years, our neighborhood had changed. New houses and condominiums stood where the park once rambled and most of them were now sinking in marshy land, and yet Ikoyi Park was still considered prime property. I found my father sitting on the veranda, reading a brief.

"My dear," he said.

"You're on your own?" I asked.

"Yes."

I sat in the cane chair next to his. "Hm. Working on a weekend. Don't tell me Peter Mukoro is in government trouble again."

My father didn't confirm, but Peter Mukoro had enough law suits to keep fifty lawyers fully occupied, I was sure.

"Where is Titus?" I asked.

"Day off," he said.

"You're lucky. I brought you *jollof*."

He made a show of being shocked. "I know it is not you who cooked that. Is this part of military training?"

I smiled. "It's my friend. She has a catering business."

"Which friend of yours does that?"

"Sheri."

"I don't remember her."

"She lived next door."

He followed my finger. "Chief Bakare's daughter?"

I nodded.

"The one who?"

"Yes, the one who, and now she's catering, so if you ever need help..."

My father resumed his reading. "Let us see if her cooking is any good."

I went to the kitchen and placed the Tupperware container into the refrigerator. Except for two bottles of water, a shriveled orange and three pots, my father's refrigerator was bare. Titus, his cook, was a myopic old man from Calabar. He could barely discern peppers from tomatoes, and yet he would come into the living room and announce, "Dinner is served." The first time I witnessed this, I asked my father what was happening in his house. Dinner was beans and fried plantain. Dinner was always beans and fried plantain, except when it was boiled yams and corned beef stew. My father replied, "Titus used to work for an English family. Let him say what he wants, so long as he doesn't cook potatoes."

My father trusted Titus, enough to leave him in the house alone. Titus sometimes corrected my English.

I returned to the veranda.

"How are you?" my father asked.

"Fine," I said.

He patted my arm. "That will end when you start work with me."

"Pay me well, that's all I ask."

"I will pay you according to your experience."

"You better not be miserly."

He pretended to be deaf. "What?"

"I said, you better not be miserly with me because there are plenty of people who would like to employ me."

"Like who?" he asked.

"Uncle Fatai," I said.

"Fatai is cheaper than me."

"Well, be careful how you treat me. One day you'll be begging me to run that place."

We watched the Lagoon. There wasn't a movement, not even a ripple around the sticks the fishermen had left to mark their fishing traps.

"We had trouble during the week," my father said.

"Eh, what happened?"

"Fishermen. They scaled over the fence and stole three chairs."

"I thought they were in the garage or something."

"They were stolen."

"What will fishermen do with cane chairs?"

"Sell them."

"We've had those chairs for years."

"I don't care about them," he said. "It's about what is happening to our country. Men who fish for a living becoming robbers. We're in trouble."

I shook my head. "What will save us in this place, Daddy?"

"When the army leaves. When we can vote in a good leader."

"But, look at the last civilian government; throwing champagne parties, embezzling, and all that."

"That was 1979."

"It is the same kind of politicians who will surface next time around."

My father nodded. "Let them come. We will drive them out with votes. Anything but this. These military boys don't care. They step in with one policy or the other, suspend the constitution, mess up our law with their decrees... detain people without charge. I'm sure they're deliberately trying to ruin the country."

"How can they benefit from that?"

"Who knows? Most of them are millionaires now. Maybe it's a sport. I don't understand it either."

My father was still passionate about politics, but one single event had catapulted me into another realm. I viewed the world with a bad squint, a traveling eye, after that, seeing struggles I could do little about. Sheri's brigadier, for instance, was he one of the military men who deprived me of my right to vote, or one of those house dictators who seriously made me wish I could beat up somebody.

"Twenty-five years after independence," my father continued. "And still this nonsense. No light, no water, people dying all over the place, before their time, from one sickness or the other."

I remembered my mother.

"I saw her last week," I said.

"You did? How is she?"

"She says the price of her medicine has gone up."

My father said nothing.

"And her tenants are late in paying their rent. Can you send them a letter?"

"It's a waste of time. I'll send one of my boys over."

"She also says the houses are still in your name."

My father rubbed his brow. "I haven't had time to transfer it to her."

"In ten years?"

"Your mother doesn't speak to me, how will she remind me?"

"Well, I'm reminding you. Please, put the houses in her name."

"She can wait," he said. "After what she's done, bad-mouthing me all over the place, trying to get me disbarred. If I put the property in her name, she will probably give it to that church of hers."

"Please," I said. "Let her have the house in her name."

"She collects rent. What difference will a name make?"

"It's hers," I said.

I didn't say any more, but wondered about him, acting like he didn't know better. I heard my mother's voice again, accusing me of always taking his side and decided to pursue the matter from then on.

I stayed with him until the sun began to fall. My father urged me to return to camp, because of armed robbers who prowled the streets at night. It was dusk as I drove up Third Mainland bridge, and the Lagos lagoon looked like a sheet of iron beneath it. The bridge was smoother than most Lagos routes, which had crevices, but there were no street-lights, and some of the steel barriers had been broken by thieves who melted them down to make forks and knives. I could smell burning wood from a village nearby. Logging was their industry. I thought of Mike. I'd missed him. He was working on a piece and wouldn't be back until tomorrow. I decided to surprise him. It wasn't that late.

There was a power cut in the area when I arrived. In this part of Lagos, houses huddled together separated by high brick walls, topped with broken glass pieces to deter thieves. A few teenagers loitered on the other side of the street. I parked my car outside the house and rattled the gates. A man emerged from the front door wearing his pajama bottoms and a white undershirt.

"Good evening," I said.

"Evuh-ning," he said, rubbing his belly.

"I'm here to see Mr. Obi."

"Obi? He lives behind."

He pointed to the back of the house. I saw someone stepping out with a lantern. It was Mike. The man returned to the house.

"Who was that?" I asked as Mike unlocked the gate.

"My landlord," he said.

He slid the fat chain through the gate's rails and pushed the gates open as though he'd been expecting me.

"Aren't you a little surprised that I came?" I asked.

"I'm happy," he said, holding my hand. "Come, I was about to start something."

He led the way, keeping his lantern up. We walked down the side of the building.

Mike's apartment was an art studio, or so it appeared. It was normally occupied by his landlord's son, a former classmate who was out of Lagos on national service. Mike was renting it from him for the year: one large room with two doors leading to a small kitchen and bathroom. In the corner, on the floor, was a mattress with a patchwork spread made from various tie-dyed pieces, and next to it was a wooden rack over which he hung his trousers and shirts. The only seating space was an old sofa, on which he had a large Fulani rug with black and red embroidery. Everything else was related to his work: an easel, a drawing board, tracing paper, brown paper, pencils, chalk, a black leather portfolio, tape. Leaning along the walls were several mosaics he'd completed, and on a table was a plywood board surrounded by colorful bottles.

"What are these?" I asked, picking one up.

"Beads," he said.

I headed for the nearest mosaic and knelt by it. "Bring the lantern closer."

He did and it cast my shadow over the mosaic. I stepped aside and looked again. It was a woman's profile. She was brown with green flecks in her eye.

"What's this one?"

"Ala."

"Who?"

"Earth mother."

"Of whose earth?"

He smiled. "She is an Igbo goddess."

I moved to the next. "Em, what is this one?"

On a wooden board almost the length of my arms out-stretched, was the form of a naked woman with muscular shoulders, in black and white beading. I reached for it.

"Can I touch?" I asked.

"Gently," he said.

I rolled my fingers over her brow and it tingled. "Beads," I murmured. "You stick them on?"

"One by one," he said.

"How long does it take?"

"Eight months for that one," he said.

I breathed in. "Is she a woman or a man?"

"Neither."

"A hermaphrodite? I once thought I was a hermaphrodite. Before my periods started."

He laughed, shaking the light all over the room.

"He's Obatala."

I screwed up my nose. "Who?"

"You're Yoruba?" he said.

"Born and bred."

"And you don't know your gods?"

"Should I?"

"We don't respect our heritage enough."

"I respect my heritage; its right to evolve and change."

He walked over to the table and placed his lantern on it. "The Yoruba religion is the most exported African religion. Cuba, Brazil, Haiti."

Yeah, yeah, yeah, I said for each country. He ignored me.

"Everyone knows about Aphrodite, but ask them about Oshun... "

"Who dat?" I interrupted.

I smiled. I'd been teasing him from the start. What was he saying? He was Catholic, and he wasn't even Yoruba. How much did he really understand about our gods? And my Yorubaness was like my womanness. If I shaved my head and stood upside down for the rest of my life, I would still be a woman, and Yoruba. There was no paradigm. Every civilization began and ended with an imperfect human being.

"Oshun is your Aphrodite," he said.

"And this Obatala?"

"The creator of the human form."

"Yet you've made him a woman."

"Some cultures, I think the Brazilian descendants of Yorubas, worship him as a female."

"Why is she in black and white?"

"They say all things white belong to him: milk, bones."

I tapped the edge of the mosaic. "I like her," I said. "Although, I'm a little scared."

"Of what?" he asked.

"Evoking gods."

"It's art, not idolatry."

I shook my head. "It's not right."

He walked to the wooden board on his table.

"Who's to say what is right? The Yorubas believed that the

world was water. The gods came down on a chain carrying a calabash filled with soil, a cockerel, and a chameleon. They poured the soil over the water. The cockerel spread it around, the chameleon walked around to make sure it was safe, other gods came and the world was born. A beautiful story. Less believable than a story of two naked people in a garden? I don't know."

I dodged an imaginary lightning bolt. Between my mother's worship of religion and my father's disinterest, I, too, had found my own belief, in a soul that looked like a tree covered in vines: vanity, anger, greed, I stripped them off before I prayed. Sometimes I wouldn't make it before I fell asleep. God was the light toward which my tree grew. But the God of my childhood, the one who looked like a white man, eight foot tall with liver spots and wearing a toga, kind as he was, he was still a God I feared, beyond reason. I was not ashamed to say it. Those who wanted to challenge Him were free to. I'd been burned before, on one finger or the other, and I did not want to feel that all over my body, for eternity.

"Come here," Mike said.

I walked toward the table.

"Pick a bottle," he said.

I chose the red beads.

"Open it," he said.

I unscrewed the top.

"Now, take a few in your palm and cast it over the board."

"Over it?"

"Yes. They will stick wherever you throw them. There's glue on the board."

I poured some beads into my palms and cast them over the wooden board like an Ifa priestess. "I'm an oracle," I said, looking at the spray of beads on the board.

Mike took my hand. "Now, stand here and tell me. What do you see?"

I looked at the beads. "Beads."

"Look again."

I squinted for a moment. "Nothing," I said.

He drew me closer and wrapped his arms around my waist. "Think."

I felt his breath on my neck. He was like a blackboard behind me.

"A sky," I said.

"Are you sure?"

"It's a sky," I said.

"That is what I will do next."

"My sky?"

"Your sky."

I clapped. "Mike, you're the true son of your father."

Mike worked like a seamstress. His fingers moved fast as he dived in and out of the board. He had had one exhibition in Enugu already. There was talk about an exhibition in Lagos, from a French woman he met at the consulate. "I think she just wanted to sleep with me," he admitted. The woman commissioned work from him, so did some of her friends. He wanted to experiment with murals. It was what he'd been searching for, the opportunity to go beyond designing homes.

Soon he began to stalk the board, murmuring to himself. I felt like I was intruding on a confession, so I went to his sofa to lie down. There was a cigarette wrapper tucked in a corner.

"I didn't know you smoked," I said.

"I don't," he said.

I pushed it further in. If it belonged to him or to someone else, I did not want to know.

"You're getting tired," he said.

"I can't believe I have to drive back to camp tonight."

"At this time of the night? You're not going anywhere."

"It's only past eight."

"Still, you're not going. You've forgotten already? Armed robbers?"

"I have nothing with me. No spare clothes."

"You can wear one of my shirts."

I propped myself up." I don't want to go. But your landlord..."

"He minds his business. Your worst fear is your new car outside. We should bring it in."

Mike went to his bathroom to wash his hands and afterward, we went outside to park my car behind his. Returning to his apartment, the air seemed heavier.

"It's hot," he said, as if reading my thoughts.

"Hope they bring back light tonight," I said.

We settled on the sofa. He placed the lantern on the table and drew me to his side.

"Rest your head."

I place my head on his belly. It was as tight as a drum.

"What did you do all day to make you tired?" His voice resounded within him.

"I went to see my father," I said.

"You had fun?"

"I always have fun with my father."

"What else?"

"I went to see an old friend."

"An old friend. Which old friend?"

"Sheri Bakare. My best friend when I was small."

I listened to his heartbeat for a moment.

"And you?" I asked.

"I went to see my uncle."

"Your uncle. Which uncle?" I mimicked him.

"My uncle, the architect I was going to work for."

"Until?"

"He gave me a job that changed my mind."

110

"What job was this?"

"Some man who wanted his house extended."

"What's wrong with that?"

"I saw the house. It's a series of extensions. Like an anthill inside."

"Why does he keep extending it?"

"New wives. More children."

I smiled. "So you feel artistically compromised?"

Mike sighed. "Here is a man, who has in his living room a portrait of himself inside his aquarium."

"No."

"I swear to God."

"He gave you the job, I'm sure."

"Bent over, eyes closed."

I slapped his arm. "Mike! Everyone needs a job in Lagos. Everyone needs a car that works."

He wrapped it tighter round me. "I'm not doing it anymore, not after this. The pay is not good, and the work is lousy. My parents never had much money, but they were satisfied with their jobs."

I could easily have told him that was years ago, that they lived on campus, in a house provided by the university.

"So you'll concentrate on your art work?"

He nodded. "Teach for national service, find small work to pay my way. My rent is not much, and I pay monthly."

"That's brave. I'm not sure I want to practice law full-time, but I'm too frightened to think of it."

"Why study law at all?"

"Who knows? Father's business, only child. But it's not bad work. Though he doesn't pay me enough and it pains me that I can't have a place of my own."

"Find another job. Move out."

"A daughter? It's not done."

111

"What is this 'it' that's not done?"

I sat up. "Don't be difficult. You know where I'm coming from."

"Thousands of single women are living on their own, all over town."

"Well, I am not them and they are not me. I will go back to England penniless before I live in a Lagos slum. What kind of country is this anyway? You graduate and you're privileged to live off your parents, or some old sugar daddy or some government contract. He should at least pay me enough. It's only fair. It's only fair, Mike."

He smiled, satisfied that he'd made me look beyond my small world. Yes, I was acting like a brat, but he hardly ever had to consider his parents and they were not sanctioning his every move. I was curious.

"Tell me about when you were small," I said.

"What age?"

"Eleven," I said, placing my ear to his belly.

As he spoke, I fell asleep dreaming of him, an eleven-year-old boy with khaki shorts holding a rifle made of sticks, dancing to high-life music with his mother and learning how to drink palm-wine from his father's calabash. His parents played card games lying on the floor. It was like a bed-time story.

When I woke up there was light in the room. I was startled by how bright everything seemed. Stretching, I asked. "When did they bring it back?"

"An hour ago," he said.

"And you sat here?"

"Your head," he explained.

"I'm sorry," I said, getting up. "Which door leads to your bathroom?"

He pointed.

Inside, I looked at his shaving cream and toothbrush on the

sink. The blue tiles on the shower wall were powdery white from scouring powder. Black mold lurked between them. In the corner was an aluminum bucket for bathing because water pressure in Lagos was too weak to drive showers. I washed my face, came out and found Mike lying on the couch with his shirt off.

"You can pick any of my shirts," he said, pointing to his rack of clothes.

"I don't want a shirt," I said, unbuttoning mine.

He watched me undress and I pulled a face. I walked up to him, willing myself to be confident.

He kissed holes down my back. I cried, only from his tenderness. Later, as he slept, I crept to the bathroom and filled the aluminum bucket with cold water, and washed myself clean. I slept with my nose in his armpit.

Military camp ended in a parade attended by government and military officials. Some members of our platoon were chosen to participate in the event, but Mike and I were not among them. We stood in the stands and cheered instead.

Monday, after the parade, I started work at my father's firm. I was a sleeping partner, he said, no matter how hard I worked. "Five years' time and I will be dead according to the latest statistics! Still nobody serious to hand my business over to! This is my lot in life!"

In time my father had become bona fide miserable, not surprisingly. His business was to appease acrimonious freeholders, after the fist fights and juju. Another rental agreement, an old one breached, a reminder letter to an expatriate who had not paid his rent, or a Nigerian tenant who was certain to throw the letter away and still not pay. Court case after court case over property disputes, land disputes, split families, brothers who had not spoken for years, since the old man died.

113

My father had two senior associates working for him. Dagogo John-White, a quiet man whose name we loved to tease (Da go go, Da come come, Da going gone, and for the brief period he found religion, Da kingdom come, Da will be done.) I made no mention of his white john, left that to Alabi Fashina, a quick tempered man we dared not tease. Whenever my father was away, Dagogo and Alabi sometimes argued about their home cities. Alabi was from Lagos, Dagogo from Bonny Island in the Niger Delta. "Bushman from Lagos," he would say.

"Bushman from Bonny," Alabi would reply. "Hm. Bonny women. They are the most forward women on earth. I visited once. Women were crawling all over me like ants on a sugar, crawling all over me. I did what a man had to do."

"Our man Flint!" Dagogo would say.

"It was a precarious operation."

"007!"

"But I had license to kill."

Our very own double act. They would end with a handshake, snap their fingers and call each other *"man mi,"* my man. Dagogo was tall with a neck at least six inches long; he naturally looked downward. Alabi was stocky with a one inch neck; he looked upward. Different temperaments, but if they faced each other, they always saw eye to eye.

Thankfully, they were rarely in the office. The others, I saw more of: Peace, the receptionist and secretary whose gymnastics with bubble gum broke new boundaries every day. She would not speak clearly on the phone, because she did not want to smudge her lipstick, and was occasionally off with General Body Weakness—her bones were paining, if you asked her to describe the symptoms of this officially recognized illness. Mrs. Kazeem, a woman who handled the company secretarial work. Her expression was naturally vexed, and we called her mother of twins, because she was expecting some. And finally, Mr. Israel, the lugubrious driver. We called him Papa sometimes, because he was as old as Moses. He spoke Yoruba to everyone, even to Dagogo who couldn't understand a word.

"Who wants groundnuts?" I asked, looking around the office.

Dagogo raised his head momentarily, Alabi said no, and Peace popped her bubble gum. Mr. Israel and Mrs. Kazeem were out. I pulled some dirty naira notes from my bag and went outside to the woman who sat by our gate, selling roasted groundnuts by the bottle.

My father's office was designed like a classroom, without a blackboard. We sat behind desks, facing his room and whenever he came out, it was hard not to react as one might to a school master. He was a different person in the office and kept his face as closed as one of the hardback books he'd stashed along his shelves. I'd also discovered just how stingy he was. He had not increased lunch allowances in over five years and I really wasn't surprised. I couldn't ever remember having much pocket money to spend as a child. My father always told me he had no money. The oil boys were the rich ones, he would say, referring to the handful of lawyers who were counsels for international oil companies. Lawyers like himself, they had to scrape a living.

My father had scraped enough to acquire a large estate. If he worked these days, it was only because he wanted to. He had shed most of his staff now, except for his senior associates, but still, he didn't pay well. I placed the bottle of groundnuts on my table when I returned and invited everyone to eat. Then I headed for his door.

"Come in," he said.

He was scribbling on a sheet of paper.

"What can I do for you?"

"Are you busy?"

"I'm always busy," he said, without looking up.

"Shall I come back?"

115

He placed his pen down. "No."

I sat in the client chair. "Three things, please."

"Yes?"

"Our lunch allowance."

"What about it?"

"It's too little."

My father's knuckles locked like a zip. "How so?"

"One hundred naira a month?" I said. "I've just bought a bottle of groundnuts for ten naira."

"Please, get to the point."

I spoke slower. "Our lunch allowance needs to be increased, in line with inflation at least."

"In line with inflation," he repeated.

"Yes," I said.

My father sat back. "We'd be doubling allowances every year. Did my staff ask you to do this?"

"No."

"My dear, I've been running this place for over thirty years and..."

I raised my hand.

"Let me finish," he said. "I've been running this place for many years and I think, by now, I know how to run it well. My benefits are fair. Ask my people outside. If any of them are dissatisfied, they will leave."

I thought of the scruffy lawyers who stood outside the courts, begging for affidavit work.

"To go where?" I asked. "You think it's easy to find work these days?"

"I'm busy," he warned.

"Just think about it," I said.

"The next thing was?"

"I've drafted the transfer letter," I said.

"What transfer letter?"

Of his houses, to my mother, I explained. My father listened without commenting.

"The third thing?" he asked.

"Can Sheri do the catering for your dinner party?" I gabbled the words. "She's very professional. Please. Her father died, and her uncle took her inheritance. And she has no job. And Titus cooks so bad. Sheri can do better. Please."

My father looked irritated enough to throw his pen at me.

"You're wasting my time," he said.

"Thank you," I said, getting up. "Thank you. I knew you would say yes."

Back at my desk, I lifted the bottle of groundnuts and found it half empty.

"Who ate my groundnuts?" I asked.

No one raised their head.

"How are you coping?" I asked Sheri.

Our kitchen was unusually clean. She wiped the water around the sink, and grease from the stove. There wasn't a dent in her gown, not even a stain, while my own dress was creased from shoulder to hem. I was glad I was wearing black because I'd spilled wine on myself.

Cooking was a skill, I thought; an art form. In our country, we appreciated the end result, but not the craft, perhaps because we didn't have fancy names. Paring was "cut it." Julienne was "cut it well." Chopping was "cut it well well," and so on till you had puree, which would probably be "mash it." And, if anyone was measuring any ingredient in a kitchen, it meant that they really didn't know what they were doing.

Sheri was preparing what she called a continental dinner for my father's party: chicken curry with coconut fried rice, grilled fish, shrimp kebabs, and a bowl of Nigerian salad that would put any niçoise to shame. It had tuna, baked beans, potatoes,

117

eggs, and dollops and dollops of mayonnaise. For dessert, she'd made a pineapple crumble and a platter of sliced mangoes and pawpaws over which she sprinkled lemon juice. I checked one of the bowls.

"Shall I take this to the table?"

"Please," she murmured.

She folded a dish cloth to take the crumble out of the oven. In the dining room, I checked the table. Sheri had insisted we used another table for the food. The guests would have to serve themselves buffet-style, she said. I agreed only because I wasn't that interested in the logistics of a dinner party, or entertaining. Growing up with my father, I rarely stepped into a kitchen, and my father was easily satisfied with meals his cooks prepared. Tonight the food would at least be edible, I thought. His guests were out on the veranda and I would call them in soon.

I wondered about Mike. He was meeting my father for the first time and we planned to sit on the veranda during the dinner. The doorbell rang again as I adjusted the napkins on the table. It was him.

"I was just thinking about you."

He was in traditional wear: a white tunic and black trousers. He bent to pick up something leaning against the wall and dragged it into the doorway. It was a mosaic of different colors, like a jagged rainbow.

"My sky," I said.

"I didn't say I was going to give it to you," he said.

I steered him toward my father, who was talking to Aunt Valerie, a Jamaican woman whose voice skipped like calypso. At first my father looked as if he were under siege, then I presented the mosaic to him. My father perched it on a table.

"What a stunning piece," Aunt Valerie said. "Did you do this, young man?"

"Yes," Mike said.

118

"He's an artist," I said.

"That's wonderful," she said. "Sam, come and look at this."

Her husband, a baldheaded man, walked over with Uncle Fatai. Uncle Fatai's wife, Aunty Medinot, hovered in the background. In support of my mother, she rarely came to the house. Just seeing her made me feel guilty, but my father had invited my mother, and she refused to come. "For what reason?" she asked.

"This young man did this, Sam," Aunt Valerie said. "Isn't it wonderful?"

"It looks like a sunset," her husband said.

"Or fire," Aunt Valerie said, throwing her head back.

"Both," Uncle Fatai said.

I drew close to my father.

"He's an architect," I said, "but he does this on the side."

"Really," my father said.

Mike approached us with an apologetic smile. "I never thought they would... "

I patted his shoulder as we returned to the living room. He deserved to be embarrassed for bringing a gift for my father.

"That woman says she wants to see my work," he said.

"Show it to her," I said. "But save Obatala for me."

I snatched the mosaic from him and carried it to my father's room. There, I smoothed my dress and dabbed some cologne behind my ears.

I hurried back. Peter Mukoro had arrived in my absence. A huge man with a thick black mustache, he was already holding court.

"Our last regime claimed they wanted to wage war against indiscipline, and yet they couldn't fight it among themselves. Military coups are the worst form of indiscipline. No respect for the constitution. No respect for those in power... "

"Our people are indisciplined," Uncle Fatai said.

"How?" Peter Mukoro asked, stroking his mustache.

"You're driving and someone tries to run you off the road."

"Trying to avoid potholes," Peter Mukoro said.

"Speeding through traffic stops?"

"Running from armed robbers."

"Teachers not showing up for class?"

"Can't afford transportation."

"Hospital staff selling supplies on the black market?"

"Benefits in kind."

"Bribery?"

"Tipping," Peter Mukoro said.

He continued to speak as though he were making a toast and twirled his cigarette. I edged toward Mike. "Come, let me introduce you to Sheri. This man won't stop talking. He loves his voice."

"I've already met her," he said.

"When?"

"She came in here when you were away."

I sat on the arm of the chair. "What did you think?"

"She seems... reserved."

"Sheri?"

"To me, she was."

I stood up. "Excuse me, I have to check on the food."

Inside the kitchen, I found Sheri pouring curry into a big ceramic bowl. Her waiter was standing by to take it into the living room. I could smell the coconut rice and sweet ginger of the pineapple bake in the oven.

"Is everything ready?" I asked.

She nodded. "You can call them in now."

I paused by the door. "You met Mike?"

"Yes," she said.

"What did you think of him?"

"He's nice."

Throughout the evening, they showed nothing but courtesy for each other. I'd expected some interest, some camaraderie even, but soon I realized that they shared nothing in common. Mike would find Sheri too old. She would find Mike far too young.

Peter Mukoro continued to dominate the conversation meanwhile. He was predicting the demise of our country under the new military government. They were making plans to devalue our currency, and to scrap foreign currency regulations. Most of us who needed foreign currency for business or travel welcomed this. We envisioned a time we no longer had to succumb to black market rates. There were places in Lagos you went to buy US dollars and pounds sterling, from hawkers who loitered like drug dealers. You had to be sure you were buying the real thing.

"We're finished," Peter Mukoro was saying. "The naira will be like toilet paper now. And if we take the IMF loan we can kiss our independence goodbye."

My father seemed to be enjoying his tirade, rocking back and forth. I refilled his wine glass. "Fill my friend's as well," he said, pointing to Peter Mukoro's.

Reluctantly I did.

Peter Mukoro tapped my arm. "I was calling that lady, that yellow lady in the kitchen, but she ignored me. Tell her we need more rice. Please."

"Her name is Sheri."

"Yes. Tell her we need more rice. And beer. Wine is like water to me. I'm an African man."

I delivered the message to her word for word.

"He can't be talking to me," she said.

"Who then?" I asked.

"He must be talking to his mother."

I laughed. Titus had already annoyed her, asking her to serve guests from the left and not from the right. Sheri wore her head

121

tie turban style and it dropped over her eye brows. Her profile was hysterical. She was taking her work too seriously, I thought. I could snatch the head tie and make her run after me. I carried a bowl of rice back to the dining room with a cold bottle of beer.

"Ah thanks," Peter Mukoro said. "Brother Sunny, you must ask for a hefty dowry for your daughter. Look at her, good hostess, lawyer, and all that."

"I would be glad," my father said, "if someone would take her off my hands for free."

They laughed hyuh-hyuh-hyuh, as only men with too much money should. I ignored them and returned to the veranda.

"Something wrong?" Mike asked.

"Peter Mukoro," I said. "Every single time he opens his mouth."

Mike smiled. "He's a man's man. Your father seems to like him."

We looked toward the dining room. Sheri had come out of the kitchen and was leaning over my father.

"He seems to like Sheri, too," he said. "Unlike me."

"Close your mouth," I said.

By the end of the evening, my head was full of wine. I saw Mike off and he kissed me so hard he pulled me through his car window. We spoke against each other's teeth.

"Come back with me."

"My father will kill me."

"You're not a child."

"I am, to him."

"Nonsense."

"Hmm. Where are your sisters?"

"Locked up at home, where they belong."

The road was empty, except for a few parked cars. Before he drove off, I did a strip-tease. I flashed a breast, turned to wriggle, only to find Peter Mukoro standing by the gates. "Ah-ah?" he said. "Are we invited? Or is this a private reception?"

He laughed as I hurried past.

I smoothed the creases from my dress before I walked into the house and kept my face as straight as a newscaster's. Sheri and my father were in the living room. My father was writing a check.

"That young man," he said. "What did you say his name was?"

"Mike."

Count one against him: his name wasn't Nigerian. This could mean his family didn't have enough class to uphold our traditions.

"Obi," I said.

I expected his next question to be which Obi.

"An artist, you say?" he asked.

"Yes." Count two.

"And he's given up architecture?"

Count three. I hesitated. "Not really."

My father peered over his glasses. "That's no good."

"Why?" I asked.

He turned to Sheri. "Tell her. Please. If I say anything to her, she thinks I'm old-fashioned."

Sheri laughed. "You have to admit, Enitan. An artist in Lagos?"

My father handed the check to her.

"Thank you," he said. "It's been a pleasure."

I saw her to the door.

"Well done," I whispered. "Now I won't rest in this house. Why did you have to say that?"

"*Aburo*, the artist has jujued you?"

"I think I've outgrown that name by now."

She raised her hand. "I won't use it if you don't like it."

"Thanks."

"Bye yourself," she said, cheerfully.

I shut the door gently and faced my father. He removed his glasses, which usually meant he was about to give a lecture. I braced myself.

"You know," he said. "I may not know much about youngsters today, but I know a few things and I don't think you should be making yourself so available to a man you've just met."

I crossed my arms. "In what way?"

"Your demeanor. A woman should have more... comportment. And you can stop following him outside unchaperoned, for a start."

"Unchaperoned?"

"Yes," he said. "He might think you're easy. Cheap. I'm telling you for your own good."

I walked away. Unchaperoned indeed. Look at him. Just look at him, and that Sheri, calling herself my sister. "This is modern Lagos," I said over my shoulder. "Not Victorian London."

"This is my house," I heard him say. "Don't be rude."

During national service, I received a monthly stipend of 200 naira from the government. This, I spent usually within a week. In return for my stipend, every Monday, I took a day off work for community service. For community service, I met with other national service participants who lived in my district to complete half-day chores. Sometimes we picked litter off the streets; other times we cut grass in local parks with machetes. Most days we begged our team leader, a man who reminded me of Baba, to let us go. He stood over us, gloating as we pleaded. The machetes were heavier than I expected and the grass left my legs itchy. The experience gave me respect for the work Baba did in our garden every week.

Now that he had decided not to work for his uncle, Mike was teaching art classes at a free education school near his home.

One morning, after community service, I visited him there. The free education schools in Lagos were the legacy of a former governor of Lagos state. Several years later, and still underfunded, they were teeming with children and lacking teachers. Most of the classrooms were unpainted and some were without windows and doors. I passed a classroom and heard children reciting alphabets; passed another, and heard them chanting multiplication tables. Through the door, I saw a teacher standing by a blackboard with a whip in his hand.

The next room was the teachers' mess. Inside, a woman sat on a chair. She was eating an orange. Her skin was bleached and her hair was sectioned into plaits. In the corner, a man placed both his feet on the table. He flexed his whip at a school girl of about fifteen years who knelt facing the corner with her arms raised. The girl's armpits were stained brown and her bare soles were dusty. There were welts across the back of her legs.

"Good afternoon," I said.

"Afa-noon," the man said.

The woman eyed my jeans.

"Is Mr. Obi around?" I asked.

The student turned to look at me. Her face was wet from tears.

"Turn your ugly face to the wall," the man shouted. "Look at you. Tiffing mango from the tree when you have been warned consecu... " He whipped her legs.

"Consecu... " he whipped her legs again.

"Consecutively." He sucked his teeth. "Tiff."

"Is Mr. Obi here?" I asked.

He picked his teeth. "Obi?"

"Yes, Mr. Obi, the art teacher. Please, do you know where he is?"

I spoke with an English accent to offend him. He would immediately think I was trying to be superior.

"In class," he said.

"What class?"

He pointed. "Outside. Fork right, then right again."

"So kind of you," I said.

He reached over and flicked the girl's shoulder with his whip. She straightened up.

Mike's class was the last on the adjacent corridor and smelled like a puppy's pen. There were about twenty-five children in a room, intended for half that number. Their desks were pushed to the walls and they were gathered around five large wash bowls. They squished the contents with their tiny fists. Mike was walking around them.

"Behave yourselves," he said.

"What's going on?" I asked.

"They're making papier-maché," he said.

There was gray mush in the bowls. One of his students, a skinny boy with dusty knees scrambled over.

"Mr. Obi?"

"Yes, Diran," Mike said.

"Pitan fell me down."

"Pitan!" Mike yelled.

Pitan's large head popped up. "Yes, Mr. Obi."

"No more pushing," Mike said. "This is the last time I'm warning you. If one more person gets pushed, you will all run round this school, you hear me?"

"Yes, Mr. Obi," they chanted.

Mike turned to me. "They're getting on my nerves."

I smiled. "I thought you wanted to teach children."

"I've made the biggest mistake of my life."

"I thought you never had regrets. And what kind of teachers are you in this school? I was in your teachers' room and one man there was beating a girl for stealing fruit. You should have seen."

"That's Mr. Salako, our agriculture teacher."

"He's horrible."

"Her mother probably beats her more. Most of them in here, they leave this place and go home to spend the rest of the day selling something. They think I'm a fool because I don't whip them. Everyone else does."

The children's heads bobbed like a sea of life buoys. Their parents beat out of love, it was said, with love, so that they wouldn't grow up misbehaving anyhow-all-over-the-place-willy-nilly-shilly-shally. Teachers beat, neighbors beat. By the time a child turned ten, the adults they knew would have beaten out any cockiness that could develop into wit; any dreaminess that could give birth to creation; any bossiness that could lead to leadership. Only the strong would survive; the rest would spend their lives searching for initiative. This was what it took to raise an African child, a village of beaters, and yet if someone put their hands around a child's neck, and applied the slightest pressure, someone else would accuse them of wickedness, because strangulation had nothing to do with discipline.

Diran sidled up to Mike again. He scratched his head.

"Mr. Obi."

"What is it?" Mike asked. "Why are you scratching your head? Do you have lice?"

The children laughed.

"Pitan banged my head," Diran whined. "Now my head is broked."

Mike clapped. "All right. No more."

There was murmuring around the class. Mike walked to the center of the room.

"I can see you're all begging for punishment today."

Pitan raised his hand. "Mr. Obi?"

"Shush!" Mike hissed. "I mustn't hear my name on anyone's lips again. No more. Now push your bowls to the side, return to your desks and line up to run around the school."

The children giggled as they dragged their bowls to the corner. We heard the school bell ring.

"God saved all of you," Mike announced. "Come on, let's get out of here," he said to me.

We drove back to his place and ripped our clothes off. Mike had a collection of Bob Marley albums, and we joined in the wailing. We made love on the mattress and then on the floor. He began to talk the way he talked about football. Could I feel it? It was a fusion of time and space. We were the reggae and soul generation. Our parents were the jazz generation. The next would be hip-hop.

"Stop talking," I said.

He wouldn't stop. I wrapped my legs around him.

"Enough," I said. "You like sex too much."

He grabbed my foot and began to tickle it. His landlord, the whole neighborhood, the whole world even, was about to know how much sex he liked.

"They'll think I'm a slut!" I said. "Please! They'll think I'm... shit."

I was hoarse from screaming. I went to his bathroom to wash myself when I heard a knock on the door.

"Would you like a beer?" Mike asked. "I'm going round the corner."

"No," I said.

I knocked the bucket of water over. Mike walked in.

"Are you all right?"

I stood up.

"What is it?" he asked.

I wanted to tell him, but the story was never mine to tell. I was hurt only by association.

"What?" he asked.

I began anyway. The faster I spoke, the easier it became: the picnic, the rain, the lagoon, the van. The boys.

I sounded fake to my own ears. In my mind's eye, I was standing there, that day, thankful to be safe, glad to be untarnished.

"Come here," Mike said when I finished.

He wrapped his arms round me so tight I thought my fear might drip out. He took the bucket from me, filled it with water and brought it to the shower. He lowered me and began to wash me. I shut my eyes expecting some pain, some probing, something.

The last person who washed me was Bisi, our house girl. I was nine. "Spread your lecks," she would say, and I would spread them hating her sawing motions. But Mike washed me with the gentlest motions, like a mother washing her baby. I felt sure my fear was like any other fear; like the fear of a dog bite, or of fire, or of falling from heights, or death. I was certain I would never be ashamed again.

We didn't drink beer. We drank the palm wine from his refrigerator instead and ate the remnants of a peppery stew with yams. The stew had mellowed nicely, and after about two glasses, the wine made my eyes slip.

"Who taught you to cook?" I asked.

"My mother," he said.

"You'll make a good wife," I said.

I reached for my glass. Of course he was right for me. Even Obatala seemed to be winking at us.

The Bakares started their catering business. As I predicted, it wasn't a difficult transition for them. Their house in Victoria Island was spacious and part of their back yard was conveniently cemented. Their hands were many. Sheri's stepmothers took charge of the cooking, while she handled the money. Her brothers and sisters took on smaller tasks. The back yard was used for cooking, and they converted their chalet into a cafeteria with locally carpentered benches and tables. Most of their customers were office workers from surrounding banks who came in for their meal of the day. I visited once, only because I hadn't entirely forgiven Sheri for siding with my father, and also because the drive to Victoria Island was too long for my one-hour lunch-break.

Nearing lunch time in the office one afternoon, Mrs. Kazeem looked out the window. "Our friend is here," she said.

"Who?" Peace asked.

"Miss Nigeria," Mrs. Kazeem said.

We looked out of the window to see Sheri.

Sheri was one of those women. Other women didn't like her, and I'd often wondered if she noticed. She rarely came to our office, but whenever she did, the women behaved as if she'd come in for a fight. The men, meanwhile, found excuses to come to my desk. Today, the men were out and only the women remained. Mrs. Kazeem crossed her arms over her belly, Peace clicked her gum. Sheri opened the door.

"Enitan," she said. "Will you come out for a moment?"

I got up, aware that the others were watching me. Not greeting was considered rude. Outside, the sun warmed my head. We crossed over to Sheri's car, parked by an orange seller who sat with an infant strapped to her back. She was peeling an orange with a rusty pen-knife.

"Why didn't you greet the others?" I asked.

"Those jealous women," Sheri said.

"No one is jealous of you."

"Who cares? I've lived with this too long, and I didn't come here to see them anyway."

"What did you come for?"

"Are we fighting?"

"No," I said.

"Why haven't you contacted me?"

"I've been busy. My father keeps me busy. All morning I've been drafting letters."

"Don't you go to court at all?"

"He tries to keep me here," I said.

"I'm surprised."

"You don't know him. He runs this place like an army."

We heard a cry from the road.

"Pupa! Yellow!"

A taxi driver was leaning out of his window. He was holding the window lever he would pass to passengers who needed to "wine down." One of his front teeth seemed longer than the rest.

"Yes, you with the big *yansh*," he shouted.

Sheri spread her fingers at him. "Nothing good will come to you!"

"Whore," he jeered. "Wait till I get down on you."

"Don't let me curse your mother," she said. "You'd better use that long tooth of yours to push down your windows. It might straighten it out, and your passengers might not suffocate from your stinking armpits."

I lowered my head.

"And you, *Dudu*," the taxi driver said.

Startled, I looked up.

"Yes you with the black face. Where is your own *yansh* hiding?"

I glared at him. "Nothing good will come to you."

He laughed with his tongue hanging out. "What, you're turning up your nose at me? You're not that pretty, either of you. Sharrap. Oh, sharrap both of you. You should feel happy that a man noticed you. If you're not careful, I'll sex you both."

Sheri and I turned our backs on him.

"Fool," I said.

"Penis like Bic biro," she said.

We huddled together laughing.

"So what happened?" I asked.

"Ibrahim wants me to stop my business," she said.

"Because?"

"He doesn't want me going out."

"Is he willing to give you the money?"

"No."

"Then, why are we wasting time talking about this?"

"I wanted your opinion," she said.

"Since when?"

"Please," she said.

"Drop him," I said. "You don't need him."

She raised her hand. "What will happen to me when my rent is due? Where will I live? I can't go back to my father's house. Have you seen the place?"

The day I went, it was teeming with customers and friends. I wondered if they ever had private moments.

"Bide time," I said. "Until your next rent is paid. After that, find more clients. There are weddings, burials, christenings, every weekend in this place. Next year you'll be paying your own rent. But this, this, I have to tell you, is rubbish. You're bright, you're young, and this man is treating you like his house girl."

"It's easy for you to say."

"You asked my opinion."

"You've never had to worry."

"If ever I do, please talk sense to me."

She turned away.

"Sheri," I said.

"What?" she snapped.

"It's for your own good," I said.

"How? I'm not even sure we can continue the business. My uncle comes to the house, complaining that we are misusing his property. He wants to take the house from us, I'm sure."

"He can't do that."

"Why not?" she said. "He took everything else under native law as my father's rightful heir. Why would the house be different?"

"Whose name is the property in, now?" I asked.

"My father's."

"Did he leave a will?"

"No."

What place did the law really have in family matters? At law school I'd learned those indigenous set of codes collectively called native law and custom. They existed before we adopted civil law, before we became a nation with a constitution, and they established individual rights under inheritance and marriage. A man could marry only one wife under civil law, but he could bring another woman into his home under native law. It was polygamy, not bigamy. If he pleased, he could beat up his wife, throw her out, with or without her children and leave her with nothing. His relations might plead with him to show her mercy, but she had no claim over his property. If he died, under some native customs, his son would inherit his estate instead of his widow. Sometimes, a widow couldn't inherit land at all. Even with the progressive customs, widows inherited according to how many children they had, and sons could have double the rights of daughters.

The courts determined how to share a man's estate, according to how he lived his life: the traditional or "civil" way. In reality, his relations could come into his house, "drive his wife comot" and sit on her front porch threatening to put a hex on her if she dared to challenge them. Of course there were exceptions; women who fought in and out of the law courts and they nearly always won.

"There are steps you can take," I said. "But the most important thing is to find a good lawyer."

"Your father's a good lawyer," she said. "Can I ask him?"

I wasn't sure I wanted Sheri to ask my father about this.

133

I wasn't sure I wanted her to ask my father about anything, especially as he had not settled the matter with my mother.

"Yes," I said, since I'd opened my mouth.

"Thank you, my sister," she said.

As she drove off, I turned to the street seller who had finished peeling her orange. A complete spiral of green orange skin bounced off the edge of her pen knife. The infant on her back had his mouth wide open.

"Mor'ing," she said.

"Good morning," I said.

They began with Peace, the events following Sheri's visit to my father's office. They began and ended with Peace. She brought the magazine to the office one afternoon and announced, "Come see, our client Mr. Mukoro in a love triangle."

We gathered round her desk. It was a copy of *Weekend People*, a gossip magazine. Peace bought it monthly and I borrowed it each time. Sometimes Sheri appeared as a former Miss Nigeria, "Veteran Beauty Queen Steps Out" and such. On the front page of this issue, was a photograph of a woman with a head tie. The camera had caught her sneer. The headline read "Mukoro is a hypocrite."

The woman was Peter Mukoro's wife. They had been married for 22 years and he had recently taken a second wife. Peace improvised her way through the woman's allegations of affairs, adding gasps and squeals. The highlight of the interview was the story of how Peter Mukoro came home with a bald patch in his pubic hair. His lover had helped herself to a sample while he was asleep. The proceeds went to a medicine man to brew a potion to ensnare him. Alabi kept laughing, Dagogo pretended to be above it all, but he was stapling the same sets of papers together. I had to show it to my father.

"I don't want to read it," he said.

Then he read the whole page.

"Can you believe it?" I said.

He looked bored as he pushed the magazine toward me.

"The woman disgraced herself."

"Him," I said.

"Only herself," he said. "She has nothing better to do, going to the papers with this nonsense."

"He goes to the papers," I said, "For everything. He calls himself a social critic."

"It's not the same," my father interrupted. "This is a private matter."

"Oh," I said, taking the magazine.

"What is 'Oh'? You have something to say?"

I shook my head.

"Speak your mind now," he said "Since you've already come in here."

"I don't think it's a private matter," I said. "A social crusader practicing bigamy. I think it is good that people are being told."

"By *Weekend People?*"

"Yes," I said. "It's good they consider the story newsworthy. And really, I don't know why we continue to follow native law anyway, when civil law is in existence. It has no moral grounding, no design except to oppress women... "

My father laughed. "Who's oppressed? Are you oppressed?"

"I didn't say me, but yes, in a way."

"How?"

"I'm part of this... "

"This what?"

"This group, treated as chattel."

"Let's not get hysterical."

"Show me one case," I said. "Just one, of a woman having two husbands, a fifty-year-old woman marrying a twelve-year-old boy. We have women judges, and a woman can't legally post bail. I'm a lawyer. If I were married, I would need my husband's consent to get a new passport. He would be entitled to discipline me with a slap or two, so long as he doesn't cause me grievous bodily harm."

"You've made your point," he said. "Your grandmother was married off at fourteen, into a household with two other wives, and she had to prove she was worthy of her dowry by cooking better. I'm not sure what your gripe is. I made sure you had a good education, encouraged you to fulfill your career goals..."

"Can you change our culture for me?" I asked.

"What?"

I had not meant to be hysterical. I came in to laugh. Now my heart rate was rising, and I wasn't even sure why and my argument was a mess.

"Can you change the culture?"

My father placed his hands together, still looking bored. "We know there are problems with native law and custom, but these things are changing..."

"How do we know? The women don't come to court, and when they come, it's men like you who conspire..."

"Me? Conspire?"

"Yes, all of you, conspiring."

He laughed. "When did I conspire? I can't believe I spent money sending you to school. This would be endearing, if you weren't getting old."

"I'm not old."

"Accusing me of conspiring. You are not oppressed; you are spoiled. Very. At your age, I'd bought my house already, I'd started my practice. I was supporting my parents. Yes. Not the other way around."

At his age there was less competition for lawyers. At his age there wasn't an economic recession in our country. It was easier to be a kingpin, and most professionals from his generation were.

They substituted the colonialists' sir-and-madamism for theirs, stood by while military men led us into a black hole. Now, we their children were dependent on them. I didn't say any of this.

"Why won't you take me seriously," I grumbled. "Even as a professional. For three years I was respected, paid well. I come back home, you treat me like an idiot, pay me nothing... "

My father stopped laughing. "Shouldn't you be working?"

"It's lunch time," I said.

He leaned back in his chair. "Get Dagogo in here before you disappear for lunch. And stop reading trash."

"It's not trash," I said.

"Yes, it is," he said. "And I hope you're not using an article in *Weekend People* as a springboard for discussing the plight of women in this country."

"Why not?"

"You shouldn't even be discussing the plight of women at all, since you've done nothing but discuss it. How many women do you know anyway, in your sheltered life?"

I felt my heart racing, unnecessarily, and told myself I must never argue with him again, not over this. It was a stupid article, anyway.

"Discussion is a start," I said, steadying my voice.

"Get Dagogo in here," he said.

At his door I said, "I think Peter Mukoro is a hypocrite, too," and quickly stepped out.

The others welcomed me with glances. I knew I had to say something. I handed the magazine back to Peace and said, "Men like Mr. Mukoro should be... "

"Should be what?" Mrs. Kazeem asked, looking me up and down.

"Sued," I said.

They all laughed.

"So sue the lawyer who is representing you," Mrs. Kazeem

said. "Sue the judge hearing your case. Sue the driver who carries you from court to your house after your case has been dismissed. Then, when you get home, sue your landlord."

"Sue everybody," Dagogo said.

"Sue God," Alabi said.

Peace clicked her gum and sighed.

"Welcome home," Mrs. Kazeem said.

"Kukuruku," people say in my country, whenever they imitate a rooster's crow. Kukuruku. Some might say a rooster sounds more like cock-a-doodle-doo, even though roosters all over the world make the same sound.

It wasn't that I no longer belonged, that I'd become a stranger. Being overseas never changed what I instinctively knew before I left. What had changed was other people's tolerance for me. I was old; too old to be deceiving myself.

Sheri took my advice and began to cater for more social functions. As she predicted, her uncle did take her family to court over possession of their home and my father agreed to represent them. The day she called to tell me, I could do no work. I'd been trying to get my father to sign the transfer letter to my mother for weeks. "All I need is five minutes of your time," I kept saying, but he said he had no time.

I tried again.

"Have no time," he said.

I hovered by his desk. "It's just a signature."

"Have to read it first," he said.

"Why?"

"You're asking me this? You're... asking me this?"

I waited for him to calm down. "Can I leave it here, until you're ready?"

"No," he said. "I have enough papers here."

I retrieved the letter from his table.

"Sheri says you're going to take their case."

"Who?" He looked up.

"My friend, Sheri Bakare. She called today to say you're going to take their case."

"Yes, Miss Bakare."

"Are you?" I asked.

"Am I what?"

"Going to take the case?"

"Yes I am."

"Do they have a chance?"

"There's nothing to prove. Their uncle doesn't have a chance. He swindled them out of their inheritance. The children and the wives, they own that house."

"Under native law?" I asked.

"You should know this. They share his estate amongst his children, according to how the man lived his life."

"Not according to how the wives wish to live theirs?"

"Wives are not always in agreement. These women just happen to be. They want to incorporate and transfer the property to the company."

"They do?"

"What do you think? They're Lagos women. They were trading before you were born. Give them the options and they will do what they have to."

I peered at his papers. "Are you really that busy?"

"Why?" he asked.

"If you're busy, why are you taking a case like theirs?"

He put his pen down.

"I take whatever case I want, Enitan, and at least your friend is a respectful girl, unlike some."

It was like trying to trap a tadpole. I reproached myself, but the next time Sheri came to the office, I watched her as closely as the other women did. She came to my desk before stepping into my father's office. She stayed ten minutes in there and came out.

"He's so nice," she said. "He's not charging us anything. Can you believe it?"

"Let's hope he's doing it out of kindness," I said.

My father never did pro bono work. He too came out of his room smiling. He never smiled in the office. If you do such a thing, I thought, chase my friend, you will never forget what I have to say to you and after that, I will have nothing left to say to you.

It wasn't improbable, he with a younger woman; Sheri with an older man. There were men in Lagos who chased their daughter's friends. You called them Uncle and curtseyed before them. There were women in Lagos who would chase their best friend's father for money.

Sheri smiled. "Why else would he do that for us?"

"He alone knows what he does," I said, "and why."

As a child, I knew that he strayed. I chose not to think about it. These days, when he brought women home, I treated them like any of his friends. It was hard to discern if he was interested in one or the other. I did not care to know. I discovered that after one of his clients, a married woman, started visiting him regularly. I thought her visits were work-related, until I met him at the airport after a trip abroad and saw her there. My father was a tricky man, I thought. Tricky enough to warrant an ambush. One afternoon, I arrived home early hoping to catch him. I found him in the living room with Peter Mukoro.

"Hello," I said, deliberately fixing my gaze on my father alone.

I couldn't bear my finger nails scratching a blackboard, the tips of my teeth running along cotton cloth. Peter Mukoro's mocking looks, I couldn't bear them either. He was stroking his mustache and watching me.

"You're back?" my father said.

"Yes," I said, heading straight for my room.

"Enitan," my father called after me.

"Yes," I said.

"You can't see Mr. Mukoro sitting here?"

"I can see him."

I knew I was in trouble. I almost welcomed it. My father came to my room after Peter Mukoro left.

"I've been watching you," he said. "Frowning all over the place and I've been very patient with you. Whatever you think is bothering you, never, ever again do that in my presence."

"I don't like him," I said.

"I don't care if you like him."

"Why won't you sign the transfer letter?" I said. "One minute you're helping someone else. Sheri, this... awful man."

"What has he ever done to you?"

"Sign the letter."

"When I am ready."

"Do it. Now."

My father stepped back. "You think we're equals? You think we're equals now? I treat you like an adult and you repay me this way? Your mother always said I was lax with you. But that will change. If you can't respect me in my house, you're 25 now, go wherever you want."

"Sign the letter."

"I won't tell you again. This has nothing to do with you. I've given you a choice. You either do as I say, or you leave this house."

He left me staring at my door. Leave my friend alone! I wanted to shout.

It was there; an old anxiety. But I was too old to be playing child and he was too old to be playing parent. If we forced the old ways upon ourselves now, we were liable to come to blows.

141

Sheri was counting old naira notes into separate piles on the desk in her office when I arrived. She licked her thumb and dealt them like cards. "One minute," she said.

"Take your time," I said.

It had taken me most of my lunch break to drive, but the anxiety was out of control. It was keeping me up at night. I wanted it to stop.

There were two stacks of boxes in the corner of the room: Peak milk, Titus sardines, Tate and Lyle sugar. A portrait of her stepmothers and another of her father alone. A pile of old mustard colored curtains were folded under the window. The green mosquito screen had ripped in two places. Dust. Everywhere. Sheri could not bear the mess, I was sure. She finished and flopped back in her chair.

"How come you're here today?"

"I came to see you," I said.

"Did you see the people outside? Did you see them?"

"I saw them."

"We're making money."

"I know."

There was a large lunch time crowd. They would have to wait for seats and their cutlery would not be clean or dry. Some would cut fried meat with spoons. If they complained, the cooks would ignore them. They had the same expression as cooks in the best food spots in Harlem, Bahia, Kingston: *Do not bother me*. The people came regardless. The food was good: black-eye peas, fresh fish, rice, vegetable stews with cow foot, intestines, lungs, and all manners of innards because in this part of the world we wasted no meat.

Sheri's nails galloped over the table.

"I'd better get back to work," I said.

"But you've just come," she said.

"Lunch-break over."

She laughed. "Why did you bother?"

"I was passing. I wanted to see your face."

If we didn't share our childhood, would I like her? Sheri was rude and vain. Sheri had always been rude and vain, except that as a child it was endearing. And whatever she said, it was clear that she did not think much of herself. She liked rich men. Yes, she did. In Lagos we used the word "like" this way. You liked to stare, you liked to criticize, you liked to make appointments and not keep them. There was an assumption, bad English aside, that if you did something often, you liked it.

If you do that, I thought, chase my father, I will have nothing to say to you. It would be sufficient, more than sufficient, to know that you think so little of yourself.

"You've seen my face," she said in Yoruba.

"It's the same face," I said.

We walked together to my car. Outside, the lunch-time traffic blocked the road. Someone leaned on a car horn. The sun was fierce. I shielded my eyes.

"Has my father been here?" I asked.

"No."

"Did he say he was coming?"

We faced each other. Sheri looked beyond me at the road.

"I hope he doesn't come," she murmured. "This place is a mess. Look, this man is going to... "

A Peugeot had moved too quickly on the road and rammed into the back of a Daewoo. The Daewoo driver got out and smacked the Peugeot driver through his open window. Mr. Peugeot jumped out and grabbed Mr. Daewoo's shirt. Mr. Daewoo was bigger. He slammed Mr. Peugeot against his car, held him by the scruff of his neck.

"Are you mad?"

"You're crazy!"

"Bang my car?"

"Slap my face?"

"I'll kill you!"

"Bastard!"

People came from the surrounding buildings to watch: men, women and children, elders so old their backs had given way. On a Lagos street, justice happened straight away. You knocked someone's car and they beat you up. The people would come out to watch. You knocked someone, and the people themselves would beat you up. You stole anything, and the people could beat you until they killed you.

The drivers on the road blasted their horns in frustration. They were as gridlocked as my mind; tight and going nowhere. The horns were never about this, two men beating themselves senseless over a dent in a bumper, and after a while, the horns had nothing to do with the delay, at all.

It was like pressing on a painful bump. I could not stop. The phone in my father's office rang one afternoon. Peace was out for lunch so I answered it. It was the receptionist from his travel agency. I told her he was in court.

She dragged her words. "His tickets are ready for collection."

"I'll tell him when he gets back," I said.

I knew my father was traveling, but I'd dropped the phone before I realized she said he was traveling with someone. I found the number of the travel agency, and waited for a dial tone. My father still had not updated our phone system. We waited up to two minutes for a dial tone and every month when we received telephone bills with phantom charges to Alaska, Qatar, places we were not even aware of, he threatened to have our phones disconnected.

The line was busy. I slammed the phone and tried again.

"Star Travel, good afternoon?"

"You called Mr. Taiwo's office?"

"Yes."

"His tickets. Whose names are they in?"

My heart was hammering. She put me on hold, consulted someone who asked who I was. I said I was his secretary.

"One is for Mr. Taiwo," she said.

"Yes," I said.

"Second one is for em, Mr. Taiwo."

I frowned. "Who?"

"Sorry, Dr. Taiwo," she said.

No such person, I thought.

"Dr. O. A.," she said. "Initials Oscar Alpha?"

"There's no such person," I said.

"Hold on," she said.

A man's voice.

"Hello, Peace? Why these questions?"

I wasn't Peace, I explained.

"Who are you?" he asked, brusquely.

"I work here," I said.

"Oh," he said. "Well the tickets are for Mr. Taiwo. And his son Debayo. Are you new?"

No such person, no such person, I thought.

"Peace will know. Tell her. Mr. Taiwo and his son are traveling. Their tickets are ready. She knows about it."

I dropped the phone. It was like shrapnel, being pulled out, I was sure.

Guilt never did show in my father's face. I'd seen. It was how he won cases. It was how he'd driven my mother to distraction. I'd seen that also.

My parent's mothers were both in polygamous marriages. My mother's mother was a trader. She saved money for her children's education under her mattress. One day my grandfather took the money she'd been saving and used it to pay the dowry for a second wife. My grandmother died broken-hearted for her money. My mother herself had never gotten over the shock. A pampered child, she disguised her embarrassment with snobbishness from then on. My father's mother was a junior wife. The two senior wives would deny my father food, hoping that if he were skinny enough, he would amount to nothing. That was why he didn't eat much; that was why he never gave in to my mother's food threats; that was why, years later, he still preferred to have an old man in his kitchen.

I waited for him that afternoon. My head felt like a shaken jar. Each time I opened it up, I didn't know which emotion to pull out. It wasn't uncommon for married men, especially of his generation, to have children outside. But this? Lying for years? I recalled how he punished me for lying as a child, how he would not forgive me for sneaking out with Sheri. It wasn't her—it was him I couldn't trust.

The joke was that a man's families discovered each other at his burial. That they fought until they fell into his grave. In reality most men who could still afford to lead this kind of double life confessed or were caught long beforehand. What were the requirements for being successful, after all? Telling one family, Don't call me at home, keep away from my real family?

It was nonsense.

He returned late in the evening. I opened the door.

"Do you know a Debayo Taiwo?" I asked.

My father placed his brief case down. "Yes."

"Is he your son?"

He straightened up. Yes, he said. Debayo was his son, four years younger than me. He lived in Ibadan. So did his mother. No, they were never married. He was in medical school there, finished last year. He was born a year after my brother died.

"I would have told you myself," he said.

"When?" I asked.

146

"I wanted you two to meet. Not like this."

I began to count my thoughts out on my fingers. If I didn't, I wouldn't have known how to speak. But I spoke calmly. He was not going to take control of this argument.

"That I thought I was your only child, I can live with that. That almost everything I've done comes back to it, was my own choice. That I have a mother who despises me because I stayed with you, is my own lot. So is the fact that I live in a place where all sorts of asinine..."

"Be careful how you speak to me," he said quietly.

"Asinine behavior is passed off as manliness."

"Be very careful."

"But don't tell me it is time I meet your son. That is not my choice. Not my lot, and I don't have to live with it."

"I have not asked anything of you."

"Does my mother know?"

He did not answer.

"Does she know?"

"No," he said. Shame had winded him. His voice was too low.

"You see?" I said, just as quietly. "You're the one who did the wrong thing, not her. Not her."

"You do not speak to me like that. No child of mine speaks to me like that."

I turned away. "I'm not staying here."

"Where are you going?" he asked.

"To my boyfriend's house," I said.

My father pointed. "Walk out of that door, and you won't be welcome back here."

"Liar," I said.

I packed a bag, didn't even look at him as I walked out. For all I cared, he could take my hymen, stretch it out, and hang it on the wall next to Mike's mosaic.

The road to Mike's house was choked. I kept punching my steering wheel. Perhaps it was a sign. Daughters didn't walk away like that. It was sacrilege. Costly, too. Under my breath, I cursed our economy that didn't give me freedom to sustain myself.

I had always believed my mother chose to depend on my father. The evidence was there in her dusty certificates. Other mothers walked out every day, to work, but she didn't. Now I felt no different from her, driving the car he had bought. My father would give a car, but he would not pay me enough to buy myself one. If I were taking the car with me, I deserved it. If my mother took a house, two houses even, she deserved them. The power had always been in my father's hands.

I stopped at a junction. A battered Peugeot crossed the main road before me. The driver was gaping at me. He drove as slow as if he were taking time to masturbate. I could not imagine why. A more bitter face than mine, I had not seen.

I banged on my horn. "What are you looking at?"

He scratched his head and accelerated.

When I arrived at Mike's house I rattled the gates. He came out wearing nothing but shorts.

"You didn't say you were coming," he said.

"I didn't know I was."

He opened the gates and I slid through.

He spotted my bag. "What's this?"

"I need a place to stay," I said. "I beg you. Tonight."

He walked ahead of me and I thought nothing of it because he might have been working or playing football. Climbing up the stairs, he stopped by the door.

"You didn't say you were coming, Enitan."

"You want me to leave?"

"No, no. I'm not driving you away."

"You won't... have to," I said, studying him. His shoulders

148

were hunched. "Do you have someone with you?"

He looked away.

"Mike, I'm talking to you."

Still, he said nothing. I brushed past him and opened the door. Lying on his sofa was a girl wearing nothing but a shirt. His shirt. I recognized it. Her hair was cropped like a boy's and she had bronze lips and eyes so haughty they didn't even blink. She was so dark and so beautiful I could have wet myself from grief. She drew on her cigarette.

Mike's hand closed over my shoulder. I wriggled out of his grip and hurried down the stairs. He ran after me, grabbed my waist and I elbowed him. We locked into a knot, breathing heavily into each others' faces. I was tempted to spit at his.

"Let go of me!"

He gripped me tighter and dived lower. I kicked him. He released me.

"Don't open your mouth," I said, pointing at him.

I remembered how I'd called him a liar when I first met him.

"Pretentious bastard." I said, walking away. "You're shallow and your work is shallow."

He followed me. I fumbled with the lock of the gate, then kicked it. It rattled in protest.

"Open this damn lock," I shouted.

The gates fell apart. I pushed him aside and walked out. I reached my car, jabbed my key into the key hole and yanked the door open.

"Listen," he said.

"Why?" I asked. "Tell me? Why should I listen to a single word that comes out of your mouth."

"I don't know," he said.

"You don't?" I said. "Well, neither do I."

He was one of those people. They were either living as they pleased or they were the greatest pretenders. In a room of ten people, how many would call him a berk? I sort of knew. I'd always sort of known.

The thought seized me. She couldn't go free. If I got in my car and drove away without letting my rage go, it would rupture me.

I got out of the car and began to walk back to the house.

"W-where are you going?" Mike asked.

"I don't know," I said, wagging my finger.

He hurried after me. At the top of the stairs, I saw the girl peeping from the doorway. She took one look at me and dashed back inside. I heard a door shut and realized she was running from me. Stupid girl. She was running from me.

I ran up the stairs.

I headed straight for Obatala, grabbed her, seemingly, by the ear and dragged her out. Mike was standing at the foot of the stairs. He was staring at me as if I held a gun in my hands. I raised Obatala high above my head, smashed Obatala over the banister, heard her beads pitter-patter down the stairs. Mike clamped his hands over his head. I placed the broken board on the ground, and walked down the stairs.

"Tell her," I said. "Tell her she should be running away from you, not me."

"Not my work," he said.

"Not my life," I answered.

I drove away. Through the gate I saw Mike's landlord, standing with his mouth open. I could almost read his thoughts: Good women didn't shout in somebody's house. Good women didn't fight on the streets. Good women didn't come looking for men. Good women were at home.

My fingers trembled over my steering wheel and tears pricked my eyes, but they wouldn't fall. I drove fast till I reached Sheri's house. The traffic favored me.

There I cried.

Sheri asked me to reconcile with my father. "These things are nothing," she said. I was not the first and I would not be the last. Half of Lagos had an outside family, and the other half wasn't aware. I refused and arranged a transfer to work with the Federal Ministry of Justice for the rest of the year. While my father was at work, I went home and packed a suitcase.

The day I met my new boss, I waited an hour before she arrived, and waited another thirty minutes while she ate yam and eggs out of a Tupperware container. My boss was one of those people—asking questions was unnecessary fussing. Her favorite complaint was that her duties belonged to someone else. Over the next months, I would go to court with her as an assistant, prosecuting in federal cases. The first time I had to address the bench, I tried to adopt an impressive voice. The judge, a middle-age woman, asked, "Young lady, is this some sort of new style?"

"No," I said.

"Speak in your normal voice, please," she said. "This is very tiring."

It was a hot day in court, especially under our wigs, which were made from horse hair, so we never washed them and they itched. The judge's salary would never compensate for the procession she had to witness: a tattered clerk, an illiterate criminal, my boss who was ill-prepared and asking for an extension, "if my lord pleases."

This particular my lord was not pleased. She had to take notes because there was no stenographer. She was taking the notes in longhand and oh Lord, the different ways of speaking. Then there would be traffic on her way home.

Fraud rackets had recently increased. Overseas they were calling it "Nigerian Crime." Here we called it "419," after the criminal code. Drug trafficking had also increased, and if the latest reports were true, Nigerian drug rings were now one of the largest suppliers to the US and Europe. Foreign embassies were reluctant to grant us visas, and those of us who received them risked being strip-searched for drugs at airports. Many of the accused were single women, mules, who were caught en route to Europe or the US from the Far East. Some had swallowed condoms crammed with heroin and cocaine; others had squeezed them up their vaginas. There was a case of a woman who stuffed a condom of cocaine down her dead baby's throat and cradled him on a plane. She was caught when an air hostess noticed the baby wasn't crying.

I hated coming out of court to find relations pleading to spare their son or daughter, old men and women prostrating. In one trial, the accused, a nineteen-year-old girl, claimed she didn't know what she was carrying. Another woman had handed the package to her, then disappeared. The court found the girl guilty. A month before, the new regime had shot people for the same crime, as part of their war against indiscipline. The executions were carried out retroactively, to punish those who had been tried and convicted before the law came into effect, but following a public outcry, further executions were deferred.

The girl's face haunted me. The way her glasses kept sliding down, I imagined her as a school librarian in her hometown, coming to Lagos to earn a better living. When I actually began to believe her story, I realized I was not detached enough to be successful at litigation. I wasn't even sure I enjoyed being in court. The proceedings took too long, relied on too many people. I viewed them through bleary eyes and my heart throbbed like a toothache.

I had lost weight, even with Sheri's cooking. Whenever I remembered Mike and my father, not being able to say a word, I dropped my head. I cared for someone and I enjoyed showing them courtesy. The worst was to be deprived of giving it. I carried some of their shame. Soon I began to keep the same hours as my boss and learned how to disguise my tracks. I didn't even mind the bad looks I was receiving from other colleagues.

Living with Sheri, I saw how she survived as a sugary girl. She limited her involvement in the family business to please her brigadier. She tidied, after me and after her nephews and nieces who came to spend time with her. She dusted with cleaning rags, sometimes with her fingers. She plumped cushions if she stood up, picked fluff from her carpet, listened to the saddest Barbara Streisand songs. The rest of her time she spent preparing for Brigadier Hassan: her hair, her nails, dabbing perfumes and cooking meals. There wasn't a coy bone in her body to spare for the outrage of others, especially those from homes like mine, with errant fathers and mothers who prayed good and hard about which good families their daughters would end up in.

In a bizarre household arrangement that appeared incestuous to me, Brigadier Hassan's wives were trying to recruit her as a third wife. They knew their husband had a number of girlfriends and thought that if he had to remarry, it would be to someone who wasn't liable to sit around the polo club chukka after chukka, wearing expensive sunshades. Sheri found polo boring. Their daughters liked her. She was less than ten years older than the eldest and would never tell if they visited boyfriends. They had all attended finishing schools in Switzerland, and their marriages were to be arranged. Their father also thought they ought to remain virgins until they left his house. The eldest claimed that horse riding stretched her. Meanwhile, he was taking Sheri to Paris, to Florence, first class. Sheri, who had trouble remembering: "That place in Florence with the gold market," "that street in Paris with the shops," "that watch, starts with P? Exactly, Pathetic Philip." I could remember every single trip in Europe, even the names of each poxy pensione I'd stayed in, and if someone had bothered to buy me an expensive watch, I would at least try to remember.

Where two cultures diverged Sheri had chosen which to follow. Her grandmother, Alhaja, had seen to that. A woman widowed in her thirties, Alhaja headed a market women's union and earned enough to educate her children overseas. She was disappointed when her son ended up with a white woman, but she raised Sheri herself so that no other wife would mistreat her. When the other wives did come, they would worry more about Alhaja's rage than their husband's. She would visit their home, if she heard they were fighting. There, she threatened them. Her son had had a white woman, and he would get rid of two squabbling Africans in no time! She would go to the houses of her daughters if their husbands beat them. The husbands would end up begging her. When she learned about what happened to Sheri at the picnic, she visited each of the boys' houses with a mob in tow. The mob started with the watchmen, or whoever was unfortunate enough to open the gates. They broke down doors and windows. As they went for furniture, Alhaja went straight for the boy's crotches. She wasn't letting go until their mothers, fathers, their grandparents even, lay flat on the floor to beg her granddaughter. After, she visited her medicine man to finish what was left of their lineage.

Sheri was her grandmother's true daughter. I once tried to explain the Tragic Mulatto syndrome to her. She said it was nonsense. All sorts of people tried to find their identity. Why was the mulatto tragic? There was nothing tragic about her. At the Miss World contest, a girl from Zimbabwe told her the word "half-caste" was derogatory; "colored" was what Sheri would be called in her own country. Sheri said she didn't care what anyone called her. In the Yoruba-English dictionary there was a whole sentence to describe her: "the child of a black person and white person," and it suited her fine.

It wasn't always that clear to her. She was eight years old when, fed up with a boy at school who laughed at her features, she ran home one afternoon and cut off her hair, trimmed her lashes to stubs and rubbed brown shoe polish on her face. Her grandmother Alhaja found her standing before the mirror and ordered her back to the boy. He was singing that Yoruba song, "I married a yellow girl" when Sheri grabbed him. "I beat him up," she said. "Then I emptied his school bag on his head and pushed him into the gutter. I will never forget his name. Wasiu Shittu."

Like a proper Lagos Princess, nobility surfaced once you got in her way. A fist fight? A person would have to kill Sheri first before she let it rest. Drop an insult? Yes, she would, as fast as she was provoked. Chop a person down in three glances heads, torso, and legs. In no time, if they turned their noses up at her. And whoever they were, she was about to give them their life history: "From where are you coming? From where?"

Still she wouldn't eat pork. And every morning when she said her prayers with a scarf wrapped around her head, she had a humble expression. The humblest she would have all day. Haughty and bored it would be from then on. The kind of haughtiness that came from being a favored child and the kind of boredom that came from not having enough to do.

I avoided her brigadier altogether, catching only the smell of his cigars and finding it strangely seductive. I imagined him according to the stereotype: dressed in a long white tunic with a Mao-style collar, gold cufflinks, fat diamond watch on his wrist. His hands would slip in a handshake. His trousers would flap around his ankles. His feet would be small in his leather slippers. Absolutely no conversation. He would not be used to talking to women. Not that way.

But I dared not say a word, not even about his drinking and smoking as a strict Moslem. I was living in his apartment, the very place I'd urged Sheri to move out of. Whenever he was visiting, I would go swimming at Ikoyi Club, and she was pleased. "Forget that stupid artist," she said.

I swam regularly. My body pressed on. Then it seemed that my mind, which had been lagging behind, soon began to say, "Wait for me. Wait for me."

I was swimming one evening when a tall man with legs like an Olympic swimmer joined me in the club pool. He dived in and paced himself fast. He made me feel slow and clumsy. Once or twice I crossed him in the middle of the pool, but most times we were at opposite ends. Soon I paused to rest in the shallow end. He came to a stop and rose from the water like something aquatic. "Hello," he said.

His smile was the color of ivory. One side tooth popped out a little.

"You too," I said.

He splashed water over his chest. "Would you mind if I told you something?"

"I would," I said.

He tucked his chin in. "Why are you being rude?"

"Listen, I come here to swim."

"So do I," he said. "All I wanted to say was that you have mucus."

"What?"

"Mucus. Hanging out of your nose."

He pointed.

My hand clamped over my nose as he hoisted himself out of the pool. I shrugged and continued to swim. Fool, I thought.

I was walking up the stairs, two evenings later, from the changing rooms to the pool shower, wearing my swimsuit. He was walking down the stairs from the pool bar to the same shower.

"Sorry," I said, in embarrassment.

I was usually alone in the pool in the evenings. The children, mostly expatriates, were gone. There were married couples at the pool bar, having soft drinks. Most of the activity was in the main club house, where beer and spirits were served, or in the squash courts full of the regular players. I never expected to see him again. He gestured like a cattle herder, I thought, to move me along.

"At least say thank you," he said, when I didn't.

"Why," I answered.

I stepped under the faucet with my backside to him, didn't even care if he saw my stretch marks. He wasn't perfect either. Good legs maybe, startling height, weakish chin, and his stomach could be tighter.

He made a sound, "hm," as my father would, like a warning. Not as women did, stretching the sound and turning their mouths downward. That was the sound I made in response.

"Any time," he said, as I walked away.

We swam as if we were each alone in the pool that evening.

Again I bumped into him. This time, in the main club house, after swimming another evening.

"Miss Rudeness," he announced.

"I'm not rude," I said.

He walked past and I turned on a whim.

"Excuse me?"

"Yes," he said.

"My manners are mine," I said. "You don't have to remind me of them, or my mucus for that matter. It has nothing to do with you. And whenever you see me, try not to say anything, if you really want to avoid an insult."

He smiled. "Let it go. Let it go."

"What go?"

"Bitterness," he said. "It eats you up."

I looked him up and down. "I see your mouth is sharp."

"So they tell me."

"What do you know about me? You know nothing about me. All I'm saying is, stop passing comments whenever you see me."

"Let it go."

We were both smiling now, except he was making fun of me. There was no need to be angry with him, I thought. He was a big fool.

"What's laughing you laugh?" I said.

He continued to smile and I wanted to shock him.

"Would you like to have a drink?" I asked.

He cupped his ear.

"I said would you like to have a drink?"

"I come here to swim," he said.

"After you swim," I said.

I pulled a face behind his back. I'm not afraid, I thought. Of any of you. If I want a drink, I will have one.

He joined me in the club house. We sat at the bar, while the bartender gave me disapproving looks.

Niyi Franco. He was a lawyer, though he was now a manager in an insurance company. His grandfather was a lawyer. His father and four brothers were lawyers. His mother retired from nursing the year he was born. He swam for Lagos State, and thought he would do so for the rest of his life. Then he cracked his head on a diving board, and his parents banned him from entering a pool for life.

"Africans can't swim," I joked.

"I'm a Brazilian descendant," he said, lifting his chin.

"My friend," I said. "You're African."

I told him about my recent experiences in court, saying little about my family. We walked to our cars together and it was hard to keep up with him because he took such long strides. This time we were talking about lawyer's wigs and gowns. There was much debate in the press about changing the uniform to reflect our heritage.

"We'll never change it," he assured me.

"I hope we will," I said. "Those wigs look terrible."

"Thank God I don't have to wear one."

"When was the last time you did?" I asked.

"A year after I graduated," he said.

"When did you graduate?"

"'77."

I stepped back. "No."

"Yes," he said.

That was the year of the Festival of Arts and Culture we called Festac. Stevie Wonder came to play at our national theater, Mariam Makeba, Osibisa, every African person in the world represented in Lagos. I thought I would die because I was in boarding school in England. We had color television for the first time in our country, and everyone was growing vegetables in their back yards in support of the government's Operation Feed the Nation. My mother grew an okra patch, my father said the whole regime, its Operation Feed the Nation and Festival of Arts, was all nonsense.

"See my eyes," he said. "I never lie. I have a six-year-old son."

My mouth fell open. "You're married?"

"Divorced," he said.

"You're married," I said.

As far as I was concerned.

"Well," I said. "Nice meeting you."

"You too," he said.

"I'd better get home."

"I've enjoyed talking to you."

"You're welcome," I said, without thinking.

I almost curtseyed. How old was I in 1977? Seventeen.

I was determined to find out about his wife the next time we met. This time, we sat in the drinks lounge.

"You must miss your son," I said, as we waited for our beers to arrive.

"Yes."

"You get to spend time with him, I'm sure."

"No," he said.

"That is a pity," I said.

I thought I should give up prying. It was not my business.

"He's in England with his mother," he said.

"Your wife's in England?"

"She's not my wife."

Our waiter arrived with the beers. Niyi immediately reached for his wallet and paid. The waiter obscured his face for an instant.

"You drove the poor woman to England?" I said.

I reached for my bottle.

"She left," he said. "I was twenty-three. Let me see... she was pregnant, still in medical school. I was working for my father. My parents are strict Catholics, but I didn't get married because of that. My father was not an easy man to get along with. He kept threatening to sack me. One day I said, 'I've had enough' and walked out. That was the beginning of our troubles.

"I found a new job, but it was hard. She was working in the teaching hospital, we were living in Festac Village. My son is an asthmatic. One day her car was stolen, this, that, you can imagine. But she had this group of friends. Like rats those women, shoe-and-bag girls. They were always wearing something, traveling somewhere. She wanted all of that. One day her parents gave her a ticket and she took off. She went to England with my son. She didn't even call until she found a job then she phoned crying and asking me to come and join her."

"What did you say?"

"I had a job here. I wasn't qualified over there. What was I going to do? Who would employ me? She was a doctor, and I would be what? All the time we were in Lagos, she was telling everybody I couldn't provide. Now she wanted me to go to another country and take an odd job?"

"That would have been difficult."

"I could have gone, for my son."

"Would she have done the same for you?" I asked.

As he drank his beer, I watched him. Every movement he made was large.

"No," he said, rubbing his forehead. "She knew exactly what she wanted. She always knew what she wanted. She wanted to get married. She wanted to travel. She wanted to work in England. She just wouldn't admit it. Women do that, you know."

"What?"

"Dribble past you and score. Phoosch! Mental football."

I smiled. "You generalize."

"You're not like that?"

"I'm not perfect."

"Tell me your faults," he said, smiling.

"I trust too fast," I said. "I don't forgive easily. I'm terrible, terrible with that, and I'm scared of death."

"Yours?"

"Mine, and others."

"That's not a fault."

I pictured myself as a drunken woman, ramming my head into a wall, thinking I would eventually walk through. I was always hopeful about men.

"I'm hopeful," I said.

"That's good," he said, taking another drink.

I glanced at his hands.

"Do you play the piano?"

He studied them, looking pleased. "How come you know?"

I brought my glass to my lips.

"How did you know?" he said. "You must be a mammy-water, hanging around pools, looking for men to entice and wagging that ass of yours."

My beer went down the wrong way.

Sheri was sitting on her bed. I stood before her mirror, wearing work clothes: a black skirt suit that always needed to be coaxed down.

"You can't go out like that," she said.

I checked my lipstick. "Why not?"

"To the Bagatelle? People dress up to go there. Your suit looks un-ironed."

"Who's looking?"

She walked to her wardrobe and began to sift through.

"You'll never find anything in there for me," I said.

"Wait and see," she said.

"I won't like it, Sheri. I know I won't, and I'm not going to change to please you."

Always. She asked if I'd eaten. She fixed my hair as I walked out of her door, made me iron my clothes. I told her she had an old woman's soul. She said that was why she was wiser. She pulled out a black gown with a large gold print. It was narrow and the neckline was a little wide, Senegalese style.

"Tell me you don't like it," she said.

I wore it. Niyi arrived early. I thought he would have made an effort, but he was wearing work clothes. Sheri was looking forward to meeting him, and he ended up not staying. We were running late, he claimed, then he later confessed he was hungry.

"How long has she been living here?" he asked as we drove out of the apartment complex.

"Two years," I said.

"She's come far," he said.

"What do you mean?"

162

We approached the junction leading to the main road.

"Living here and no job," he murmured.

I watched one car whiz past, then another. I was about to answer when he whistled. His gaze followed a red car which looked like a miniature space ship on the antiquated road. The car slowed by the gates of the large apartment complex across the road. "What?" I asked.

"The new BM," he said.

"BM what?" I asked.

"W," he explained.

He stared at the red brake lights. The gates opened and the car rolled in.

"Em, can we go, now?" I asked.

The main road was clear. He gave it a cursory look before coming out.

I sniffed. "So materialistic."

He looked me up and down. "You don't like good things, Madam Socialist?"

I turned my face to the window.

He patted my knee. "It is good to see that your politics doesn't affect your dressing. You look nice in your black and gold."

I kept my face to the window. I did not want him to see me smile. How the man annoyed me.

But I knew he joked because he thought he was flawed. Not flawed the way most people were, secretly, for their own self-obsession, but flawed publicly, so that everyone could see: a wife who had walked out on him, a son he was not raising. Anywhere else in the world it would be hard to deal with, more so here. A woman was used to humiliation by the time she reached adulthood. She could wear it like a crown, tilt it for effect even, and dare anyone to question her. A man would wear his like an oversized cloak.

"Move your broken down car," he shouted.

He drove terribly, as if we were rushing to the airport for the last flight out of Lagos, and accused other drivers of sleeping.

"Please," I said. "Don't crash us."

The Bagatelle was one of the oldest and best run restaurants in Lagos, owned by a Lebanese family. Throughout dinner I was laughing. Niyi ordered falafel as lafa-lafa. When it arrived, he said it would give him gas. I asked if any food pleased him. He said home cooking.

"I'm sorry, I don't cook," I said.

"Serious?"

He contemplated my confession for a moment then thumped the table.

"I'll marry you, anyway."

"Oh, Lord," I said, holding my head. If I did, I would be in trouble.

"Eat up," he said.

"I'm full," I said.

"You're wasting good food," he said. "I thought you were a socialist."

"You've been calling me names since you met me."

"Eat up, o-girl."

"Please, let me digest."

How the man annoyed me. He had a wicked mouth, even to kiss.

I was surprised to find Sheri's door ajar when I returned. I pushed it open and peered into the living room. There was a pot on her sofa, overturned. I slipped and realized there was okra on the floor.

"Sheri," I said, placing my hand to my chest.

I walked around the sofa, found more stew on the floor. In the kitchen, I saw a bag of yam flour lying half empty on the floor.

"Sheri!" I said.

Her voice came from her room. I hurried there and found her lying on her bed.

"What happened?"

She propped herself up slowly.

"Nobody hits me. You hit me and I will hit you back. God no go vex."

There was yam flour in her hair.

"Who hit you?"

She patted her chest. "Telling me I'm a whore for going out. Your mother is the whore. Raise a hand to hit Sheri Bakare, and your hand will never be the same again. Stupid man, he will find it hard to play polo from now on."

"Sheri, you beat up the brigadier?"

With a pot, she said. The Civil War hadn't prepared him for her. She beat him for every person who had crossed her path in life. I told her she didn't have a drop of white blood in her. Anyone who had white blood wouldn't beat up a whole brigadier, like that, with a pot of okra stew.

"I was raised in downtown Lagos," she said. "Bring the Queen of England there. She will learn how to fight."

She swept the yam flour off the kitchen floor.

"You know you will have to leave this place," I said.

"I know," she said.

"And you know he might send people over to harass you."

"Let him send the president," she said. "United Nations troops, even."

"You're prepared to die?"

"I know people who will beat him up for ten naira alone," she said. "And I know things about him that will land him in Kirikiri maximum security prison for the rest of his life, if he tries any nonsense. The man is a coward. That is why he hit me. He won't dare send anyone here. If he does, he will read in *Weekend People* how a woman beat him up."

I shook my head.

"Me and you, I don't know who is crazier."

"After what my eyes have seen? If I'm not crazy, what else will I be? The man is jealous of me. Can you believe it? He's jealous of my success. With all he has. He wants me to have nothing, except what he gives me. He says he will take it all back. I said take it! All of it! I did not come to this place naked."

I looked into the living room.

"What about your furniture?"

"We don't have tables and chairs in my father's house? Let him keep them. All I want is my Barbara Streisands."

I could see she was struggling with the broom.

"Let me do that," I said.

She dragged a chair as I gathered the flour into a pile.

"Enitan," she said after a while. "I'm telling you this, not because of what happened tonight, and I hope you will listen."

I was about to kneel. "Yes?"

"My mother is not dead. My father told me she was, but the truth was he took me away from her."

"What?"

"You know how England was in those days. Black people were like monkeys to the *oyinbos*. He had just graduated. She was working in a hotel. She used to bring him food. They never married, and he wanted me to know our traditions."

I whispered. "Traditions of what?"

The man didn't even bother to raise Sheri. He handed her over to his mother and then to his wives.

"Alhaja told me everything before she died. She apologized. I told her it was in the past. Stop looking at me like that. I'm not the first or last. At least he didn't leave me in England like some did, and anyway, I have two mothers."

"But your real mother… "

"The person who never came to look for me. That isn't a real mother."

I shut my eyes. "What your father did was wrong. Wrong!"

"I can accept it; so can anyone else. Are you trying to tell me you feel my pain more than me?"

She was smiling; I knew not to probe.

"Sorry."

"Just make up with your father. That's all I'm asking. It's enough now. I'm moving out of here tomorrow, and I'm going back to my family. I think you should do the same. These things happen in families. They happen. It's what you do afterward that matters. Your father raised you. He never abandoned you. Don't be stubborn."

"I have a right to be angry."

"So you deny the person who raised you."

"It's more than his lies."

"What more?"

"I can't trust him. Not even with my friends."

"Which friends?"

I pointed.

Her eyes widened. "You think your father is after me?"

I imitated him: "'My dear this, my dear that.'"

"He does the same to you."

"Well, I know him. He thinks I don't, but I do."

I stood up, aware that I was sounding like my mother.

"This is Lagos," she said. "You can't behave like this. You won't be the first, and you won't be the last. Our fathers, we know what they're like. We just have to accept them as they are."

I emptied the dust pan into the large waste bin.

"Enitan!"

Walking down the graveled path, I felt ashamed. Daughters were meant to listen and I hadn't listened. I paused before I rang the door bell; rang it twice and heard footsteps. The door opened. Her hair was completely gray. Perhaps she'd forgotten to dye it. For the first time, I worried that my mother would die without forgiving me.

"It's you?" she said.

"Yes," I said.

"Come in," she said.

She listened to what I had to say.

"You were rude to him," she said, "You will have to apologize. That is taboo, to call your father a liar."

She kicked her bedroom slippers off. They were originally light blue, but her feet had left brown imprints and the fabric was matted with dust.

"He was no good. After you were born, I told him I didn't want another child. God had blessed us with a healthy child. Why risk having another? But his family wouldn't hear of it. He had to have a son, so they started threatening that he would take another wife, and his mother, that woman who suffered so much herself, threatened me too. Your father never said a word to support me.

"I was very reserved, you know. Aloof. Your father liked that. Sunny, he always felt he had to be above others. Maybe because he was so neglected as a boy. And I did not mind wearing what he bought, clothes, jewelry. I had it all, but when your brother was born, who cared about them? Imagine the pain for a child? He would scream and scream and we couldn't touch him. I couldn't touch my son. For what? For a man who wouldn't be kept. Going out all the time, as if my son didn't exist, as if I didn't exist. He said I stopped looking after myself. I did not have time for myself. He said I was angry all the time. Of course I was angry. It was like swallowing broken glass. You can't expel broken glass from your body. It will tear you apart. It's best that it remains inside you."

"Never make sacrifices for a man. By the time you say, 'Look what I've done for you,' it's too late. They never remember. And the day you begin to retaliate, they never forget. Pray you never know what it means to have a sick child, either. You don't know whether to love them too much, or too little. Then as they become sicker, you love them the only way you can, as though they are a part of you.

"The day your brother died, your father was out. I took your brother to church. We were praying. How we prayed that day. Your father wouldn't forgive me, kept talking about hospital. Why didn't you take him to hospital, why didn't you take him to hospital. What can hospital do? Hospital can't take sickle cell out of a child, hospital cannot make a dying child live. I am not an ignorant woman. There isn't a mother in the world who wouldn't believe that faith can heal her child after medicine has failed, even the young women of today, who are so smart about family planning."

I nodded. In those days, couples took chances. These days, couples who could afford it, traveled overseas for a test in their first trimester. If the result showed a sickle child, the woman would have a quiet abortion. We believed in reborn spirits no more than we believed in the sanctity of early life.

"Yes," my mother said. "A son, you say. I'm not surprised. It was a question of time before he surfaced. I'm glad I know. All those years, I wanted your father to admit he was doing wrong. He never did."

I tried to picture my brother. He was scrawny; always being tossed in the air and tickled, even by me, except when he was sick. Sometimes I wanted to know how it felt to be sick. Once, I tried to pretend that I was having a crisis. He laughed and poked me off my bed, screamed until my mother rushed in.

"You think it's funny?" she said to me.

The day of his funeral, none of us attended. My parents didn't, because parents couldn't bury their children, according

169

to the custom. I stayed with them because my father said I was too young. Years after, I fantasized that my brother was playing another prank, this time, pretending to be dead. I wanted to see him again, getting me into trouble and sneaking peeks to gauge my reaction, but I was afraid of ghosts. My brother was the brave one, I thought. Whenever he was in hospital, I preferred to hide under my bed than to visit him, and after he died, I worried that he would visit me like an ugly masquerader. For a while, death became the logical conclusion to every situation. My head itched, so I would scratch it, so I would bleed and bleed until I died. A spider on the curtain, so it would fall into my mouth, bite my throat, my throat would swell up and I would die. As I grew older, the links between events became less precarious.

There were things I remembered about my mother also, how she brewed lemon grass tea whenever I was ill and checked on me several times a night, like a nurse, without pity: "Open up. Good." In another country, she might have sought help through counseling or therapy. Here, people were either mad or not mad. If they were mad, they were walking the streets naked. If they were not mad, they remained at home. My mother once had thirty-three bottles of perfume on her dressing table, before she started wearing those church gowns smelling of bleach and starch. I counted them. I could still remember the glamour days, the velvet caftan with circular mirrors. I imagined her with broken crystals in her stomach. They were there in her eyes. She was a beautiful woman. I had long forgotten.

1995

People say I was hot-headed in my twenties. I don't ever remember being hot-headed. I only ever remember calling out to my voice. In my country, women are praised the more they surrender their right to protest. In the end they may die with nothing but selflessness to pass on to their daughters; a startling legacy, like tears down a parched throat.

The first time I spoke to Niyi about marriage, I'd discovered my mother was scavenging our trash bags for my used sanitary towels and taking them to church for prayers. Her priest had said I would remain childless otherwise. She was still a member of his church, a senior sister now. She lit candles in the mornings and evenings to pray, mumbled to herself and hummed church songs. Her front door was padlocked by six o'clock and her curtains drawn. I would go out to see Niyi just to escape from her, from her house where I often felt shackled by afterbirth. It was hers now, since my father relinquished it. That happened three weeks after I moved in with her. I received a transfer letter from him with a covering letter accusing me of de-camping. I replied, thanking him for raising me and reminded him that I was never given a chance to decide what camp to be in. I apologized for my rudeness meanwhile. Really, I shouldn't have called my own father a liar.

My mother began to boast to her church friends that I'd seen his hypocrisy first-hand. I watched her disappear every Sunday only to come back and accuse these same people of meanness. I pretended to listen. I knew that she hurt because of the sacrifices she'd made in her marriage. I finally understood why she turned her mind to church with such fervor. Had she turned to wine or beer, people would have called her a drunkard. Had she sought other men, they would have called her a slut. But to turn to God? Who would quarrel with her? "Leave her alone," they would say. "She is religious."

I had watched my mother worship, and seen the way she waved her hands and exaggerated her smile. Whenever she said amen, I thought she might have well have been saying nyah-nyah. She had tricked us all. Her fixation with religion was nothing but a life-long rebellion. Faith had not healed her and I hoped that one day, the birth of a grandchild would.

But when I told her I was going to marry Niyi she said they had madness in his family. Oh yes. One of his aunts was always washing her hands, and another one, pretty thing like this, had a baby and would not touch it for days. "Imagine that for a mother," she said. I told my father about my engagement and he, too, suddenly became religious. "Not allowed," he said, raising his forefinger; not allowed by the Pope, he meant. Niyi was a divorced Catholic, so he would not give his blessings. Not until Uncle Fatai persuaded him would he agree to the wedding, then he lectured Niyi about how our marriage would have to work. That ended any father-son relationship they could have developed, and Niyi, disturbed by my mother's church activities, avoided her as if she were a sorceress.

On the day of my traditional engagement, I knelt before him according to the rites. He presented a dowry to my family, of hand-woven cloth and gold jewelry. I did not want a dowry and I did not want to kneel. Niyi, who was reluctant to participate in rites that would proceed as if he were 21 and without a child of his own, did not want to be there at all. During the ceremony my parents argued. My mother refused to sit by my father. He told her she was quite welcome to stand outside his gates. A week later, at the civil ceremony, I almost suffocated from the ill-feeling in the Ikoyi registry.

I did not shed a tear over leaving home. I, who cried easily. After the final rites, when a bride knelt before her parents and they blessed her, she was supposed to cry. An entire wedding party waited for this moment, so that they could say "Ah, she wept. She wept, that girl. She loves her parents no end." But I'd always been suspicious. What were the tears for, on cue like that? One bride, almost 40, gray hairs all over her head, she was crying as if her parents had sold her. They had all but given up on her. What was she crying for? I was not bitter about my parents. We had healed the way most families did, enough to hold us together from one day to the next, but liable to split under any great stress. I still had not met my father's outside son, my half-brother. At first it was about letting my father know I hadn't forgotten about his deception. Then it was about being loyal to my mother. After a while, it was really about having other matters to worry about, like work.

At the time, I was working for the Ministry of Justice and supplementing my income with the odd business incorporation. After we got married, Niyi introduced me to some of his friends in banking and I found a job in credit control. I was not prepared for my new environment, handling large sums of money within tight deadlines. On the one hand, I had the hustlers from treasury pushing me to pass deals; on the other, management cautioning me to check credit lines. The treasury guys would come ten minutes to cut-off time, tallying exactly how much the bank would lose if I didn't approve their transactions. I would get heartburn from arguing with them. Then, one day, I mistakenly approved a deal with an insufficient credit line and manage-ment hauled me in for a reprimand.

After work I drove home crying. Niyi took one look at me. "You have to be tougher than this, o-girl," he said. "You can't let people push you around. Tell them to go to hell if they pressure you."

"You have no idea," I said. Bankers were not like lawyers. We were accustomed to waiting for due process. We expected delays. Niyi pulled my nose. "Stop," I said and slapped his hand away.

He patted my head. "That is what I want to hear."

I was able to face work the next morning. From then on, Niyi led me through similar rites. Months later, when the company secretary left, I stepped into her position.

At work I consciously tried to imitate him. How he said "no" without moving his head; how his eyes, once locked, wouldn't shift. At home, he had me howling with things he would do and say with that look. He played pieces on my piano and dared to call them jazz. I thought they sounded like a petrified rat scurrying back and forth over the keyboards. He walked around with nothing but Y-fronts on. On more than one occasion, he turned his back and pulled them down; to check. He had hemorrhoids, at least two episodes a year. I told him it said something about his personality, that he had a hidden weakness in his gut. He said I should get used to it, the pesseries and the ointments. I would eventually grow accustomed to this and other marital surprises. I didn't know a man could have his own way of squeezing toothpaste. I didn't know I could come close to lunging across the dining table to throttle a man, because of the way he chewed. Then there were more serious times, when Niyi's brows knotted and I knew that silence would follow. This happened whenever he was reminded of his grudges, against his ex-wife, against their friends who had taken sides and his own family. That I would never get used to.

After he left his father's firm, Niyi's brothers avoided him for fear of offending their father. Only his mother sneaked visits to him. Then his wife left him. The day she found a new boyfriend, their son stopped calling. Now, years later, although they were all on speaking terms, Niyi swore he would never forget each person's role. Whenever he wanted to speak to his son, I was the one to call his ex-wife. He was wary of his father and brothers, and he protected his mother like an egg.

Toro Franco. She was one of those women who swallowed her voice from the day she married. She was a nurse, and yet her husband and sons, all lawyers, thought she couldn't grasp the rudiments of Offer and Acceptance, so she acted like she didn't. She called "precedence" "presidents," walked around with her underskirt hanging out. Whenever she tried to join in their legal discussions, they teased her, "Mama, look at you. Your Saturday is sticking out of your Sunday." They laughed as she adjusted her underskirt. If they mentioned the word hungry, she ran into her kitchen and began to boss her house boys around. Soon she would summon me to help. I knew that she watched me botch my kitchen duties, dropping spoons, recoiling from hot handles, slicing my fingers.

"It's hot in here," I would say.

"Don't worry," she would say.

"The boys should help."

"Boys? What can boys do?"

"They know how to tease you."

"Who else can they tease?"

Once, I tried to trick her into a confession. "Don't you ever feel lonely in here, ma? Isn't the kitchen the loneliest room?" She looked at me as if I'd offered to strip.

"Enough," she pleaded. "Enough now."

I continued to stir her stew, imagining her in a mortuary, on a slab, underskirt hanging out, husband and children saying how nice she was.

Everyone said my mother-in-law was nice. I wouldn't believe them until I'd heard a true word pass her lips. Her husband was a man who liked his stews prepared the traditional way, meat fried in thick groundnut oil, and he loved his wife so much he wouldn't eat stews prepared by anyone but her. Forty-five years later, he had bad arteries and her hands were as dry and shriveled as the meat she fried. Francis Abiola Franco, Esquire. The first time we met he asked, "You're Sunny Taiwo's daughter?"

"Yes, sir," I said.

"Good breeding always shows," he said.

"I'm a horse?" I asked Niyi later.

"He's a horse," Niyi said. "An old nag."

He was one of those Senior Advocates of Nigeria, though he was now out of touch with the Law, and with reality. He asked his sons to dial if he needed to make a phone call. He sat in the back seat of his car, always, even when one of his sons was driving. He stopped speaking to me after I challenged him on a point of law. I disagreed with him just for the sake of it. I didn't care much for him, but my brothers-in-law, I loved. They would all troop into my house, all four of them looking like Niyi with the same dark skin and thin nose, and I would kiss each of them feeling a rush of libido and motherliness as they greeted me, "Enitan of Africa!" *"Obirin Meta!* Three times a girl!" *"Alaiye Baba!* Master of the earth!" It was like welcoming my husband four times over. I didn't even mind sitting with them as they scratched their groins and christened women's parts: her foward, her backward, her assets, her giblets. About Sheri: "She's, em, very talented. Hyuh-Hyuh-Hyuh."

I knew. They were petrified of women, though they denied it. "Who? Who's scared of chicks?" they asked.

"Sneaking," I said. "Lying. Lying on your last breath. Then you cannot even face somebody to say a relationship is over? That is petrified."

"If you say so. Hyuh-Hyuh-Hyuh," scratch, scratch, scratch.

Sometimes they brought girlfriends who disappeared by the next visit. Sometimes they played hide-and-seek games with their girlfriends. I once asked, "Are you boys waiting to marry your mother, or what?"

"Of course," they answered, including Niyi.

"Well, em," I said. "Don't you think you should drop your standards a little?"

"No," they said, except Niyi.

Niyi bullied his brothers the same way he bullied me, but he could easily become vexed in the middle of our playing. Then he would call me aside and warn, "Better watch what you're saying. Next thing they'll be calling me woman wrapper." Wrapper was the cloth women tied around their waists. Woman wrapper was a weak man, controlled by his woman. I thought he was paranoid. I said it was too bad. He was the very person who had encouraged me to be strong at work. He was asking me to fly within specified perimeters. I would have shouting fits about this and he would remain totally silent. He said he wasn't used to arguing that way. "In our family," he said, "we don't raise our voices."

The Francos were one of those Lagos families, descendants of freed slaves from Brazil, who once formed the cream of Lagos society. They considered themselves well-bred because their great-grandfather, Papa Franco, was educated in England. In his time, Papa Franco acquired a huge estate which survived the slum clearance that wiped out most of the Brazilian Quarter in Lagos. Some of the buildings now looked as if a giant fist had come down from heaven and punched them into the ground. Those that remained standing were rickety with tall shutters and wrought iron balconies. Nothing had been done to improve the drainage system: gutters and pit latrines dating back to colonial times. They were occupied mostly by street traders and market people.

Papa Franco's only son, Niyi's grandfather, had twenty-six children by three different women who died before him and there had been several documented court cases over his estate. Each faction of Franco occupied separate pews in the Catholic church they attended. Their church reminded me of my mother's: the incense, white robes, and chants. When the collection tray passed, they gave very little. Oil wealth hadn't touched their palms and civil service wages were paltry. The

Franco men tilted their noses heavenward, the women fanned their cleavages laden with gold and coral beads, their clothes reeked of camphor balls. They had the pride and lack of ambition of a generation that wealth would skip, and ignored each other because they thought it was common to quarrel openly. That was how they settled differences: Aunty Doyin, The Pretty One, locked herself in a room until her father allowed her to marry a Protestant; Niyi's father stopped speaking to him for a year after he left Franco and Partners; Niyi, himself, would ignore me for days.

The first time this happened, we'd argued over drinks. Drinks. His brothers were visiting and I had just returned from work. As usual, he asked, "Enitan can you get these animals something?"

Niyi claimed he was totally inept inside kitchens. His favorite trick was to feign panic attacks by the door, clutching his throat and keeling over. Normally I humored him, because we had house help, but this evening, I only wanted to stop trembling from the lack of sugar in my blood. I'd spent the day fending off the treasury guys.

"You have hands," I said.

"My friend," he said. "Show some respect."

"Go to hell," I said.

In my 29 years no man ever told me to show respect. No man ever needed to. I had seen how women respected men and ended up shouldering burdens like one of those people who carried firewood on their heads, with their necks as high as church spires and foreheads crushed. Too many women, I thought, ended up treating domestic frustrations like mild cases of indigestion: shift-shift, prod-prod and then nothing. As far back as my grandmother's generation we'd been getting degrees and holding careers. My mother's generation were the pioneer professionals. We, their daughters, were expected to continue. We had no choice in the present recession. But there was a saying, and I'd only ever heard it said by other women, that books were not edible.

It was an overload of duties, I thought, sometimes self-imposed. And the expectation of subordination bothered me most. How could I defer to a man whose naked buttocks I'd seen? touched? Obey him without choking on my humility, like a fish bone down my throat. Then whoever plucked it out would say, "Look. It's her humility. She choked on it. Now she's dead." This may have been my redemption, since my husband needed a wife he could at least pity. Later that night, he called me aside to say, "Why did you have to say that in front of my brothers?"

"Well, why can't you ever get them drinks for once?" I answered, "Why can't you go to the kitchen? What will happen if you go? Will a snake bite your leg?"

He did not speak to me for two weeks and I contemplated leaving him for that alone—he could at least have remembered his age, even though I deliberately bumped him and poked my tongue behind his back. But no one I knew had left a man because he sulked, and I wanted a family, and I'd seen how Niyi grieved for his. I knew him down to his breath in the mornings. When we were not quarreling, I liked to watch him writhing to one whiskey-voiced woman or the other, like the one he called Sarah Vaughn. I could not tell one scat from another, but she said just about everything I wasn't prepared to, using ten words:

Sometimes I love you
Sometimes I hate you
But when I hate you
It's becau-au-au-ause I love you

I got pregnant and shortly after had a miscarriage. I was at work when I felt the first contraction. By the time I arrived home, it was too late, I'd passed a blood clot. I cried until I soaked my pillow. Nothing is worse than the loss of a child, even if the child is never born. If a child dies in your care, people understand that you feel responsible. If a child dies within you, they immediately try to absolve you: it is God's way, there is to be no mourning. You never understand why.

I got pregnant again. This time, the baby grew out of my womb and could have killed me had it not been for one smart doctor. I had to have an emergency operation. The doctor told us my chances of having a child after that were reduced. "But keep trying," he said. A year later, we still were. Niyi's relations began to press, "Is everything all right?" They looked at my stomach before looking at my face. Some scolded me outright. "What are you waiting for?" My mother invited me to her vigils; my father offered to send me overseas to see other doctors. I asked why they harassed women this way. We were greater than our wombs, greater than the sum of our body parts. "For God's sake," my father said solemnly. "I'm not playing here."

Sheri suggested I tried fertility drugs. Didn't I know? Everyone was taking them. They were? I asked. "Of course," she said. "One year and nothing is happening? Six months, even."

"Six months!"

She began to name a few women. One who didn't have children. Another who had two, but both were girls. One who did it to trap a man. Where did they get the drugs? I asked. "Doctors," she said. Infertility specialists? I asked. Um, she didn't know, but they treated infertility all the same. Where did the doctors find these drugs? Black market, she said.

Multiple births, laparoscopies, drug cycles. She gave me details, asked if I wanted a telephone number. I only wanted to be left alone, I said. At least my husband had a son of his own. No one could accuse me of ending the Franco lineage.

I never once doubted that I would become a mother. Not once. I just didn't know when it would happen, and I didn't want to be a guinea pig until then. Two more years passed and Niyi and I were still trying. I finally agreed to see a gynecologist who specialized in infertility. He made the appointment and I stuffed my head under a pillow as he spoke to the receptionist, but he refused to use a fake name. "It's not a VD clinic," he said. We arrived and saw the number of cars parked on the street, walked in and I saw that some of the women were as old as my mother. I was one of the few with a man by her side. The doctor arrived an hour later, chin up, stomach forward. He grunted in response to our greetings. I ducked a little, like the other women. Didn't even know why.

In no time at all Niyi and I began to quarrel about the fertility regime. It made us feel like mating animals. Every minor event sparked an accusation, and I shrunk to the size of my womb. I stared at other people's children imagining their soft, sticky hands in mine, worked myself into false morning sickness and cursed out loud when my periods started. Sometimes they didn't, then I'd be buying pregnancy kits and peeing on the sticks. Soon I convinced myself that it was a punishment; something I'd done, said. I remembered the story of Obatala who once caused women on earth to be barren. I made apologies to her. I remembered also, how I'd opened my mouth once too often and thought that if I said another bad word, had another bad thought, I would remain childless, so I swallowed my voice for penitence.

That was how my thirties found me, in a silent state. I felt as though I'd been running in midair for years. The realization had me laughing at myself. "Satisfied?" I asked myself aloud one morning. When I could hear no answer, I said, "Good."

I would not delve below that; I preferred to balance my home on a pin than to delve.

The day I got pregnant, I sat on my bathroom floor crying over a stick. "Thank you, God," I said. "God bless you, God." I waddled to Niyi, already imagining my stomach big, fell into his arms and his eyes filled with tears.

"I thought we were finished," he said.

"We are never finished," I said.

We promised not to argue. This time, my doctor suggested bed rest for three months and I resigned from work because my managing director, the one with the bad sinuses—who once told me I was segsy, very segsy indeed and he would have chazed me but for my sginny legs—he had been looking for an opportunity to move his cousin into my position and refused to approve my request for time off. "Mizeez Frango," he said. "Our bank can ill-afford an abzent company segretary." The bank couldn't afford my lawsuit either, I threatened. This wasn't a position to let go without a fight. I considered suing for a while, then I gave up on the idea because really, I wanted to be a mother more than I wanted to be a company secretary. I knew this when I would vomit into a toilet bowl in the mornings, look at myself in the mirror and smile. I accepted my father's offer for partnership instead.

During my first month of bed rest, I read local newspapers I normally didn't have time to read while I was working. Mostly I read stories in less reputable papers: *Woman gives birth to snake. Hundreds flock to vision of Mary on latrine window.* I also read the obituary pages: *Rest in peace, O glorious mother and wife, died after a brief illness. In loving memory of our father.* Here was the real news, I thought. The obituaries were always timely and uncensored, expect when they were hiding deaths from AIDS.

Sometimes I read editorials about the future of democracy. It was over a year since June 12, 1993, the day on which our country's third transition to democratic rule was to begin. That ended two weeks later when the military government annulled our general election and stepped down. A transitional government lasted three months before there was another coup. This new regime partially restored our constitution; placed a ban on political parties, disbanded both houses of senate and representatives, then instituted something called a constitutional conference to bring about democratic reform.

Of the pro-democracy activists campaigning, one was my father's long time client, Peter Mukoro, now editor of a magazine called the *Oracle*. Over the years, Mukoro had gained a wide readership because of the kind of reports he pursued: exposes on drug rings, oil spills in the Niger Delta, cults and gangs in universities, religious wars in the north, Nigerian prostitution rings in Italy. When Peter Mukoro wrote people read, so, quite often, Peter Mukoro was in trouble. He'd had several law suits against him. My father continued to represent him. Some they lost, some they won, others were pending. Peter Mukoro's house was burgled twice, although nothing was stolen. Then there was that mysterious fire in his office. After that Mukoro declared himself "the unluckiest man in town" because, even by Lagos standards, his life was "well and truly jinxed." When he ran an editorial calling for the reinstatement of the general election results he himself was detained. His magazine went underground. He was not formally charged, but his detention was made lawful under Decree Two, that decade-old military decree under which persons suspected of acts prejudicial to state security could be detained without charge. Even I felt sorry for him. At least he wasn't one of those journalists who were government critics until they landed a government job. Mukoro would not work for a state-owned paper. He would not work for anyone with military affiliations.

My father immediately published a statement in the *Oracle*, saying he would continue to petition until Peter Mukoro's release. I worried about my father's safety, given that under Decree Two, any arrest could be justified. These days, my father was going as far as to ask the military regime to step down. I, too, wanted them out, especially after they gunned down protesters during the political unrest. But there were thousands of other ways people were being killed in my country: unseen pot-holes in the roads, fake malaria medicine. People died because they couldn't afford an intravenous drip. People died because they drank contaminated water. People died from hardship: no water-no light, we called it in Lagos. People died because they got up one morning and realized they were ghettoized, impoverished. 1995 had me giving thanks for the calamities my family and friends had escaped, not protesting against the government. I was almost two months pregnant and thought, like many Nigerians, that my priorities were best kept at home. What I hoped for, at the beginning of the year, was to have my baby in peace.

Niyi handed the latest copy of the *Oracle* to me.

"Read," he said.

"What is it?" I asked.

"Your old man," he said. "He's talking again."

He left our bedroom and I read the article. My father had given an interview about recent detentions under Decree Two. He was advocating a national strike. I tossed the magazine on the bed and put some clothes on. Niyi was surprised to see me coming downstairs. He lowered his paper. "You're going out?"

"Yes. To see my father. Talk some sense into his head."

"What about bed rest?"

"I'm tired of resting."

He pulled his paper up by the shoulders. "Be careful."

I assured him that I would. As I drove to my father's house, I breathed in deeply. It was a while since I'd been out on my own and during the harmattan season the evenings were cooler. I could see no more than half a mile down the road because of the dusty haze. It shrouded leaves and blew into people's eyes. Children were still calling conjunctivitis Apollo.

I should have planned what to say to my father. I found him indoors. He no longer sat outside on the veranda in the evenings, not since thieves visited the house next door by boat.

"What are you doing out of bed?" he asked.

"I'm not ill," I said.

Over the years, his hair had whitened considerably and the pupils of his eyes had faded to a grayish-brown. His shoulders were also hunched, as though he were permanently grumbling.

"You're supposed to be lying down," he said.

I held the magazine up. "I read your interview, Daddy."

"Yes?" he said.

"You're calling for a national strike?"

"Yes."

"Suppose they pick you up?"

"Did you come here to visit or to fight?"

"I came to visit."

"Then you are welcome to stay. If not, find your way."

He picked up a cushion and gave it several blows before sitting. I settled in his sofa. I could smell the wood wax on the floor. Every month my father's floor was polished. He would never give that up. On his walls there were three fake crystal clocks that looked like corporate gifts. They had all stopped working: quarter to five, half past seven, twenty-seven after two. My father could not be bothered to replace a battery and he surrounded himself with clutter: unhung paintings, lava lamps so old they were fashionable again. The spot where my piano had stood was now a storage space for records and gifts. From the mess he would pull out a bottle of port, a biography, a Nat King Cole or Ebenezer Obey record.

"How shall I beg you?" I asked.

"For what?"

I didn't have to explain. "You know."

He waved his arm. "So I mustn't talk? An... an innocent man is locked up and I mustn't say anything?"

"Just be careful is what I'm saying."

"Of what should I be careful? Walking outside? Driving down the road? Sleeping in my house? Eating food? Breathing air."

"Don't make fun."

"But you are funny, all of you, Fatai and the rest. 'Don't do this. Don't do that.' Maybe I'm the one who's ruining this country."

"We're worried."

"Well, worry yourself with your own worries. Let me worry about mine."

He was not ready to listen.

"Do you have any idea," he said, in his normal voice. "Do you have any? One hundred million of us, less than ten thousand of them and they want to run this country... " he searched for words. "Like it's a club that belongs to them?"

"Yes, I do."

"Then they tell us." He patted his chest. "Tell us that we can't talk? We can't say anything, or we'll be locked up? Fatai, too, comes here this morning telling me that I should be careful. I'm disappointed in him. He is afraid like a woman."

He noticed my expression and pulled a face to imitate mine.

"What? How come your husband let you out of the house anyway?"

I laughed. "I'm not a pet."

"You modern wives."

"I see everything is a joke to you."

He folded his arms. "Humor is all I have left."

His anger was not controlled. He was like a child with a bloodied nose, waiting for the opportunity to strike back.

"So," I said. "Nothing I say will change your mind."

"Nothing," he said.

"Activists end up in prison."

"I'm not a criminal. Why should I fear going to prison? Anyway who's calling me an activist? Have you seen me join any pro-democracy group?"

"No."

"Do you see me running off to Amnesty International?"

"No," I said.

"Well then. I'm only doing my job, as I've always done. My business is to look after other people's legal business and I can't let this go, not as easily as they want. They must free Peter Mukoro. He has done nothing wrong."

There were lawyers who made their names in the struggle for human rights. My father was not one of them. He never cared for groups and had lost favor with some in the bar association, because of his association with Peter Mukoro, who had called senior advocates "senile advocates."

"Now, look at the situation we're in," he was saying. "Older people afraid to talk, the young ones too busy chasing money. Doesn't the situation bother the youth at all?"

"It does."

"Yet none of you are saying anything?"

"We worry about no money, no light. You form your groups and they beat you up and throw tear gas in your face. What can we do?"

"Women," he grumbled. "We never hear from them."

"Women? What do you want to hear from women for?"

"Where are they? More than half our population."

"We have our own problems."

"Like what? More important than this? People ridiculing our constitution?"

I began to count on my fingers. "No husband, bad husband,

188

husband's girlfriend, husband's mother. Human rights were never an issue till the rights of men were threatened. There's nothing in our constitution for kindness at home. And even if the army goes, we still have our men to answer to. So, what is it you want women to say?"

"Two separate issues," he said.

"Oh yes," I said. "Bring on the women when the enemy is the state. Never when the enemy is at home."

My father eyed me. Whenever I stood on my soap box, he wanted me to step down. When he stood on his, it wasn't a soap box; it was a foundation of truth. I smiled to annoy him more.

"Is everything all right at home?" he asked.

"Shouldn't it be?"

He glanced down at the sofa. I knew he was looking for his reading glasses. He simulated fist fighting movements. "You're too... "

"Me?" I said. "I'm not like that anymore."

"Since when?"

"I'm a peaceful woman now."

"You gave me *wahala*."

So did you, I was tempted to say.

"Just don't end up in prison," I said. "I won't come to visit you there."

He found his glasses between cushions. "I don't need your warnings."

"You're not getting any younger."

He slipped his glasses on. "If you came here to remind me of my age, then you've wasted your time and mine, because I know how old I am."

"I've told you, Daddy."

"I heard."

"You'll be sorry."

"I can't be sorrier than I am now."

We spent the rest of the evening discussing our plans to work together after my baby was born. "Practice some real law," he said. "Instead of taking minutes or whatever you do in a bank."

My father was suspicious of my generation of bankers, with their MBAs and other qualifications. Slick and rude, he said about them. They wanted to run before they could walk. Time had proven him right. Some managing directors I knew had been locked up under a failed bank decree.

On my way home, I passed Lagos Lagoon. I could smell animal cadaver, sweet fruit, and burnt tires. Smells were still strong though I'd managed to overcome nausea. A motorcycle growled past. The rider hunched over his handle bars. The woman behind him held on to his waist. Her white scarf blew like a shrunken peace mast. I touched the hard mound below my navel and imagined my child curled up. Nervous bubbles popped inside me. It had to be good this time. I could not bear another mishap.

I drove past a row of houses with balconies and green pyramid-shaped roofs. They were concealed behind high walls, above which coconut and oil palms grew. In this part of the suburbs, there were a few free-ed schools. Uniformed children walked around in shin-high socks. They came from nearby slums. From here, only their El-Shaddai and Celestial church spirals were visible. I stopped by the vigilante gates of our housing estate. Street hawkers sat behind wooden stalls in a small market along the front wall. They were Fulani people from the North. The men wore white skull caps and the women wrapped chiffon scarves around their heads. Their stalls were illuminated by kerosene lanterns. They talked loud in their language, and together they sounded like mourners ululating. Recognizing my car, the guards pushed the gates open. "Evening, madam," one of them said.

"Evening," I said.

Our estate, Sunrise, was on the outskirts of Ikoyi, though people here claimed to live in Old Ikoyi. They were mostly young couples in well paid vocations. Plot one was a banker and his wife was a lawyer. Plot two was also in banking and his wife sold Tupperware and baby clothes. No one knew what Plot three did, but he wore good suits and his wife Busola ran a Montessori school from a prettily painted shed in their yard. We lived in Plot four and so on. Our roads had no names.

There was a lot of gossip in Sunrise: who was earning less than they claimed, whose husband was shooting blanks, who owed money to the bank. Whenever we came together, the women sat on one side, and the men sat on another. The men chatted mostly about cars and money; the women about food prices, pediatric medications, work politics, and Disney toys. The advertising world may not have been aware of us, but we bought the merchandise they targeted at others nevertheless, whenever they arrived in our country and when we traveled overseas. We bought to hoard, to show off, to compensate for affairs, for ourselves. We bought what someone else had bought, what everyone else was buying. Consumerism was someone else's embarrassment; we felt privileged to be able to be part of a circle that didn't change much, except with fashion.

Some would say we were New Money. But I thought all money in our country was new, because our money itself, the naira and kobo, was new, devaluing fast and never able to make our country work anyway. So what car was anyone driving? To where, with craters in our streets? What watch was anyone wearing, when a thief could grab it from their wrist? What stereo system; what shoe; what dress. And no matter how much money a person had, they would find their bowel movements floating around in their toilet bowl, not going anywhere, because there was no water to flush our toilets.

We were living in enviable conditions, pre-fabricated homes

worth millions of naira, because the naira was worth so little. We were in the middle of another water shortage. On Tuesdays a tanker brought water which we stored in large drums, for flushing toilets and bathing; for cooking and cleaning teeth. Drinking water we bought by the carton. Sometimes we found sediment in it. We drank it anyway. There were no phone lines on the estate, so we carried mobile phones. Power cuts turned our meat rotten and our pots black with kerosene soot, unless we owned electricity generators. At night, mosquitoes bored holes into our legs and every year there was another death to mourn: someone shot in the head by armed robbers; someone crushed by a wayward lorry; someone suddenly taken ill with malaria, typhoid, they-don't-know.

Afterward we congregated in the deceased's house to mourn. Mostly we came together to celebrate: birthdays, holidays, and christenings. My one rule, whenever I was hosting, was that the women should not serve their husbands food. That always brought a reaction, from them: "Well, you always speak your mind." From their husbands: "Niyi, your wife is a bad influence!" From Niyi himself: "I can't stop her. She's the boss in this house."

I contributed to that illusion, claiming to be free from domesticity, and encouraged our friends to argue about division of home duties. The men would profess how they took charge of manly tasks like programming videos, opening jars, and changing light bulbs. The women would respond with such halfhearted attempts to appear indignant, that I would be tempted to take the men's side, just to stimulate a real discussion. But I wouldn't. Then from the opposing side would come an accusation so venomous, I'd almost fall backward from the force of it: feminist.

Was I? If a woman sneezed in my country, someone would call her a feminist. I'd never looked up the word before, but was there one word to describe how I felt from one day to the next?

And should there be? I'd seen the metamorphosis of women, how age slowed their walks, stilled their expressions, softened their voices, distorted what came out of their mouths. They hid their discontent so that other women wouldn't deprive them of it. By the time they came of age, millions of personalities were channeled into about three prototypes: strong and silent, chatterbox but cheerful, weak and kindhearted. All the rest were known as horrible women. I wanted to tell everyone, "I! Am! Not! Satisfied with these options!" I was ready to tear every notion they had about women, like one of those little dogs with trousers in their teeth. They would not let go until there was nothing but shreds, and I would not let go until I was heard. Sometimes it felt like I was fighting annihilation. But surely it was in the interest of self-preservation to fight what felt like annihilation? If a person swiped a fly and the fly flew higher, would the fly become a flyist?

I thought not, but that was before, in my twenties. These days, if ever I carried on that way, on my soapbox, it felt like an exercise in vanity, childish, in the scheme of dangerous living.

The houses in our estate lined up along the road trying to assume separate identities within cramped spaces. One had a palm tree in its front yard, another a thatched gazebo. Several had wide satellite dishes perched on their roofs to capture CNN and other television programs from overseas. All had barred windows and doors. My headlights beamed on our iron gates. Beyond them was our house with a bush of violet bougainvillea. Our gate man unlocked the gates. His prayer beads hung from his wrist. I realized I must have disturbed his prayer. Soon it would be the Moslem fasting period, Ramadan.

"*Sanu,* madam," he said.

"*Sanu, mallam,*" I replied in the only Hausa I knew.

"How now," Niyi said.

He aimed his remote at the stereo system. The sound of trumpets jarred my ears like Lagos traffic. He was trigger happy, my husband, and listening to jazz again.

I dropped my car keys in my bag. "How now," I answered.

"What did he say?"

"You know him. He won't listen."

He pressed a button to lower the volume. "He has to this time."

"I'm nervous about working with him again. The man doesn't compromise."

Niyi was busy nodding. He liked the women who sang or the men who played. Never the other way around. What if a woman could blow a horn? I would ask. "Can't," he would say. What if a man could sing? "Can't," he would answer. He dreamed of buying a Bang and Olufsen by the year 2000 so he could hear each instrument clearly. I only hoped he would be satisfied with our Hitachi in the year 2000. Our savings were geared toward replacing our electricity generator since it had broken down.

I slipped my shoes off, and turned down an offending light. Our living room was furnished with black leather seats and glass tables that matched the keyboards of my old piano, on top of which were financial magazines. The room reminded me of a chess game. We had plants, but no flowers, because flowers flopped within a day. I owned nothing except a framed print of gazelles from the Ivory Coast and an ebony stool on which Niyi rested his feet.

I turned the music down and walked toward him. Niyi placed both feet on the floor and his knees jumped up. There was never enough space for him wherever he was.

"You have giant in your genes," I said, placing my hand on his head.

"Good. I will pass it on."

"What if she's a girl?"

"She will be a giant, too."

"Who will go out with a giant?"

"She won't go out with anyone. But she will be beautiful and she will look like me."

"Big feet and a skinny nose?"

He turned his profile. "It's my foreign roots."

My laugh rushed through my nostrils. "Foreign my ass."

Niyi liked to remind me of his Brazilian ancestry the way an English person might say he were part French or part something else. He grouped himself with black people who had a direct claim to foreignness: West Indians and African-Americans. I kept reminding him that there wasn't a single black soul who hadn't descended from Africa. His ancestors would be rejoicing. They were back where they belonged.

I watched him in amusement. With his bald head he could pass for one of those American basketball players, but a girl who looked like him would be finished in a place where men loved small shapely women.

"Did you get through to London?" I asked.

He nodded. "That crazy woman answered the phone."

"What did she say?"

"He's doing it for attention."

I shrugged. "Well, teenagers. Maybe he is. It's tempting to play your parents against each other."

He'd been trying to reach his ex-wife all day. Their son was refusing to call his stepfather "Daddy." His mother was insisting that he did, and Niyi was saying the boy never should have in the first place.

"Stupid woman," he said. "I stayed with him while she was working. She practically kidnapped him. Now she's complaining he's difficult. I told her if she can't live with him, she should send him back here. He can go to school here. I didn't go to school abroad and there is nothing wrong with me. She didn't go to school abroad and there is nothing wrong with…"

He realized he was about to pay her a compliment. He straightened his leg so fast he kicked my wooden stool over.

"Foolish woman. If she were here, she'd be begging me to see him."

"Don't break my one piece of furniture in the world," I said, smiling.

Two disgruntled men, one evening. The truth was that neither was used to feeling powerless. Niyi would not rise above anger for his son's sake. He preferred to disrupt the boy's life and bring him home twelve years later.

"She doesn't know how lucky she is," he muttered.

"For the sake of this child," I said. "Forget how much you hate her. It doesn't matter who is right or wrong."

"Why do people say that rubbish?"

"Okay, it does matter. But try to make your own phone calls from now on. I didn't escape my parent's home to become a mediator in mine."

He did not answer and I thought I'd been insensitive.

"At least," I said. "Give me a chance to despise her, or to be jealous of her or whatever it is I'm meant to feel for her, instead of acting as your counselor. Look at you, you worry, you phone, you write, you listen. There is no better father than you. It is her loss. No one can come between father and son. Have you eaten?"

I asked only to appease him.

"Nothing to eat."

"Did you bother to look?"

"It's stale. I don't want any of it."

I waved my free hand regally. "Hm. Maybe someday I can sit with my feet up and grumble about food. I will have to go shopping this weekend, since my lord and master is not pleased with the food I have at home."

"Woman, what d'you think I paid your dowry for?"

"Good sex," I said, strutting away. Since I was out of bed and running all over the place, he said, I would have to perform my wifely duties and give him some.

"You speak like that to the mother of your child?"

"Your breasts have grown."

"So have yours, and you'll be lucky if I ever have sex with you, after all the sex I've had to make this baby."

"What about my needs?"

"Handle your needs yourself," I said.

I had married a man I could fall asleep with, not a man who would keep me up at night. I told him, the only way he could make me scream in bed was if he farted under the covers. I would repay him my dowry one day, have a ceremony and return his gifts. I went to bed dreaming of market shopping instead. Sex my ass.

"Give me another tray," Sheri said.

The market woman passed her a tray without looking. She neatened the tray of tomatoes Sheri had rejected.

"How much?" Sheri asked, surveying the new tray.

"Twenty," the woman said. Her hair was bound in thread and her cheeks were lined with facial marks.

"You must be joking," Sheri said. "Twenty naira for this? Fifteen only."

"Fifteen is not possible," the woman said.

She swatted flies from her ware. The sun bore holes in my back. I dipped under the corrugated-roofed shack and swiped flies from my braids. The flies swarmed the marketplace, perching on mangoes, between spinach leaves and lumps of cow flesh. Later they would settle in the gutters and clotted drains and fly back to the food. I had left Sheri to bargain. She was better at it. Sometimes the women misjudged her and she immediately told them, "Do you know where I'm coming from?" One woman answered, "It's not my fault. I've never seen a white person who acts like you."

In the same shack, another woman sat behind a wooden table laden with okras, cherry peppers, and purple onions. She had tattoos on her arms. A naked infant sat on a mat by her feet. Spit drooled from his lips and yellow mucus dangled from his nostrils. His eyes were lined with kohl.

"How much is this?" Sheri asked.

"Ten naira," the first woman said.

"Ten naira!" Sheri exclaimed.

It was a game. I watched the second woman. She lifted the infant and sucked on his nose. The infant gasped as the woman spat his mucus into the gutter. The first woman wrapped our tomatoes in the obituary pages of a newspaper.

The marketplace was a series of meddlesome shacks like this, built row by row for a square mile. They were topped with rusty iron sheets and had no light except for sunlight. A small tarred road, wide enough to contain a car, separated the east side from the west. Cars and bicycles were not allowed in. They were parked by the entrance, near a high rubbish dump that smelled of rotten vegetables. Shoppers filled the road, walking in one direction like pilgrims. Above their voices I heard car horns from nearby streets.

At the butchers, I preferred to stand in the hot sun, rather than stand near the stall. I couldn't bear the smell of cow's intestines. From a distance I watched Sheri giving the butcher instructions. He laughed and hacked through a cow's flank with a machete. Soon he paused to wipe sweat from his forehead using the neckline of his bloody undershirt.

Sheri returned to me. She had lost some weight and it showed in her face.

"You're skinny," I said.

"You think?" she said.

"Are you fasting?"

"It's my gym. I never fast."

I fanned my face with my hands. The sun seemed to be melting me.

"Everyone is going to the gym these days," I murmured.

I'd heard men say that women like Sheri didn't age well: they wrinkled early like white women. It was the end of a narration that began when they first called her yellow banana, and not more sensible, I thought. Thankfully, Sheri never relied on their praises, so she didn't pay attention to the insults. She was not one of those retired beauties who walked into a room and immediately began to assess who was better looking than her before she could relax.

We stopped by a fabric stall across the road, then loaded our bags into the trunk of my car and drove out of the market. By the exit, a hawker sat before a gutter selling roasted corn.

"Want some?" Sheri asked.

"No," I said.

I couldn't risk getting typhoid. She stuck her head out of her window and beckoned to the hawker. I drove into the usual Saturday traffic. Cars formed two lanes on the narrow one way street. Some stopped by hawkers on the side walk, causing temporary bottlenecks. Shoppers scurried between them. Before us, a yellow bus staggered along. A conductor hung from its door, shouting the destination of the bus: "C.M.S! C.M.S!"

C.M.S. was the Christian Missionary Society school near the Marina. Only two people came out of the bus and about ten hurried in. There would be no space for them inside. Lagos was getting more crowded. Most of it resembled a shantytown. Buildings were never repainted, roads never repaired. My car began to make grinding noises. Ten years old, it gave me a reason to visit my mechanics almost every month, though in its present state, it could fetch three times the amount it had cost. I still used it for what I called my rugged trips. These days, people budgeted for cars the way other people in the world budgeted for houses.

"Niyi is talking about a party for my birthday," I said.

"He is?" Sheri said.

"Yes. I've told him it has to be small and only people I want. Will you cater for us?"

"Yes."

"Discount?" I asked.

She finished her corn and threw it out of the window. I would get my discount, she would help cook, but Sheri would not come to my party. She was not interested in people who would gossip about her or boast about their possessions. And the people I knew, Sunrise people in particular, scrutinized her whenever they saw her, for unhappiness, sexual frustration, and other deprivations, so that they could say her life was well and truly ruined. Sheri, who had always divided people into those who would die for her and those who were jealous and wished for her downfall, ignored them in a way that made me want to jump up and cheer, so desperate was I to rise above our social circle.

Niyi wasn't home when we arrived. "He's at work," I explained as we separated our bags in the trunk of my car.

"Your husband works too hard," she said.

"Everyone works too hard," I said. "I'm about to work too hard."

"You must take care of your husband's home," she teased like an old woman.

"Ah, I hate it," I said, peering into a package. "And for a man who won't even take a glass to the kitchen."

"He won't?"

"I've never seen anything like it before. The man behaves as if I'm his personal servant."

I told her about our living room, how I found beer glasses left overnight, stuck to our glass side tables, stuck so hard I could lift the tables. In our bedroom, I picked up his clothes as he dropped them. In our bathroom, I found stains around our toilet rim, which looked like beer stains, except they were misdirected urine.

"You must have known before," she said.

"I haven't been at home this long before."

"It's his mother, I'm sure."

"The statute of limitations has run out."

"Show him sense, *jo*."

I handed her a bag and sighed. "These are peaceful times."

Our conversation was as idle as conversation was in Sunrise. We separated parcels of vegetables wrapped up in censured news. Sheri recounted how she'd seen a man knocked down by a car the week before. The driver who hit the man drove off for fear of being mobbed. Four passersby carried the man off the street, one for each limb. They were shouting and the man himself was shouting, from pain.

"Please," I said. "Why are you telling me this?"

She sighed. "How-for-do?"

I ruffled through more bags.

"You must break fast with us this year," she said.

"You don't fast, Sheri."

Allah had to forgive her. She couldn't go an hour without eating.

"Still come. We're going to cook."

"I'll be there."

She sighed. "Hopefully we will have light that day. All this talk about democracy. I will take any kind of government that can guarantee me electricity."

"Any government?"

"A communist regime even."

I knew she wasn't serious.

"Only electricity?"

"That's all I need," she said.

"Some people don't have power lines."

"Who? People in the villages? What do they care? They light their fire at night, the smoke drives mosquitoes away. At night they quench the fire and sleep. Clean water to drink is their problem, not electricity. Guinea worm? Can wipe out a whole village."

Two children rode past my gates on bicycles. They pedaled fast and screamed.

"We're still better off," I said.

Sheri handed a package to me. "I wonder."

I arched my back. "Have to be grateful, Sheri, for everything. Good health, food, roof over your head and bed to lie in."

"With a grumpy husband," she said.

"At least he's not one of those running around."

"No other woman will have him."

"You see? What more do I want? And at least I have a car of my own. Even if it hardly works, I can still get up and go. Someone can't knock me dead on the streets. Hm-hm. What are we going to do? 1995 and we still have no decent ambulance service in this city. No decent hospitals. No nothing."

"I'd rather die on the streets than go to any hospital here."

"I'm telling you. If you get a headache, start packing your bags."

"If you can afford to get out," she said.

"If not," I said. "Start digging your grave."

"Gather your family for last rites. And oh, don't forget, on your tombstone: 'The wicked have done their worst'."

We laughed. Sheri handed me a tight obituary parcel.

"But people suffer," I said.

"Country hard," she said.

Our bags were finally separated.

"My sister," I said, tapping her back.

"Greet Papa Franco," she said.

Sheri called Niyi "Papa Franco" behind his back, because he was always scowling, she said. I couldn't tell her he scowled because he thought she was bad company. "Used-up like dry wood. That's why no one will have her." I would get hoarse arguing with him. Sheri didn't need any man. I was there when she walked out on her lousy brigadier. "Yeah, yeah, she has a past," he would say.

"Has a future," I would say.

When she took money from her brigadier, she wore evening shoes in the day, bought any ornament with flower motifs and didn't even stay abroad too long because it was too cold. Now that she earned her own, she watched it like an accountant. I envied her freedom to spend as she wanted; her business knowledge, which came from bargaining. Sheri said she didn't have a head for books, but she saw a clear margin before a deal started. It was true that she rarely read anything, not even the gossip magazines I sometimes read. She said they were written by idiots, for idiots, especially on the rare occasions she was captured by the handful of tiresome Lagos paparazzi at the society events she catered for. "A half caste and a half" one recently called her. Sheri only ever read the romantic novels she'd been reading since she was a child. She used leather bookmarks to save a page. It took her several weeks to get through one, and yet trading came naturally to her. A wake, a wedding, a christening, she was there, haggling and keeping her client's dirty secrets as a doctor would. Within a year of starting her business, she was able to buy herself one of those second-hand cars people called "fairly used" and after two years, she was able to rent a place of her own.

No, Sheri didn't love men or money. What she loved was food. She was always munching on fried meat, corn, biscuits. She could suck down a dozen banana ice pops and her eyes grew wide as food entered her mouth. I was there when her worship of food began and it didn't make sense because I was learning to starve myself through my tribulations. Now I knew some women did exactly the opposite. Sheri had gained weight from it over the years: English size 16, American 14, Bakare household size 2, she would say. But she had shed most of her childhood spirit, and I often remembered the time she laughed till hibiscus toppled out of her afro. It still brought tears of laughter to my eyes.

She was my oldest friend, my closest friend. We had been absent friends, sometimes uncertain friends, but so were most sisters and she was the nearest I'd come to having one in this place where families were over-extended.

In my kitchen I removed the food and stored the plastic bags away for future use. My kitchen was equipped for preparing local meals, nothing else. There was a wooden table, two collapsible iron chairs, an electric cooker, a kerosene stove, in case of power cuts, a deep freeze large enough to store a human body, and a refrigerator with an ice maker I'd never used. In my store room, I kept plastic bags, which were hard to find in Lagos, kegs of palm oil, groundnut oil, sacks of rice, yam flour, dried ground cassava, a bundle of dusty yams and sticky plantains. On the shelves there were piles of dishes, Tupperware, enormous steel pots, plastic bowls and calabash quarters for scooping. The door leading to our back yard was barred. The windows were also barred and covered in green mosquito netting. The netting garroted mosquitoes, trapped dust and raindrops. Sometimes, if the wind blew, I smelled all three and sneezed.

Pierre, my present house boy, began to wash the vegetables in a bowl of water. He was a burly boy about nineteen years old from the neighboring Republic of Benin. French was the only language we had in common. He spoke it fluently with an African accent, and I vaguely remembered it from secondary school. Pierre couldn't cook. He cleaned, fetched water, and thought himself a lady's man in between. Unable to get the French accent quite right, we pronounced his name, "P'yeh" and Niyi said it served him right anyway, because Pierre was lazy and never around when you needed him.

I needed Pierre to place the okras on the chopping board. "*Ici*," I said pointing. "Over there, please."

Pierre raised a brow. "*La bas*, madame?"

"My friend," I said. "You know exactly what I mean."

It was my fault for attempting to speak French to him. Now he raised his eyebrows twenty times a day.

"I beg, put am for there," I said.

Our continent was a tower of Babel, Africans speaking colonial languages: French, English, Portuguese, and their own indigenous languages. Most house help in Lagos came from outside Lagos; from the provinces and from neighboring African countries. If we didn't share a language, we communicated in Pidgin English. Night watchmen, washmen, cooks and gardeners. The general help we called house boys and house girls. It was not our way to feel guilty and adopt polite terms. If they had friends over, we worried that they might steal. If they looked too hard at our possessions, we called them greedy, and whenever they fought we were amused. We used separate cups from them, sent them to wash their hands and allowed our children to boss them around. They helped with daily chores in exchange for food, lodgings, and a stipend. Most were of working age, barely educated, but some were of pensionable age, and many were children. In good homes, they could be treated like distant cousins; in bad homes, they could be deprived of food, or beaten. I had more than once suggested that they were a few degrees separated from blacks in old Mississippi and in apartheid South Africa. "But that's racism," someone would say.

Pierre began to chop the okras. I ground the peppers and onions. Later he washed and cut the meat and I braised it. We worked together, cutting and frying, stirring and pouring. My eyes streamed from pepper and palm oil fumes settled in my braids. Steam scalded my wrists. Three hours later, we'd finished four separate stews. Pierre scooped them into Tupperware containers and placed them in the freezer. I handed him a plate of lunch and decided to have a wash.

Behind our bathroom door, we kept a drum of water. I filled my bathing bucket and topped it up with boiling water from a kettle. But for the bump under my belly button, my body was the same as it was before I became pregnant. I'd finished soaping myself when the electricity generator next door began to roar. "Shit," I said, remembering the food in my freezer. Quickly, I scooped bowls of water from the bucket over my body and came out. Niyi was coming upstairs.

"No light?"

I stamped my foot. "It's just gone."

"Why are you getting angry?"

He looked just as irritated.

"I've been cooking all day."

"You cooked?" he said. "Good."

He headed downstairs as I grumbled on: "Someone ought to call a national conference for diet reform. The day an African woman can prepare a sandwich for a meal, that will be the day. I've spent the whole day in that bloody kitchen... "

"Where is this food?" Niyi interrupted.

I leaned over the banister. "When you are truly hungry, those bearings of yours, you'll find them very quickly."

He knew how serious I was. If he liked, he could try me, then he would see the African version of the girl from *The Exorcist*.

Electricity returned before midnight and my food was saved. Niyi said it would taste so much better if only I learned to cook with a sweeter disposition. "The trouble is," he said, before we went to sleep. "You are not a domesticated woman. You just don't have that... that loving quality."

He pinched his fingers together as if I couldn't grasp the essence of what he was saying. He was lying on my side of the bed. I pushed him over.

"I'm very loving," I said. "What do you know? Move, I beg."

I was a scrotum shrinker, he said. And I would not stop until he was as small as raisins.

"What are you doing for my womanhood?" I said, spreading my arms. "Am I not a temple of the miracle of creation?"

Every picture, advert, film, I'd seen of pregnant women, showed their partners rubbing their feet and such. I didn't ask that of him; never once expected him to tell me I was beautiful. It was a miracle, I had to admit, that he never complained when I came to him in the mornings with a puffy face after vomiting. That was his best loving ever; his best romance from the time I met him.

We held hands to sleep. The next morning, we shared the Sunday papers, though Niyi remained downstairs while I stayed upstairs reading what he handed to me from time to time. I was flicking through a government-owned newspaper. A group of army wives had founded a program for women in a village. They promised to train the village women to eradicate infant dehydration. On the front page, an army wife was put on display with a gold choker around her neck. I turned the page and a man had thrown acid into his lover's face. On the next page was a charity drive for a boy's eye. He had a rare type of cancer and would have to be flown overseas for treatment. Underneath, a bank director in tortoiseshell glasses was discussing capital investments. A page later there was an update on our peace-keeping troops in Liberia, directly over the story of a child hawker who had been molested. She had had difficulty expressing herself during the court case, and untied her wrapper to show where the man had touched her. The magistrate ordered her to cover up. The caption read, "No Need for Nakedness."

Niyi walked in. I held the paper up.

"Have you read this?" I asked.

His mouth was open. My heartbeat quickened.

"What?" I asked.

"They've arrested him," he said.

"Who?"

"Your father."

I grabbed my head. "No."

"This morning. Baba came to tell us. He's downstairs."

I scrambled out of bed. "I told him. I told him."

I ran down the stairs. Baba was in the dining room. His eyes were yellow and watery. A fly settled on his white lash and he brushed it away with a trembling hand. "I was doing my work," he said. "Doing my work, as usual. A car came. Two men. I let them in. I went back to work and time passed. Then your father called me to the veranda. 'Tell Enitan,' he said. 'Tell her they've taken me. And let Fatai know, too.' Then he got in the car and they drove off."

"Policemen?" I asked.

"Like policemen."

"What were they wearing?" Niyi asked.

Baba ran his heavily veined hands down his chest. "Em, something. Something... "

I was trying to recall the last detainees I'd read about. Ten-millimeter names, blurred photographs, newspaper phantoms. People invited for questioning by state security. They disappeared for months.

The rest of the morning, we tried to telephone our friends

and family. I couldn't recall any telephone numbers and Niyi had to find my address book. My mother still didn't have a phone. We called Uncle Fatai, then Niyi's parents. Later, Sheri. By lunch time, they were in my home.

They eased into my father's disappearance the way people in Lagos eased into death. At first there were the usual questions. How? What? When? Then resignation set in. My father-in-law began to talk about other people who had been detained: journalists, lawyers, a trade union leader. "I know him well," he said.

He talked slow and savored his pronouncements. Whenever my father-in-law spoke, he lifted his chin as though he was making a great contribution to humanity, and kept his eyes shut, confident that when he reopened them, someone would still be listening. My mother-in-law always was.

Niyi walked over to me. "We should get them lunch at this rate."

"Lunch?" I said, as if he'd suggested horse manure.

"Yes. They've been here all morning."

I began to gabble. "Pierre has his day off and I don't know if... "

"I'll help," Sheri said.

Niyi tapped my shoulder. "Thanks."

I was getting lunch, Niyi told everyone. I stood up and my mother-in-law stood up, too, but I waved her down. "No ma, Sheri will help."

My voice was unnaturally high. It was nothing but a minstrel show, I thought, except no one bothered to watch as Sheri and I headed for the kitchen.

Inside, I slammed an empty pot on a stove. "What am I doing here?"

"Where do I start?" Sheri asked.

"My father is detained and I'm cooking?"

209

"People have to eat."

She looked around as though searching for a weapon. I imagined us finding plates and breaking them; both of us banging pots.

Sheri beckoned. "Be quick. Where do you keep your cutlery?"

I did not eat. My father-in-law and Uncle Fatai sat on opposite ends of the table. Their chewing inspired me to imagine new ways of throttling.

"I want to talk to you," Uncle Fatai said, as I collected his plate. Niyi and his father inclined their heads like world leaders at a conference. On a whim I asked, "Can you help?" Niyi looked up like a world leader confronted by his mistress at a conference.

My father-in-law cut in, "The young lady can do that."

Sheri stood up hurriedly and nudged me through the kitchen door.

"I want them out of my house," I whispered. "Out."

Sheri touched my shoulder. "They won't stay here forever. Go and speak to your uncle. Go on."

She pushed me through the door. I joined Uncle Fatai at the dining table. He pressed his hands together and his knuckles dimpled. "Who will mind your father's business now?"

"I will," I said.

"Good," he said, covering his mouth.

"Is there anything we can do meanwhile?" I asked.

He rubbed his mouth with a napkin. "Nothing."

"Shouldn't we try to look for him?"

"Where?" he asked.

"I mean, can't we contact someone?"

He noticed my expression and leaned forward. "Enitan, your father knew what he was doing. You understand? I'm sorry but this is the result of a decision he made on his own. When he started saying things, I told him, be careful. All we can do now is to make sure his practice continues. You understand?"

The aftermath of his belch hung between us.

I nodded. "Yes, Uncle."

"By the grace of God he will be out soon," he said. "Now, I will need a bowl of water."

His knuckles dimpled as he held his hands up.

"To wash my hands," he explained.

I couldn't sleep. All that my father had told me about prisons came to haunt me: the darkness, damp, smell of stale urine, cockroaches, rats. There were no beds, no ventilation, too many inmates. Some were arrested for being out on designated sanitation days; others belonged in mental institutions, cemeteries.

At dawn I forced myself to imagine my father. I could see only his hands and they were covered in sores. "Look where I've landed myself," he said. "We sleep in each other's urine in this place. The food is like the bottom of a pit latrine. I have not touched it."

"Your hands," I said.

He lifted them. "It's going around. Itches like mad, but they won't get a doctor. They keep sending the prison matron in. That woman doesn't know what she's doing, but the men love to see her."

"Men?"

"I'm not alone. I have friends. An armed robber, Tunji Rambo, he calls himself. Too much heroin in his blood and too many American movies in his head. He says that he's no more a murderer than a general here who fought in the Civil War and killed Biafrans, than a government minister who embezzled money set aside for healthcare. He says that God will judge them the same."

"Death is death."

"The general used to be a fat man, now he's thinner than

you. They put him here for plotting a coup. He could have been our president. Today, he's just another criminal. He prays with the librarian. That one we call Professor. The man has more knowledge than an encyclopedia. He was picked up for wandering on a sanitation day. Now, he prostrates to rats and calls them gods."

"Please don't end up like him."

Monday morning I went to my father's office. Peace began to cry as soon as I mentioned the word detention. I felt dishonest standing there and promising them that their jobs were secure. What did I know about running my father's business? I'd worked in a bank since national service. My experience in estate transactions was limited and outdated.

"We will just have to continue until he returns," I concluded.

As they dispersed, I gritted my teeth. My father's table was littered with papers. He never shared what he called sensitive information and his filing system was held in his head. Mr. Israel, the driver, walked in. "Someone to see you," he said.

"Who?"

"Journalist."

"Tell him to come in."

The journalist was a woman. Her smile was so benign, she could pass for a Bible seller.

"Grace Ameh is my name," she said, extending her hand. "*Oracle* magazine. We interviewed your father last week. We had another appointment this morning and I hope you won't mind speaking to us."

She had a gap between her front teeth and her gums were the color of dark chocolate.

"What about?" I asked.

"His detention. The driver, Mr. Israel, told me. I'm sorry to hear about it."

"It happened only yesterday."

I wasn't ready to confer with a stranger. She was thick-set from her waist up. Her dress had a butterfly collar and she carried a wrinkled brown leather portfolio. She removed a notepad from the portfolio.

"All I need is a few words from you, about what transpired."

There was a drum roll in my chest. "Is it safe?"

"To talk? It's never safe to talk."

"I haven't done this before."

"You're afraid?" she asked, glancing up.

"I'm not sure you should be here."

She waited for me to recant my statement. I was first to look away. Grace Ameh was older, self-assured, and her disapproval was beginning to cloud up my father's office. She had an intense stare.

"That's a pity," she said. "I would have thought you would be willing."

"Last week," I said, "my father spoke to your magazine. Today he's in detention."

"Perhaps we started off on the wrong foot... "

"I don't know who 'we' are."

"Please, let me tell you what we're facing." Her voice remained calm, but her lips moved with a hint of impatience. "Our reporters are being dragged in every week, no explanation given. They're kept in detention for weeks, questioned, or they are left alone, which I'm told is worse. Nobody speaks to you in detention, you see. If you don't cooperate, they transfer you to a prison somewhere else, packed with inmates. Sick inmates. You may end up with pneumonia, tuberculosis, and you won't get proper medical attention. Jaundice, diarrhea— food in Nigerian prisons isn't very good. I'm sorry. I'm sorry. Am I upsetting you?"

"No." But she was.

"I want you to understand why people must hear from you. This can happen to anyone these days. Your father had no reason to be involved. He could easily have been silent, too. So, are you willing to talk to us?"

I nodded reluctantly. "Yes."

"Thank you."

Her hand whisked shorthand notes over her notepad.

"My father is not a criminal," I began.

I visited my mother in the afternoon. Uncle Fatai had promised to tell her about my father, but I could not be sure. When I arrived, her neighbor's daughter was sitting on top of their gate. A girl of about seven with dusty knees, she was wearing a white T-shirt with the words "Kiss me I'm sexy" across her chest. She had top teeth missing. Behind her, two of her brothers played a loud game of table tennis; a third brother twisted his mouth in time to the ball. The girl looked liable to fall.

"Kiss me I'm sexy," I called out. "Be careful sitting up there."

Her brothers collapsed over the tennis table laughing.

"My name is not Kith me I'm Thexy," she said.

"Sorry," I said. "What is your name?"

"Shalewa."

"Shalewa, you have to get off."

She scowled. Her brothers were dancing around the tennis table singing: "Kith me I'm Thexy!" One of them tugged the corners of his mouth. I felt bad for causing them to laugh at her.

Shalewa hopped down from the gate. Her spindly legs trembled. "Bombastic elemenths!" she said.

My mother opened her door. "Those children are so rowdy."

"They're your tenant's children?"

"I've had enough of them. But at least their mother is pleasant."

Over the years my mother's expressions had become one: sad

that a good thing had happened, happy that a bad thing had. I could smell menthol. As usual we spoke in Yoruba.

"Fatai told me about your father," she said.

"Yes," I said.

"It happened yesterday, he said."

"That's all we know."

"So," she said. "What is being done now?"

"We can't do anything. We don't know where he is. A journalist I spoke to this morning thinks he might be in one of the state security offices."

I pressed my temples. My mother watched my hand movements.

"What journalist is this?"

"From *Oracle* magazine."

"You spoke to him?"

"Her. I gave a statement."

"You're giving statements now? You're giving statements to the press?"

"It was nothing."

"Not in your condition," she said, clapping her hand. "Not for your father, either. God forgive me, but that man caused his own problems. Fatai told me. He said he warned him. He said you too warned him. Now what are you going to do? Get yourself locked up, too?"

"I'm not going to get locked up."

"How would you know? The government has been doing what they want for years. What do you do? You leave them to it, that's what you do. Does your husband know about this?"

I didn't answer. My mother coughed and rubbed her chest.

"Be careful," she said. "This kind of thing is not a woman's place. Not in this country. You don't need me to tell you."

"I want my father out of there."

"What if they take you, too? You're pregnant, are you not?

Do you or do you not want this child?"

"Yes."

"So," she said. "You've waited this long. None of this. You hear me? Not for a man who... who showed me nothing but wickedness."

I was about to answer when a girl about twelve years old came out of her kitchen. She had robust cheeks and a pointed chin. The hem line of her dress was askew.

"Ah, Sumbo," my mother said. "You've finished in there?"

"Yes, ma," she said.

"Good. You can go now."

The girl disappeared. Her bare feet scraped the floor like sandpaper. There were cracks in her soles.

"You've got a new girl?" I asked.

"Yes," my mother said. "But I need to train her. She never washes her hands."

"How old is she?" I asked.

"Her parents say she's fourteen."

"She's young," I said.

My mother shrugged. "The parents brought her here themselves. Look at her fat cheeks. She's better off. She eats well and sends money home. She's not too young. She's probably seen more than you have. Turn your back on that one and she'll be dipping her hand in your bag or following men."

"Mummy."

"It's true."

I saw her regularly, out of choice. I was capable of deciding my answers and silences. If I remembered the bad times, I stopped myself from thinking about them. Whenever I felt overly criticized, I knew the feeling would pass. I did not retaliate in any way, and I wasn't analyzing how or why I had this reserve. To me, it was like picking fresh fruit from a basket of mostly rotten ones.

"Your new tenant," I said. "Is she paying her rent on time?"

"No problem with that."

"That's good," I said.

My mother looked me up and down. "You look tired, Enitan. If I were you I would go home and rest."

"I'm not that tired."

"Still go. You need your rest. Let Uncle Fatai run around for your father, if he pleases. After all, they are friends."

"Uncle Fatai is busy."

"Then it is too bad. Too bad for your father. He can't keep a family together, now he wants to save his country?"

My father couldn't even save himself, she said. She began to recount their past battles. I did not say a word. When I left her house, Shalewa next door was drawing circles in the ground with a stone. Her tongue jutted out from the side of her mouth. Her brothers were nowhere to be found. They must have abandoned her, I thought.

"What time did she come?" Niyi asked.

I was sitting at the top of the stairs, watching him through the banister. He placed his briefcase down.

"About ten," I said.

"Ameh," he said.

"Grace," I said.

"She must be from Benue with a name like that."

I wrapped my dressing gown tighter. What did I care where in Nigeria Grace Ameh was from? Our air-conditioner was too cold. I was shivering.

"Where are they publishing from now?" he asked. "Didn't they close down?"

"They're underground."

"What does that mean?"

"I don't know."

"How do you know she was one of their reporters?"

"She said she was."

"Did you ask her for an ID?"

"No."

"Suppose she was state security?"

"She wasn't."

"How do you know?"

"She wasn't."

He would know if he'd seen Grace Ameh himself, and why was he questioning me? He threw his keys on the dining table.

"You should have called me first."

"I didn't have time."

"What if they pick you up, after the article is published?"

"They won't pick me up. Not for this."

"She took advantage of you. I'm sorry. The woman knew exactly what she was doing. They will do anything to get publicity, these journalists."

"What publicity?"

"Asking you to give a statement, jeopardizing your safety at a time like this. You shouldn't even be going to work."

"I shouldn't be entertaining people, either, but I did."

"What?"

"Yesterday," I said.

"I'm serious," he said.

"So am I," I said.

There was no precedent for this, nothing to draw on. We went to the authorities to report crimes. Where could we go when the authorities committed one? It was as if I'd opened a Bible and found the pages blank.

"Call me next time," he said.

Wednesday morning I paid my father's staff their salaries: Dagogo and Alabi first, and then the others. I was surprised—Dagogo and Alabi's paychecks were a fraction of what I had earned at the bank. I'd heard them joke before about eating two meals a day, about substituting beans for meat. It was the principle of "at least" on which people persevered in Lagos: at least they had food in their stomachs, at least they had a roof over their heads, at least they were alive. People said there was no middle class in a country like ours, only an elite and the masses. But there was a middle class, and all that separated us was a birthright—a ridiculous name for a right, because there wasn't a person dead or alive who hadn't been born at some point. We were a step-down society compared to those by which we would be defined. The Nigerian elite were middle class people. Few had the sort of wealth that would rank them amongst the world's elite, and they were usually government or ex-government officials. The middle class, in turn, were working-class people, and the masses were poor. They begged for work and money, served, envied and despised the elite, which actually made the elite feel more special and important. But for Lagos, always reminding me where exactly in the world I was living, I grew up feeling like I was part of landed gentry in England. That uppity.

I left the office that afternoon with my head down. How could my father be paying his senior associates so little? I asked Niyi at home.

"It is the cost of living that's high," he said.

"Don't employers have a responsibility to compensate?"

He rubbed his eyes. "It's the northerners. They are responsible for the problems in this country. They've completely ruined the economy."

"Beggars on the streets, our night watchman, he's from the north. The hawkers by our gates, they are from the north. I don't see them ruining any economy."

Niyi wasn't convinced. "Who heads our government? Northerners. Who heads the army? Northerners. One southerner wants to be president and they lock him up. Come to my office. The whole place is full of them. Barely educated and yet they want to bring in more of their people. They've completely ruined the economy. How can men like Dagogo and Alabi survive?"

Increasingly, I was hearing this type of sentiment; north versus south. We had the oil fields, the northerners had enjoyed the revenues for so long. Some southerners were calling for a secession. I thought it could end in the kind of bloodshed we'd seen in the Civil War. From his little experience with office politics, Niyi had come to distrust northerners, and Moslems, if he cared to admit. He called them Allahu-Akhbars. His chairman, a northerner and Moslem man, had little education. He bypassed senior staff for another northerner. Round them up and shoot them, Niyi would say. "Then what?" I once asked. "No one will ever bother you at work again? No official will ever dip their hands in our treasury and deposit half the proceeds with the Swiss? Please."

I imagined my father in a prison cell again. Under a detention order he would have no right to know the reason for detention, no access to his family, or legal counsel. The detention orders were renewable and the law courts could not review them. Some detainees were released after a few weeks; others were held for longer periods and no one could decipher why. It didn't matter to me if a northerner or southerner was responsible for this.

"Do you think they will let him out soon?"

"Yes," Niyi said.

"What if they try to kill him?"

"They won't," he said.

I moved closer toward him and rested my head on his shoulder.

"If anything happens to him," I said, "someone will pay."

He stretched and the leather sofa grunted.

"You're tired?" I asked.

"Exhausted," he said.

He put his arm around me. Family rifts, losses, absences. The stress brought us closer. Niyi's heartbeat was almost in time with mine when our air-conditioner shuddered to a halt. We were sitting in the dark.

"Jesus," he said.

We heard the electricity generator start next door. He went to the kitchen and brought back a huge battery-operated lamp. I watched the stark light, like the moon. Outside crickets chattered. I began to feel hot.

"It really is more than north and south," I said. "We have all played a part in this mess, not caring enough about other people, how they live. It comes back to you. Right back. Look at us in this house, paying Pierre pittance..."

"Pierre's lazy," he said. "I work harder than him."

"Living in quarters..."

"He's lucky to have a roof over his head."

"Bad ventilation and a pit latrine? Would you like to live there?"

A mosquito buzzed around my ear. I swiped it away. If I wouldn't like to live in our quarters, why would anyone else?

Niyi turned to me. "Why are we talking about Pierre? Don't we have enough problems of our own?"

The skin on my belly was beginning to feel moist. Niyi once said I was guilty of thinking too hard. I told him that it wasn't possible, even with a million thoughts, colliding with each other, my thoughts wouldn't be enough. I envied his ability to be certain.

He placed his hands behind his head. "You live in this country, you suffer in some way. Some more than others, but that's life." He noticed my expression. "That's life, o-girl, unless you want Pierre to come and sleep in our bed tonight?"

I resented him, enough to shift inches away from him, then I shifted back again because none of it was his fault anyway. If people didn't care, it was because there was so much to care about. After a while the suffering could seem like sabotage; salt in your sweet pap. A beggar's face at a car window could appear spiteful, a house boy's clumsiness deliberate. Sheer wickedness could begin with the need for self-protection.

We slept without electricity that night. The next day, Niyi returned from work with two potted plants. "Anything?" he asked.

"Nothing," I said.

He shook his head. "Man... "

I walked toward where he stood in the veranda. We'd had the same conversation several times during the day: Anything? Nothing.

"All day," I said. "People were calling the office. I had nothing to tell them. I mean, if you detain someone, shouldn't you at least tell their relations?"

I held his hand as it came over my shoulder. What little garden we had, Niyi was responsible for: the golden torches I liked, the spider lilies he liked. He bought them from a nearby nursery and performed tricks with them: cutting up the leaves and replanting them, halving a plant to make two. I'd even found him polishing the leaves of a rubber plant. These new plants were pinkish-white and waxy. I couldn't remember what they were called.

"You love this house so much you bring her flowers every week," I said.

He rolled his shoulder. "Hm."

"You strained something?" I asked.

"It will go," he said.

"You should have asked Pierre to help."

"What, I'm not a slave driver today?"

I'd been looking forward to seeing him. What I wanted was to share every thought I had during the day.

"No one is calling you a slave driver. I'm just saying, maybe we can't see things the same way. Not anymore."

I expected an answer, instead he began to punch the air with his free hand.

"How was work?" I asked.

"Same. Akin called, just before I left."

My mind was drifting. Between phone calls at work, I was thinking that the one person I could ask for advice was the one who needed help. My father. There was no one else.

"He and a group of other guys," Niyi was saying. "They are starting a firm. Stock-brokers. They are looking for people who want to join. It seems like a good idea, I mean, privatization is bound to happen soon. Can you imagine? If it means we can have an electricity system that works in this country, a telephone system that works... you're not listening." He tugged my chin.

"Sorry," I said. "I was thinking."

"Yes?"

"All day I've been thinking. So many things. Decree Two. You remember when they first passed it? You remember? I didn't care then, and I called myself a lawyer. Now... " I waved my arm around. "Now, we don't have a safe country. Not even to have a thought."

"So?"

"So, this is the result, can't you see? Nothing, nothing will get better if we don't do something. That is what I was thinking."

His hand dropped. "Something like... "

I stepped back. "It is blood money if they privatize. I wouldn't join a firm like that. What is it? These military bastards are always on to something: Indigenization decree, Structural Adjustment Program, Operation Feed the Nation, War Against Indiscipline, National Conference for Democratic Reform. Now, privatization. I'm sick of it. Their damn initiatives. Someone gets rich and people continue to drop dead. What, are we to rejoice because a group of generals and their friends are about to buy up what the public owns in the first place? Let them privatize if they want. They can't deceive the people anymore."

I could have been bragging about an old boyfriend the way Niyi was looking at me. He worried more about the loss of financial power than any other. But I was not interested in the profit ventures of my father's captors; not even if it meant a career change for him.

"I take responsibility for what I have done," he said. "Only for what I have done."

"And what we have not done?" I asked.

I was hoping he would tell me I was right.

"At some point," he said, "We have to let it go."

Letting it go. My father, backdoor house boys and house girls, child hawkers, beggars. We saw their faces every day and we were not stirred. There was a feeling that if people were at a disadvantage, it was because they somehow deserved it. They were poor, illiterate, they were radical, subversive, and they were not us.

How did we live comfortably under a dictatorship? The truth was that, we in places like Sunrise, if we never spoke out, were free as we could possibly be, complaining about our rubbish rotten country, and crazy armed robbers, and inflation. The authorities said hush and we hushed; they came with their sirens and we cleared off the streets; they beat someone and we looked the other way; they detained a relation and we hoped for the best. If our prayers were answered, the only place we suffered a dictatorship was in our pockets.

I should have reached the end of my self-examination, but I didn't until Friday morning. I arrived late to work. It was a few minutes past eleven. Everyone was present in the office, except for Mrs. Kazeem who was normally late. I was in my father's office when his phone rang. I thought she was a client. "This is Grace Ameh," she said.

"Yes?"

"I have news. About your father. Please, don't say anymore."

She would not give details. I scribbled her address down.

"Is he... how is he?" I asked.

"Come to my house," she said.

I telephoned Niyi's office as soon as I had a dial tone.

"It's me," I said. "That journalist, Grace Ameh, has heard from my father. I'm going to her house."

"When?"

"Now."

There was silence.

"Hello?" I said, impatiently.

"You think you should?"

"Yes," I said.

Again, silence.

"Okay, but be careful."

"I will."

As though I had any control.

"And call me afterward."

"Don't worry."

They made me nervous, the way close families made me nervous. They talked loud to each other and walked around in disarray. Behind us was a shelf stashed with books. Grace Ameh was by my side on a sofa. She was a wife and mother now. Her hair was in four chunky plaits, and she had the habit of scratching her bra strap as she spoke. Her husband dragged his flip-flops across the room. He was wearing faded blue shorts and his white undershirt clung to his belly. Their daughter, a girl of about fourteen or fifteen, watched her brother who sat before a computer. He looked a couple of years older.

This was Grace Ameh's study, she explained as she escorted me upstairs, but it was where her family had been coming to escape from the people who were dropping by since her release from detention. The room, with one fluorescent light, gave the appearance of a store room. The rest of their house was too spacious for a family of four, and under-furnished. They'd either rented or inherited the property. This part of Lagos had residential buildings abandoned in various phases of completion and during the day armed robbers ambushed residents as they drove through their gates. At the top of their street there was a Viligante barrier.

"Joe," Grace Ameh said to her husband.

"Grace," he answered without looking at her.

"If any more reporters show up, tell them no more interviews."

He picked up a newspaper from her desk and walked out.

"I suppose I was talking to myself," she whispered.

His head popped back in. "My wife writes. She doesn't get royalties, instead she gets locked up. You see my trouble?"

"Joe," she warned.

"I too suppose, that it could be worse for me. I could be cuckolded."

"Joe!"

"I'm going," he said.

She turned to me. "Don't mind him. He thinks he's married to a renegade. Now."

"Mummy," her daughter interrupted. "Isn't *'Nkosi sikelel' iAfrika'* God bless Africa in Swahili?"

"Swa?"

"Hili," her daughter said.

"No, it isn't."

"I told you," her son said.

Her daughter looked angry. "What is it, if it's not Swahili?"

Grace Ameh sighed. "Xhosa, Zulu. Why are you asking me? *Na wa,* can't you children take pity on me? Why are you here anyway? You know this is my quiet room."

"Sorry," her daughter said.

"Both of you," Grace Ameh said. "Go downstairs, in the name of God, before I lose my head."

As if by cue, they disappeared. Their legs were too long for their bodies and they had the same teenage slouch.

"I can't wait until they graduate," Grace Ameh said. "Now. I was at Shangisha last night, State Security Service headquarters. I was coming back from a conference in South Africa. They read one of my manuscripts and said I was in possession of seditious material. I asked how my work of fiction can be seditious. They took me to Shangisha to explain why I made mention of a military coup in a work of fiction. I begged them. What else was I to do with philistines? I was not going to stay in that place. I asked them to take pity on me, left with the names of some of the people they had in there. They said your father was there, but he has been transferred. No one knows where."

"You didn't see him?"

"No."

"Should I go there?"

"To Shangisha?" She shook her head. "Don't do any such thing, my dear. These days if they can't find you, they take your family. What will they do with you if you present yourself? They don't interrogate prisoners in detention; they torture them. Nail pulling, ice baths. If you're one of the lucky ones, they will throw you in a cell and leave you on your own. Mosquitoes? Plenty. Food? Unbearable. Grown men cry inside there. They cry like babies and run away from the country to avoid it. I told you, I begged them on my knees."

I pinched my mouth. She had become a blur.

"At least you know he is alive," she said. "This is better than nothing, isn't it?"

I couldn't tell.

"Dry your tears. You have to be strong."

"Yes," I managed to say as she rubbed my shoulder.

"She sounds strange to me," Niyi said.

He had listened to my experience at Grace Amehs' house as though it were a party he missed. I thought he sounded resentful.

"She wasn't," I said.

"What does she write anyway?"

"She writes for the *Oracle*."

"I've never heard of her before."

"Well," I said. "She writes."

We were sitting on the floor in the living room. He winced as he struggled to his feet. Sometimes his knee joints gave him trouble.

"She's brave though," he said.

"Yes. She was begging them and thinking of a way to outsmart them."

His stomach groaned loud enough for me to hear.

"Man," he said. "I'm hungry... "

He had that dazed expression, as if he expected food to appear magically. I ignored him and dragged my forefinger around the carpet.

"I have to tell the people at my father's office about this."

"I wouldn't do that."

"Why not?"

"The last thing you want is to tell anyone about this."

"Why?"

"It is not safe."

I stood, supporting myself with the chair and walked toward him.

"Whose safety are you worried about?"

He raised his hand. "We'll talk about this later."

"When?"

"Later."

He was near the kitchen door. I hurried there and blocked his way. "You know I hate for you to walk away."

He reached for the handle and I placed my own hand over his.

"Talk to me now," I said.

He laughed. "Out of my way."

"No," I said. "What do you want in there anyway? When have you ever entered a kitchen before?"

"I'm a hungry man."

"You're always hungry. Answer me."

"Okay!" he said. "Who the hell are these people?! They come to your office and you speak to them. They call you and you go. How do you know they won't get you into trouble?"

"Do you see me in any trouble here?"

"That is exactly what your father said. Now look where he is, and I'm surprised... "

"Surprised that what?"

"You are pregnant."

"I know."

"You've already had one miscarriage."

"I. Know."

"You don't seem to care."

I wagged my finger. "Not from you will I hear a thing like that."

"This has nothing to do with us!"

"Why didn't you say that before? That you didn't want to be involved."

"You. I don't want you involved."

"I am involved."

"Not yet," he said. "But the way you're going, you will be, and yes, I am scared, but I don't have to announce it before you're satisfied. Now please."

He made shooing movements with his hands.

"No," I said, jabbing him several times.

Niyi checked his torso as if it had sprung leaks. "Is something wrong with you?"

"Don't you dare speak to me like that."

His voice dropped. "Listen, I'm not used to this... this melodrama."

"Ah," I said. "Just because one person chose to live like a zombie in your family doesn't mean you didn't have problems of your own."

He put his fist against his mouth. "Step away from the door."

"No," I said.

"I won't tell you again," he said.

Niyi was as tall as the door. He moved closer and I stepped aside.

"Go," I said, as he walked through. "See if that solves anything. And when you've finished in there, why don't we buy our way through our problems as we always have?"

I heard him slam the refrigerator door. He marched back with a bag of frozen bread. "If you had any concept," he said, "any, of what it means to pray for money, like most people do in this country, you wouldn't be standing there making such a stupid statement."

I pointed at the kitchen door. "Isn't that why we spend half our lives inside there? Cooking this, cooking that, so that you can take charge, at a time like this?"

He was struggling with the knot in the bag. "Say what you like. You're heading straight for trouble and I'm not going to let you."

"Let?" I yelled.

"Yes," he said. "If you have no sense in your head, at least I do. What, I should walk to the presidential palace and ask them to release my wife's father? Should I? 'Please, sir. My wife's father is locked up. Please release him, sir.'"

"Have no electricity," I continued. "Buy a generator. No water, pay for a bore hole. Scared? Hire your safety. Need a real country to live in? Buy a flag. Stick it on your roof. Call it the republic of Franco."

"And while you're living here," he said, "don't even think of trying to ruin it for everybody by playing... "

"Playing what?" I shouted.

He ripped the bag apart.

"Fucking political activist," he said. "Or any of that shit."

He said nothing to me for the rest of that evening, and I moved into the spare room, vowing to stay there until he apologized. People like my father, did they come from a different place? Were they born that way? Ready to fight, tough enough to be imprisoned? I checked the doors and windows twice before going to bed. I fell asleep after midnight. When I woke up three hours later, my gums throbbed and my mouth tasted as if I'd been chewing on iron beads. Going downstairs to get a drink of water, I saw a strip of light under Niyi's door. No, I thought, this wasn't one of our house fights. I would give him time. He just hadn't accepted it yet. We were all under attack.

My memory liked to tell lies. Huge lies. Sometimes, I remembered my father standing tall, my mother cracking jokes. My memory could blank out all but one sensation: a sick feeling in my stomach, a smell, a taste, like the creamy sweetness of banana ice-pop in my mouth. Then there were times my memory became a third eye, watching from a distance. This was always how I remembered the conquering moments; the moments I transcended myself: my first free rotation on a bicycle, my first paddle without arm bands, first plunge into a pool.

My father was standing in the shallow end. I was on the very edge, swimsuit in my butt crack and nose streaming. I crouched like I was about to pee, then flopped in.

He grabbed me. "You see? It's not so bad."

I buried my face in his chest. The water had smacked me good and hard. My father had given me my first swimming lessons, though he wasn't a good swimmer himself. Half of it was a lesson in courage, he said.

I couldn't shift the feeling that I had failed him. I told my friends and family about Grace Ameh, and no one else. Uncle Fatai said we could do nothing but wait for his release.

I waited. In the silence of my home I waited, as harmattan season passed and the Moslem fasting period, Ramadan, approached. Those who could afford time and money began to look forward to the day of the new moon on which Moslems feasted. Niyi's silence continued as the mound in my belly grew. My thirty-fifth birthday came and went like any other day. I was relieved.

As soon as the February issue of the *Oracle* came out, I drove to nearby Falomo to buy a copy. As usual there was a traffic jam there. Traffic to and from Victoria Island converged in the same place, under the bridge at Falomo. On one side there was the Church of Assumption; on the other, the local council had built a line of concrete stalls by the police barracks. Mammy Market, it was called. The road was filled with potholes. The barracks looked like slum dwellings over the marketplace: dusty and gray from cauldron smoke, wooden slabs for windows, barefooted children. Hens.

This was suburbia. A vagrant woman scraped ash from a burnt pile, using a piece of cardboard. A man hawked small plastic bags filled with drinking water. Someone had hung four fake Persian rugs over a public wall, for sale; another displayed a set of children's tricycles on the sidewalk. A man walked by with a sewing machine on his shoulder, ready to fix a zip or tear. There wasn't a corner free from baskets and wooden stalls. A watchman performed ablution into a gutter, another peed by a wall that said *Post no Bill*.

While people moved slowly, they were not idle. They were skewering meat, pumping tires, hawking suitcases of fake gold watches. If no one would employ them, they would employ themselves. The State gave them nothing, not even what they paid for. Sometimes they were begging, and sometimes the beggars were children. A girl stood with a tray of coconut slices on one side of the street. Next to her, a boy carried a board: *Please help me. I am hungry.* Billboards told the story of trade: Kodak was keeping Africa smiling; Canon was setting new standards in office copying; Duracell lasted up to six times longer. Redeemed Church, rug cleaners, Alliance Français. A bank, vet services, a nursery of potted plants, *fresh salad sold here.* No pesticides or dyes so cucumbers were small and oranges were yellowish-green.

Initially, finding myself unexpectedly nervous, I couldn't read the article, but driving back home, I pulled into a private driveway to search for it. It was a three-inch column: "Sunny Taiwo's daughter speaks out." Grace Ameh recounted the events as I'd told her, and then finished with: "When asked to comment on her father's detention, she stated, 'My father is not a criminal.'"

I placed the magazine on the passenger seat and drove off. A few meters down the road there was a police check-point. Two policemen stood by rusty oil drums placed on either side of the road. Their rifles were hanging over their shoulders. One of them flagged me down and I came to a stop. He searched the interior of my car.

"Your lishense," he said.

I reached into my glove compartment. He flicked through breathing heavily and handed it back.

"Insh-wurance?"

I passed my insurance certificate and he held it upside down.

"Sistah, why you stop like dat?" he asked, giving it back.

"Where?" I asked.

"Yonder."

He pointed down the road where I'd stopped.

"I was looking for something."

"What?"

"My glasses," I said.

He scratched his chin. "Is not allowed to stop like dat, Sistah. Is not allowed. You almost caused accident for dis side."

His eyes landed on my handbag under my legs. There wasn't a traffic sign on the road. I knew not to argue with the police. Give them money, or apologize. Move on.

"That is not true," I said, quietly. "There are no traffic signs, nothing to say I can't stop there."

"Eh," he shouted. "Who tol' you dat? Comot. Comot."

He banged on my car door. I got out of my car and stood before him. Across the road, his partner glanced at us and carried on watching traffic. The policeman screwed up his face attempting to look angry. "Sistah, you no fear? I can arrest you right now."

"What for?"

He snatched my arm and I snatched it back.

"I'm a pregnant woman. Be careful how you handle me."

His gaze dropped.

"Yes," I said. "I am."

His face creased into a wide grin. "Why you no talk before? You for enter labor small time."

I didn't answer.

"Begin go," he said waving me into my car. "Go on. You're

234

very lucky today. Very, very lucky. It could have been another story."

His mouth hung like a hammock from his ears. The dead and the pregnant, I thought.

Niyi was sitting on the couch with his legs propped up on my ebony stool. As usual, he was listening to his noise. I heard a clarinet.

"How now," I said.

Drums.

"The article came out today. We have nothing to... "

Trumpets.

"Worry about."

The instruments clashed like a marketplace brawl. Niyi nodded in time to the bass. I placed the magazine on the dining room table and went upstairs.

The spare room seemed smaller. I imagined it was the same size as my father's cell. I drew the curtains and lay down. Slowly, I rubbed my belly, trying to picture my child inside, skin stretching, bones forming. My palms ached from being snubbed, but I was no longer alone.

My father appeared leaner in my imagination, with yellow eyes. I strained to see him. The rest of him was a shadow.

"I spoke to the *Oracle* about you," I said.

"You did?" he said.

"They are calling you a prisoner of conscience."

"They are."

"Do you think I was right to speak to them?"

"Do you think you were?"

"Yes."

"Nothing left to say then," he said. "Let your mind be at rest."

Downstairs I heard the thud of a bass. Outside I could hear children playing. There was a hush over my country. I heard that

235

too, and in my frustration, it sounded like men learning how to be women.

In my first year of marriage, there was a hawker who sat by the vigilante gates of our estate. She was one of those Fulani people from the north. We never said a word to each other: I could understand her language no more than she could mine. But I would smile at her, she would smile at me, and that would suffice.

Fulani people, traditionally, were cattle herders, but those who lived in Lagos worked as stable hands, night watchmen, craftsmen, or as street hawkers. Lagos people would say they spread tuberculosis because they were always spitting. Their elite were the sort of people Niyi held responsible for the demise of our country, the power hawkers. They were Moslems, influenced by Arab culture, and wealthy. Sheri's brigadier was one of them.

This hawker sold confectionery out of a portable display box: Trebor mints, Bazooka Joe gum, Silk Cut cigarettes, local analgesics, and I would often find her crouched over her box, arranging the contents of her display, as if she were playing a solo chess game. Occasionally I stopped to buy something from her and I soon began to call her "my woman." She pressed her palms together whenever she smiled, and I thought she was truly graceful and enjoyed seeing her, the way a person might a beautiful tree, or a view.

Niyi asked if I was a lesbian, calling her that. I told him that I'd always wanted men, but women interested me. Still, one day, I came back from work and my woman was not there. I thought she might be preparing for prayers, or resting in the dilapidated building where she and others in her community squatted at night. I asked a gate man and he confirmed that she'd gone. I wondered where. I watched the other Fulani women. They were lighting kerosene lanterns for night time and perching them on their display boxes. I imagined a story about my woman. Her name would be Halima. She would be the wife of a stable hand.

His name would be Azeez. One day Halima got tired of being stationary in Lagos. She left on foot, walked to Zaria up north, crossed the Sahara desert in her robes and chiffon wrap. During the day, the sun beat her head, but she never, ever died, and at night, her gold hoops made music with the wind.

February began with the season of Ramadan and a petrol shortage. Sunrise Estate was full of angry residents, none of whom could leave their homes to go to work. The first day, we telephoned each other: What kind of country were we living in? How would we ever get out of our homes? By the second day, children were ecstatic. Two whole days and no school! The third day, and they were driving their parents crazy. Solutions began to emerge fast. A bank was sending a bus around. Someone knew an employee of an oil company with petrol to spare; another somebody knew somebody who knew somebody else who was selling petrol at black market rates.

The queues were three days long. A few petrol stations had opened. They were selling petrol from oil drums using nothing but funnels to get the petrol into car tanks. I stayed at home until the shortage was over. I doubted any of my father's staff would show up. Public transportation had not fully resumed and fares had quadrupled. I saved what little petrol I had for an emergency which never occurred.

Niyi went to work every day. His company driver came for him. Our home was ridiculous. He was carrying on his standoff and I'd retreated fully to the spare room. Silence had become noisy: doors clicking, curtains rolling, and at night, jazz and crickets. Sometimes I heard Niyi laughing on the phone. I wanted to tell him that a heavy plug had settled at the base of my womb. I wanted to tell him that I was finding it difficult to sleep on my belly at night. I wanted to talk to anyone about my father.

On the day of the Moslem festival, *Id-el-fitr*, I left home for the first time that month to break fast with the Bakares. The streets were crowded with vehicles and the heat was heavier than I was prepared for. Harmattan ended in Lagos and we expected something new, the way the rainy season left colors deeper and cleaner and shinier. It was always easy to see that a well-meaning season has passed after the rains. But after harmattan, all that remained was humid heat. Gutters dried up as if they couldn't remember why they started flowing. The dry season was nothing to look forward to in Lagos, and it lasted most of the year.

As I drove through their gates, I heard a ram bleating in the back yard of the Bakare's house. It had been tied to a mango tree for two weeks and would be slain for the *Sallah* feast. I parked, walked past the lunch time cafeteria and emerged in a cement square. Sheri and some of her family members stood around the square. They were watching a butcher untie the ram. Nearby, a bandy-legged butcher's aide waited with his hands on his hips. I headed straight for Sheri's stepmothers and curtseyed.

"My child, how are you?" Mama Gani said.

"Long time we haven't seen your face," Mama Kudi said.

I apologized. It was the petrol shortage. February had been a quiet month because of it.

"How's your husband?" Mama Gani asked. Her gold tooth flashed.

"He's fine," I said.

"And your mother?"

"She's well, thank you."

"Still nothing about your father?"

"Still nothing," I said.

She clapped her hands. "*Insha Allah*, nothing will happen to him, after the kindness he's shown us."

There wasn't a line on either of their faces, as though they hadn't aged from the day I met them, but they were fatter, with the same lazy walks, high cheek bones, watery eyes, and chiffon scarves wrapped over their heads. Perceptions of beauty had changed over the years, between satellite and cable television and overseas travel, but not for women like these. They wanted to be fat, they enjoyed being fat and worried about foreign women who cried on television because they were fat.

Their husband had married the same woman twice, I thought, regardless of their characters. Mama Gani was the one who had ordered me to kneel before her when I was a girl: the wicked one, but nice. Her wickedness saved their family in the end. She was always disagreeable and confronted her dead husband's relations. She was the one who would fight on cue, Sheri said, remove her head tie to land a slap. Mama Kudi was younger and she spoke three languages: Yoruba, Hausa, English, and a little Italian for bargaining, but she hardly said a word. She was also the one with a boyfriend.

I wondered how they could live according to their traditional roles. I had wondered, also, how they could stay together without the man who had brought them together in the first place. Sheri once said that they rarely quarreled; that they took turns to sleep with her father without once coming to blows. In her uncle's house, the wives fought and tried to poison each other's children, but that was because the man himself was no good. "This one-man-one-wife business," she said. "If it's so wonderful, why are women so heartbroken?" "We don't break our own hearts," I reminded her.

Children of polygamous homes, this was their refrain, that civil marriages didn't work anyway. They boasted about their numerous relations, elevated their mothers to sainthood. "Pity your own self," they would tell me, "we are not unhappy with our family arrangement." They rarely confessed about domestic battles: who got more money from Daddy, which mummy had more sons, whose children performed better in school. I suspected they were embarrassed by their fathers, who had bigger sex than brains. But how successful were civil marriages meanwhile? Couples bound by legal certificates, confused by romantic love. So and so whose husband had an outside child; so and so who slept with her boss, because her husband was sleeping with his subordinate. If this was a country struggling with religious and government structures imposed on us, it was also a country struggling with foreign family structures. On our estate alone, there were affairs from day to day, and above it all, Niyi judging other people as only a jilted man could. It was sad to see women acting out like their fathers, because they were so determined not to be like their mothers; worse, to see women joining born-again churches, seeking refuge from their marriages as some mothers had.

Sheri's younger siblings greeted me as I walked across the cement square.

"Hello, Sister Enitan."

"Long time no see."

"*Barka de Sallah*, Sister Enitan."

I felt awkward smiling. I was about to respond when the ram slipped from the butcher's grip and charged forward. Sheri and I collided. The others fled. Within a moment, the butcher had grabbed the ram. His aide tackled the hind legs. The ram bleated louder and I shut my ears to drown out the noise.

"Are they about to kill it?" I asked.

"Yes," Sheri said.

"I can't watch," I said.

The aide wrestled the ram off the cement square and the butcher brought out a knife. He pulled the ram's head back and dragged his knife across its throat. Blood poured into the dark soil. The younger children shrieked and huddled closer. Sheri's stepmothers laughed.

"I hate this," I whispered.

It reminded me of the fowls Baba killed for my mother. He

240

beheaded them and allowed their bodies to run around headless until they dropped. It reminded me of Sheri being strapped down by two boys.

The ram lay dead on the floor and the butcher began to slit its belly.

"Let's go," I said, tugging Sheri's elbow.

We sat on the balcony overlooking the cement square. The butcher castrated the dead ram and placed its testicles next to it. They looked like hairy mangos.

"Not once have you fasted," I said. "Yet you celebrate *Sallah*. What kind of Moslem are you?"

"If I don't fast until I die, I will get to Heaven," she said, cheerfully.

"Are you sure? I hear none of you in this house will inherit the kingdom of God."

"Why not?" she scoffed.

I smiled. "It's what the Christians say."

A woman poked her head through the sliding door. She was bouncing a baby boy.

"Sister Sheri, sorry I'm late. It's the baby again."

There was a coin taped to the baby's belly button to tame his hernia.

"What happened?" Sheri asked.

"He hasn't gone for days," the woman said.

"You've given him orange juice?" Sheri asked.

"Yes," she said.

"Bring him here," Sheri said.

Sheri prodded the baby's belly. "You, you're not supposed to give your mother this much trouble."

"He's been so fussy," the woman said. "I haven't been able to leave his side."

Sheri handed the baby back to her. "He's all right."

The woman left, cuddling her baby.

241

"You're a pied piper," I said.

"Don't mind her, *jo*," Sheri said. "She's just pretending. Every time it's the same with her, one excuse after the other. We can't get her to help with cooking."

"Who is she?"

"Gani's wife."

"Don't you have enough help downstairs?"

"Ehen? She knows how to eat, doesn't she?"

"Leave the woman alone," I said.

Our country was full of passive-aggressive wives like her, finding ways to challenge their in-laws.

Like her grandmother Alhaja, Sheri expected her brother's wives to run around for their family functions. Sheri's stepmothers expected the same. Through them, the spirit of Alhaja was alive, keeping the next generation of wives in check.

As Sheri read the article, I watched the proceedings on the cement square through the balcony railings. The ram's guts were displayed and the butcher and his aide were contemplating how to carve the body. Nearby, Sheri's stepmothers were supervising the women who had come to cook.

Sheri once said she was not interested in who held the power in our country, the military or the politicians. She had witnessed their corruption first hand, mixed with the underworld of people who got rich on their backs. She who slept with an important man to get her directorship. He who slept with the same important man and received a multi-million naira contract. It was enough to make me doubt we had any legitimate businesses in our country that were not somehow linked to corrupt or lustful government officials. But her stepmothers loathed the military, because they supported the wife of the man who would be president, Kudirat Abiola. Abiola was campaigning for her husband's release, and for a reinstatement of our general election results. She was a southerner, a Moslem, and a Yoruba woman, like them. They loved her, and my mother said of her, "Oh, she just wants to be First Lady," which was ironical to me, because Kudirat Abiola was in an openly polygamous marriage. 1994 had given us our greatest symbol of hope in post-colonial Africa with the inauguration of Nelson Mandela. Rwanda was our despair. Kudirat Abiola had become the symbol of the Africa I'd been at odds with since my return, a senior wife, fighting for her husband's political freedom.

"Well done," Sheri said, after she read the article.

If Sheri sympathized, she never showed it.

"How's work?" she asked.

"A mess," I said. "You should see. Papers all over the place. I will have to start sorting them soon."

"One day at a time," she said.

For a while, we watched the carving of the ram. The butcher skinned the ram and then cut the meat. His aide washed the blood away with boiling water.

"How was your birthday in the end?" Sheri asked.

"Quiet," I said.

"Papa Franco didn't do anything?"

"Doesn't even speak to me."

"Eh, why not?"

I tapped the magazine. "Over this. He didn't want me to talk to them. The man hasn't spoken to me for weeks because of it."

"Hey-hey, I think I would prefer a beating."

"I hate the silence."

"It is my friend," she said.

Most times, I could only guess what was going on in her mind. Sheri had become guarded about her personal life, as unmarried women our age were; as the long-term unemployed were about their job prospects.

I turned to her. "I mean, how can I decide what to do about

243

my father from a kitchen? Come to think of it, how can I decide anything with a mini Idi Amin sitting right there in my home?"

She smiled. "Papa Franco? He's not that bad."

"Yes, he is. Sulking, sulking."

"If he frowns, just don't look at his face."

"I wouldn't be bothered with it, any of it, if I were on my own."

She shook her head. "It is not easy on your own. Men thinking you want them; women pitying you and not wanting you around their homes. Your own mother talking about you as if you have terminal cancer: Ah, Enitan, she's still with us. Ah, Enitan, we pray."

"Nothing can be worse than this, Sheri. We see each other in the morning and no hello even."

"Ignore the man."

"He is so childish."

"Don't let him affect you, or anyone else. The people in your house that day, do you think they knew, or cared, that you were angry?"

I patted my chest. "Asking me to make lunch."

"The day my father died, the people who came to give their condolences wanted to eat."

"What did you do?"

"My stepmothers cooked. Some people even asked for more." She laughed.

"I don't think it's funny, Sheri. We laugh and one day we will be laughing in our graves."

"Ignore the man. He can't do anything. And stop letting people upset you. It's not good for you or your baby."

I could have predicted her advice. Sheri once taught me a lesson when she knelt to greet her uncle who had tried to disinherit her family. "How could you?" I asked, sure that I couldn't muster a nod for him. "It's easier to walk around a rock," she said, "than to break it down, and you still get where you're going." I saw that in the past I'd been inclined to want to break rocks, stamping my feet and throwing tantrums when I couldn't. Acting without grace. So cynical was I about the core of strength an African woman was meant to possess, untouchable, impenetrable, because I didn't possess one myself.

The Bakares had not forgotten how to enjoy themselves. After lunch, I watched them do a line dance called the electric boogie. During the dance there was a power cut, which brought on more laughter: no electricity for the electric boogie.

Close families had affectations, I thought. In Niyi's family, they spoke hush-hush; in Sheri's family, they worried about food: Have you eaten? Why aren't you eating? Are you sure you don't want to eat? I thought it was best to say yes to whatever they handed me. They quarreled with people over food-related misdemeanors, like refusing to eat what they offered, or not eating enough. As they danced, I imagined them in the aftermath of a nuclear attack, no home or hair to speak of, still worrying about food.

Niyi was out when I arrived home, and a sneer met me at the front door. It poked my shoulder and prodded me upstairs, spread its ugly mouth across my bedroom wall. In the distance, I heard sounds of Lagos: car horns, motorcycles, street hawkers. From here, the noise sounded like tin cans colliding on hot asphalt. I sat on my bed. There was a fly perched on my mosquito netting. I couldn't tell if it was resting or trying to pass through. I faced the walls again. At one end, silence could defeat a person, a whole country even. At the other end, silence could be a shield, used as Sheri did. An attack and a defense, and yet people always said silence was peaceful.

My phone rang. It was Busola from next door, inviting me to dinner.

"We're having Bomb Alaska," she said.

I really couldn't, I said.

"I saw your husband at the club today. I couldn't believe it. I said, 'You? Here? Where's your best half?' He looked at me, as if to say, 'This girl, you're certifiable.' I know he hates me."

"He doesn't hate you."

"Oh, I know he doesn't like me."

"He doesn't... "

"Anyway he's one of the decent ones and he works hard, unlike some lazy buggers in this house. Come on, to cheer yup."

"I can't," I said.

Busola was someone I'd known from my student days in London. She socialized with a few Nigerians who drove Porsches to lectures and snorted cocaine for extra-curricular activities. They were called the High Socs, and Oppressors, and they were the envy of those who had time for such emotions after studying and socializing. I'd always thought her crowd was a little tragic: their cocaine habits, the inevitable drying out, which could mean they were in a clinic in Switzerland, or being exorcised by the whip of a juju man in their hometowns. Wasted brains, and the boys nearly always ended up beating their girlfriends.

"Any Rhoda," she said.

The gossip about Busola was that her husband had married her because of her good English and secretly he chased women who could barely string two words together without breaking them. Her father was a retired government minister and my father handled part of his large estate. While the rest of us were filling out university applications, Busola was planning a year in Paris. A year stretched to two years and she returned to London wearing short skirts and saying she was in public relations. No one could understand it. We had to go to university. But Busola didn't, and her parents brought her back home when they discovered she was dating an English boy. Now she was married to a Nigerian whose sole purpose in life was to wear good suits and attach himself to the polo-playing clique in Lagos.

I liked Busola, down to her Chinese hair wigs and bags from Milan. I thought she was stylish, smart even. She had conned a whole bunch of people into submitting their children for her Montessori classes, hosted art exhibitions for artists she knew nothing about, dabbled in interior design. All these things required skills, I told Niyi who started calling her "the blockhead next door." From the day she described the houses on our estate as glorified storage space, he'd lost patience with her. Her father had robbed the treasury and she was not afraid to open her mouth, he said. "Why do you always befriend women that no one else can stand, like that Sheri?" he asked. Sheri, who having spent a mere ten minutes with Busola, asked, "Come, what was she talking about? Is she a joker?"

Being generally offensive was what I had in common with both women, and there were a handful of jokers in Lagos, enough to keep the dinner parties going. They cherished their foreign ways, not like the bumbling colonial copycats of our parents' generation. They were much too savvy for that. They gave their children Nigerian names, wore traditional dress, spoke our languages, and pidgin. They were not that different from me, to be fair. But I lacked their affectations, to be fairer still. I imagined them being accosted by state security men at Busola's party. She would drop her Bomb Alaska and run screaming through the gates of Sunrise.

She was nice. The kind of nice that she would say of her husband: "He took my car, went out and didn't come back till morning, and I was furious. So, so furious. You know what I did? I looked at him. Like this. So he knew how furious I was."

Each time I heard a car that night, I went to the window.

How free was I, really, in my marriage? Niyi got in a bad mood and in no time, so did I. When I met him, I followed his eye movements, to see if he would stray. Now that I was sure he didn't, I still worried if he was out late, and not just because of his safety. Infidelity was always my limit. For Sheri it was any form of physical force. But there were other things a man could do. My father-in-law had tamed his wife, almost as if he'd scooped out her brains and left just enough for her to keep on obeying him. His son acted like I was invisible until he liked what he saw.

I went downstairs and padlocked the front door, tossed the key with a flourish. Beaters, cheaters, lazy buggers. The worst were the so-called decent. No one would ever encourage a woman to run like hell from them. Fortunately, my mother had shown me the power of a padlock. Whenever Niyi returned, he would have to wait a while before he entered his own home. Mosquitoes could keep him company outside meanwhile.

It was past midnight when I heard the door bell. I opened the door in my crumpled night shirt. My face was swollen. I had not slept. Niyi dropped his keys on the dining table as he normally would. I sat on the bottom stair. I was determined to make peace with him this time. The floor felt cold under my feet.

"Busola says she saw you," I said.

He raised his brows as if to say, "And so?"

Niyi's face was easy to read when he was angry. This was not the case. He was not sulking; what he wanted was a surrender. I'd almost forgotten that he was a man who believed in absolutes: he wouldn't chase other women but he would break my heart for my own good.

"I'm not asking you to talk," I said. "Just listen. I know you're scared for my safety. I too wish my father were not involved. He and I, there are questions I could ask him, but none of it

248

matters now. What if I never have a chance to speak to him again? God knows what is going to happen, but my life has to change, and you have to help me. Please. This is too much for me. Look at me."

Niyi looked as if he wished I were still upstairs sleeping.

"You hear me?" I asked.

His expression didn't change. I gave him time.

"So," I said. "This is how it is. I can't tell a lie—you're hurting me. I've tried my best. Don't forget to lock your door."

Anger was heavy in my hands that week, weighing them down, and I didn't know where to place it. I would stab a table with a pencil, drag a curtain by the nose, kick a door in its shin. Sometimes I passed Niyi along a corridor when he returned from work. I felt like reaching out to push him, with both hands: "Bombastic element!" But I wasn't going to give in.

I visited Grace Ameh again, hoping for some impartial advice on what to do about my father. She was dressed as I last saw her, in a colorful up-and-down.

"My dear, any news?"

"No," I said.

"*Na wa,* what a pity. Well, come in."

She placed her hand on my shoulder. We found our way to her study. This time I looked around. There were piles of paper in bundles, an ancient computer, a typewriter, two ebony busts used as book ends. I recognized some of the authors on her shelf: Ama Ata Aidoo, Alice Walker, Buchi Emecheta, Jamaica Kincaid, Bessie Head, Nadine Gordimer, Toni Morrison.

"You write here?" I asked.

She looked confused. "What?"

"Write in here," I said.

"You'll have to speak up," she explained. "I'm deaf in one ear. That's why everybody shouts in this house."

Now, it was obvious she was lip-reading, not scrutinizing, me. I repeated my question.

"Not recently," she said. "I feel their presence too strongly, on the tip of my pen. I want to write a word and I think of treason. I'm too upset to write since I came back. Have you ever been to South Africa?"

"No."

She screwed up her nose. "I didn't feel comfortable there. Racial tensions and all that. I don't understand, wherever I travel, beautiful countries, better countries than ours, countries that function, I am always eager to come home for a reason. What do I get on my arrival?"

I smiled. "Arrested."

She folded her arms. "What is it you do? I never asked. I assumed you were a lawyer like your father."

"I am a lawyer."

"I hear that's curable."

I touched my stomach. "I've been out of practice for a while. I was in banking, and then maternity called."

"How many months?"

"Four."

"*Na wa*, congratulations. My mother was a midwife. She worked in Lagos Maternity. She gave up the day she learned that rats were eating the women's afterbirth."

She caught my expression.

"Afterbirth is nutritious," she said. "But it makes the rats fatter, and she couldn't bear that."

"My husband wants to know what you write about," I said.

I could not forget him for a moment, I thought.

She glanced at me sideways. "You've heard of my play 'The Fattening House?'"

"No."

"You've never heard of my play 'The Fattening House?'

Two sisters locked up in their home and force-fed by their grandmother?"

I smiled. "No."

"Look at you," she said. "That was my first play. I made such a loss. Yes, those were the days. At least we were able to express ourselves freely. I write plays for the stage and television. I'm also the arts editor for the *Oracle*. Now that they've driven us into hiding, I do what I can to make sure they don't completely silence us."

I seized the opportunity. "My father says women are not vocal enough."

"He does?"

"About what is happening."

"Not many people are, men or women."

"I can see why women are silent."

"Why?"

"The usual pressure. Shut up and face your family."

"I don't subscribe to that."

"Neither did my father, but it's reality."

"Not mine."

"Your family must support you."

"I wouldn't have it any other way."

Was she being smug or trying to get information out of me? After all, she was a journalist.

"Not everyone has the will to defy people they care about," I said.

"You?"

"Yes. I hear the warnings all the time. 'Don't get involved,' 'Don't say anything.' Sometimes it's easy to forget who is at fault."

She nodded. "Yes, yes, but you have a voice, which is what I always try to tell people. Use your voice to bring about change. Some people in this country, what chance do they have? Born into poverty, hungry from childhood, no formal education. It amazes me that privileged people in Nigeria believe that doing nothing is an option."

"Don't you think I should at least try to get my father released?"

"If you stand with others. But on your own, you are nothing but another victim. Those men I begged at Shangisha, they could easily have harmed me."

"You managed to trick them."

"That doesn't make me a willing hero. Make no mistake, I am not about to be recognized posthumously, as they do over here, people forgetting you and nothing ever changing. I may not be able to write freely with the threat of treason over my head, but I cannot write if I'm dead, eh?"

"You still believe I should avoid Shangisha?"

"Yes."

"It is frustrating, just sitting around."

She reached for a sheet of paper on a side table and handed it to me.

"See. Maybe you would like to come. They've invited me to speak. They are a good group. They work with writers overseas to spread awareness of what is happening."

It was an invitation to an event in support of journalists in detention. Peter Mukoro was one of them.

"A reading," I said.

"There are people there who are involved in the campaign for democracy, human rights and civil liberty organizations. No one will expect you to be silent."

"Thank you," I said.

She smiled. "Hm, so you came here to see me?"

"Yes."

"Petrol shortage and all that?"

"Yes."

"*Na wa*, I'm flattered. It is nice to see your face again. You should come to the reading if you can. It will be good to have support. They say that great minds think alike, but in this country it is the stupid ones that have a consensus."

I decided to go to the reading. I wanted to be around people who had taken a stand against our government. At home, Niyi's silence was upsetting me, and I couldn't forget about my father's detention. I invited Dagogo and Alabi. They said they weren't wasting precious petrol, driving somewhere to listen to poems or whatever.

Looking back on the choice I made to go, I really wasn't interested in attending a literary event either. I never even realized writers in my country held readings, except within academic circles, or except when one retired senator, general, diplomat or the other, wrote his memoirs and threw a large party afterward to raise funds. I'd heard that there were published writers who had not yet seen a royalty, because publishers just didn't pay. My library at home was short on their books, because in an economy like ours books were scarce, if they were not banned by the government. If ever I did come across a book by an African author, it was in London, in a neighborhood where I'd gone to buy plantains, in a bookshop with kente cloth drapes. None of the books I encountered had characters as diverse as the people I knew. And African authors, it seemed, were always having to explain the smallest things to the rest of the world. To an African reader, these things could appear over-explained. Harmattan for instance. You already knew: a season, December–January, dust in the eyes, coughing, chilly mornings, by afternoon sweaty armpits. Whenever I read foreign books, they never explained the simplest things, like snow. How it crunched under your shoes, kissed your face both warm and cold. How you were driven to trample it, then loathed it after it became soiled. All these things! No one ever bothered to tell an African! This never occurred to me, until an English friend once commented on how my accent changed whenever I spoke to my Nigerian friends. That was my natural accent, I told her. If I spoke to her that way, she would never understand. She looked stunned. "I don't believe you," she said sincerely. "That is so polite."

After I'd come to terms with how polite I was being, I became incensed at a world that was impolite to me. Under-explained books, books that described a colonial Africa so exotic I would want to be there myself, in a safari suit, served by some silent and dignified Kikuyu, or some other silent and dignified tribesman. Or a dark dark Africa, with snakes and vines and ooga-booga dialects. My Africa was a light one, not a dark one: there was so much sun. And Africa was an onslaught of sensations, as I once tried to explain to a group of English work mates, like eating an orange. What single sensation could you take from an orange? Stringy, mushy, tangy, bitter, sweet. The pulp, seeds, segments, skin. The sting in your eyes. The long lasting smell on your fingers.

But people concentrated on certain aspects of our continent: poverty, or wars, or starvation; bush, tribes, or wildlife. They loved our animals more than they loved us. They took an interest in us only when we were clapping and singing, or half naked like the Maasai, who were always sophisticated enough to recognize a photo opportunity. And for the better informed: "How about that Idi Amin Dada fellow, eh?" That Mobutu Sese Seko fellow, that Jean-Bedel Bokassa fellow, as though those of us who just happened to be living in the same continent could vouch for the sanity of any of these fellows.

We had no sense of continent really, or of nation in a country like mine, until we traveled abroad; no sense of the Africa presented outside. In a world of East and West, there was nowhere to place us. In a graded world, there was a place for us, right there at the bottom: third, slowly slipping into fourth world. A noble people. A savage culture. Pop concert after pop concert for starving Africans. Entire books dedicated to the salvation of African women's genitals. If only the women themselves could read the books, critique them: this is right; this is incorrect; this is total nonsense. If only Africa could be saved by charity.

Niyi said it was as simple as economic prowess. Economic prowess equaled respect and love. If we had economic clout the rest of the world would love us; love us so much they might even want to mimic us. Why did I think England was beginning to resemble an American colony? Why did I think the most stylish people in the world were forcing themselves to eat sushi? He made sense, I had to admit.

The reading began at 7:00 P.M. but I arrived late, Lagos-style. It was held in a small hall that normally served as a venue for wedding receptions. The hall was the size of a school assembly hall, with folding doors, which, once fully pushed back, allowed air to flow freely from one side to another. Two white fans were suspended from the ceiling. There was a low wooden stage where I expected various brides and grooms had been set on display during their wedding receptions together with ribbons and balloons. The lighting was poor. I sat at the back, under a broken light by the door, wanting to observe. I hoped no one would notice me.

There were about forty or so people present. They were mostly men. One of them caught my eye because he was smoking a pipe. He looked about my father's age. Another, a skinny tall man, walked around with a serious expression. He was handing out leaflets. I saw Grace Ameh. She laughed and patted her chest. She was chatting with the man seated next to her. The skinny man got on the stage. He talked about activism and writing. His voice was so soft it made me wonder if he breathed. He spoke about a rally he had attended, where state security agents had arrested people. They arrived during the first speech and none of the speakers had been seen since. His friend, a writer and journalist, was one of them. He himself wrote poetry and he didn't believe that writers had any special obligation to be activists. "Why must I write about military tyranny?" he asked. "Why can't I write about love? Why can't I just write for the rest of my life about a stone if I want?"

The next reader was Grace Ameh. For a while people adjusted their chairs and she waited for the noise to die down. "In this state we're living in," she said, "where words are so easily expunged, from our constitution, from publications, public records, the act of writing is activism." The audience clapped.

She begged our forgiveness if she was out of touch, but she hadn't read the papers since her return. The news was so heavily censured and she hated to come across the words "socio-economic" and "socio-political," which were over-used by her colleagues in the media. This brought on jovial hisses from the audience. I was surprised Grace Ameh didn't talk about her arrest, only about her trip to South Africa. She said she felt like an honorary white, drinking South African wine and discussing literature. She feared the world would judge Winnie Mandela as a woman, not as the general she was in the war against apartheid.

Grace Ameh was an entertainer. She was also openly self-absorbed, as if she'd decided to crown herself because no one else would. She flirted and quoted from English poems and Zulu sayings. She dared to move daintily. After her, the man with the pipe read an excerpt from his short story about a surgeon with a missing finger, followed by another man who read a poem full of words like sweat and toil. I imagined it had something to do with the demise of farming in our country.

I was in awe of the people I was listening to, that they wrote without recognition or remuneration, and more so that they denounced injustices as a group, at the expense of their freedoms and lives. At the same time, I thought that none of them could be fully conscious of the implications of speaking out. They would have an awareness only; an awareness that manifested itself in whispers, omitted names, substitute names when people discussed politics at gatherings or over the phone. I had lived with the awareness so long, it had become normal. But what made a person cross the frontier of safety? It wasn't consciousness. Anger, I thought. Enough to blind.

The evening ended with a question-and-answer session. I would have stayed, but I was already feeling hungry. These days my hunger was as fierce as thirst. I took note of the next reading, slipped out of the back door. Outside, I hurried to my car in the dark. I'd parked by the gates because I expected to be boxed in. The grounds of the property were over an acre wide with a huge flame-of-the-forest tree in the front court. There were no lamps in the lot, so it took me a while to find my car keys. When I finally did, the headlights of three cars blinded me. I kept perfectly still, recognizing the familiar Peugeot shapes. One car stopped before me and the others carried on toward the hall. The back door of the car before me flew open. A man jumped out. I raised my hands. He was carrying a rifle.

"Don't move," he warned.

They threw us into a cell, Grace Ameh and I. They said we had disobeyed public orders.

The police stormed the reading and ordered people out at gun point. They arrested Grace Ameh; she was the one they came for. They arrested the four men who came to her rescue. I was arrested because I was the first person they saw.

"Why?" I asked the police officer.

"Inside de car," he said.

"Why?"

"Inside de car," he said, pushing me in.

Through the back window I saw the other policemen running into the hall. They aimed their rifles and shouted orders; I shut my eyes and blocked my ears. I thought they were about to shoot the people inside. I heard Grace Ameh screaming, "Don't touch me." They marched her into the car. I felt so ashamed; I wanted her to be quiet, but she wouldn't stop until we reached the police station, telling them what cowards they were.

There were twelve other women in the cell they threw us in; fourteen of us in a space intended for seven, with ventilation holes on an area the size of an air-conditioning unit. There was no air, no light. My pupils widened in the dark. Outside crickets chattered. Mosquitoes buzzed around my ears. The women lay on raffia mats, overlapping each other on the cold cement floor. One woman had been ordered to fan the others with a large cardboard sheet. Another sat by a shit-bucket in the corner, carrying on a conversation with herself: "Re Mi Re Do? Fa So La Ti Re. La Ti La Ti... "

Grace Ameh stood by the cell door. I was crouched behind her, as far away from the shit-bucket as possible. The smell was already in my nostrils, in my stomach, churning it over. My breath was coming in gasps.

"Get away from the grill," a loud voice said.

It was the woman who seemed to have assumed control of the others in the cell. She had been giving orders to the fanner: "Face north. Face south. Quicken up. Why are you slowing down? Are you crazy?"

Her voice was full of mucus. I was able to make out the roundness of her face, but not her exact expression.

"I stand where I want," Grace Ameh answered.

A woman of words, her voice had broken in her rage.

"I've told you, madam," the loud woman said. "Get away

from that grill. You're disrupting everything inside here since you came, and I don't like disruptions."

"I'm not part of your little brigade," Grace Ameh answered.

She was spent from screaming. One or two people slapped mosquitoes from their legs. Someone coughed and swallowed. I gritted my teeth to control my nausea.

"You think because you're educated," came the woman's voice again. "You think you're better than me. I'm educated, too. I read books. I know things. You're no better than me. You and your butter-eating friend in the corner who can't take the smell of shit."

"Look at you, treating people so badly in here," Grace Ameh said.

"Don't speak to me like that," the woman shouted. "You're no better than me. Not in here. We sleep on the same floor, shit in the same bucket. I'll deal with you in a way you least expect if you insult me. Any of my girls here will deal with you in a way you least expect. Even Do-Re-Mi in the corner. Ask her. She kills people and can't even remember. Ask her. She'll tell you."

"How can she tell me if she can't remember?"

"Eh?"

"If she kills people and can't remember, how can she tell me that she's killed them?"

The woman was silent for a moment, then she laughed. "Madam, you know too much. More than God, even. Holding cell must be full again, otherwise I wouldn't have to deal with the likes of you."

She lay down and I shut my eyes. Who would know I was here? Who would think to look for me? All night here, by morning then what? I thought of Niyi at home, waiting.

Do-Re-Mi began to talk louder: "Fa So La. Ti Mi Re? La So La So... "

"Do-Re-Mi, keep the noise down," the loud woman ordered. "And you, fanner, face south again. The women over there need air."

The fanner did an about turn. She was moaning that her arms ached.

"What is wrong with her?" Grace Ameh asked.

"She's lazy," The loud woman answered. "She never wants to do her turn."

"Do-Re-Mi, I mean."

"She's a witch. She hears voices from the other world. They tell her what to do and she does it."

"Schizophrenia?"

"Only you knows, madam. Skipping-freenia. All I know is she's a witch."

Grace Ameh sighed. "I think you know."

"All right, all right!" the woman said. "She's sick in the head. What am I to do? Half of them in here are sick in the head. Listen. Who art thou?"

A voice answered. "I am that I am."

"I say who art thou?"

"I am that I am?" the voice mumbled.

The loud woman laughed. "*In nomine patris, et filii, et spiritus sancti*. I call that one Holy Ghost. She thinks she's God, quarter to her grave, from the day they brought her in, old as a rag, soon to be six feet under. Looks like she really suffered. I mean under Pontius Pilate. But she obeys, she obeys..."

Someone began to pee in the bucket. I heard her grunts, followed by a trickle. My stomach tightened.

"What are you here for?" Grace Ameh asked.

"What is your concern?" the loud woman answered.

"I only ask."

"Don't concern yourself with me. Concern yourself with yourself. We've all done something. Some of us don't even know what, because they haven't told us yet."

"They haven't?"

"Six years. Six hundred, even. Awaiting trial."

There was mumbling and more slapping. Someone complained about the smell from the woman who had gone. Tears welled in my eyes. I sank lower. If I had been made to lick a toilet bowl, I could not feel sicker. The bile twisted my insides, shot up to my temples. My eyes criss-crossed.

I reached for Grace Ameh's leg.

"The smell... I can't... "

She knelt beside me. "My dear, are you okay?"

"You think it smells of perfume here?" the loud woman said.

"She's pregnant," Grace Ameh said.

The woman sat up. "Eh? What are you saying? The butter-eater is pregnant? No wonder she can't stand the smell of shit."

"Try and keep calm," Grace Ameh said.

"I've had a miscarriage before," I whispered.

"Butter-eater," came the woman's voice again. "Who impregnated you?"

"Enough of that," Grace Ameh said to me.

"I thought you were too good for sex."

"Don't mind her," said Grace Ameh.

"What's going on over there?" came the loud woman's voice again.

"Nothing," Grace Ameh said.

The loud woman laughed. "Is your pregnancy still intact? I hope so, because I know you butter-eaters, small thing and babies start falling out of you, plop, plop."

In the dark, I despised her. Plop plop, she kept saying.

"Your baby dead," she said between laughs.

I vomited, wiped my mouth with the back of my hand and sat

next to my mess. My head felt clearer. I used my sleeve to clean my tears.

The first protest came from the far corner. "You don't have to speak to her like that."

"Why not?" the loud woman asked.

"After all, she's expecting."

"Is she the first to expect?" the loud woman answered.

"It's not Christianly," came a whiny voice. "It's not Christianly. She doesn't deserve to be here, a pregnant woman."

"Do I deserve to be here? Do any of us, bloody dunces. Fanner!"

The fanner had slackened again.

"Do I have to tell you again? Or do you need a slap to remind you?"

The whiny voice continued. "It's not Christianly what you do. It's not Christianly. You blaspheme... " She sounded like a broken whistle.

The loud woman stood up. "Sharrap. Are we equals? Are we? I thought not. Christian it isn't, Shit-stian it is. Where are your best friends hallelu and hallelujah since you've been calling them? I don't see them here. On the day of judgment those who don't know will, so keep your trap shut until then. Thou shalt not speaketh unless you are speaketh to. Take that as your eleventh commandment and commit it to memory."

The whiny voice continued. "It's ungodly what you do. You treat us terribly, as if we don't have enough trouble. We are children of God."

The other women took up the chorus. Yes, they were children of God. They sounded wretched. Weak.

The loud woman stood up. "So. You have little loyalty to me in this place? Two new people and you begin to question me like this?" Her voice broke. "After everything I've done."

She began to weep. The women protested. They were not

against her. They only wanted her to show some sympathy for the pregnant woman. She stopped and cleared her throat.

"Where is she even?"

She made her way toward Grace Ameh and I. The smell of stale urine was stronger than ever as she stood over us like a shadow. I stopped breathing.

"You're turning everyone against me," she said.

"She has a point," Grace Ameh said. "We are in here together."

"Born again? What does she know? Fertile and dumb. She has so many children she can't even count. Christian *ko*, Shit-stian *ni*. Before she came in here what was she doing? Prostituting herself to feed her family. Half a dozen men a night. Stinking crotch. If she scrubbed it with limes, it still wouldn't be clean. Now she says she's born again."

She knelt.

"Butter-eater... "

Grace Ameh moved her hand over my belly. "Don't touch her."

Someone in the far corner shouted, "It's me and you if you touch that pregnant woman. You know you have little strength for fighting, only for talking."

The loud woman slapped her head. "Ah-ah? You think I would do something like that? Do I look like an evil person to you? Let me speak to her, that's all I want, woman to woman. I remember when I was expecting."

"You have children?" Grace Ameh asked.

"Twins," she said.

Her spit sprayed my face. She stroked my braids.

"Butter-eater, you ever had twins?"

I gritted my teeth. Her breath was like a bad egg.

She laughed. "It is like shitting yam tubers. This one is a real dunce. Doesn't say much..."

"You think you're speaking to a child?" Grace Ameh said.

"She's a lawyer."

The woman's hand left my head. "A lawyer? And she's never seen the inside of a prison cell before? That's a focking lawyer." She laughed. "A very focking lawyer indeed. I used to work for a lawyer, just like you. A proper African-European. She spoke like she had a hot potato in her mouth: *fyuh, fyuh, fyuh*. She was always afraid: I'm afraid this, I'm afraid that. She was even afraid she couldn't take a telephone call, bloody dunce. Em, my Lord, if it em, pleases the court, can you tell me why, according to articles my left foot, and my right buttock, why 'whereas' a good woman like myself was living my life peacefully and 'whereas' my life story was straight, all of a sudden my life story got k-legs?"

I blinked once, twice. She expected an answer.

"Monday morning," she said, "my husband dies. Tuesday morning, they shave my head and say I must stay in a room. Alone. Naked. I can't touch my children. Twins. Twins, I had for that wretched family."

She began to cry again. The women begged her to be strong. She cleared her throat and continued.

"They say I can't see my twins. Instead they give me the water they used to bath my husband's corpse, to drink, to prove I didn't put a hex on him. I say I'm a secretary typist. Qualified 1988. I'm not going to drink it. They say I killed him."

"That's why you're here?" Grace Ameh asked.

"I didn't kill my husband. They said I did. The day I killed somebody, they said they were surprised. No one in their family ever did that."

She laughed and rocked. "I had not bathed for days after my husband died. I was walking around in one dress. One dress on my back and nowhere to go. No food to eat. They had sent me out and left me with nothing. I was walking the streets. One foolish man approached me. He called me Hey Baby. I said I'm not Hey Baby. I'm a secretary typist, qualified 1988. Maybe he thought I was a prostitute like Born Again over here, or a crazy like Do-Re-Mi. You know some of these men will go with the crazies to get rich, and some of these crazies will go with men. Crazy in the head but not so crazy in the crotch. The fool touched my breast, I slapped his face. He pushed me to the ground."

She cleared her throat. "I grabbed a stone, whacked his head. I couldn't stop whacking. He was shouting, 'Help! Help!' Before I knew it, he died there on top of me. The police came and carried me to prison."

"That is terrible," Grace Ameh said.

She used her wrapper to wipe her tears. "Yes. What was I supposed to do but kill him? Answer me that."

She reached for my braids again. Her hand felt rough.

"Doesn't this one speak?" she murmured. " Or is she dumb?"

I cleared my throat and steadied my voice.

"I'm not," I said.

"Eh? She speaks?"

"Yes, I do."

I sounded calm. My heart was beating fast.

"So tell me why, according to your law articles, this happened to me."

"You should not be awaiting trial this long," I said.

She stopped stroking my braids.

"And only a court can decide if you're guilty."

The woman started stroking my braids again. "That's very good," she said. "That's very very good, indeed. You're a Yoruba girl?"

"Yes," I said.

She began to speak in Yoruba. "A European one. I can tell. I never thought I'd see one of you in here. Smelling so clean, so clean...Your friend isn't Yoruba?"

"No," I confirmed.

"You keep answering in English. You are not a lost child of Oduduwa, I hope. You can speak the language?"

"Yes," I said in Yoruba.

"Tell me, since you've come in here, smelling so clean and speaking such good English, if I came to your office to see you, would you turn your nose the other way? Say that I smell? Ask someone to show me out? Would you drive past on the streets when I was walking and wonder? Had I eaten? Had I rested? Did I have a roof over my head?"

She tugged my braids.

"That is enough," Grace Ameh said.

"Would you?" she asked.

"You have to let me go," I said.

She released my braids.

"You see? You don't consider us your equals, you butter-eaters. You see us and you think we're no better than animals."

"That is not true," I said.

She turned to Grace Ameh. "You're saying this one is not a child? This one who can't even answer a simple question. Telling me only a court can decide and nonsense like that?"

Her saliva droplets hit my face again. I wiped them away. She got up and began to make her way over the bodies lying on the floor.

"You have not grown up," she said. "You're still a child."

"I am not responsible for your being here," I said.

"Shame on you. Shame. Bringing another child into the world."

"I did not arrest myself."

I tried to stand, but Grace Ameh's hand came down on my shoulder. "Don't listen to her. Can't you see? It is how she has control."

I stood up. It was not anger that propelled me, it was

266

humiliation. She could be a client, and I would not allow her to ridicule me.

"What do you know about me?" I asked.

"I hope you're not trying to think you can follow me," she said. "I sincerely hope not. You dare not provoke me. I'm not nice when I'm provoked."

I climbed over another body. "I'm not scared of you."

She laughed. "Shaking like a fowl from the minute you walked in. Ooo, Ooo. Can't take the smell of shit. Will your baby's shit smell sweet? Your baby's shit won't smell sweet. That's what I know about you."

"You ask me a hundred questions. You don't even give me a chance to answer."

She began to rock back and forth, mimicking me. "O dearie me. O my goodness. O my goodness gracious."

"Ignore her," Grace Ameh said.

"No," I said.

She would bury me unless I faced up to her. I waited until her dance was over.

"You've finished?" I asked.

"You still have not answered my questions," she said.

I moved closer. "I answered one. You insulted me."

"Don't take a step forward," she shouted.

"Why not," I said.

"I will damage that precious pregnancy of yours."

"You will have to kill me afterward," I said. "Because if there is a heartbeat left in me, I will kill you."

It was a gamble. She was a bully, nothing more.

She was waving her arm in the air, breathing heavily. I heard women mumbling. Mother of Prisons. Wouldn't she ever stop?

"What have I done to you?" I asked.

"You talk too much," she said. "You should have shut up. You should have shut up, in the first place. Only a court can

267

decide. You think this is a joke?" Her voice broke. "All these years I've been in here. The one thought that stopped me from becoming like these crazies, is that nothing, nothing, can be done for me."

She began to cry. This time she sounded genuine.

"This is the kind of hope you have?" I asked.

I looked around. A few of the women were sitting up. They thought we were about to fight. I heard some more grumbling. Mother of Prisons, she was always fighting, and she had no strength, only for talking.

But how could I have answered her question honestly? A government dedicated to eradicating opposition. A country without a constitution. A judicial system choking, even over commercial matters. Sluggish, sluggish as an old man's bowels.

"I'm sorry, " I said. "I should have been quiet."

"I have no quarrel with you," she said.

I took her arm. Her skin felt damp.

"S'all right!" she said.

We lay on the floor. Grace Ameh by my side, Mother of Prisons next to her. She said she was not sleeping next to any stinking people, and there were many in this cell. Someone protested. "Sharrap," she said. "Watch your step, butter-eater," she said to me, as we found places to lie. "Easy, easy now. We don't want any accidents. Don't worry, I will take care of you."

There was not enough space for us, unless our legs and arms touched. My eyes were wide open. I listened for every creak outside. Soon, someone would come in to free us. They would open the door and let us out.

No one came. I remembered the last time I was in a police station. It was during my national service year, when I worked for my father. A client called. Could he send one of his "boys" over to Awolowo Road station? One of his expatriate tenants was there with a hawker he'd caught trespassing.

I went with Dagogo, only for the drama. We arrived to find an Englishman drenched in his gray lightweight suit: Mr. Forest. His hair was wet with sweat and his nostrils flared. He reminded me of every impatient boss I'd worked with in England—I made a suggestion and they ignored it. I made a mistake and they told everyone. I cracked a joke, and they asked, "What on earth are you talking about?"

It was hard not to feel vengeful.

"D-dagoggle?" Mr. Forest asked, for confirmation, and Dagogo answered to the name. It turned out that the hawker had been trespassing on Mr. Forest's lawn, to see her cousin who lived in the servants' quarters in the house behind his. He had warned her, but she wouldn't stop. Every time he looked out of his window, there she was, trespassing again. I studied the police officer on duty, a rotund man with perfectly white teeth. He listened with a grave expression. I suspected he was daydreaming. Dagogo meanwhile questioned the woman. Why did she trespass? Didn't she know it was wrong to trespass? The woman, a popcorn and groundnut seller, looked as if she couldn't understand what was happening. I knew she would do it again and still look just as confused. We advised Mr. Forest to let her go, he'd scared her enough. "She's really, really sorry, Mr. Frosty," I said.

My legs began to itch from mosquito bites. The cement floor pressed into my shoulder. My stomach groaned. I was hungry; hungry enough to forget the nausea that seized me when I first entered the cell. I pulled dry skin from my lips and swallowed it until I tasted blood. My lips stung. I turned to relieve my shoulder.

"Can't you sleep?" Mother of Prisons asked.

"No," I said.

"Me too," she said.

The others were asleep. There was some snoring and two women were coughing incessantly. The rhythm was disturbing. Grace Ameh was awake, though she wasn't talking. She had confessed that this was her worst nightmare, to be locked up, and I was sure she could not hear our whispers.

Mother of Prisons said, "I can never sleep at night, only during the day. By evening, I'm fired up."

How long could people stay in a place like this before they broke down. One week? I thought. Two? How long before their minds broke down irreversibly? I felt the need to tell her.

"My father is in prison," I said.

"Eh?"

"My father is in prison."

"What did he do?"

"Nothing, nothing. Like you."

"Where is he? Kalakuta or Kirikiri maximum security?"

"No one knows."

He was a political prisoner, I explained. The new government was detaining people under a state security decree. I explained it to her in simple terms, wondering why I felt the need to treat her like a child. She would know that a man like my father would never be in prison unless he was a political prisoner.

"I know nothing of our government," she said. "Or our president, or any African leaders for that matter. I don't care to know. They are the same. Short, fat, ugly. Not one ounce of sense in their heads. How long has your father been in detention?"

"Over a month," I said.

"He's done well," she said.

There was a loud snore. She sucked her teeth.

"Who was that? These women, worse than any drunken husband... "

"You must miss your husband," I said.

"No," she said. "Focking ass couldn't keep a job."

"But you… "

"But me no buts. My whole life was ruined by one but."

I smiled. "But you married him."

"Doesn't mean. You're a woman, aren't you? We marry anybody for marry sake, love anyone for love sake and once we love them, we forsake ourselves. Make the best of it, till they die or till we do. Look at me. Everything, everything, in that house I bought, and I was sending money to my parents in the village, sending money to his parents."

"You must have had a good job."

"A shipping company. Paspidospulus, or however they pronounce his name, these Greeks. You know white people, they pay well, unlike our people."

"He treated you well?"

"Paspidospulus? The kindest man ever. He gave me his wife's old clothes to maintain a professional appearance, though her trousers never fitted my ass."

"Goodness."

"Then like a fool I was telling everyone that it was my husband who was providing, you know, to boost him up. Then he started telling everybody that, yes, he was taking care of the family, he was providing. Providing what? Five hundred extra mouths to feed? Ate like a focking elephant, that man. Greediness killed him, not me."

She began to laugh, and her laughter turned to grunts as she spoke.

"It's my children I miss. Not him. You eat like that, you bear the consequences, God rest his soul. He ate my food store empty. Buy a week's beans and he demolishes it. *Pfff!* A month's meat… "

"Please," I said, waving an arm. Her grunts were funny and my head was light from hunger.

"Gone in a day," she said. "Can eat fried ants if you put

271

them on his plate. He won't know the difference. Paspidospulus couldn't have paid me enough… "

I felt laughter in my belly, and a sweet pain lower down. My bladder was full.

She kept on grunting. "Paspidospulus couldn't have paid me enough. I'm telling you, tomato. Tomato, I tell you. This was when tomato was becoming expensive. The focking ass… "

"Please," I said. "Stop, otherwise I will have to go."

"Huh?" she said. "Go where? Who released you yet?"

"To toilet."

"Piss in the bucket," she said. "What do you think?"

I could not let her down. She was enjoying our friendship, and I thought she might begin her tirade again. The bucket was available, she said. For whatever business I had to do. We were all women in this place. There was no reason to be proud. Worse things were happening here, worse than I could imagine. One woman was rotting away. Couldn't I smell it?

"What?" I asked.

"Her cancer," she said. "It's terminal."

I had not taken a step before the familiar wave forced me over again. The back of my neck tightened, bile rose from my stomach and singed my throat. I'd gotten up too fast.

"What's going on?" Mother of Prisons asked.

My mouth opened again, involuntarily. I crouched between two bodies, held my sides.

"Are you all right?" Grace Ameh asked, sitting up.

"She's miscarrying," Mother of Prisons said. "Help her."

The bile tasted bitter on my tongue. Nothing else came out. I was trying to say I was fine. The women rose in varying stages of alertness. They circled me, the sick and the mad with their sores and ringworm and tuberculosis. Their body heat enveloped me. I stretched one arm out, to prevent them from falling over me. I took shorter breaths, shut my eyes.

"Let her breathe. Let her breathe," Grace Ameh was saying.

They kept on pushing.

"She's miscarrying," Mother of Prisons said.

Do-Re-Mi began to talk to herself again. "La So Fa Mi. Ti Ti Re Mi…"

A whiny voice recited a psalm. *"He that dwelleth in the secret place of the most High shall abide under the shadow of the almigh-tee…"*

"Please, please let her breathe," Grace Ameh said above the noise. She sounded anxious. I was all right, I wanted to tell her.

"He shall deliver thee from the snare of the fowler, the noisome pestiii-lence…"

There were hands on my head. Someone kicked my back. I curled up.

"Thou shalt not be afraid of the terror by night. Nor for the arrow that flieth by day. Nor for the pestilence that walketh in darkness. Nor for the destruction that wasteth at noonday…"

They would suffocate me, I thought.

"A thousand shall fall at thy side. Ten thousand at thy right hand…"

There was loud banging on the door and shouting from outside.

"What is happening in there? What is happening?"

"Thine eyes shalt thou behold and see the reward of the wicked…"

The cell door creaked open. Light shone on our faces. The noise died to a few mumbles. The psalm stopped.

A stocky warder appeared. She was the one who had led us in. She spoke in a resigned voice. "Mother of Prisons, are you making trouble again?"

As the women dispersed, I finally saw her face, Mother of Prisons. Her hair was in patches. Sores had eaten into the corners of her mouth. She was shaking like an old woman. She was about my age.

"Trouble?" she said. "Which trouble? You see me making trouble here?"

The light made me squint.

"What are you doing with the new prisoners?" the warder asked.

"Me? It's you. You should be ashamed of yourself, locking up a pregnant woman. If she had miscarried, the blood of her child would be on your head. Right there on your head. It was I who looked after her. I alone. If not for the kindness in my heart, it would have been another k-legged story in this place."

She waddled back to her spot scratching her armpits. The others lay down. They looked like twisted tree branches. The warder walked between them.

"How is our sick prisoner today?"

"What do you think?" Mother of Prisons answered. "Why haven't her people come for her?"

"They say they can't afford the treatment."

"Take her to hospital. She hasn't opened her eyes for days."

The warder sighed. "Give her pain-killers."

"She won't take them."

"Crush them with your teeth and feed them to her. You did it before."

Mother of Prisons raised her fists. "Are you listening to me? I say she's nearly dead. How will she swallow? The whole womb is rotten now. We are choking on her smell."

The warder was silent for a moment.

"I've done my best," she said.

"Not enough," Mother of Prisons said.

The warder pointed to me and Grace Ameh. "You, you," she said, in a resigned voice. "Follow me."

I was prodding myself to check for wetness between my legs. I rose with my back bent over and breathed steadily to keep my nausea down.

"Better get a doctor inside here," Mother of Prisons said, as we walked out. "Before we have another wrongful death in this stinking place! If you think I will ever stop talking, you must be focking joking!"

The warder asked us to hurry back to the hall, "should-in case" armed robbers stole our cars, "plus-including" the men, we were free to go. She released us, no explanations given. She warned Grace Ameh not to participate in further political activities.

Grace Ameh's husband was waiting for us outside. We drove back to the hall and I occasionally caught his scowl in the rearview mirror. I did not know who he was angry with: me, his wife, or the people who had detained us. I did not care to know. I only wanted to get back home. I breathed in fresh air through the back window.

"I'm sorry I involved you in this," Grace Ameh said before we parted. "I suspected they were watching me but I didn't think they would go this far. Go home and stay home." She patted my shoulder and I had a feeling she'd left some-thing of herself on me.

I arrived home at four in the morning. Niyi was waiting for me in the living room. He got up as I walked through the front door.

"What happened? I've been waiting five hours now. I thought you were dead."

I began to undress. My clothes fell to the floor as I told him.

"I can't believe this," he said.

"I swear."

"We were living normally, in this house, a few weeks ago. They were making political speeches. Why didn't you leave?"

I was in my underwear, surprised that this was what he couldn't believe. I mumbled, "One person. One person said something."

"What if they beat you up inside there?"

"They didn't."

"What if, I said."

"They didn't."

He raised his arms. "Come on. Wasn't it enough to be in prison?"

"I didn't ask them to arrest me."

"You're not hearing me. It's not just about you anymore."

"It's me they arrested. You weren't there."

"I'm talking about the baby."

I couldn't tell if he was holding back from slapping or hugging me.

"I'm sorry," I said.

"How are you?" he asked.

"Fine," I said.

"I don't know what else to tell you. I don't know what else to say. Your life means nothing to them. Can't you see? What will I tell people if something happens to you?"

"Please," I said. "Don't tell anyone."

He brushed past me to lock the front door. "You're confused, o-girl. It's not them I care about. It's you. You, and you're the one opening your mouth, not me."

I went upstairs to have a bath, then I lay on my bed in the spare room. I begged my child for a second chance. I could still smell the prison on me.

Niyi would never tell anyone about my arrest, and I would not tell anyone. I would take my time in prison and put it away. Do-Re-Mi, Mother of Prisons, Born Again, Holy Ghost, the woman with the rotting womb. Gone. Niyi went to the police station the next morning. They told him my arrest was an unfortunate incident. Two weeks later when I read in the papers that the hall had been fire-bombed and some of Sheri's customers complained because they would have to change venues for their wedding receptions, I said nothing. I didn't blame the police; I blamed myself for putting my child at risk for another miscarriage. No, they shouldn't have arrested me, and yes, people should be allowed to say what they want. But it was one thing to face an African community and tell them how to treat a woman like a person. It was entirely another to face an African dictatorship and tell them how to treat people like citizens.

I wasn't inviting trouble, that evening. Niyi knew, Grace Ameh knew, which was why she spoke to me with the sincerity of a mother telling her war-bound son, "Make sure you come back alive."

The day after my release, I saw my doctor for an unscheduled check-up, then I closed the office for a week after he cleared me. I went back to work the following week only because I knew my father's staff would have to earn their livings, even for as little as two hours a day, and also because I realized that wherever I was in Lagos, I was no longer safe. Like a joke, like a joke.

If February seemed long that year, March was beginning to feel longer. At work, jobs dried up as my father's clients shied from dealing with me; at home, Niyi's silence continued. I shuttled between the two locations feeling anesthetized. Only on occasion would I feel breathless for my father's safety and I would immediately fight the feeling down. I dared not think otherwise. Each moment carried me to the next and I no longer imagined prison cells because I'd seen the inside of one. I also promised myself that I would no longer speak for women in my country, because, quite simply, I didn't know them all.

One morning, I came in determined to tidy my father's drawers. His letters were in no order, and I was sure he kept them separate so his staff could not gain access to them. I sorted the bank letters first, then the letters from his accountants. The folder where I found salary details needed tidying, so I flicked

277

through. I discovered my parents' divorce papers: *"Take notice that a petition has been presented to the above court by Victoria Arinola Taiwo instituting proceedings for a decree of dissolution of marriage and also seeking orders with respect to the custody of the one child... "*

My mother had given her reasons for falling out with my father: a neglectful and uncaring attitude; withheld house-keeping allowance; on several occasions did not return home and gave no reasonable answer as to his whereabouts; influenced her child to disregard her; disrespected her church family; made wicked and false allegations about her sanity; colluded with family members to alienate her; caused her much embarrass-ment and unhappiness. There was something about a car. I could not read on.

Peace came in.

"Someone to see you," she said.

"Who?" I asked.

"Your brother," she said.

I refused to allow my heart to jump. I had not done anything wrong. "Please tell him to come in," I said.

My brother looked like my father, although he was taller. He had big eyes and that wasn't from my father. He was wearing blue khaki trousers and a striped yellow shirt.

"Debayo," I said.

"Yes," he said.

He had a widow's peak. That was my father's.

"Uncle Fatai called me," he said. "I've been meaning to come."

I watched every move he made. He frowned at a spot on my father's desk, rubbed his thumb over the top of his lip. I held on to my pen with both hands. He did not know if he should come, but his mother would not forgive him if he didn't.

Outside the sound of sirens deafened us temporarily. It could have been a government official passing, a security van escorting money from the Central Bank, or a Black Maria van carrying prisoners.

"What kind of doctor are you?" I asked.

"Pathologist," he said.

"Eh? Why?"

"It's not so bad," he said.

"A doctor of dead bodies."

"I wanted to study law," he said.

"Why didn't you?"

"Two of us, in here. It would have been difficult."

He was smiling. Where he found the grace, I could not imagine.

"You have a right," I said.

He shrugged. "I'm over that now, wanting to work for Sunny. I had people pushing me in that direction. The way I see it, Sunny decided for me."

He called our father Sunny. He was not as cordial as he appeared.

"Debayo," I said. "I'm sorry, I don't know where he is, and the little I know, I don't know if it will put your mind at rest."

"What do you know?"

I told him. He gave me a telephone number and asked me to contact him if I heard anything else. He was visiting Uncle Fatai later that evening. He didn't seem worried and spoke as if he was relieved to have fulfilled his obligation to his mother. I walked with him to his car and we stood facing the road. His ears stuck out a little, and that was from my father. I shielded my eyes from the sun.

"Where are you staying?"

"Cousins," he said, and then he added. "My cousins."

"How is your mother taking the news?"

"My mother? They are not together anymore."

"No?"

279

"For many years now."

"I didn't know."

He turned to me. "You must know I'm the youngest in my family."

"I didn't."

"That I have three older sisters?"

"No."

"He didn't tell you anything about me?"

"A little. Did he tell you anything about me?"

"No," he said.

"You never even stayed with him?"

He smiled. "Once. Only once, one summer, when my mother caught me smoking, and it was lecture, lecture, lecture..."

"What were you smoking?"

"Cigarettes."

"Why didn't you tell him to leave you alone?"

"Him?" he said. "I was scared of him."

"You were?"

"Weren't you?"

"No," I said. "Not really."

He rubbed his thumb over his upper lip again. He was double-jointed. His fingernails were square and they reached his finger tips. That was my father.

It could have been different for a son. Debayo had not offered his help in any way, I thought, and I wouldn't either if I were him.

"You must be the only doctor left in Lagos," I said.

"No," he said, taking me literally. "We're many. Some of us don't want to go, even though the temptation is there. We keep hearing about those abroad, doing well, especially in America."

"Why do you stay?"

"Steady work."

"For goodness' sake," I said.

I sensed that he had delivered that line many times before, and I sensed he was enjoying my disapproval. My brother knew everyone in the office. He gave Dagogo and Alabi that manly handshake, before he left. *"Man mi,"* they called him. When I returned to the office I asked Alabi, "You know my brother this well?"

Alabi nodded. "He's our paddy."

"Our paddy-man," Dagogo said.

"I'm not your paddy-man?" I asked.

They laughed.

"Face like stone," Dagogo said.

"Worse than BS," Alabi said.

I recognized my father's initials. Bandele Sunday. In his office, I resumed my task. Some school bills caught my eye. They were not from schools I'd attended. I flicked through. There were school reports, letters from a principal. I read them. They were my brother's. He was an above-average student, played field hockey. He was good at math. Once he was in trouble for playing truant. My brother. It was a start.

My mother's first thought was that he had come to do me harm. "What's he coming for?" she asked. "Suddenly he wants to see you? Don't take anything from him, you hear me? Whatever he gives you, straight into the bin. It's all well and good. If he wants to find out about his father, let him go to Uncle Fatai and find out what he needs to know there."

I was sitting next to her at her dining table. She slumped over it.

"No water no light," she said. "Now this. Ah, I'm tired."

"At least Sumbo is here to help," I said.

"Sumbo?" she said. "She's gone."

"Where?"

"She ran away. Two weeks, now."

"Back to her parents?"

"Those parents who sent her away in the first place? Who knows? I had to send word to them that she's disappeared. I woke up one morning and she wasn't there. I went everywhere searching for her. I even went to the police for that girl. Not a thing. These people, it's always something or the other with them. "

It was easy to distract her. My mother had bought a few baby rompers. She spread them on her dining table and held a yellow one up.

"I'll get some more," she promised.

"I've never seen you like this before, " I said. "Don't finish your money."

"Why not?" she said. "I spent money on my church and what thanks did I get? For the first time in how many years last month my tithes were low. They were complaining. I told them I had other obligations. They said I must put God first. I told them I am putting God first. He gave me a grandchild, and I must thank Him by preparing."

I smiled. "Why do you stay in that church?"

She raised her hand. "I didn't ask for your opinion."

I raised my hand, too, in surrender. I was tearful. The rompers, the light in my mother's eyes. I worried about her as if she were a teetotaler with a glass of wine in her hand. It would have to be good this time. If not for me, for her.

As we talked and folded the rompers, my mother told me the story of a faith healing gone wrong. A man in her church, deaf from birth, claimed he could hear after going through cleansing. My mother spoke to the man afterward to congratulate him. "Couldn't hear one word," she said. "And I've asked Reverend Father before, 'You say that only those who love God will be healed from cleansing. Shouldn't a person who loves God be eager to die as quickly as possible in order to be with Him? Why would they want healing?' He couldn't give me a straight answer to that. 'As for me,' I told him, 'when my God calls, I'm ready to go.'"

My mother's analysis surprised me. No one satirized the people in her church as she did. Half of them were sinners, she said, and fault-finders, and they gave cheap gifts at Christmas. I couldn't fold from laughing. She was a total gossip. She asked me to return an aluminum bowl to her new tenant, Mrs. Williams, so that I could meet her. Mrs. Williams was a divorced woman who worked for a large fishing company. "She is high, high up in the company," my mother confided. "They say her husband drove her out because she was always going out: parties, Lioness meetings, this and that. You should see her, pretty thing and slim. Now they say she's found herself a boyfriend."

"That's good," I said, wiping tears from my eyes.

"Quick-quick, like that? It's not good."

"You should try it yourself."

She eyed me. "Don't be rude."

"Why not? It will keep you looking fresh. Just make sure he's young and... "

"Will you stop?"

Fresh, fresh, I kept saying to tease her. She eventually smacked my arm.

"Leave this house, Enitan."

As I walked to Mrs. Williams's house, I was thinking that I was due for another sex talk and this time I would be just as shy. At what age was a woman content to be celibate? No one ever said. If they caressed themselves, the pleasure they got, they would never say. The thought made me wince. I was twenty when I first saw my father kiss a woman. He did it properly, the way they did in films. He circled her waist with one hand, bent his knees, straightened up. I covered my eyes with my hands and screamed silently. Then I avoided him for the rest of the day, in case I smelled perfume on him or something. I had never seen my mother kiss a man; not even my father.

"You must be Enitan," Mrs. Williams said, unlocking her gate.

Her hair was weaved in intricate patterns that ended in a miniature crown of plaits on top of her head. She was wearing one of those up-and-downs, which dipped in at the waist and flared like a tutu. It made her look as slight as a teenager, but I was certain she was in her late forties. Her eyes were that composed.

"You're so pretty," I said.

"You," she said.

Her gate opened.

"I've heard a lot about you," she said.

"Good or bad?" I asked, walking in.

"Your mother and I are friends," she said, knowingly.

"She says thank you for the fish."

I placed the bowl over my stomach like a tortoise shell. She glanced at it.

"Would you like some? Come in and get some."

We walked to the back door that led into her kitchen.

"I'm with Universal Fisheries," she explained. "I'm sure your mother told you. They give us senior officers frozen fish every holiday. But we've had light on and off for two days now and it will spoil if I don't give it away." She kicked a toy car by the kitchen door. "Watch out for that. I keep telling my children to put their toys away before they go out."

"They are not in?"

"They're with their father."

There was a collapsible iron table in Mrs. Williams' kitchen that took up most of the space. Behind it was a large freezer like mine. She removed a slab of frozen fish.

"See?" she said. "Melting already."

I stood back as she wrapped the slab in several sheets of newspaper and placed it in the bowl.

"Here," she said, handing it to me.

It was heavier than expected.

"This is your first?" she asked.

"Yes!"

"You should put that down," she said. "The fish. You should put it down if you're not ready to leave."

I placed it on the table next to her. "I saw your children. Your little girl, Shalewa, told me off for not calling her by her name. I think she was upset the boys were not playing with her."

"Don't be fooled. She bullies her brothers. The minute they touch her, she's going to tell her father. Even me she reports."

"She's so cute. Forgive her."

"Her? It's not her I have to forgive. But, you know, the day you've had enough, your legs just carry you... "

She was explaining her own circumstance, but I didn't mind listening. It was good to be reminded that everyone, smiling or not, had overcome adversity.

"I'm sorry to hear about your father," she said. "I hear you're the one running his practice."

"Yes."

"That must be hard."

"I try."

"It's all you can do," she said. "In this place. Look around you. Not one of us asked to be in the situation we're in. My children, they keep complaining, oh they want to go to their father's house, oh they want to play video games and watch cable. I told them, 'The children without video games and cable, you think they're from a different planet?' Before we moved here, they were always indoors, staring at a screen from morning till night. Now they're outside playing. They're getting fresh air."

"They won't want to hear that."

"I know, but sometimes I think the sooner they learn the better. The disappointment is less. There are no more ivory towers in Lagos. The waves just keep coming one after the other. When they do, you raise your head higher. If you don't, then what? I was used to my comforts. I'm used to being without them now."

I smiled. Yes, we were the city of broken survivors, children included.

"Condition," she said.

"Hm?"

"Condition make back of crawfish bend," she said.

During the week the government announced they'd uncovered a coup plot. The details in the press were sketchy and the latest issue of the *Oracle* barely dedicated a column to the story. I wondered why. Then the rumors started coming in, this really wasn't a coup; this was an excuse to arrest more government opponents. A former military ruler and his deputy were detained. There would be more.

The government had warned the newspaper editors not to speculate about the coup. People began to joke in that senseless way that a beaten people might: "You're speculating? Why are you speculating? You've been warned not to speculate. I'm not speculating with you."

I buried my head in token stories and editorials meanwhile. A woman had been murdered by her house boy. He left her body indoors and used her car for taxi services. I couldn't get that image out of my mind. A cannibal was out on the loose, another story said. Was this a modern Dahmer-style murderer or a throwback to paganism, the editor speculated, since he could speculate on nothing else. Someone had accepted radioactive waste from overseas for a tidy sum and dumped it in his village. The villagers were placing their radios on trees, hoping that the radioactivity would recharge their batteries. More jokes about that.

I read the most disturbing stories to escape from my own life, and two visits surprised me at the office later that week. The first was from Uncle Fatai, who came in after lunch, just at the time I'd kicked my shoes off, because my feet were beginning to swell. When he walked in, I stood up. He waved me down and squeezed into the visitor's seat. For the first time, I noticed how much he wheezed as he talked.

"I'm traveling to London," he said. "For a check up."

"I hope... "

He waved. "Annual. It's nothing to worry about. Half my problems would go, if I wasn't so fat. Do you need anything?"

"No, thank you."

Nigerians still made pilgrimages to London like no man's business. Over there, only our money was welcome.

"Any developments about your father?" he asked.

"No."

Dimples appeared in his knuckles as he placed his palms together. "He will be out soon, Old Sunny... em, staff paid?"

"Yes," I said.

"That's very good," he said.

"What about his clients?"

"They don't call anymore."

"That is to be expected."

"Debayo came here, Uncle," I said.

I watched for a reaction. There was none.

"Yes," he said. "I saw him myself. And how is your husband?"

"He's fine," I said.

"Your mother too. I have not had time to visit."

"She's fine, thank you."

"That's good," he said.

Uncle Fatai was not used to extending more than the usual

287

courtesies to me. He ran out of questions and ended up asking after my mother again and again. When he finally heaved himself up, I could easily have rushed to his rescue the way he was tottering. He brought out a handkerchief and wiped his forehead.

"You know, em, you're not a child anymore, Enitan. Your father, he em, always felt bad about your brother... that he wasn't there when your mother took him to church like that."

"Yes," I said.

"Sunny always treasured you. He never stopped seeing you as a child. That was his mistake. But you know, an African man cannot die without leaving a son."

I could hear my colleagues talking behind the door. I wanted to say that I didn't know how to think like an African woman. I only knew how to think for myself.

"Yes, Uncle," I said.

"It is time you met your brother," he said. "I always told Sunny to bring you two together from the start, but Sunny makes his own mind up."

"Yes, Uncle."

"Take care of yourself."

"Safe journey, Uncle," I said.

The next visit was from Grace Ameh, who came first thing in the morning. She smiled as she did the day I met her and I was relieved to see her.

"You're out and about already?" I said, hugging her.

She was wearing a dress again. This one was pale yellow with a pleated skirt, and she carried her brown portfolio. She patted my back like a comrade.

"My dear, I can't let them stop me."

"I hope they're not still monitoring your movements."

"They must be tired of me. I've been up and down."

"Wicked people."

She placed his portfolio on the table. "I've been meaning to speak to you."

"Yes?"

"I was wondering if you would be interested in joining a campaign, for Peter Mukoro and our friends who have been detained, your father included. There will be more detainees, I'm sure, after this latest coup fiasco."

"Yes."

"A group of wives will spearhead this one. I think they feel left out of the wider campaign. They're looking for someone, anyone, who can be their spokesperson. I think you will be an ideal candidate."

"Me?"

"You're the most qualified. The other lady is a bank clerk and she works full-time, and she has three young children. Bear in mind we're in the early stages. We don't have many members. Ten at most."

"They want me?"

"I know you had reservations the first time we spoke, but that must have changed by now."

I remembered Niyi's warning. "Yes, I want my father out of detention."

"You may need to do more than want now. If they're conjuring up coups, they can conjure up coup plotters."

"My father?"

"Any of the detainees. I've always said, men fight for land, and women fight for family."

I was unable to agree, but she was in journalist mode again, stirring me in a pro-democracy direction.

"I don't know," I said. "But let me be honest. I know your magazine's agenda, I read it regularly and I will not campaign for deposed politicians, if that is what you're really asking."

Her eyes flickered with impatience.

"I'm sorry," I said. "They don't care about democracy. They never have, only about power. My memory of them, throwing cash to villagers, rigging elections, setting opposition groups on fire, making themselves richer... "

"The military enrich themselves. They've always done."

"We didn't vote for them, but politicians, we do. The last elections, I voted only because there was an election. No other reason."

"Our elections were the fairest they've ever been. And no one is campaigning for politicians. It's the process we're interested in. Let the process begin. Good will will take care of itself."

"What happens if there's another coup? There's nothing to stop the army from coming in again."

She knew the facts better than I did. Coup after coup after coup, especially on the west coast of Africa. 1963, Slyvanus Olympio of Togo, killed. 1966, Tafawa Balewa, our first Prime Minister, killed. The same year, Kwame Nkrumah of Ghana. After that, it was non-stop. No one in the world recognized that African soldiers had fought against Hitler, but almost everyone was aware they spent time deposing their own rulers, heading civil wars from Somalia to Liberia, fueling civil unrest from Algeria to Angola.

She asked, "You're suggesting we never seek democratic rule because of the threat of military coups?"

"I'm saying we may never have a democratic government if we have an army."

"Every country needs an army, to protect its people."

"Evidently, in Africa we need armies to kill our people."

She smiled. "Your views are impractical. Politicians with pure intentions and a country with no army. *Na wa*, I hope you're never thinking of running for office."

"No."

"So, will you settle for our small campaign, instead?"

This time I was thinking of my time in prison.

"I have a child to think about in a few months," I said.

"I wouldn't put you in a compromising situation."

"Tell me. What situation are you putting me in?"

"Let me see, a group of wives, coming together once a month, in someone's house, doing what women do best. Gossiping." She winked.

"I've never passed up the opportunity to gossip."

She smiled.

"Please," I said. "Give me time."

"Of course," she said.

They, too, would need time, she said, to raise funds. Their aim was to increase local awareness about detentions. The wives felt that only important people were being spotlighted. Grace agreed. "Not all detainees are equal."

She would be out of Lagos, meanwhile, covering a story in the Delta. There had been more detentions following protests against oil companies. "Peter Mukoro is from those parts," she explained. "It was his story to tell. He's the son of an Urhobo farmer."

"Wasn't he in a family dispute over the farm?"

"No, his dispute was with an oil company. They destroyed his father's land. The irony of it is that Peter Mukoro was offered a scholarship by the same company. He rejected it and became a journalist."

"I didn't know."

"Not many people do. He's a true son of the soil."

"They say it's a wasteland in the Delta."

"You should see," she said. "Oil spills, barren farmland, villages burned down. They don't pray for rain anymore. When it rains, it shrivels their plants."

"Oil."

"It's always been about the oil. The control of it. They tell us we can't get along, ethnic tensions, Africans not ready for democratic rule. We know exactly where we want to go in this country. A few greedy people won't let us get there."

I thought about Niyi again. "My husband says he can name five men in our country who can pay off our national debt, and a hundred companies overseas who earn a higher turnover than our oil revenues. I think that it will be better when the oil finally dries up. Maybe then we can have leaders who will get on with the business of running this country."

"Maybe. But meanwhile their greed is our problem. Here and in the rest of Africa."

Drought, famine, and disease. There was no greater disaster on our continent than the few who had control over our resources: oil, diamonds, human beings. They would sell anything and anyone to buyers overseas.

Grace Ameh reached for her portfolio.

"You have to go?" I asked.

"Yes," she said. "To be honest, I don't know how much longer we can continue. We hold editorial meetings in churches and mosques these days. The government has warned us not to speculate about the coup. You've heard?"

"I don't speculate."

"They will arrest anyone who does."

"What keeps you going?" I asked, escorting her to the door. "You have a family to think of, and yet you risk your life to tell a story."

She smiled. "Because they detain us and fire bomb our offices? You can't kill a testimony of a country and of a people. That's what we're fighting for, a chance to be heard. And the second thing is, I love my country. "

Did I? I believed I could live nowhere else. I hoped to be buried nowhere else. Was that enough to say that I loved my country? I barely knew the place. We had thirty-six geographical states, from the triad of North, West, East regions the British created before I was born. My father was from a town in the middle belt of Nigeria; my mother, from the West. They lived in Lagos. I was born here, raised here. Privilege never did blind my eyes, but there were parts of the city I'd never visited, parts I never needed to. Most of my country I had not seen, not even the Delta Grace Ameh spoke of. I only spoke one of our languages, Yoruba.

There were times I'd felt my hand leprous, bringing out my Nigerian passport, in case an immigration officer mistook me for one of those drug smugglers who were giving us a bad name around the world; other times I'd felt happy to wave a flag for women in my country; African women. Black women. What was the country I loved? The country I would fight for? Should it have borders?

Walking to the window, I caught a glimpse of Grace Ameh leaving our premises. She stopped to buy sugar cane from one of the women who sat across the road. The woman had been there from morning, would probably be there all day. Her ware couldn't be worth more than twenty naira. The cheap pen in my hand was worth more. "People are hungry," people liked to say, especially when the political debate heated up, "People are starving *out there!*" I'd heard it said, with some pride, that we didn't have the same type of hunger as other African countries where people died because their bodies eventually rejected food. Hunger in my country always looked like a child with a swollen belly, and I strongly believed that no one, except those who were hungry, should speak of it. The rest of us, unless we were prepared to give up half our food, were only entitled to shut up. But this woman selling sugar cane, would she eat better on the promise of a vote? And if her children were hungry, could she tear up her ballot to slip into their mouths? I was almost certain she didn't vote, but the result of the general election was considered to be the will of the people. Some brave people caught bullets in their chests defending this will. I was not one of them. I stayed at home that day. The government had warned us not to participate in the protest, and our mothers reiterated the message at home. What freedom was worth dying for? Soweto, Tiananmen Square. Remember.

I was lying on my bed. One arm was over my belly, the other was behind my head. Through the mosquito netting across my bedroom window I could see a huge satellite dish perched on the house across the road. It was the sort of afternoon that made me want to rip my clothes off. We had no electricity.

I was thinking of campaigns, military decrees, consti-tutional rights. In a democratic system, with a constitution in place, a citizen could challenge injustices, even if the system itself was flawed. With the military in power, without a constitution, there was no other recourse besides protest, peaceful or violent. I was thinking of my country, which I'd done nothing for. If she were a Lagos woman, she would be laughing right in my face. "Did you give me food to eat? Did you put clothes on my back? No. So, clear out of my sight, with your miserable face."

Downstairs my mother-in-law chatted to Niyi about *frajon*, a dish prepared for Good Friday. "Enitan can't make *frajon*?" she was saying. "I'm surprised. It is so easy to make. All she needs to do is soak the beans overnight, boil them till they're soft, then grind them with a blender, then stir in coconut milk, boil it with nutmeg. But she must wrap the nutmeg in muslin cloth. Remember how your uncle broke his tooth? You don't want that to happen, eh? So. When the *frajon* is boiled, then she can make the fish stew. You have fish? Not too bony fish, and I prefer not to fry mine, but that is her choice. *Frajon* is easy to make. In my day it was real work. We used to have to grind the beans and coconuts on slates, sift it..."

I turned over, imagining they had wrapped me in white muslin cloth and dipped me in scalding *frajon*. When I died, I would be called to give account of my time here on earth. What a pity if I said I cooked and cleaned. What a pity, even, if I couldn't give account of a little sin.

I imagined I marched downstairs to where they sat, banged my fist on the kitchen table and yelled, "Get out of my house!" Filled my lungs so our president could hear it in his presidential palace: "Get out of my country!"

I got up and stripped naked. The mirror on the dressing table was short so I could see my torso only. I liked the swell of my stomach; the roundness, tautness, softness of my hips; stretched nipples, darkened. I had not been touched in four months.

"Enitan?"

My mother-in-law stood in the doorway. I hurried over to my bed to retrieve my clothes. I was tripping and huddling over.

"Sit," she finally said.

She patted the bed, and I sat next to her, disheveled. She spoke without mixing her words. "Niyi has told me everything. I don't want you two to fight anymore. It's enough now."

"Yes, ma," I said.

She took my hand.

"I was not born into this family. I married into it. It was not easy for me as a young bride. I'd just finished nursing when I met Niyi's father. He was a difficult man. Difficult. The Franco men are difficult. But you know, my dear, when two rams meet head on, nothing can happen until one backs down."

"I know, ma."

"So. What you did for your father, that was right. But you were wrong not to consult your husband first. He is the head of the house. He has a right to know. Now. What happened later, I think Niyi was wrong. To ignore your wife because she made a mistake like that. That was wrong, I told him, 'You cannot,

cannot treat your wife that way. Say your piece to her, as a man and let it go.'"

"Yes, ma."

"You yourself, you must learn that a woman makes sacrifices in life. It shouldn't take anything out of you to indulge your husband for the sake of peace in your house."

"Yes, ma."

"So, let this be the end of it. You hear me? I don't want to lose another daughter."

She hugged me and I held my breath. I did not want to be that close. She drained me the way soft-hearted people did. Somehow I ended up deferring to her, as if to do otherwise would be taking advantage of her. She was fasting for Lent, she said, for the new baby.

"Thank you, ma," I said.

Niyi and I escorted her to her car. After she drove out of our home, we faced each other in our small driveway. "I'm sorry," he said. "I couldn't let you take a risk like that. I prefer that you hate me."

He twisted his soles on the gravel and stood up with his hands in his pockets. Four months separated us as if I'd licked my forefinger and drawn an indelible line in the air. Where would I begin?

"I don't hate you," I said.

I dreamed that night, in the spare room, clear as a prophesy. I was holding a newborn baby. "He's dead," my mother was saying. I tried to console her, but the more I did, the more her sorrow. I realized the baby was mine. I woke up in such pain. I waddled into our bedroom and switched on the bedside lamp.

"What's wrong?' Niyi asked.

"The baby," I said. "It's kicking."

He patted my side of the bed and I slid in. I moved close to him, to calm my heartbeat. He placed his arm over my belly.

"What's going on in here?"

My eyes were wide. "Is it normal?"

He patted my belly. "Yes, it is. Whoever you are, let your mother rest."

On Good Friday I made *frajon* with my mother-in-law. She invited family members and I invited Sheri. Sheri and I sat at the kitchen table as Pierre washed dishes. Stacks of dirty plates surrounded him. We were surrounded by empty bottles of Star beer and Coca-Cola. We were tired. Sheri had brought her cousin's children, Wura and Sikiru. Sikiru, we banished to the living room. He sat there rocking himself in a persecuted manner. A more falling-down four-year-old I had not seen, with a head so long he could pass for Nefertiti. Outside, he'd collided with pots, grazed his knees, bumped his head on a washing line pole. "Sikiru! Sikiru!" we cried out every time we heard his yelps. After a while, we sounded like pigeons, or one of those old aunts we thought we'd never become. His sister, Wura, sat with us, a five-year-old with her hair pulled back like a rabbit's tail. She eyed my stomach until I got nervous and asked what she wanted.

"Coca-Cola," she said.

"I was not allowed to drink Coca-Cola at your age," I said.

"My mummy lets me. From when I had chicken pops."

"Chicken?"

"Yes. And my froat was paining me, that's why."

She held her neck.

"Throat," Sheri said.

"Troath," she said. "And my body was pops, pops, pops."

She pinched her forearm and wagged her forefinger. "But no scratching. No scratching, because that is the rules. And if you scratch, your pops will only grow bigger, like a balloon."

She stretched her arms wide and mistook my amazement for sympathy.

"It was terrible," she said, in a husky voice. "Now, can I have my Coca-Cola?"

I started breathing as if I'd gone into labor. When I served Wura *frajon*, it was, "Ee-yack, I don't like this Free John thing." "*Fray*-John," I corrected her. "Can I have fish?" she asked. I gave her some of the stew I made from Mrs. Williams's fish. "Ee-yack. Too much pepper in this fish," she said. "Aunty, do you have biscuits?"

I handed her a Coca-Cola. She drank it clean, burped, and went in search of her brother with caffeinated eyes. Dear Wura. "May I be askewed?" she asked. When I said yes, she said, "Fenks." I immediately forgave her.

"Are all children like this?" I asked Sheri.

"Be prepared," she said.

Pierre dropped cutlery in the sink. I placed my bowl aside. I had already had two helpings of *frajon* and some of her stewed crabs, so tasty I'd hidden them from everyone.

"I will be a terrible mother," I said.

Sheri stretched. "You're not looking forward to it?"

"I am. But I have not had time to think about it."

I did not feel comfortable discussing motherhood with her, but I was aware of a presence within me, as infinite as God. I did worry that I might spoil my child rotten.

"It's hard work," she said.

"I can see."

Niyi came through the door. "Pierre, water to drink. Quick."

He placed his hand on my shoulder and Sheri watched him the way she watched men, arching her brows and keeping her eyes on his midriff. Niyi rubbed my shoulder and left.

"Is he talking to you now?" Sheri asked.

"He is."

"You're not still angry with him."

"I need time."

Time really wasn't enough, I thought. Forgetting would be enough.

Sheri sat back in her chair. "It is good that you met your brother."

"I can get to like him."

"I hope so," she said.

"I don't have to like him, Sheri."

"I didn't say you did."

"But I know what you're thinking. In your family, everyone sticks together... "

"I never said we were perfect. We just happen to like each other, and thank God we do, because I don't know what would happen in the little village my father left."

"You're confessing something?"

"If they keep to one woman our lives would be simpler."

"Ah."

"But we, too, are just as guilty for what we do to each other. I've never met a man who had an affair with himself."

"No."

"So. The blame is on two sides then. I keep telling my sisters. Stop letting these boys treat you badly. They tell me, 'But we're not strong like you.' Strong. I don't even know what that word means. But look at the way we were raised, two women in one house, one man. Mama Kudi's turn to cook for Daddy. Mama Gani's turn to sleep with Daddy. A young girl shouldn't grow up seeing such things. But that is my family. I've accepted it."

We accepted the world we were born into, though we knew what felt right and wrong from the start. The protesting and detesting could come afterward with confirmation that our lives could have been better, but the acceptance was always there.

Pierre left the kitchen with a bottle of water and I dared to cross a line.

"Are you curious about your mother?"

"Hm." Her lips were thin.

"Enough to look for her?"

"Not like that."

"Why not?"

"What if she doesn't want to know me?"

"What if she's thinking what you're thinking?"

"I'm not ready. I'm not."

"I'll be behind you when you are."

I couldn't imagine being that estranged from my own mother. We listened to the Francos' chatter in the living room for a moment.

"Can you see yourself married?" I asked.

She shrugged. "If I meet someone with sense. But what I've seen so far: rich man wants to own your future, poor man wants to own your past. Some are just plain untidy, and you know me, I can't stand the mess. Some must have children, and, well... "

"Aren't you sometimes angry?"

"Why?"

"Looking back."

"I'm a today-tomorrow woman. I can't look back. I have my business, plenty of children around me. Someone will always chase me. I still have a pretty face. *Abi?*" She sucked her cheeks in. "It's other people who worry about me. Me, I have no worries, except when I die."

"Why then?"

"Because who will bury me?"

"I will," I said, poking my chest.

"What if you die before me?"

"Then my child will bury you," I said.

Sheri had two mothers. Why couldn't my child?

"What I really want," she said. "Really, really, *sha*, is to work for children. You know I practiced saying that for Miss World? I memorized a whole speech even, children are our future, all that. I didn't care about one word. I was annoyed the judges eliminated me before I had a chance to use it. Then one day I was thinking about the speech. Children beg on the streets here and people drive past them. Everyone is fed up. You open the papers and someone is asking for their child to get treatment abroad. Why not raise money for them? I started thinking... "

"About?"

"A charity. I'm good at asking for money, I know people and these photographers are always snapping me somewhere. Why not use them? The one thing that has stopped me is that I can't stand people knowing where I am and what I'm doing. But I think I can get used to that. It's a small price."

The work suited Sheri more than she thought. A charity. Her unfriendliness was an asset. People were intrigued by her. Those she approached would feel privileged. She would thrive.

"You have to do it," I said. "You will be so good and you'll be surprised how much you've missed being around. You're not a background person. What, you want to hide for the rest of your life because people talk? Let them talk. One day they will ask themselves what they're doing with their own lives. Any social event in this place, people will come whether or not they care about your cause. They will buy tickets, give money, so long as they're recognized. You have to do it, Sheri. If you had told me this before I would have sat on your back."

"I've been thinking seriously, end of this year hopefully. I need to find a name and trustees... "

"Put me. We will arrange the paper work for you at the office. You'll be the best charity in Lagos."

Her birth mother and motherhood taken away from her, and she wasn't thinking of tearing her clothes off and walking naked on the streets. She was stronger than any strong person I knew. The word strong usually meant that a person was being short-changed emotionally and physically and had to live with it. I had always been motivated by fear, of lowliness, of pessimism, of failure. I was not strong.

Sheri was planning to make the next pilgrimage to Mecca. I couldn't imagine her becoming an Alhaja. She would have to get a gold tooth, at least, to fit my image of a Lagos Alhaja. More guests arrived and she decided it was time for her to leave. I saw her to her car and when I returned to the kitchen, my mother-in-law was serving more *frajon* for them.

"I'll do that, ma," I said, reaching for the bowl.

"No no," she said. "You've done enough."

She tugged at the same time I did, and we found ourselves fighting over the bowl. I stood back as she bent over the pot. I thought she was searching for her life, the unborn child, who had given birth to everyone but herself. She too was strong; strong enough to live with a man who wouldn't even look at her when she spoke to him. She was a human shock-absorber.

Pierre walked in with more dirty plates and jiggled cutlery around in the sink.

I headed for the living room. Niyi was sitting on the floor by his Uncle Jacinto's feet. Uncle Jacinto was leaning over him, talking hush-hush as the Francos did. I imagined it was like sticking my nose into a petrol pump. Uncle Jacinto was a retired law professor and the reigning king of Latin phrases: *de jure, de facto, ex parte, ex post facto*. He enjoyed his spirits, though the word "drunk" had never been mentioned in relation to him.

Niyi nodded politely. If our friends were here, this was about the time he would be stirring up trouble, either on his own or in support of me, telling someone or the other I was the boss in the house. As soon as they left, it was Enitancanyou? With his family Enitancanyou began while they were around and I couldn't challenge him, because they would hate me for controlling him, he said. Watching him, I felt sorry. It was no lie, he was protecting me. I was protecting him too. I didn't want anyone to call him a weak man, even though I thought the sooner his family hated me the better. From then on I could do exactly as I pleased.

There were about twenty of them present and any family as large as that was bound to have the usual array of people: Uncle Funsho, who rubbed my bra straps whenever he hugged me; Aunty Doyin, the pretty one who locked herself in a room. She still wore wigs and pale pink lipstick of the early seventies. She wasn't so pretty anymore, because the man she had locked herself up for ended up punching her face whenever another man looked at her. There was Simi, her daughter, braids down to her butt, sassy as Brazilian Samba. Too cool to smile or be pleasant. What was it about this new generation? I loved their bad attitude. Simi walked around with a T-shirt and exposed her navel. After she pierced her nose the Francos said she would get pregnant, but she didn't. She was studying to be an accountant, though her university was closed after a student protest. There was Kola, her brother, who always looked weighed down because his family had called him a dullard for so long. "Won't learn a thing, keeps taking photographs and thinks that will suffice," they said. I knew he was dyslexic. And Rotimi his first cousin. Rotimi, whose voice was high. Niyi and his brothers tried to slap his manhood into his back, punch it into his skinny ribs. "Speak like a man! Speak like a man!" I warned them, "You'll kill this boy before he discovers his sexual preference." Now he had a girlfriend, and his voice was still high.

Gnarled and plump people, the Francos, I thought. The old and young. I could well be jealous of them. When did we ever have family in our home? My mother's family was her church. My father avoided his because they were always trying to extort money from him. "Big Foot," I said.

It was Niyi's youngest brother, the tallest and skinniest.

"Yep?" he answered.

"Gerrin here," I said.

He walked toward me looking like some sort of willow tree. Big Foot was my favorite—clumsy, and his feet were size fourteen.

"We need help in here," I said.

"Who needs help?"

"Your mother, who gave birth to you, needs help."

"Doing what?"

"Serving food."

He frowned. "I don't know how to do that."

"No one knows how to do that. They learn. So you better gerrin here or else those girls you keep bringing around here, trying to impress, I will start talking."

"You won't do that."

"Just ask your brother what a wicked woman I can be."

"You women's liberation-nalists," he mumbled.

He tackled his mother for the bowl. "Relax woman," he told her.

She sat by the kitchen table watching him. "Big Foot knows how to do this? Big Foot? You know how to do this? I thought you were useless, like the rest of my sons."

Big Foot spilled stew on his shirt and yelled.

That evening, I found a dress in my wardrobe. It was not one of mine. It was made from tie-dyed fabric and newly sewn. I thought I'd stumbled on infidelity.

"What is this?"

I held it up. Niyi was lying on our bed.

"I can't even have a girlfriend in this place," he muttered.

"Whose is it?"

"You were not supposed to see it. It's yours."

I lifted it. "Mine?"

"For Easter."

"You've never given me a present for Easter before. Who made it?"

I placed it against my body.

"Your seamstress," he said.

"You went to my seamstress?" I leaned forward. "You went to my seamstress?"

He nodded. "Now I know where our money goes. That woman has a bigger fan than ours in that shack of hers."

Niyi called me Jackie O. I ran to my seamstress more than any other woman he knew, for all my principles. Well, he was a big fat liar, but it was true that new clothes could make me salivate. I sniffed the dress. I could still smell the sweat of my seamstress' fingers on the cloth.

"Thank you," I said, using the dress as a shield.

"You too," he said. "You did a lot today."

"I know," I said.

I also clipped his toe nails before we slept. I always did because he wouldn't and he would end up scratching my legs. As I wrestled with three months' nail growth, I was finally able to tell him about meeting my brother.

"These men," he said. "I don't know how they do it. I didn't choose to have two families and most days I feel like half a man."

"Since when did you feel like half a man?"

"Watch what you're doing."

"What will I do with half a man? I want you to be double man. How many years now, and we've been fighting. I want you to be my greatest ally."

"I am."

"You're not."

"Here we go."

"Keep still," I said.

"Don't amputate my foot!"

He wasn't kicking me and I was cutting him up. We were

talking again.

"My love for you is much," he said. "You just don't know."

Baba came to collect his monthly salary the next day. He was still tending my father's garden on Sundays, and on Saturdays worked at a house nearby.

"Compliments of the season," I said. "How are you?"

I spoke to him in Yoruba, addressing him by the formal you, because he was an elder. He responded with the same formality because I was his employer. Yoruba is a language that doesn't recognize gender—he the same as she, him the same as her—but respect is always important. "We are fine," he said. "Hope all is well with you. Have you heard from your father?"

"No word yet."

"I will be there to work tomorrow."

"Please excuse me," I said.

He waited by the kitchen door as I went to get his money. When I returned, I felt a slight breeze through the mosquito netting. I handed the money to him.

"It's cold," I said.

"It's going to rain," he said.

"Rain? So early? The rain is strange these days."

"Yes," he said.

"You'd better not get caught in it," I said.

"I will hurry."

I rubbed my arms as goose bumps appeared. Walking upstairs, I imagined Baba trudging to the nearest bus stop in the rain. He had withered so much, it was hard to believe he was the same person who had chased me round the garden when I was small. I told Niyi I would give him a lift, then visit my mother. "She hasn't been well," I said.

"Again?" he said.

"It's not her fault," I said. "She prefers to be well."

306

He, who listened to his father's self-praise without yawning. I'd asked him to stop finding every excuse to leave home whenever my mother visited. Mostly, he said he had to go to the office. She worried that he was overworked.

I found Baba by the gates of our estate, and drove him to the nearest bus stop. We passed a marketplace. The sky had turned gray and the market women were clearing up in anticipation of the rain. They placed plastic sheets over their wooden stalls and secured them with rocks. Children scurried with full trays perched on their heads. Some were giddier than the wind with excitement. Their trays were colorful with tomatoes, cherry peppers, purple onions, okras, and bananas. A sign post on a shack caught my eye.

We specialies in
Gonerea
Sifilis
AID
Watery sperm

"I didn't know you lived on the mainland," I said.

"I moved," Baba explained. "Ten years now. I used to live in Maroko. They drove us away and flattened our homes. Your father let me stay in the quarters, until we found a new place."

"I didn't know."

"You were with your mother. They came to us that day with coffins, and told us that if we didn't leave, we would end up inside them."

When Baba said "they," he meant anyone in uniform: the army, the police, traffic conductors. He would have seen different rulers under the British, First and Second Republics, and military governments.

I slowed for a group of hawker women to cross the road.

"Did you vote at the elections?"

"Yes. They told me to put an "X," I put an "X." Now they're

307

telling me my "X" is nothing. I don't understand."

He said "hex" instead of "X."

"They're following their predecessors," I said.

"These ones?" he said. "They have surpassed their predecessors. For the first time, I'm looking at them, and saying, it is as if… "

Baba took time to finish his sentences. I waited until he was ready.

"It's as if they hate us," he said.

I dropped him at the bus stop. It began to rain as he boarded his bus. The rain coursed down on my windscreen; the wipers barely cleared my view. I drove slow and noticed the sign post on the shack again.

We specialies in
Gonerea
Sifilis
AID
Watery sperm

My face was wet and steamy. The gutter in front of my mother's house flowed like a muddy river. My mother didn't come to her door when I rang her bell, so I rushed to the back door to check if it was open. It was. I walked upstairs cleaning the rain from my arms, knocked on her bedroom door.

I smelled her death before I saw her.

"Mummy!" I screamed.

She was lying on the floor, before an empty candle holder. I reached for her shoulder and shook, bent to listen to her heart. There wasn't a sound. I ran out of her house and swallowed rain.

On the front porch of Mrs. Williams' house, Shalewa stuck her toe into a puddle. She took one look at me and froze.

I rattled the gate. "Shalewa, where is your mother?"

"Upstairs."

"Please. Open the gates."

Shalewa ran into the rain.

"Tell her it's Enitan from next door. Tell her I need to see her. Please."

She unlocked the gates and I followed her indoors.

Mrs. Williams didn't think it was wise to call an ambulance. "They may come, they may not come," she said as though discussing the month's profit margins. "We will have to carry her to hospital in my van. Shalewa?"

"Yes, Mummy."

"Get me my phone, my sweet."

"Yes, Mummy."

She'd been skirting around, trying to hear our whispers. As her mother made phone calls in the dining room, I sat in the living room with her. She moved a place mat around a side table, and sang a pop song; not one I recognized, "Treat me like a woman," occasionally peeping at me. She knew I'd been crying.

Mrs. Williams returned to the living room.

"I've found help," she said. "I'd better call the hospital now. You stay here and I will come for you when we're ready."

Who would carry my mother? I thought. Her arms, her legs. They would have to carry her with care, as if she were sleeping, as if she could wake.

Once her mother left, Shalewa resumed her game with the place mat. I wanted to tell her not to worry, but children knew when they were being lied to and she would think she was responsible for my sadness regardless. She continued her song. "Treat me like no other... "

Her mother returned.

"Shalewa," she said. "You want to go to Temisan's house?"

Shalewa nodded.

309

"That's my girl. Go upstairs and get your shoes. Her mummy is coming for you."

Shalewa ran upstairs, half-smiling. She tripped on a stair and exaggerated her limp.

"Will she be okay?" I asked.

Her mother nodded. "I'll explain to her later. We'd better go."

I noticed the mobile phone in her hand, but mine were shaking too hard to make a call. I asked her if she would.

On the way to the hospital, Mrs. Williams kept talking to herself, "I hope the police don't stop us. You know, these checkpoints... "

Her windscreen wipers hypnotized me. They tore the rain apart each time and I hugged myself, not because I was cold, but because my mother was lying in the back of her van, wrapped in white bed sheets. Above us the rain beat proverbs on the car roof:

Let our tears help us see clearer

He who denies his mother rest will not rest himself

Below us the rain beat the earth.

"I knew there was something," Mrs. Williams murmured. "There had to be something. The rain, pouring like this, coming so early."

My mother had been dead a day. Going through her medicines later, I discovered a batch which appeared to have been re-dated. I did not know where she'd purchased them, or how long they had expired. I imagined she'd bought them because they were cheaper.

Mrs. Williams washed her. The nurse's aide in the hospital would not.

"There are others," she said. "She will have to wait."

"But she's waited too long," Sheri said.

Sheri was anxious; Moslems buried within a day. The nurse's

310

aide shrugged. Her eyes were like a dead fish's, sunken and gray. Too much, they were saying. I've seen too much, can't you see? Whatever your story is. I don't care.

"Is there someone else?" Sheri asked.

"Only me," the aide said. "Only me is here."

Irritation crept into her voice. She was shifting, wanting to resume her task. Who were these people? Coming down to the mortuary, getting in her way?

Sheri turned to Mrs. Williams. "What will we do?"

I stood by the door with Niyi. I'd been waiting upstairs for three hours. Niyi arrived first and Sheri after him.

"I can wash her, " Mrs. Williams said to me.

I felt Niyi's hand. He led me into the corridor outside.

A week later we buried my mother, in Ikoyi cemetery next to an angel with broken wings. The cemetery was filled with decapitated statues. Thickets grew higher than the head stones. It was where my brother was buried, but the plots next to his had been filled. I paid the local council for a plot by the entrance. During the funeral the pallbearers we'd hired to carry her casket refused to carry it further until we'd paid their money.

"You will burn in Hell for this," our priest told them.

"Reverend Father," said the stocky man who'd snatched the money from Niyi. "Hell and Lagos? Which is worse?"

He squinted as he counted the notes. One of his mates yawned and scratched his crotch.

For two days after my mother's funeral, I stopped eating. On the third day Niyi accompanied me to my pre-natal check up and at the end of it, the doctor told us, "I don't like what I'm seeing. This baby isn't growing properly."

"Enitan hasn't been eating," Niyi said.

"Why not?" the doctor asked.

"She's lost her appetite," Niyi said.

"How can we get it back?" the doctor asked. "Can't her mother cook her something nice?"

He was an old man and tended to talk to people as he pleased. Normally I didn't mind because he was also one of the best ob-gyns in Lagos. Niyi began to explain but I tapped his arm. I could barely form the words because my mouth was dry.

"My mother is dead," I said.

We arrived home and Niyi headed straight for the kitchen to cook a meal. I was lying in bed when he brought it to me. Fried plantain. They were golden brown and cooked right through, unlike the charred, half-raw pieces I usually handed to him. He picked one up and carried it to my mouth. He pried my lips open with his forefinger and thumb. The plantain slithered into my mouth, warm and sweet. I shut my eyes as it clung to the roof of my mouth, pulled it down with my tongue and began to chew.

As a child, whenever I had malaria, I would have a bitter taste in my mouth, after my fever broke. I hated that bitter taste. It tainted everything that went into my mouth, but the bitterness meant that I was cured: no more bouts of nausea, no more pounding headaches. I did not like the taste of the plantain in my mouth, but I began to eat from then on.

My daughter Yimika was born on the morning of August 3. Between the time crickets sleep and roosters wake, I tell her. After my water broke, I begged to be gutted like a fish. Then I saw her. I burst into tears.

"She's beautiful," I said.

Like a pearl. I could have licked her. I had only one wish for her, that she would not be disinherited in her lifetime. I chose Sheri as her godmother. She would understand. Following Yoruba tradition, Yimika could have been called "Yetunde," "mother has returned" to salute my mother's passing, but I decided against it. Everyone must walk their own path unencumbered. Hers wouldn't be easy, born in a motherland that

312

treated her children like bastards, but it was hers. And I didn't worry that she wasn't born in a more fortunate place, like America, where people are so free they buy stars from the sky and name them after their children. If you own a star from the day you are born, what else is there to wish for?

My milk took me in a tackle, tugging on my shoulder, and tearing through my chest. I sat up in bed and unbuttoned my nightgown. Yimika's tiny mouth snatched my nipple and dragged. Bluish-white milk spurted from my free nipple. I covered it with a tissue from the box on my bedside table. The air-conditioner blasted cold air over my face; I lay back.

As my breast softened in her mouth, I eased it out and transferred her to the other. Yimika grabbed it with the same hungriness and I bit my lip to overcome the pain. Her palms traveled up my ribs. Her own ribs were separated from mine by her soft pink cotton romper. I wriggled her toes.

The night she was born, I was too tired to do anything but hold her. The day after, I was overwhelmed by visitors in my hospital room. The day after that, I braved my sutures and came home. "We won't need to press this one's head," my mother-in-law said. "It's round already."

She suggested that we wash her the traditional way, smothering her with shredded camwood and stretching her limbs. I refused and settled her in a crib by my bed; gave her a top and tail instead. Afterward, I checked her ears. They were as dark as my hands, which meant that she'd taken after me. I traced down her spine where Mongolian spots had left her skin black and blue. I dressed the mush on her navel, felt the pulse under her ribs. I imagined her heart pink and moist and throbbing. There was a tiny bald patch on her head, which worried me, though her doctor said it was nothing but a birth mark. I told him to be sure, because if anything happened to her,

313

my faculties would close down and there would be no begging me out of that state.

I remembered my mother. There were times I still felt tearful, and I found that if I placed Yimika against me, she soothed me. She was tiny, but as heavy as a paper weight on my chest. I stared at her face for hours. She had taken her father's eyes, shaped like two halves of the moon. I knew she would shine.

Niyi shuffled in wearing his pajamas. He was sleeping in the spare room because Yimika was keeping him up at night. He scratched his shoulder. "How are you feeling?"

"It hurts," I said. "My whole body hurts, like she's sucking out my marrow."

"Why are you smiling then?"

I'd heard that some women cried for days after childbirth, because their bodies were out of control. But I had not shed a tear. If women cried, perhaps it was because we were overwhelmed by the power granted to us.

Niyi sat on the bed and began to stroke Yimika's head.

"She's tiny," he said.

"Too small," I said, opening her fingers one by one.

"Fatten her up for her debut."

I pressed her closer. It was four days to her naming cere-mony. I touched his cheek. "I can't believe this is happening. We must make sure we behave ourselves from now on. We will be the best family."

For a while, he watched as if he were supervising.

"Is Sheri coming again?" he asked.

"Yes," I said.

"She's really helped."

"She's good with children."

"I feel so bad. The things I've said about her."

"Really?" I said.

He shook his head. "Nope."

He had to go to work. Sheri arrived when the hairdresser who had come to undo my braids was almost through with her task. She brought pounded yam and okra stew from her family's restaurant.

"Your hair has grown," she said.

The hairdresser pulled another braid and began to poke it loose with a comb. Her price had increased since the last time, but so had the price of food, she said. The veranda floor was littered with hair extensions. Yimika slept in a pram stationed next to Sheri. Sweat trickled down my back and I shook my gown down. I studied my reflection in the hand mirror and was surprised by how long my hair had grown, and by how much my face had changed. I had a shadow over my cheeks from where my skin had darkened.

The hairdresser loosened the last braid. I lifted my hand mirror to inspect her work.

"Oh-oh," I said.

Sheri edged forward. I lowered the mirror as she inspected my hair line.

"You have white hair," she confirmed.

"I'm only thirty-five."

"I've had mine since twenty-nine. Dye it."

"I won't dye it," I said. "Why should I?"

The hairdresser pulled my hair back. She hadn't said a word since she started her work, but it was obvious she was enjoying my discomfort.

I paid her and she left. Yimika cried in her pram and I hurried over to check her. She was still asleep, smiling too. I preferred to think she was having a good dream, but Sheri had told me that it was wind. There was sweat in her hair. I couldn't help but pick her up. Whenever she was sleeping, I missed her. Her arms flopped over my hands and her mouth opened.

"*Alaiye Baba*," I whispered. "Master of the earth."

She looked like one of those plump empresses who had slaves peeling grapes for them. I bent to kiss her. Her lashes unlocked.

"Our friend is awake," I said.

Sheri came over and eased her out of my arms. She made clucking sounds and began to rock her. We were standing by the bed of purple hearts and I surveyed them as though I'd just planted them. A red-head lizard slithered across the veranda floor. It slid between two pots of mother-in-law's tongue and disappeared into the garden.

"Congratulations, mummy."

I turned around to see who had said that. It was Grace Ameh.

From the moment she stepped into my home, her eyes were darting around. "I went to your office to look for you. Then they told me about your mother. My sincere condolences. I'm terribly, terribly sorry."

I felt shy now that she was on my turf. We were like strangers who'd been forced to use the same bathroom.

"I'm surprised you had time to find your way here," I said.

"We closed down last month. Our final issue."

"That's a shame," I said.

"Yes," she said, in her usual neutral manner. She down-played her struggles, so successfully one could almost believe she dismissed them.

"You must eat with us," I said.

It was a joy to watch her, the way she dipped and separated, and swallowed. She talked between gulps about journalists and activists who had been sentenced following the alleged coup in March. They were charged with being accessories after the fact of treason.

"It's a farce," she said.

I placed my fork down. "They say the Commonwealth ought to impose sanctions."

316

"Commonwealth," she huffed.

"Don't you think that will work?"

"Our problems are ours to solve, not anyone else's. I'm not one of those who believe in crying to the West. They still haven't got it right themselves. Freedom of speech, human rights, democracy. Democracy, some would say it's for sale. Besides, their leaders are constrained. They can't help us if helping us will hurt their constituents. We will always have to look within for our own solutions. I have faith in Africa, anyway. A continent that can produce a Mandela? I have faith."

Instead, she looked weary, and I did not entirely agree with her. Intellectuals like her resented foreign intervention. It was the same with the Nigerian elite and foreign aid, always complaining about how patronizing that was, when Nigerians who really needed help could not care less where it came from. Sheri was discovering just how hard it was to get money from wealthy Nigerians. They pledged their support to her charity and then they disappeared. I wasn't sure about the extent of foreign intervention in our local politics—CIA-backed coups and assassinations included—but was it too much to expect other countries to take an interest in our well being, if most of our stolen wealth was invested in their economies?

"Economic sanctions," Sheri said, "Let's be realistic. Who will they hurt—Brigadier Big Belly or Mama Market?"

"Exactly," Grace Ameh said.

"You know there are detainees who have nothing to do with politics," I said.

"I don't understand," she said.

"Half the people in prison," I explained.

"I know," she said. "Most of them are awaiting trial. Some of them die before they ever see a court room."

I thought I had badgered her enough.

"When do we start our campaign?" I asked.

"As soon as you're able."

My heart beat faster.

Grace Ameh stayed for a while after we finished eating. She wanted to avoid the lunchtime traffic. I cleared the table when she left as Sheri watched over Yimika.

"You never told me about this," she said.

"Ah, well," I said.

"What does Niyi think?"

I wiped the table using circular motions.

"He doesn't know."

"Will you tell him?"

"Today."

She laughed. "You're joining the ranks, *aburo*?"

I made my circles smaller and smaller.

"Small by small," I said.

I washed my hair and braided it into two, sat in a bowl of brine to heal my sutures. I had to shake my head to shift the fuzziness that plagued me since Yimika was born. By the time Niyi returned from work, I was ready.

I watched as he undressed in our bedroom. He hopped out of his trousers, placed them over a chair. As if he remembered I'd asked him not to, he took the trousers off the chair and laid them on the bed. The gesture made me sad. How caustic we were to each other, and we'd wasted time over what we didn't want, and what we didn't like. Was it simply that we knew not to ask for what we wouldn't receive? Our jokes saved our marriage, I realized. When we shared them we were within a safe zone. But we had no jokes to spare now, except the one about the man who had chosen the wrong women twice.

"Grace Ameh came here today," I said.

"Who?"

"Grace Ameh, the journalist from *Oracle* magazine."

"What did she want?"

"She wants me to chair a campaign for my father, Peter Mukoro, and others."

"What did you say?"

"It's a small one."

"What did you tell her?"

"I said that I will. That I want to. It's the chance I've been waiting for. I'm hoping we can meet once a month... " My voice trailed off.

He released his tie. "Not here I hope."

"We can meet at my mother's house. It doesn't really matter."

He walked toward the bed.

"We've talked about this already."

"No. We never talked. At least we never agreed. And nothing is safe around here, anyway. Robbers could break in as we speak. The police, the army, whether or not you are looking for trouble, they give it you. I've thought it through. We will appeal to the government. There are women and children involved. Yimika. You know I won't take chances with her."

He pulled his tie through his collar. Yimika whined in her crib. I could feel my milk in my chest. I rolled my shoulders. I was not ready to feed her.

Niyi undid his cufflinks.

"I care about my family," he said. "Only my family."

"So did I," I said. "Once. But that has changed now. I wasn't worried about my mother. Who are we fooling? The state our country is in affects everyone."

He didn't answer.

"Are you listening?" I asked.

"No," he said.

"No what?" I asked.

Yimika began to cry. My milk began to leak into my bra. It seemed to be dripping from my armpits.

"No, I can't allow that," he said. "I am sorry."

No one's "no" was more final than Niyi's, but I pressed further. I was not looking for a compromise. He had to change his mind. I was desperate enough to force him. From childhood, people had told me I couldn't do this or that, because no one would marry me and I would never become a mother. Now, I was a mother.

"I'm not the same," I said.

"What?"

"I'm not the same as I used to be. I want you to know."

I shook my blouse down. My milk had stained it.

I listened to many voices that night. One told me I would be dragged to one of those far-off prisons: Abakaliki, Yola, Sokoto, where harmattan winds would brittle my bones. I hushed that. Another told me I would never see Yimika again; that she would grow up, like Sheri, without a mother, Niyi would replace me and I would fall sick from heartbreak. I let that talk and talk before I hushed it. When the last hush was hushed, I listened.

I, alone, had beaten my thoughts down. No one else had done that. I, believer in infinite capabilities, up to a point; self-reliance, depending. It was internal sabotage, like military coups. Wherever the malice came from, it would have to go back. Yimika began to cry. I checked her but she wasn't wet. I rocked her back to sleep. My eyes grew heavy and I shut them. I could agree with Niyi; at least the tiredness would go away.

"Everyone has at least one choice," my father said, whenever I talked about women in home prisons. He was shocked. How could one make such a false and simplistic comparison? Likening a handful of kitchen martyrs to people confined in Nigerian prisons. Some prisoners set free would choose to stay on, I argued. My point was about a condition of the mind. Most days, I was as conscious of making choices as I was of breathing. "I raised you better," my father said. "You think," I said.

Yimika was dressed in her white christening gown. Sheri cradled her. I offered a calabash of kola nuts to my father-in-law. He picked one, split it in half and took a bite. My mother-in-law sat next to him, also chewing. I was wearing traditional dress: a white lace blouse, and red wrapper tied from my waist down. Around my neck were coral beads and on my head was a scarlet head tie with gold embroidery.

Because of my mother's death, only family members were invited to Yimika's naming ceremony, but they filled our living room. I placed the calabash on an empty stool and bit my kola nut. It was a gesture of affirmation for our prayers. Initially, all I could taste was bitter caffeine, then I tasted a slight hint of sweetness at the back of my tongue.

A few china bowls were laid out on the dining table: honey and salt for sweetness in Yimika's life, water for calmness, peppercorns for fruitfulness, palm oil for joy. She had received four names: Oluyimika, God surrounds me; Omotanwa, The child we waited for; Ebun, Gift; Moyo, my middle name, I rejoice.

Niyi's grand aunt began to pray in Yoruba. She was the oldest in the family and the other family members responded, "*Amin,*" each time. I joined the prayer for my daughter, then added a prayer for the place she'd arrived, that leaders would find their way to children, and our customs would become kinder. After our last amen, Niyi's grand aunt poured libation and raised a glass of Schnapps to her mouth, to salute her ancestors. Her lean body stiffened as the alcohol shot down her throat. She adjusted her head tie. It was time to eat.

In the kitchen, one of Sheri's cooks sat on a chair with a wooden mortar between her knees. She scooped lumps of pounded yam from it using a calabash quarter and wrapped them in cellophane. Blue bottle flies swarmed the sink where someone had knocked a can of mango juice over. A second cook served fried meat onto small plates. They worked together like big band players, rehearsed and indifferent.

"Are you ready?" I asked.

"It's done," the first cook said.

They were not ready. As I left the kitchen, my mother-in-law hurried toward me.

"What about the food?" she asked.

"They're almost finished, ma," I said.

"The guests are hungry."

"Don't worry, ma," I said.

"Where are you going?" she asked.

"Upstairs, ma," I said.

I could not wait. There were babies who stayed in their mother's wombs too long. By the time they were born, they were already dead. There were people who learned to talk on their death beds. When they opened their mouths to speak, they drew their last breaths.

The staircase in my house had never been a staircase. Often, I walked up imagining I was making an ascension, into heaven even. I was rising above a miscarriage, my mother's death, casting off malaria fever, rage, guilt. My mother-in-law's disapproval, I cast that off, too. My peace surpassed her understanding.

Niyi gave me a wave when I almost reached the top. He was making sure everyone had wine. I tried to steady my smile. What story would I tell him for making him less than half a man? That would be a k-legged story.

In my bedroom I removed my head tie and retired it among my jars of pomade and perfume. Along the parting between my braids, white hairs stood out.

Sheri walked in. "People are... what's happening here?"

I wondered how to tell her. Downstairs, the people began a thanksgiving song:

My joy overflows
I will give thanks every day
My joy overflows
I will rejoice every day
Will you?

The women arrived late for the first day of the meeting.
Lagos was recovering from another petrol shortage and public
transport had just resumed. Some sat on the edge of their seats;
others as if this were their first opportunity to sit. One pregnant
woman asked to put her feet up. There were seventeen of us
now: wives, mothers, sisters of journalists.

We appointed a treasurer and a secretary. I took my place
in the middle of the room and announced that those who had
something to say should speak; those who had come to listen,
should. The surprise visitor was Peter Mukoro's wife. The one
who had exposed him to the tabloids. She asked us not to call
her Aunty, Madam, or any of that nonsense. Her name was Clara,
Clara Mukoro.

The others were quick to tire of Clara and her trouble. I tried
to retaliate with kindness. One day, she said, "You. Don't you
ever get angry?" I answered, "If we both are angry, Aunty Clara,
where will we get?"

Clara and I soon became close, enough for me to ask why
she would fight for a man who had humiliated her. She had a
square-shaped face with eyes I only expected to see on a woman
from the Far East, and whenever she talked, she narrowed them.

"I knew Peter from primary school," she told me. "My father
was headmaster of our school, Peter was in my class. He helped
me with my school books. I was there when his father's farm was
ruined. I was there the day Peter turned down the scholarship.
When he left for Lagos, I left with him. My father disowned me.
It was Peter who supported me through university. That is the

323

Peter I remember, not the Peter running around like a little boy in a sweet shop. He is still the father of my children. Besides, if anyone should be locking Peter up, it should be me."

We would write letters to our president, asking for the release of our relations, whether or not he read them. We would not stop until our relations were freed. There were other campaign groups like ours, and they often appeared in the press. Some were petitioning for the release of women journalists. We gained strength from their voices. The threat of state security agents hung over us, but surprisingly, they never came.

If we didn't try, we would never have known.

If we didn't try, we would never have known, I still say.

I was born in the year of my country's independence, and saw how it raged against itself. Freedom was never intended to be sweet. It was a responsibility from the onset, for a people, a person, to fight for, and to hold on to. In my new life, this meant that there were bills to pay alone; memories to rock and lay to rest; regrets to snatch and return; tears, which always did clear my eyes.

These days, I stretched. I spread my legs wide on my sofa, flung my arms wide over the back. I lay like animal hide on my bed, face up, face down. Niyi was so tall, I'd always thought he deserved more space. The shrinkage I experienced was never worth it. He came to see Yimika almost every day, and nearly always left slamming my front door which made me miss him less and less. But I didn't blame him. He was fighting as though we were vying for the same cylinder of air: the more I breathed, the less there was for him. I did not sit too long with his family members either, not even my brothers-in-law. It wasn't out of ill-will: I had little energy for that. But I knew that given half the chance, they would confuse me with their advice, and nothing would be left of my original thought.

One morning I found an old picture of my mother and me.

She was carrying me and I was about six months old wearing a dress with puffy sleeves. She was wearing a mini dress and her legs were as skinny as mine. My mother once said she whispered words of guidance into my ear, when I was born. She never told me what she said. She said that I had remembered. I whispered into my daughter's ear like that, in my mother's house. I told her, "I love you. You have nothing to do but remember."

Sheri wouldn't stop nagging me about feeding her later that day. "This child is hungry! This child needs to eat right now!"

"You're driving me crazy," I finally told her. "She's my baby."

I was running around trying to prepare a feeding bottle. Yimika screamed loud enough to put us both in a state of panic. Sheri rocked her. It was no mistake that the smallest, weakest person in the room was in control.

"All you did was push," Sheri said.

"No praise for a mother."

"Someone mothered you."

"I praise my mother. I praise her from when I suffered labor pains."

"Stop exaggerating. You had only seven hours labor. Feed my child, please."

"Your child didn't want to be born, and I don't blame her. You hear me? I don't blame you, my baby. All you did was arrive here on earth. Henceforth a state of confusion. Can't even get milk on time."

"What confusion? She will know what there is to know. Hurry up with this bottle."

"Shit, I can't do the cap!"

When people speak of turning points in their lives it makes me wonder. I can't think of one moment that made me an advocate for women prisoners in my country. Before this, I had opportunities to take action, only to end up behaving in ways I was accustomed, courting the same old frustrations because I was sure of what I would feel: wronged, helpless, stuck in a day when I was fourteen years old. Here it is: changes came after I made them, each one small. I walked up a stair. Easy. I took off a head tie. Very easy. I packed a suitcase, carried it downstairs, put it in my car. When situations became trickier, my tasks became smaller. My husband asked why I was leaving him. "I have to," I replied. Three words; I could say them. "What kind of woman are you?" Not a word. "Wouldn't you have tried to stop me too?" he asked. Probably, but he wouldn't have had to leave me to do what he wanted. My old neighbor from Sunrise Estate, Busola, a smile for her when she confided, "Everyone is talking about you. They say you left for no reason. He never beat you, never chased. I know he's moody, but he went to work for God's sake. What would you do married to a lazy bugger like mine?" And Sheri had this to say: "You wait. You just wait. Your father will ask when he's out, 'Why did you leave your husband?'"

My husband, our home and small suburban community like a busybody extended family, I had these reasons to stay. But I was lucky to have survived what I believed I wouldn't, the smell of my mother's death. I couldn't remain as I was before, otherwise my memory of her would have been in vain, and my survival would certainly be pointless. Anyone who experienced such a trauma would understand. The aftermath could be a reincarnation. One life was gone and I could either mourn it or begin the next. How terrifying and how sublime to behave like a god with the power to revive myself. This was the option I chose.

It would be another two months before I heard from my father. He had been in detention for ten months and our country was at the center of an international uproar over the hanging of nine environmental activists from the Niger Delta, including the writer Ken Saro-Wiwa. Greenpeace, Friends of the Earth, Amnesty International were protesting their murders. Our government remained unrepentant meanwhile. I was beginning to despair. One family in our campaign was facing eviction; another had welcomed a new child without their father.

That afternoon, Shalewa from next door had been with me, helping to watch Yimika. I was tidying my mother's living room, relieved that Yimika had finally fallen asleep when my mobile phone rang. I dashed for it, but it was too late. Yimika began to cry again. I picked her up then reached for the phone.

"Enitan?"

It was my father.

"Daddy? Daddy, is that you?"

His voice cracked. "I'm out!"

Tears filled my eyes.

"They released me today. Mukoro and the others. I thought I must call you first. Is that the baby? Is it a boy or a girl? This one cries like a fog horn. How is everyone, your husband, your mother? Fatai? You must bring the baby over. Where are you? I have so much to tell you. Enitan? Enitan, you're not talking. Are you still there?"

"Yes," I said.

I wiped the tears from my eyes.

"Where are you?" he said. "What my eyes have seen, I will never be the same again."

"Me too," I said.

I had to tell someone. Sheri was the first person I thought of. It was a humid afternoon. My back was wet with sweat and my windscreen heavy with dust and dried gnat legs. The sun burned through it.

My brother told me, once we began to talk freely, how he saw people's insides before he saw anything else. If he met a smoker, he saw their black lungs. If he met a woman with a huge chest, while his friends were getting cross-eyed, he could see the yellow fat deposits under her skin. Whenever he saw children, he saw their hearts, pink. I thought it was a strange view he had of the world. He said he did not have an imagination. He did not dream either, and had a hard time understanding women, though he grew up in a house full of them. But he loved cars. Once when he asked how I was feeling, and I said that I felt as if someone had tailgated me for miles, driving me off course. Suddenly I lost them, now I was lost myself, but I was finding my way home, small by small. He said he understood.

My heart was bubbling. I needed to stop; the traffic was too slow. Nearing the junction of a residential road, I pulled over. A couple of "All right-sirs" who had been sitting on a bench thought I needed their assistance to park. They began to direct me with conflicting hand signals. "To the left. Right. Yes, yes, reverse, reverse, slowly, slowly. Halt."

They seemed to be swatting flies. I acted as if they were invisible. I had no money to give. A driver behind pressed on his horn. I wound down and saw he was driving one of those private transport vans we called *danfos*.

"What?" I shouted. "Can't somebody be happy in peace?"

He pressed on his horn again. I checked my mirror. He would have to wait. I wriggled in my seat. The first song that came to me was a Yoruba one: Never dance the *palongo*. It can make you go crazy.

I sang the words aloud. The van crawled to the side of my car. I could see the passengers inside. Their faces were shiny with sweat. The driver spread his fingers. "Get out of my way!"

I stepped out of my car and began to sing to him.

"Never dance the *palongo*. It can make you go crazy."

The passengers clapped their hands in disgust. "Sistah what's wrong with you?" "Behaving like this?" "On a hot afternoon." "Grown woman like you." "Acting like a child."

I raised my hand in a fist. "Our men are free," I said.

The van driver blinked. "What? What is she saying?"

Someone relayed my message. "Our men are too free with women."

"Nothing good will come to you!" the van driver said.

"Tell him," I said. "Tell him, *a da*. It will be good. Everything good will come to me."

She repeated my message, but the driver seemed to have heard. He hopped out of his van.

"Maybe she's mad," someone offered.

One man simply hung his head. Yet another delay.

"Are you mad?" the driver asked. "You're mocking me? Is your head correct? I said move your vehicle out of my way."

My hands went up. I wriggled lower, and sang again.

"Never dance the *palongo*. It can make you go crazy."

The "All right-sirs" stood with their mouths open. The van driver looked me up and down.

"You must be a very stupid woman," he said.

"Was," I said.

"Maybe you didn't hear me," he said, flexing his arms.

I heard him. I danced the *palongo*, fearing nothing for my sanity, or common sense. I added a few foreign steps to disorientate the discontented so-and-so: flamenco, can-can, Irish dancing from side to side. Nothing could take my joy away from me. The sun sent her blessings. My sweat baptized me.

About the author

Sefi Atta is also the author of *Swallow, News from Home, A Bit of Difference, Sefi Atta: Selected Plays* and, her latest novel, *The Bead Collector.* Her literary awards include the 2006 Wole Soyinka Prize for Literature and the 2009 Noma Award for Publishing in Africa. She divides her time between the USA, UK and Nigeria.